LOAN

DOING BUSINESS INTERNATIONALLY

DOING BUSINESS INTERNATIONALLY

The Guide to Cross-Cultural Success
Second Edition

Danielle Medina Walker
Thomas Walker
Joerg Schmitz

McGraw-Hill
New York   Chicago   San Francisco
Lisbon   London   Madrid   Mexico City
Milan   New Delhi   San Juan   Seoul
Singapore   Sydney   Toronto

The **McGraw·Hill** Companies

1 2 3 4 5 6 7 8 9 0   DOC/DOC   0 8 7 6 5 4 3 2

ISBN 0-07-137832-4

McGraw-Hill books are available at special quantity discounts to use as premiums and sales promotions, or for use in corporate training programs. For more information, please write to the Director of Special Sales, Professional Publishing, McGraw-Hill, Two Penn Plaza, New York, NY 10121-2298. Or contact your local bookstore.

The Cultural Orientations Model™, COM™, Cultural Orientations Indicator®, and COI® are all trademarks of Training Management Corporation; Registration 75-652669, 75-652654, and 75-652670.

 This book is printed on recycled, acid-free paper containing a minimum of 50% recycled de-inked fiber.

Contents

Foreword

In a world in which companies are increasingly global, understanding cultures has become a prerequisite for sustainable development.

- The issue was not so acute when companies exported products that they adapted to local needs, or even for multinationals, where a central unit developed corporate strategy and was responsible for all the crucial functions (R&D, technology, allocation of human resources).

- In a global company that integrates different parts of the world, where there are multiple decision and strategy planning centers present within a dominant matrix structure, understanding cultures universally has become an essential element of competition. Here culture and cultural systems have an important impact on planning, organizing, staffing, leading, and controlling skills.

All too often, companies behave ethnocentrically, showing a strong belief in the superiority of their original culture and using certain stereotypes, but forgetting that others also behave rationally, but in relation to different systems of values. There are considerable differences in the ways in which individuals approach the key dimensions of existence. Such differences can be observed in the approach to nature itself, depending upon whether the individual wishes to dominate or to live in harmony with nature; in the approach to time, depending on whether the individual considers time to be of a fixed, chronological nature or a fluid nature; and in the approach to success, which can be perceived as an individual or a collective phenomenon.

This book provides significant input both for those who are already in business and for those who are preparing to enter business. It is scientifically based and useful at an empirical level of action. It is scientifically sound in that the authors demonstrate their knowledge of the literature on the subject and the analysis is conducted rigorously. The reminder of the foundations of culture and its impact on behavior and the treatment of emotions are well covered. In addition, there is a solid basis to the analysis of the choices with which individuals are confronted.

The book is clearly very useful on a practical level. It constitutes an excellent resource book for any individual doing business at an international level, as well as for business school students who need to place what they have learned in a multicultural perspective.

It is a lively, anecdotal book that illustrates a reality that is rarely understood by those who have not been exposed to it.

Claude Michaud
Directeur General
European Center for Continuing Education (CEDEP/INSEAD)
Fontainebleau, France

Avant-Propos

Dans un monde où les entreprises deviennent globales, la compréhension des cultures est devenue essentielle pour un développement soutenable.

- Ce problème ne se posait pas avec autant d'acuité tant que les entreprises exportaient en adaptant les produits aux besoins locaux, et même dans le cadre des multinationales, où une unité centrale dessinait la stratégie et détenait des fonctions cruciales (R&D, technologie, allocation des hommes).

- Dans une entreprise globale qui intègre les différentes parties du monde, où les centres de décision et d'élaboration stratégique sont multiples, où l'organisation matricielle règne, la compréhension des univers culturels est devenue un atout essentiel de la compétition, où la culture, les systèmes culturels ont un impact important sur les compétences en matière de planning, organising, staffing, leading et controlling.

Trop souvent, les entreprises ont pratiqué un ethnocentrisme négatif croyant dans la supériorité de leur culture d'origine, utilisant des stéréotypes et oubliant que les autres sont rationnels mais par rapport à des systèmes de valeurs différents. Or, il existe des différences considérables quant aux orientations des hommes s'agissant des dimensions clés de l'existence—qu'il s'agisse des rapports avec la nature selon qu'on veuille la dominer ou vivre en harmonie avec elle, qu'il s'agisse de la relation du temps qui peut être vécu comme fixe, chronologique ou fluide, qu'il s'agisse du rapport à la réussite, à la performance qui peut être considéré comme un phénomène individuel ou collectif.

Ce livre constitue un effort important tant pour ceux qui sont dans le business que pour ceux qui s'y préparent. Il est à la fois fondé scientifiquement et utile au plan empirique de l'action. Fondé scientifiquement parce que les auteurs démontrent une connaissance de la littérature sur le sujet et parce que l'analyse est conduite avec rigueur. Le rappel des fondements de la culture et de son impact sur les comportements et le traitement des émotions est bien fait. De même, l'analyse des grands choix auxquels sont confrontés les hommes est solidement fondée.

Utile sur le plan pratique ce livre l'est à l'évidence. Il constitue un excellent ouvrage de référence pour toute personne faisant du business à une échelle internationale comme pour tout étudiant de business school qui doit mettre les enseignements dans une perspective de culture diversifiée.

Ce livre plein d'anecdotes est en plus vivant et illustre une réalité souvent mal comprise par ceux qui n'y ont pas été exposés.

Claude Michaud
Directeur General
Centre Européen d'Education Permanente (CEDEP/INSEAD)
Fontainebleau, France

Preface

This second edition of *Doing Business Internationally* is both a revision of and a sequel to the first edition, which was published in 1995. In the six years between the two versions, our worlds and work environments have been marked by drastic developments, transformations, and events that have altered some of the discussions on culture and the importance of cross-cultural understanding.

Throughout these transformations—the events and aftermath of the September 11, 2001, attacks on the World Trade Center being the most obvious and tragic symbol— the objective of *Doing Business Internationally* has remained the same: We seek to provide executives and managers with the critical awareness, knowledge, and skills needed to work, compete, and lead in the global, multicultural environment. The updates and changes in *Doing Business Internationally* are driven to a large degree by the insights and knowledge we have gained from our consulting work with *Fortune* 500 companies—firms such as American Express, Air Products and Chemicals, AT&T, Avon Products, BASF, Berlex, Citigroup, Citrix, Corning, DaimlerChrysler, Ernst & Young, IBM, Lucent Technologies, L'Oreal, Marconi, MasterCard International, Merck, National Semiconductors, Novartis, PPG, Schering AG, and Wunderman, which have sought our assistance in managing the human side of globalization.

In 1995, the business environment was complex, chaotic, and competitive. In 2001, these complexities, ambiguities, and paradoxes have increased exponentially. Globalization has lost much of its novelty, glamour, and allure; it is now as much a condition of doing business as it is a condition of contemporary economic (and social) life itself (and an embattled condition at that). But that has not made the questions, issues, and challenges of globalization any less salient or more routine.

Over the past six years, we have been witnesses to a major financial crisis; the boom and bust of e-commerce and dot coms; the rapid transnational expansion of many firms through mergers, acquisitions, joint ventures, and partnerships; growing worldwide economic interdependence; and social, economic, and political volatility and upheaval. The sheer magnitude of what is at stake in global business, its threats, effects, and opportunities alike, has elevated the role of culture and cultural competence for the leaders and managers who have to navigate this tremendous uncertainty and complexity each day. This is particularly true in a world in which business leadership can no longer be parochially focused on narrowly defined commercial opportunities, but increasingly needs to encompass the stewardship of natural and human resources in the interest of peace, socioeconomic stability, and growth.

It is a noteworthy observation that those individuals who lead today's global corporations possess a unique set of attributes, such as the organization, technology, capital, and ideology to attempt managing the world as an integrated economic unit. After all, 50 of the top 100 economies in the world are global corporations. The executives and managers of these corporations hold the fate and fortunes of the world's population in their collective hands, as these corporations are economically more powerful than most nation-states or world political bodies.

Our book offers a comprehensive argument for the elevated role of culture in the process of organizational globalization, together with practical insights and approaches on how to achieve cross-cultural effectiveness and leverage worldwide cultural diversity for competitive advantage. While it is a contribution to the field of intercultural communications, it is primarily a companion to those on the journey of globalization as it continues to profoundly challenge worldviews, identities, and assumptions about ourselves and the world in which we live. It is a guide for those who do not want to shy away from the profound multicultural challenge embedded in everyone's work, for those who realize that, in the words of Antoine de St. Exupéry, "Mystery is all we fear. . . . We need men to go into the depth of the well, and return, saying that we have encountered nothing."

In order to accomplish this objective and build our argument, we have organized this book around key topics, concepts, and insights, beginning with an exploration of the broadest context and moving on to specific implications and applications.

In Chap. 1, "The Global Environment," we discuss economic, societal, and organizational trends that define the phenomenon of globalization. This chapter identifies the critical and changing role of culture. It discusses and identifies the elements of organizational and individual leadership and their concomitant global mindsets as key success factors.

In Chap. 2, "Culture," we demonstrate and discuss the role of culture in global business and management. We provide a refined understanding of culture on both a macro and a micro level, summarizing and exploring some of the key contributions and prevalent notions in the field of cross-cultural communication.

In Chap. 3, "The Cultural Orientations Model," we present our framework for understanding the hidden forces that guide our institutions, behaviors, actions, and interactions. This refined approach provides a practical device that enables us to understand the cultural underpinnings of the societal, organizational, team, and interpersonal contexts of our lives and work. This approach allows individuals not only to understand culture but also to identify the degree of influence that they have on cultural processes.

In Chap. 4, "A Survey of Cultural Patterns," we undertake a high-level survey of cultures worldwide, applying our cultural orientations framework to the broad diversity of cultural patterns on a geographic, societal level. It takes the reader on a journey through the major world regions—the Middle East and North Africa, Asia, Western and Eastern Europe, North America, and Latin America—describing the main business norms, cultural trends, and landscapes.

In Chap. 5, "Cultural Orientations in Communication," we extend the cultural orientations approach to our understanding of interpersonal communication and interactions. We introduce key findings of our own research and provide you with an opportunity to explore your own cultural profile. We also introduce the four key skills of cultural competence.

In Chap. 6, "Cultural Competence in Marketing and Sales," we provide a discussion of the implications and applications of cultural competence to common marketing and sales challenges by focusing on those business functions that most directly connect the business to its customers and on the inherent importance of integrating cultural competence within the skill set of those in these roles.

In conclusion, Chap. 7, "Translating Global Vision into Local Action," discusses salient applications and introduces key practices, particularly those relevant to the management and leadership of global, multicultural teams. As such teams are the conduit through which global visions become local reality, our unique perspective on team development ends our deliberations on a highly practical note.

We sincerely hope that our ambitious attempt to comprehensively discuss and explore the complexity of globalization, culture, communication, and performance prove to be both theoretically and practically valuable.

Acknowledgments

This book captures the results of our long-standing quest to demonstrate the theory and practice of culture and to raise cross-cultural knowledge and awareness for the benefit of individuals and the organizations in which they work.

Over the years, a genuine lack of appreciation on the part of managers and leaders of the importance of culture for business and effective human relationships has been progressively replaced by a deeper understanding of the value that insights into culture can bring.

In today's constantly changing business environment, the cross-cultural concepts and skills discussed in this book are key competencies for all whose work is conducted within highly diverse and/or complex global business environments.

Developing a guide with practical examples and insights requires behind-the-scene contributions from numerous individuals from around the world—too many, unfortunately, to acknowledge individually. The preparation of this book has been aided by the insights, knowledge, ideas, influence, endless discussions, and support of many colleagues—both professional and personal—whose encouragement has driven our quest to define the diversity and potential synergy within and across cultures. We are especially grateful to those who contributed in their own way to this book.

We wish to thank a long list of our colleagues, clients, friends, and family, all of whom have in their own special way contributed to the success and evolution of our approach and the genesis of this book.

At Training Management Corporation (TMC), we are particularly grateful to Dr. Richard Punzo for his research on the Cultural Orientations Indicator (COI) and for providing us with the rigorous validation of this instrument, as well as its application to the field of global project management; Robert Greenleaf for his continuous feedback on learning applications of the COI and the Cultural Orientations Model (COM); Suzanna Rosenberg for her researching and editing, and for her pursuit to improve the practical application of our approach; Esther Lewis, our graduate student from Columbia University, for her patience in research and editing and her insightful comments. Finally, our thanks to Jamie Fouss, Juliet Reiter, Susan Scherer, and Sonia Rodriguez for their excellent support.

We want to especially thank the following friends, colleagues, and clients who have contributed to this project and to our practice: Nancy Curl, Robert McGregor, Dick Richardson, and the entire IBM Shades of Blue team, particularly Sharon Johnson, Leighton Grant, Erika Kleesdorfer, Nirmala Menon, Peter Semardek, Angela Chang, and Marge Lanier, for their continued feedback, support, and enthusiasm; Robert Blondin, Barrie Athol, and Steve Davis of Ernst & Young and Intellinex, who facilitated the global testing of the COM and the COI in more than 60 countries; William Manfredi and Cindy Zimmerer of Wunderman for their relentless energy in applying our cross-cultural management concepts to strategically aligned interventions; Glenn Kaufman of American Express for his passionate ability to convert our cross-cultural management practice to a cultural asset for AMEX globally; Leticia Knowles of American Express for her insights on the application of the COI to the AMEX Global Diversity Practice; Glenn Hallam of Creative Metrics for steering, conducting, and completing the COI validation research; Hans Greuter and Katrin Adler of Novartis Europe for their review and feedback on the adaptation of our cross-cultural management process for multicultural, global teams at Novartis; Andreas Bauer and John Gutowski of DaimlerChrysler for their endorsement of our approach and the application of the COM and COI learning concepts to their global coaching and leadership development practice; Kevin Asbjörnson of the Center for Creative Leadership (CCL) for his feedback to strengthen and enhance our global leadership model; Mary Raz and Pam Edwardson of National Semiconductor for their reviews, challenges, and critical changes to create practical cross-cultural business content for all global learners; Lynn Scheitrum, Alyssa Dix, and Kimberli Pitts-Calhoun of Air Products and Chemicals for their confidence in our ability to assist in the building of global effectiveness of their organizations; and Harvette Dixon, Susan Page, and Diane Kappas at PPG Industries, who have given us opportunities to prove the value of our approach in leadership development.

Our special thanks to the numerous certified COM/COI practitioners from all over the world who have helped to firmly establish our approach and have given us the opportunity to help leaders, teams, and organizations appreciate and leverage cultural differences.

In addition, we want to thank our global partners for adapting our cross-cultural model and assessment to their practice: Daniel Eppling, Jos Velthuis, and Andre Collome of Krauthammer International in Paris, France, and Amsterdam, Holland; Guido Betz and Uta Pook of Kommunications-Kolleg, Andernach, Germany; Philippe Rosinski of Rosinski & Associates of Brussels, Belgium; François and Benoit Calicis of Mega Learning in Brussels, Belgium; Claude Michaud and George Eapen of CEDEP-INSEAD, Fontainebleau, France; and Linda Miller of DDI in Pittsburg, Pennsylvania, USA.

We are particularly appreciative of the insightful comments provided by participating managers from over 60 countries representing 50 multinational companies in TMC's Doing Business Globally, Cultural Orientations at Work, Managing Business Across Cultures, Leading Global Teams, and Managing Across Cultures workshops, among others. We are grateful for their participation and for their continued support.

Finally, we want to thank the Walker and Schmitz families: Love and thanks to Tim and Danielle's children and grandchildren. We owe special thanks to our dad, Joseph Walker, and to our family in the United States, France, the United Kingdom, and Israel for their spiritual nourishment over the years. Joerg Schmitz is grateful to his wife Latha and daughter Christina for their loving support, patience, and inspiration. Love and thanks also to Ille Schmitz and Hermann Kempkes.

1

THE GLOBAL ENVIRONMENT

Globalization lies at the heart of modern culture;
cultural practices lie at the heart of globalization

JOHN TOMLINSON,
GLOBALIZATION AND CULTURE

*C*ulture is an increasingly important element of the interactions of individuals in a globalizing world. From a distance, globalization means
increasingly complex interdependencies and the blurring of traditional
boundaries and divisions. As the Financial Times *points out,[1] economic*
and political linkages, involving the migration of money, goods, and peo-
ple across national borders together with ideas and values, have increased
the pace of change and the ubiquity of ambiguity, uncertainty, and unpre-
dictability. This state of affairs is at once a threat and an opportunity.

1

Michel Camdessus, former managing director of the International Monetary Fund (IMF), explains that what we now call globalization "is simply the continuation of the trend toward greater international economic integration that has been under way for the last fifty years. The difference is that today markets are larger, more complex, and more closely integrated than ever before. And capital now moves at a speed and in volumes that would have been inconceivable a few decades ago."[2] One could surely argue that globalization as it defines our contemporary experience is a continuation of a historical evolution that has been underway for at least the past five hundred years, with European colonialization and imperialism leading to a dynamic between parochial tribalism and global commerce that frames the modern state of affairs—a dialectical dynamic that Benjamin Barber (1996) fittingly calls *Jihad vs. McWorld*.[3] "The rising economic and communication interdependencies of the world mean that such nations, however unified internally, must nonetheless operate in an increasingly multicultural global environment. Ironically, a world that is coming together pop culturally and commercially is a world whose discrete sub-national ethnic and religious and racial parts are also far more in evidence, in no small part as a reaction to McWorld."

It is this fundamental dynamic that makes globalization, in the words of Rosabeth Moss Kanter, "one of the most powerful and pervasive influences on nations, businesses, workplaces, communities, and lives at the end of the twentieth century."[4]

Given the multifaceted nature of globalization, it may seem parochial to talk about it as a single concept. In terms of business, globalization is now so extensive that companies operating and investing on a global scale and with global vision are decisively transforming patterns of trade and shaping organizations and the interactions between them.

In response to the challenge of maintaining global competitiveness, international business must address rapid, sudden, and complex changes in the world economic environment. Assumptions about organizational structure, control mechanisms, and resources have changed and are continuing to change. The extraordinary speed and scope of change have become a factor affecting the business world as never before. Companies that are in the process of globalizing face two major issues: (1) the need to be both globally integrated and locally responsive at the same time, and (2) the need to develop an organization that is capable of transferring knowledge and learning throughout the world.

These changes have resulted in a dynamic business environment consisting of a series of complex interdependent developments: unyielding competitive pressures, rapid market shifts, major acquisitions or mergers, the lowering of trade barriers, decreasing transport costs, heightened expectations on the part of customers and employees, advances in communication and information technology, global access to capital markets, and inflation-driven staff reductions. The result is a succession of change initiatives that impose extraordinarily difficult transitions. Given the incessant competitive requirements of the marketplace, individuals and organizations have little choice—they must either change or face failure in an unpredictable, unstable marketplace.[5]

In 1998, the *Financial Times* captured the essential difficulties of defining this complex and pervasive phenomenon of globalization:

> Globalization can be defined in several ways depending on the level we choose to focus on. We can speak of globalization of the entire world, a single country, a specific industry, a specific company or even a particular line of business or function within a company. At the worldwide level globalization refers to the growing economic interdependence among countries as reflected in increasing cross-border flows of goods, services, capital and know-how. . . . At the level of a specific country globalization refers to the extent of the interlinkages between a country's economy and the rest of the world. . . . At the level of a specific industry globalization refers to the degree to which a company's competitive position within that industry in one country is interdependent to that in another country.[6]

Since the terrorist attacks of September 11, 2001, on the United States (designed to attack the driver and symbolic nerve center of globalization), we have been forced to reevaluate how the complex process of globalization will continue to evolve. These dramatic events and their immediate impact on international business illustrate that parallel to an emergent one-world market there is a psychological and social reality defined by a fundamental sense of threat. Business has rarely if ever realized so clearly that its success hinges on the protection and/or proliferation of an underlying and institutionalized value system. The fast-eroding distinctions between domestic and international markets are intimately tied to the spread of democracy and an open market system and their cultural underpinnings.

THE CHANGED BUSINESS ENVIRONMENT

It would be a fundamental error to conclude that only those organizations with international operations are affected by the phenomenon of globalization. Many companies that do not themselves have an international presence compete with firms operating both within and outside their home country, buy or use goods or services produced in other countries, and hire or contract with people of diverse ethnic backgrounds. Today multinational/global/transnational companies that manage globally and implement locally are playing an increased role in this growth and evolution process. Their commitment to direct foreign investment sustains the trend for the developing global business network as the twenty-first century evolves.

Change in a highly global environment is no longer progressive and incremental, as it was in the 1990s; instead, it is characterized by dramatic, chaotic fluctuations in conditions. The fundamental environmental conditions surrounding business continue to change at a rapid pace, as shown in Table 1.1.

Global managers today are facing new management demands as their responsibilities and tasks become increasingly more complex. The 1990s were defined by the need to meet new standards for quality, cost, cycle time, responsiveness to customers, and flexibility. Now, in addition, the need to provide global products to a global marketplace poses the dual requirements of an integrated global company presence and local responsiveness. The new market environment of the 2000s has replaced the static, hierarchical, and vertical organization structure in all markets. Companies must cope with a new set of dynamic issues as they consider the global marketplace. Some of the forces behind globalization are shown in Fig. 1.1, and some examples of how these forces affect global business are given in Table 1.2. The new environment is

TABLE 1.1   Characteristics Shaping the Business Environment

1980s and before	1990s and after
Continuity	Change
Planning	Coping with the unexpected
Adjustment	Transformation
Diversification	Focus and segmentation
Management	Facilitation
Instruction	Learning
Individuals	Project groups and teams
Knowledge	Competence
Scale and security	Flexibility, responsiveness, and speed
Uninformed customers	Demanding customers
National boundaries	Freedom of movement

Source: Colin Coulson-Thomas, *Creating the Global Company: Successful Internationalization* (New York: McGraw-Hill, 1992), pp. 2–3.

FIGURE 1.1   Forces behind globalization.

highly fluid, marked by the exchange of people, ideas, intellectual property, technology systems, processes, financial markets, and expertise. Among the key issues facing companies involved in globalization are

- Ease of access to open markets
- Demanding customers
- Sustained performance improvement
- Need for rapid, flexible decision making and communication
- Unabated growth in technological innovation
- Critical importance of relationship management
- Increase in the importance of diversity
- Difficulty of "going it alone"[7]

Globalization is a top priority in the business world, commanding the energy, time, and resources of countless corporations and their employees. To understand the breadth and scope of the way international businesses are evolving on a larger and ever-changing scale, it is helpful to identify key market trends and drivers in the global marketplace. We have selected three of these that we consider key to the expansion of the international marketplace and that are especially important for managers whose responsibilities lie within the realm of developing competitive advantage for their organizations in countries and regions around the world.

TABLE 1.2   Forces behind Globalization

Competition	Open trading systems and regional trading groups
	Collaborative structures: acquisitions, mergers, and other strategic alliances
	New levels of productivity and cost-effectiveness in many nations
Customers	Demand for immediate availability of consistent, high-quality goods
	Expectation of worldwide customer service and support
	Use of alternative, time-saving distribution channels
Governments	Trade policies, including licensing and import/export regulations
	Tariffs, quotas, export subsidies
	Local content requirements, marketing and advertising laws, product claim regulations
	Investments in technological structures
	Intellectual property rights protection laws
Technology	Greater interdependence of economies
	Basis of competition changed
	Consumer's voice increased
	Product development cycles altered
	Work accomplished differently
Markets	Emerging markets with new opportunities and challenges
	Soft markets forcing rethinking of forecasts and strategies
	Domestic market saturation forcing development of new markets

FACTORS AFFECTING COMPETITIVENESS

The key factors affecting competitive advantage in the evolving global marketplace that we have chosen to review are (1) globalization/antiglobalization, (2) technological change, and (3) learning and development. A heightened awareness of the critical dynamics at play in each of these factors can enable managers and their organizations to target and achieve higher levels of performance in the marketplace.

Key Factor 1: Globalization and Antiglobalization

Assessing globalization requires both a narrow focus and a wide-angle lens. The narrow focus looks at globalization primarily as an economic phenomenon; the broader perspective considers deeper social implications as well. The World Bank identifies the following drivers of globalization:

- Development of unrestricted international trade
- Rise of global market drivers
- Competitiveness of global corporations
- Cost-efficiency and productivity of doing business globally
- Evolution of foreign direct investment (FDI)
- Computer and information technology
- Convergence of global lifestyles and values
- Globalization of capital markets, flows, and services
- Emergence of the knowledge economy and era[8]

Undeniably, the movement toward greater reach in globalization initiatives has significance well beyond economics. Economics is only one aspect of the expansion of the human perspective over time: from a narrow focus on family, to an ever more inclusive view of clan, tribe, feudal system, and nation-state, and now to a view of the whole world. Today's cosmopolitan businessperson sees every stranger, regardless of national origin, as a potential customer, supplier, employee, or partner. Innovative companies now routinely look for solutions beyond their national borders. As consumers, we all search for bargains and quality from global markets.

The tide of globalization will not be substantially reversed despite the events of September 2001. Consumers want a broader choice of goods and services at reduced cost. Intellectuals want an expanded network of ideas. Businesses search for profit in global markets through international technologies. Investors seek new growth opportunities over the horizon. Nations have learned that they can achieve greater security collectively than alone. Globalization is not just an economic or commercial phenomenon. It is a social evolution that is bringing individuals, organizations, nations, and cultures closer together.

Given this expansion of globalization, global leaders will need to be keenly aware of the dynamics of the global marketplace and operate with a global mindset:

- *World trade* increased 6.6 percent per annum during the 1990s, a trend that the world banking and investment community forecasts will continue well into the 2010s and beyond. Projections show that by 2005 global trade levels will be equivalent to approximately 45 to 48 percent of the world's collective GNP.

- The sustained growth and economic prosperity of Asia's economies—China, Japan, India, Indonesia, and possibly a united Korea—will create extensive new markets driven by advantaged, wealthier middle classes. The spectra of growth in these economies could open vast markets for goods and services in these countries. This shift could mean that by 2015 at least four of the world's six largest economies would be Asian.

- Explosive growth is occurring in the scope and form of international business transactions—foreign direct investment and the export-import trade are now only two of many forms. Other forms include mergers and acquisitions, transfer of technology, strategic alliances and joint ventures, franchise operations, and manufacturing, to name just a few.

- Regardless of its geographical origins (European, Asian, or American), the level of *direct foreign investment*, both within and outside the United States, continues to grow at an annual rate of more than 15 percent. For example, foreign-owned companies currently employ 5 percent of all American workers and 12 percent of American manufacturing employees, notably in new automobile manufacture and assembly plants owned by European and Asian firms, such as Toyota, DaimlerChrysler, and Nissan. Conversely, American investment overseas exceeds direct foreign investment in this country: Europe is the recipient of 50 percent of these monies; Asia and Latin America each receive 18 percent; and Africa, the Middle East, and the former Soviet Union receive about 5 percent each.

- The *competitive environment* changed dramatically during the 1990s, and the United States no longer dominates the international marketplace. Foreign companies have invaded markets and made major investments within the United States; the pressures on the world economy have slowed the pace of broad-scale investment, but there is a continued high rate of megamergers and acquisitions within and across national boundaries. Key competitive drivers include open trading systems, regional groups, and collaborative structures.

- *Mergers and acquisitions* (M&A), leveraged buyouts, and joint/strategic alliances are sustained features of the evolving competitive business environment. In the two-year period 1998–1999, these transactions totaled over $6 trillion. A global merger wave of more than $3.5 trillion was announced in 2000, up from $3.3 trillion in 1999, and several of these were megamergers—Pfizer/Warner-Lambert and Mannesmann/Vodaphone, for example. In the United States alone, the volume of mergers and acquisitions increased from $1.6 to $1.8 trillion. A significant percentage of these new mergers brought together headquarters organizations from different countries: Daimler and Chrysler, Random House and Bertelsmann, British Petroleum and Amoco, Ernst & Young and Cap Gemini, S.A., Vivendi and Universal, VoiceStream Wireless and Deutsche Telekom. However, without the supercharged atmosphere in the technology, telecommunications, and media industries that propelled the volume of M&A activity in 2000, it appears unlikely that this flow of deals will continue unabated, except in those industries in which the rationale for consolidation remains strong, such as pharmaceuticals and energy.

- *Regional/open trading groups, governments, and industry associations* will continue to increase, emphasizing a regional rather than a national view of economic growth. For example, the North American Free Trade Association (NAFTA) and the Association for Southeast Asian Nations (ASEAN) represent this trend. In any of these regions, national goals and aspirations may be incorporated into bloc goals. The resulting impact on company planning and market objectives will be undeniable. These trading groups indicate the growing interdependence of countries in the marketplace. Conversely, within domestic markets there is increased foreign penetration and competition in products and market segments that were protected in the past. Competitors are investing to build scale in world markets.

  Governments affect globalization through their imposition of tariffs and quotas, nontariff barriers, export subsidies, local content requirements, currency and capital flow restrictions, and requirements for technology transfer. In some cases, protectionist policies affect the compatibility of technical standards, as different standards are often imposed for protectionist reasons. Common marketing regulations are frequently undercut by individual country requirements.

- *Antiglobalization* (the case against globalization) has its activists as well, who through increasingly confrontational protests and demonstrations are fighting for human rights and opposing child labor, low labor and environmental standards, unemployment, and global labor exploitation (e.g., sweatshops, found especially in China, Indonesia, Africa, Colombia, and the Caribbean). Since 1999, protests have been characterized as "multigenerational, multi-class, and multi-issue" and have frequently been violent, as during G8 economic summits, World Trade Organization (WTO) conferences, and Davos World Economic Forums.

  The antiglobalization movement has several objectives: (1) to prevent the growth of global trade by opposing multinational corporate power, in particular the perceived U.S. economic and political hegemony in the post-Cold War era; (2) to oppose global agreements on economic growth, targeting companies and economic institutions that, protestors charge, regulate and assess global trade practices and foster economic globalization, such as the WTO, the World Bank (WB), the Organization of American States (OAS), NAFTA, and the International Monetary Fund (IMF); and (3) to restrain the growth of powerful government institutions, which are viewed as limiting basic human rights in order to produce economic gain.[9]

Some countries, such as France, are struggling to accept those aspects of globalization that are indispensable for thriving in the twenty-first century while retaining—mainly for linguistic and cultural reasons—the practices and traditions on which they built their prosperity and identity in the twentieth century. The French often exaggerate a view of globalization that portrays it as a kind of U.S. plot to make the whole world resemble the United States. Resistance to globalization in France spilled into the streets in the case of José Bové, the French sheep farmer and antiglobalization activist who in the summer of 1999 vandalized a McDonald's restaurant under construction in southwestern France in protest against U.S. trade sanctions on Roquefort cheese. At the same time, the French realize that globalization is happening because of technology and ideas and that it is going to continue whether people like it or not. European integration actually facilitates the acceptance of globalization, as it is, in itself, a form of globalization on a limited regional scale. Meanwhile, the creation of the Euro is another reaction to globalization, shielding France and the rest of Europe from the effects of volatile international capital flows.

It is important to recognize that while fears and resentment of the role of the United States in globalization are often exaggerated, many of the traits and characteristics associated with globalization are also associated with the United States, such as flexible labor markets, free trade, open movement of capital, and human rights; in addition, English is increasingly accepted as the lingua franca of the global marketplace. Many companies around the world are fully integrated into the world economy and are thriving, despite being located in countries that object to the American accent that they perceive globalization as being imbued with. These companies are heavily involved in large-scale international trade, concluding international financial deals, adapting to American-style global capitalism, embracing and making greater use of the stock market, stock options, privatization, mergers and acquisitions, and so on. Globalization is a challenge for everyone, and yet, despite resistance to globalization even within the United States, the majority of people firmly believe that globalization is an established phenomenon that boosts economic growth and will continue to be a strong movement on a truly global level.[10]

- *Global harmonization of consumer buying preferences* will dominate certain industry—goods and services—sectors.

- The *emergence of global competitors*—direct competition from foreign companies—is an incontestable feature of business development in today's global arena. By 2005, eight out of ten American firms will face strong foreign competition. Meanwhile, the percentage of U.S. companies' gross sales realized from outside the United States is projected to grow to more than 50 percent from its level in 2000 of just below 30 percent.[11]

According to the *Financial Times*'s 2001 annual survey of the world's top 50 industrial corporations, 32 have their headquarters in North America (the United States and Canada), with 14 in Europe and 4 in Asia. In the *Financial Times*'s top 500 listing of the world's largest corporations, there are 236 in the United States, 64 in Japan, 39 in Britain, 28 in France, and 20 in Germany. In all, 27 countries have companies represented in the top 500, and 11 countries have companies in the top 50.[12]

Corporations in these major markets possess all the critical elements required to ensure competitiveness in the global market: well-established domestic markets capable of producing appropriate economies of scale and innovative manufacturing processes; familiarity with, and consequent efficiency in, dealing with the distribution and service issues characteristic of aggressively growing consumer markets; extensive experience in the management of complex organizations; and the financial resourcefulness required for collaborative agreements, such as joint ventures, strategic alliances, and so forth.[13]

Growth projections for the next five years reveal aggressive global expansion plans on the part of the major international firms. These firms are headquartered primarily in the United States, England, Japan, Germany, and France, but this concentration is clearly changing as multinationals emerge mainly from the Asia-Pacific and Latin American regions, particularly from countries like Korea, Taiwan, Mexico, and Brazil. These countries will play a more prominent role in setting the pace and direction of globalization during the twenty-first century.

- Even so, during the first decades of the new century, a high percentage of new investments will continue to flow from the mature economies in Europe, the United States, and Japan—still the richest consumer markets. However, a growing share of the world's capital is flowing into the financial centers and emerging economies of Asia, i.e., Taiwan, Hong Kong, Singapore, and South Korea. Furthermore, China's steady, although erratic, economic expansion could cost both mature and emerging economies much in competitive position. What is striking in investment trends is the diversity of capital investment, which is reflective of the opportunistic nature of multinational business operations today. International activities are tending to become more focused along rational patterns of business investment and expansion, e.g., firms in the chemical, financial services, pharmaceutical, retailing, and food and beverage sectors are investing internationally within their own sectors. This approach means seeing the world as a natural expansion of existing domestic markets and looking to sell similar products by differentiating them for wider markets globally.[14]

American domination of the world economy will continue in the first decade of the 2000s. Nevertheless, the United States' retention of its preeminent position will depend upon the corporate and government response to shifts and changes in the evolving marketplace. Under the old paradigm, competitiveness simply meant a company's being able to sell its goods and services to customers in broad, ill-defined markets. In the first decade of the twenty-first century, a two-tiered marketplace applies in what is now a truly global evolution of the marketplace. This new paradigm is based on two networks reaching around the world, one superimposed upon the other: (1) an overarching communication network, permitting information/knowledge managers to monitor, control, and change a broad variety of business processes in order to respond instantly to changing market conditions, and (2) a network of goods and services moving between production and distribution platforms and consumption nodes. Innovation resulting from the management of the information network will occur at the company-consumer exchange point—be it face-to-face or via business-to-business (B2B) platforms—resulting in discussion, decision, and strategic planning to meet supplier and customer problems and demands—people meeting and dealing with people.[15]

Key Factor 2: Technological Change
Technology, especially information technology, has only begun to transform the business world, and its spread is accelerating, with multiple and contradictory impact throughout the global workplace and workforce: (1) Rapid technological progress and increasingly fierce global competition have spurred productivity, caused jobs to be created and lost quickly, and increased the demand for highly skilled and well-educated workers; (2) market growth and economic competitiveness hinge on the availability of high- and, even more, low-skilled (and low-cost) workers across multiple industry sectors; (3) an

important shift away from manufacturing to an emphasis on services has occurred as the result of technological change, particularly in the computer industry; (4) there is the potential for migration of jobs abroad if countries fail to develop their work skills/capability at a national level or encourage, through liberal immigration policy, the influx of highly skilled workers from overseas; and (5) there is an increased demand for a workforce that is highly adaptable and flexible to cope with a changing and more entrepreneurial economy.[16]

Within this dynamic mix, characterized by an increase in the sophistication of new technologies and intense global competition and exchange, global organizations and their workforces face unprecedented market volatility. To maintain competitive advantage and succeed in the twenty-first century, companies will have to remain at the leading edge of technology applications, incorporating the benefits of these applications into strategic and tactical processes.

Among the ever-growing applications and innovations, the global manager finds that computer-automated systems and processes run today's companies. The instantaneous data and information resources available through powerful computers, using the Internet or an intranet (a customized in-company internet), are critical to organizational competitiveness; for example, management and development at the individual and organization level are increasingly being delivered by technology in a "just-in-time," desktop learning format. Exchange and interaction with colleagues around the world will become as easy as stopping to chat with one's colleague in the office next door. Some characteristics of the new technology are

- Virtual reality/interactive media/augmented reality
- Superconducting fiber-optic networks
- Artificial intelligence, neural networks, expert systems
- Digitization, miniaturization, portability
- Enhanced processing power
- New microchip development
- Mass customization
- Small, mobile robots
- Advanced software[17]

As corporations adopt global market structures, the fundamental technological revolution in computers, information/data, and telecommunications resources is rapidly moving us to the position of having the capability to satisfy almost any requirement for information.[18] The continuous change in technologies will dramatically affect the way we do business and structure our business organizations and will redefine the office work environment.

Information technology tools represent both the glue to integrate organizational operations and the lubricant to keep the flow of business moving. Technology will serve as the principal tool for coordinating global production and distribution, exercising operational control, and driving policy formulation and implementation. Companies that lack the full capability to put in place efficient communication networks supported by adequate technology will be quite simply unable to successfully compete in the global marketplace.[19]

Key Factor 3: Learning and Development

Learning is a fundamental engine for sustained, competitive business growth. Its primary contribution to business is its capacity to transform businesses' greatest resource—people—into efficient and productive human capital capable of providing peak performance through effective management of technology, knowledge, and content resources. Ultimately, the quality of an organization's human capital determines how well that business can produce, innovate, or compete. Learning and development become critical means to raise people's aspirations for self-improvement while diffusing knowledge and effective management practices to ensure the critical transition of workforce values and processes to continue along several dimensions:[20]

- Individuals, teams, and communities will replace employers/workers/ customers.
- Personalization is the key to enabling personal best performance.
- The motivation of the individual will be at the heart of knowledge creation, and the relationship between individuals and organizations will undergo profound changes.
- Working and learning will be the same thing.
- People will become in control of and personally responsible for their own development and learning.
- People will primarily identify themselves through project teams and communities of practice.
- Teams and communities will be enabled to create and increase their community knowledge.

Business recognizes that to get the skills it needs, it must continuously educate its own workforce. Corporations are now investing as much as $70 billion annually to operate their own in-house universities to train and educate workers at all levels. In 1999 there were about 1600 company universities, four times as many as there had been 15 years before, according to Corporate University Xchange (CUX), a research and consulting firm. If this growth rate is sustained into the twenty-first century, the result could be more corporate universities than traditional ones by 2010. At the turn of the century, 1 million people were studying online, a number that is expected to double by 2003.

The ultimate measure of these initiatives, bolstered by substantial capital investment commitments, is enhanced performance in the workplace. As organizations benchmark and track improvements, the lens of performance brings everything into clearer focus: The transition can be viewed as a new-age version of apprenticeship, as shown in Table 1.3.

Faster, more customized learning and communication tools will overturn twentieth-century business practices. Organizations are coming to view learning as a skill that can itself be learned. It is considered an open-ended process of discovery and improvement that is accessible to all who are skilled in acquiring, creating, sharing, managing, modeling, measuring, and applying knowledge. As such, learning is a process of development of higher-order cognitive skills, including decision making, problem solving, teamwork, critical thinking, and situational awareness. It is part of the process by which organizations—traditional and leading-edge companies alike—create and foster intellectual capital and, most importantly, build competitive advantage by responding to customers faster, more cheaply, and more comprehensively.[21]

TABLE 1.3   The New Performance Paradigm

Today ⟶	Tomorrow
Organizations	Project teams
Time to train	Time to perform
Generic technology	Job/task specific technology
Incremental improvements	Order of magnitude gains
Automating known processes	Innovative new processes
Preplanned training	Adaptive performance support
Trained	Readiness
Technology operators	Process managers

Source: H. Wayne Hodgins, *Into the Future: A Vision Paper*, National Governors' Association (NGA) and American Society for Training and Development (ASTD), 2000, pp. 19–25.

CHANGING BUSINESS FORMS

International markets beckon to corporations to become global organizations, a transformation based upon building competitive advantage and market leadership in a series of stages. Although there is no universally accepted definition of globalization, the expression "think globally, act locally" has been used to describe a global company. Such an organization is managing operations worldwide and employing functionally integrated, standardized operations, while responding opportunistically to market opportunities in specific countries or regions. The definition is less important than the economic drivers and market trends that shape companies and direct them to target certain levels of involvement on the global scene. In this regard, it is appropriate to trace the achievement of global status through a series of organizational changes within companies.

In the twenty-first century, of the six principal types of organizational business models shown in Fig. 1.2, the dominant models are (1) the multinational corporation, (2) the global company, and (3) the transnational organization. In general, organizations tend to be in a transitional stage between two organizational models, with reality often being a strong preference for the transnational model. The organizational structures of multinational and global firms are shown in Fig. 1.3. Transnational firms strategically align and integrate the organizational characteristics of both these structures to leverage the positive aspects of both to strategic advantage, as shown in Table 1.4.

The characteristics of the multinational, global, and transnational organizational forms are briefly reviewed from two perspectives: (1) a business structure point of view, and (2) the role of culture and the inherent requirements of employee cultural awareness.

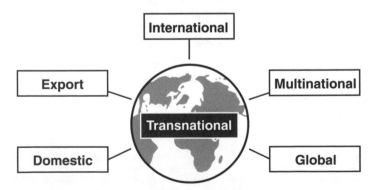

FIGURE 1.2   The six principal types of organizational business models.

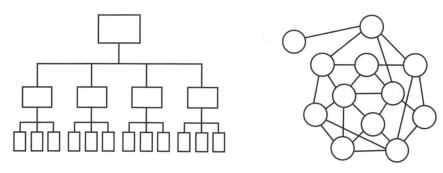

FIGURE 1.3   Multinational and global structures.

TABLE 1.4   Multinational vs. Global/Transnational Organizational Characteristics

Multinational	Global/transnational
One primary center	Many centers
Hierarchical structure	Network
Rigid geographic organization	Generally organized by products,
"Multidomestic," i.e., try to appear as a	businesses, functions
domestic company within each country	Organic
Key value is maintaining local	People are rotated around the world
responsiveness	Process
Boss/subordinate	Interactive
Chain of command	Matrix
Information is power	Information is resource

Organizational Forms: Multinational

A multinational company is one whose national or regional operations act independently of one another, causing communication problems and hindering operational efficiency. Within the multinational corporation, tensions begin to emerge between the need for national responsiveness at the subsidiary level and the need for more centralized integration at the global level, where headquarters faces multinational customers, global competitors, and requirements for larger volume to permit economies of scale. Strategic planning is completed at the headquarters level. The multinational corporation is further defined by the following characteristics:

- Has a centralized parent company or headquarters in one country that is responsible for strategy, technological structures, and resource allocation worldwide.

- Has subsidiaries, or independent business units, in other countries, each of which markets, sells, and distributes products within its own region or country.
- Encourages the subsidiaries to adapt the structures and practices of the firm to the cultural context of each country or region, so that each subsidiary looks and acts like a domestic company.
- Relies on the subsidiaries for input to the parent company's decisions on marketing, sales, manufacturing, customer service, and competitive strategies.
- Can be formed through strategic alliances and joint ventures, which strive to leverage the strengths of both parties, increase efficiency, and decrease the exposure to risk as they share rewards.
- Collects and uses information on multidomestic trends, environmental conditions, and strategic resources.
- Leverages the expertise of cross-cultural, cross-functional work teams.
- Responds and adapts to destabilizing changes by being flexible in reallocating resources across national markets.
- Requires managers to work effectively in many roles across cultures.

ROLE OF CULTURE
In a multinational company, the organization must:

- Replicate successful approaches to business used by the domestic companies in the countries where it operates.
- Rely on its subsidiaries to understand the local, national, and/or regional cultures.
- Develop cross-cultural competence at the headquarters or parent company to conduct business effectively with the subsidiaries.

Organizational Forms: Global

A global company shares resources on a global basis in order to access the best market with the highest-quality product at the lowest cost. The global multinational pushes for tighter integration at the headquarters level, while host country operations emphasize local responsiveness. In the matrix structure, authority is shared by headquarters/international division and the production entity in the host country. In this more complex business environment, the global organization faces intense worldwide competition and pressures for strategic integration and control.

As the multinational corporation evolved during the 1980s and early 1990s, certain problems of communication and efficiency of operations became evident. These problems stemmed from the clash between the need for national responsiveness at the subsidiary level and the need for more centralized integration from headquarters at a truly global level of operation, as shown in Table 1.5.

A global corporation seeks to balance structure and flexibility, global and local needs, and on-time product delivery and low costs. Finding the right balance between local responsiveness and global efficiency requires a particular mindset based on a large degree of trust in local management to "get it right." Through such flexibility of thinking, a balance can be achieved between centrally decided givens (branding, pricing, source of manufacture) and local market creativity (product range, distribution, promotional activity). This mixture of strategy integration and operations differentiation suggests a key competency requirement: managing complexity. Finding the right balance is difficult. Bob Shapiro, former CEO of Monsanto, described it in this manner: "Restructuring a company to become global is like designing an airplane while flying in it."[22]

The most common characteristics of global companies:

- The multinational corporation is extended so that national or regional boundaries are no longer barriers.
- The company makes decisions to deliver products in the best markets, at the lowest cost, with the appropriate management resources, regardless of where funds, people, raw materials, technology, etc., reside.
- The company combines a centralized global strategic intent and/or a broad-based resource, technology, and marketing allocation plan with a localized customer focus that is responsive to regional or local conditions.
- Resource allocation is free-flowing.
- The company creates global strategic partnerships, i.e., inter- and intraorganizational linkages.

TABLE 1.5   Grid of Globalization

	Process/initiative	Execution/implementation
Global (integrated)	Standardized	Standardized
Common (harmonized)	Standardized	Localized
Local (separated)	Localized	Localized

Source: "Doing Business Globally" workshop, Training Management Corporation, 2001.

- The company creates fluid conditions to be proactive and gain advantages in the marketplace.

Organizational Forms: Transnational

A transnational organization is characterized by an integration of resources and responsibilities across all business units regardless of national boundaries, yet with all business units anchored to a strong corporate identity. A key problem facing the transnational company is the complexity of decision making that results from the flexible linking of local operations in order to leverage local and headquarters capabilities. The complexity of coordination and control inherent in the formal matrix structure typical of the transnational company often creates pressures to adopt a more informal matrix structure.

As identified by Christopher A. Bartlett and Sumantra Ghoshal,[23] the transnational corporation strives to combine

- The economies of scale of a global corporation.
- The responsiveness of a multinational corporation.
- The technology transfer efficiency of the international structure.
- The localization of the domestic company.

In their work *Managing across Borders*, Bartlett and Ghoshal, proponents of this new form of global entity, describe the transnational company as a company that has surpassed the multinational and global companies by developing the capability of managing across national frontiers, retaining and leveraging local and central headquarters capabilities in a manner that achieves global integration, maintains a strong corporate identity, and communicates a clear worldwide management perspective:

- There is an integrated network that shares decision making, and components, products, resources, information, and people flow freely between its interdependent units. Every part of the organization has to collaborate, share information, solve problems and collectively implement strategy.
- Managers in transnationals use "co-option" to develop consensus; each individual must understand, share, and internalize the company's purpose, values, and key strategies. This helps avoid the danger of decision making that is limited by narrow perspectives and parochial interests. In particularly complex, multitiered organizations, this problem is exacerbated by conflicting interests and overlapping responsibilities and often leads to complex matrix structures.
- Control through a single method is insufficient. Highly formal and institutionalized control mechanisms and centralized decision making are

necessary in combination with socialization and co-option as the most effective means of coordination.

Instead of encouraging local innovations or imposing ideas from the center, the transnational allocates worldwide product responsibilities to different national subsidiaries according to their relative skills and strengths. One of the competitive strengths of a transnational is its ability to facilitate organizational learning by fostering a flow of intelligence, ideas, and knowledge around the organization.[24]

ROLE OF CULTURE

In global and transnational companies, the organization must

- Consciously develop a global organizational culture.
- Reframe diversity from a global perspective.
- Prepare employees for short- to midterm global rotations.
- Facilitate learning about cultures and their values, beliefs, expectations, and behaviors in order to be successful worldwide.
- Develop effective multicultural teamwork and structures for collaboration.
- Require that managers be able to manage, transcend, and/or leverage cultural differences appropriately and effectively.

HEIGHTENED RELEVANCE OF CULTURE

Responding to the new challenges of globalization requires clarity of vision and understanding of the behavioral role of management and organizations in this constantly changing new world. Developing leaders and managers who are capable of working across cultures is a critical challenge. The rapid expansion of global business in the last decade of the twentieth century has made it impossible to ignore the growing integration and interdependence among national economies, the tension between value sets, and the importance of a diverse, fully competent, and skilled workforce as the drivers of organizational competitiveness and strategic advantage.

At the very heart of the challenge of globalization is the *cultural challenge*, which, like a hologram, cannot be confined to one level. From the broadest societal perspective, it poses the question of how distinctive groups will collaborate to transcend and leverage their differences for their common good.

At the level of governments, it means establishing terms of engagement that can facilitate the delicate balancing of political sovereignty, economic interconnectedness, and moral/ethical convergence. The formation of regional or world bodies and agreements, such as the United Nations, World Trade Organization, European Union, and Asia Pacific Economic Cooperation (APEC), is but an initial attempt at this balancing.

At the level of those organizations that cannot but drive McWorldization, it means carefully calibrating their global moves with an understanding of the sociocultural environments across which they operate. The failure of General Electric's pursuit of Honeywell as a result of an injunction by the European Commission is a good example of divergent sociocultural perspectives on global business.

Maintaining an appropriate balance will require the exercise of global corporate citizenship with a broadly understood sense of global ethics and ethos. At the same time, the challenge of managing a global business extends far beyond questions of global citizenship. As Jeffrey Garten writes,

> Several issues arise, including how to be big enough to be a credible global player but at the same time flexible and adaptable enough to move with the rapidly changing currents that the pace of trade liberalization and deregulation, the rise of big emerging markets and the Internet will bring. How do you expand your diversity of talent and still maintain a coherent corporate culture? How do you leverage your assets around the world so that you are far more than the sum of the individual parts of a global company? And how do you lead and manage a complicated multinational firm where effective control by any chief executive may simply be out of reach?[25]

For us as individuals, the challenge of multiculturalism is part of our daily working lives: We depend on, work with, and communicate with people of different origins and backgrounds, often across communication technologies. You could work as a call center representative in Bangalore, India, responding to calls from the United States with a carefully acquired U.S. accent and concomitant identity. You could be a computer programmer working in the Santa Cruz Electronic Export Processing Zone outside of Bombay, writing software for American Express, Swissair, or AT&T. You could be a worker from Turkey assembling vehicles to be exported to Hong Kong in a Ford plant in Cologne, Germany. You could be a French research scientist working virtually in a product development team with colleagues from Mexico, Canada, the United Kingdom, Japan, and China. You could be a manager reporting to three bosses, each located in a different country that is not his or her country of origin.

The accelerating degree of contact and exchange among cultures is redefining our worlds and posing continuous personal, management, and business challenges. It is these very contacts that most tangibly bring into our daily awareness the challenges and contradiction of globalization. Successfully balancing the forces of globalization rests on the skills of leaders and managers in all areas of society to consciously take on that challenge, learn to navigate this most basic and complex phenomenon called *culture*, and develop *cultural competence*.

Given the size, scope, and weight of today's transnational/globalizing organizations (after all, 51 of the largest 100 economies are transnational organizations[26]), it is within these organizations that these skills are both most in demand and potentially the most promising and far-reaching in their application. In these organizations, managers and executives increasingly work on multifarious cultural frontiers and literally shape the future. The way to lead these organizations and manage within them is no longer rooted in what seems to be the "natural approach." It requires a global mindset, an ability to balance threats and opportunities, embrace deep personal and organizational transformation, and, in the words of Rosabeth Moss Kanter, "work at the frontiers of management." [27] In this regard, we agree with Francis Fukuyama, who, in his review of Samuel Huntington's *The Clash of Civilizations*,[28] says:

> The increasing salience of culture in the global order is such that Samuel Huntington has argued that the world is moving into a period of "civilizational clash," in which the primary identification of people will not be ideological, but cultural. . . . Huntington is clearly correct that cultural differences will loom larger from now on and that all societies will have to pay more attention to culture as they deal not only with internal problems but with the outside world. [But] cultural differences will [not] necessarily be the source of conflict. On the contrary, the rivalry arising from the interaction of different cultures can frequently lead to creative change.[29]

Cultural Competence and Competitive Advantage

A different level of awareness, competence, and skill is required to navigate the relativity and complexity of the multicultural global work- and marketplace. Most international and multinational companies have learned to integrate the most obvious elements of cultural competence into their competitive strategies. Procter & Gamble (P&G), for example, first entered the Japanese market in 1973 and had lost $200 million by 1987. Entering this market with American goods and advertising just didn't work.

By 1990, P&G had turned Japan into its second biggest foreign market (after Germany). Paying close attention to the Japanese culture and market had paid off: P&G came to understand that advertising that knocks the com-

petition is offensive to the Japanese, who value harmony and avoid direct conflict. The company found that product performance is a top priority for
Japanese customers, who are less concerned about price than customers in the
United States. It also discovered how to adapt its products to the space constraints of Japanese homes. And it quickly realized that the Japanese are also
very company-conscious and are quick to relate a product to the image and
reputation of the company.

P&G developed cultural competence and reaped success as a result by

- Understanding the customer's habits, biases, and attitudes.
- Adapting products to the market.
- Being sensitive to Japanese cultural differences.
- Penetrating the multitiered distribution system in Japan.
- Selling the company as well as the brands.

P&G's experience is only one example of what many companies went
through in the 1980s and early 1990s. As a matter of survival, they had to
unlearn key assumptions that were embedded in their products, services, and
business practices; they had to explore how to do business from a different
viewpoint. In fact, P&G's experience in Japan makes the obvious case for how
important cultural competence is to competitive advantage in a multicultural
global marketplace. It contrasts sharply with the abundance of cross-cultural
failures, including the well-known case of Chevrolet's Nova in Mexico, where
no va means "it doesn't go."

However, assuming that sensitivity and responsiveness to foreign markets
are all that there is to cultural competence would be a gross simplification.
Indeed, venturing into foreign territory and adapting to its most salient features is only the beginning of the cultural learning curve for many organizations, a learning curve that accompanies a journey into rampant complexity,
uncertainty, and ambiguity.

Within global companies, with their complex global matrix structures and
their networked, projected approach to work, a global multicultural workforce
needs to communicate and collaborate effectively in order to realize the benefits and promises of global efficiencies. The ability to attract, develop, and
retain talent globally is key to the performance of these organizations. It is the
ability of this talent to communicate, collaborate effectively, and work in virtual teams or "collaborative units" that realizes the organization's potential.

At companies such as Bristol-Myers Squibb, Hoffmann-LaRoche,
Novartis, Merck, and Johnson & Johnson, pharmaceutical research and
development rest squarely on the abilities of scientists and managers to work

in cross-functional and multicultural teams. Product development and marketing at companies like Avon or Revlon hinge on how well global teams can leverage insights into local markets to optimally coordinate development, manufacturing, marketing, and distribution. At Corning, Air Products and Chemicals, and American Express, geographically dispersed teams are creating the global IT infrastructure. Programmers and network specialists from all over the world—Russia, Israel, Germany, the United States, the United Kingdom, India, etc.—are charged with combining their innovation, creativity, and problem-solving skills. The success of these teams and of everyone involved depends significantly on how well the team members understand the differing culture-based expectations of work, workplace relationships, management, and leadership and possess the skills to transcend and leverage these expectations.

The telecommunications, Internet, and e-commerce revolution has created a new frontier for culture in a twofold way. First, the ways in which new technologies are developed, absorbed, and utilized reflect specific cultural underpinnings. Alison Maitland's *Financial Times* article "Throw the Rule-Book Out of the Window"[30] provides a good account of the cultural underpinning of e-business ventures. She investigates how cultural features such as risk taking, tolerance of failure, and flat organizational structures facilitate market leadership in e-business innovation. Understanding and managing these cultural variables may, in fact, be critical for understanding the economic creativity index that was introduced as an important part of the new competitiveness rating by the 2000 Global Competitiveness Report.[31] If competitiveness increasingly depends on innovation and creativity, those countries and companies that understand how to create the necessary cultural conditions will have an edge.

Second, communication and Internet technology have created a new arena for human interaction for which no clear norms can be discerned. Few people seem to view email, videoconferencing, teleconferencing, and ERP (Enterprise Resource Planning) systems as an improvement in communication. Each individual tends to utilize technology in ways compatible with his or her preferences, judgments, and circumstances. Frustration and confusion tend to ensue, whereas clear norms and standards would help bring about increased effectiveness and efficiency. Developing these standards and norms amounts to building a new culture, one that governs the utilization of technology and its integration into daily work practices

The challenge of developing a new culture is not restricted to teams and/or work groups; it is an organizational and leadership imperative. Edgar Schein[32] specifically emphasizes this function of leadership. The surge in international joint ventures, mergers, and acquisitions has given a new urgency to the art and craft of cultural integration. As Anne Fisher writes: "Any merger is doomed if there is no real effort beforehand to see whether the two cultures have anything in common."[33] Consequently leaders at DaimlerChrysler, Allianz, and Mannesmann/Vodafone are facing the challenge of integrating, coordinating, and separating processes; breaking down barriers to information flow and collaboration; and creating a seamless operation.

DaimlerChrysler's Juergen Schrempp observes that "there are cultural barriers to sharing, and breaking down the walls is difficult. The traditional thing was 'I'll always have something in my drawer which is private for me— my knowledge, because I want to be superior.' The internet makes it easier to break down barriers, of course, but we still have ways to go to maximize what will be possible and essential."[34] For Robert Heller, however, these statements express an unwarranted but all too common focus on technology (rather than on managerial and people processes) as an integrator. According to him, there is no worse example of managerial deterioration than that at Chrysler after the "heavy handed intrusion of supreme power from Stuttgart" injected a hierarchical structure that undercut the massive investment in managerial democratization infrastructure, namely its information and communication technology.[35] Alarming is the 1992 Coopers & Lybrand study that found that 85 percent of executives in failed or troubled mergers say that differences in management style and practices are the major cause. Here are some examples:

- Daniel Industries Companies, a U.S. gas pipeline instrumentation company, acquired Messtechnik Babelsberg, a measuring instrument firm in the former East Germany. This decision enabled Daniel Industries to reduce the land, labor, building, and start-up costs of entering the European market substantially. Yet the integration process needed to focus significantly on language issues, decision-making processes, and standards of performance management.

- U.S.-based General Electric acquired Tungsman, a Hungarian lightbulb maker, to increase its market share in Europe, establish a pan-European distribution network using highly skilled electrical design workers at comparatively low wages, and support GE's Japanese and U.S. markets with an advanced skill base. Again, successfully addressing cultural issues, such as language barriers, divergent work ethics, differences in performance management, and manager/subordinate relationships, were critical elements that determined the success of the acquisition.

- Infosys and Reliance Industries are among a handful of Indian high-tech companies that are recognized for making sweeping changes in their corporate governance and management practices by adopting Anglo-American standards. These changes, facilitated by the country's English-speaking elite's orientation toward the United Kingdom and the United States and by a democratic political system grounded in common law, are designed to make these companies more attractive partners for Western companies in need of highly skilled talent and for emerging market investors.

Whether for U.S.-based IBM or PPG Industries, U.K.-based Marconi, Germany's Schering AG, France's Alcatel, Italy's Fiat, Japan's Toyota, Korea's Samsung, Swiss-Swedish ABB, or Hong Kong's HBSC, the success of cross-border mergers, acquisitions, and joint ventures hinges on how the companies' leaders understand the process of melding different organizational cultures, recognizing the way each is rooted in its own societal environment while fully leveraging the value that each represents.

Globalizing organizations are adapting their structures, infrastructures, processes, and scopes of activities to make the worldwide market virtually local. This means creating ways in which their people can transcend the sources of distance arising from their management and business practices. The need to globalize invests culture with prime strategic importance, especially since the events of September 11. The impact of these events on the globalization process is significant, underlining the value of cultural awareness and cross-cultural skills for individuals, teams, organizations, and countries.

LEADERSHIP CHALLENGES IN A GLOBAL WORLD

It is no secret that we are in an era of global business. The rapid growth of increasingly interconnected markets, processes, and operations is affecting virtually every industry, company, and worker today. Between the increase in strategic business alliances and the proliferation of global organizations, the share of the market held by companies that span two or more business cultures is growing constantly.

These trends have changed the criteria for competitive advantage. Past success in the old marketplace does not guarantee future success in the new. Speed, responsiveness, flexibility, effectiveness, and an ever-increasing rate of innovation have become the foundations of success in today's market, and organizations everywhere have been transforming themselves to adapt to these new requirements. Most organizations now understand that competitive advantage is no longer derived from formal structures but requires a dynamic organizational culture that effectively encompasses the mindsets, competencies, and practices of the individuals who create, support, and sustain the organization, individuals who often do not share the same cultural background.

This new type of organization also calls for a different type of manager, one who can create this type of dynamic, flexible environment and draw upon her or his employees' varied mindsets and skills. The current global leadership debate involves a host of different definitions of what global leadership is and which criteria best describe the behaviors and expectations of an effective global leader in today's and the future's economic environments. It is important to consider the scope and speed of change that the globalization of business and technology—i.e., the Internet and biotechnology—will bring about in increasingly compressed time intervals. Current trends indicate that the growth of a networked global economy, heavily shaped by a revolution in IT applications, will have a substantial impact on the leadership requirements for managers of medium and small multinational businesses whose strategic vision targets sustained international development. It will be critical that managers within these organizations have leadership skills adequate to handle the key drivers shaping business growth.

To establish a set of characteristics of an effective global leader, it is necessary to first determine what exactly is required of tomorrow's leaders in terms of awareness, understanding, and skills. What managerial and leadership competencies coupled with an articulate comprehension of the cross-cultural competencies are required to manage the network of structures and systems required by organizations in the twenty-first century? Building competitive advantage will require leadership skills and competencies that are properly aligned with the forces of change.

Emerging global business policies and practices will test and change existing paradigms of global business. To be successful in the global business environment, organizations must thus constantly adjust their focus to changing realities. Key managers must lead the process, fostering new patterns of thinking to position the organization in a world without traditional boundaries and shaped by local environments. They must perform more quickly and dynamically in the face of increased organizational ambiguity, complexity, and information overload.

The rapid growth of increasingly interconnected markets, processes, and operations has made the formation of new work structures imperative and has driven organizations everywhere to transform themselves structurally in order to remain competitive. Today's globalizing organizations have found that the ability to collaborate, establish relationships, and produce results across social, cultural, and geographic distances is central to success in the new marketplace. The need for greater speed, responsiveness, flexibility, effectiveness, and innovation has thus generated matrixed, projectized, globally diverse work environments in which collaboration plays an increasingly important role. In these environments, teamwork is an ever-increasing phenomenon. Individuals from diverse cultural backgrounds, different fields of expertise, and various geographic locations are brought together for a period of time to collaborate on one or more projects.

THE KEY TO SUCCESS: DEVELOPING A GLOBAL MINDSET

Only through a fundamental shift in mindset and the translation of this shift into new ways of working can we transcend the sources of distance that pose formidable barriers to swift collective performance. The biggest challenge will be to continually develop and refine our global mindset. The tools we have learned in the past will be stretched to the limit as we examine new global industry imperatives, organizations, and resource allocation models. Figure 1.4 and Table 1.6 shows how the global mindset compares with the traditional mindset in five central areas: general perspective, organizational life, work style, view of change, and learning. The concentric rings in Fig. 1.4 illustrate how a global mindset must grow out of, but come to both encompass and supersede, a local mindset. The aim is not to abandon the traditional mindset, but rather to develop cross-cultural competence that enhances our global mindset or perspective.

With a multicultural membership and a global scope, teams operate on the frontiers of human collaboration. Competitive advantage rests squarely on how well the organization deals with culture and cultural differences.

It was once assumed that business and commerce were culturally neutral zones in which professionals from various nations came together to participate in transactions according to universally recognized norms. This is simply not true. The ways in which we manage and conduct business are extensions of our social and cultural environments and thus are deeply influenced by cultural values and associated behavior patterns. Working in the multicultural environment of the global marketplace, today's managers are confronted with

FIGURE 1.4   The global mindset.

TABLE 1.6   The Traditional vs. the Global Mindset

	Traditional mindset	Global mindset
General perspective	Functional Specialized	Cross-functional Cross-cultural Enabling boundaryless organizations
Organizational life	Forces are prioritized Conflict is eliminated Hierarchy is trusted	Contradictions are balanced (global standards vs. local practices) Conflict is leveraged as an opportunity Networked processes are trusted Global objectives are supported Influence, persuasion, and presentation skills are key
Work style	Personal self-awareness primary Individual mastery primary	Cultural and personal self- and other-awareness Networked collaboration Teamwork primary Managing in a global matrix Effective use of communication technologies
View of change	Surprises are avoided Change is seen as threat	Change is expected, valued, and actively enabled Change is seen as opportunity Change is seen as personal growth
Learning	Specific knowledge and skills are mastered Training is valued	Broad-based lifelong learning is engaged Education and learning are valued Global learning is key success factor Responsible for career development

Source: Training Management Corporation, "Doing Business Globally" and "The Effective Global Manager," seminars and coursebook (Princeton, N.J.).

this every day. The individuals with whom they conduct business and whom they manage often represent a collection of different cultures with different, sometimes conflicting practices.

The main challenge for today's global manager is to combine a repertoire of managerial and leadership skills with a thorough understanding of and sensitivity to culture. The "hard skills" of business tasks and the "soft skills" of interacting and communicating have thus become intertwined and can no longer be easily distinguished. Today's manager must be able to successfully integrate cultural knowledge into his or her understanding of how to manage business and daily work.

The process of global learning requires an ongoing commitment of time and energy and, perhaps more important, the ability to admit that you never know everything and to be always open to learning something new. The development of these competencies is a strategic imperative for today's industries and organizations; fortunately, it can also be an enormous source of personal and professional enrichment and pride for those who engage in this process as a lifelong undertaking.

As Rosabeth Moss Kanter points out, a key to the search for a new business mindset is the "triumph of process over structure." The issue is how people can work together to pursue new opportunities. Developing cross-cultural competencies is fundamental to this change process. The ability of people from different countries and cultures to think and work together is a primary element of the success of global/transnational organizations.

SUMMARY INSIGHTS

The economic landscape of the world is changing rapidly and becoming increasingly global. How successful a company is in exploiting emerging opportunities and tackling the accompanying challenges depends critically on how intelligent it is—and its employees are—at observing and interpreting the dynamic world in which it operates. Creating a global mindset is one of the essential elements for building such intelligence. Developing a global mindset is far from easy; nevertheless, it is critical. The main value of a global mindset is that it enables a company to combine speed with accurate response, building on an insight into the needs of the local market and building bridges between these needs and a company's own global experience and capabilities.

For virtually every company, in developed as well as developing economies, market opportunities, critical resources, leading-edge ideas, and competitors exist both in home markets and, increasingly, in distant and little-understood regions of the world. As companies expand in the global marketplace, they face an increasingly complex challenge of dealing with a mix of cultures both as customers/consumers and as leaders and managers.

Culture is inextricably incorporated into business, managerial practice and behavior, and economic development. As people from different cultures with different values and beliefs interact, management practice and process are critically affected, and success in the attainment of performance objectives is critically influenced by the most subtle, often invisible, yet deeply ingrained elements of the human character. Culture is a dominant aspect of the human condition, and today's manager, working in a highly competitive, ever-changing global context, must be ever sensitive to it and skilled in dealing with it.

2

CULTURE

Culture will be, as it always has been, of critical importance in deciding the relative fortunes of the major world economies. Those institutions and organizations that recognize and articulate this fact will have the lead on those that neglect it.

JOHN VINEY, *CULTURE WARS*

*I*n Chap. 1 we underscore the importance of culture to the competitiveness of societies, economies, and organizations. No organization can afford to neglect the cultural underpinnings of its performance, just as no manager or leader has the luxury of ignoring the cultural characteristics that make him or her successful. The desire to penetrate and capture foreign market space has started a journey that has increasingly moved cultural competence from the periphery of a company's business focus to the very center: the mindset and skill set of its workforce.

The challenge is to build synergy between what sets us apart and leverage differences for competitive advantage. Converting this into decisions and actions is ultimately the work of small groups of individuals with the vision, influence, and determination to effect change. These individuals share the responsibility of developing and continuously furthering cultural competence in the company's workforce at every level. In this chapter, we explore this notion and its components further. We also survey research into key cultural variables that can aid in this process.

CULTURAL COMPETENCE

The cultural competence needed in our business organizations at both the organizational and the individual level consists of five interrelated aspects that need to be honed through continuous learning and development.

Open Attitude

The first building block objective is to develop the openness of a global mindset to ensure receptivity to cross-cultural learning and to maintain a productive attitude toward difference. This requires

- Challenging assumptions
- Avoiding quick judgments
- Tolerating ambiguity and complexity
- Exercising patience
- Pursuing learning

To be effective in a global business environment, we must examine and modify our existing mindset to ensure that it is broad and conducive to learning. An open attitude is a prerequisite for the other four aspects of cross-cultural competence. It must be maintained at all times in order to ensure learning and development of personal and professional skills.

Self-Awareness

The next thing we need to focus on is the development of self-awareness and knowledge of our own cultural preferences. This requires answering questions such as

- What are my cultural values, beliefs, and attitudes?
- How are my values, beliefs, and attitudes reflected in my behavior?

- What aspects of which cultures have formed who I am?
- How do these aspects affect the way I manage and/or do business?
- What behaviors or attitudes do I engage in that might damage business relationships?
- What situations and behaviors make me feel uncomfortable and ill at ease?
- What situations and behaviors make me feel comfortable and put me at ease?
- What attitudes, behaviors, and assumptions do I have that are helpful in cultivating cross-cultural business relationships?
- How adaptable and tolerant of ambiguity am I?
- How can I increase my capacity for cross-cultural learning?

Other-Awareness

We must also focus on recognizing the cultural values, attitudes, beliefs, and behaviors of others in order to be able to develop new cross-cultural business skills. Questions to be answered include:

- What could the cultural preferences of my counterparts be?
- What values might my counterparts be expressing in their behaviors?
- What are the needs and expectations of my counterparts, tacit or open?
- How do these needs and expectations affect the way my counterparts do business?
- What cultural disconnects are affecting the interactions between me and my counterparts?
- What is our cultural common ground?
- How willing are my counterparts to learn about my cultural preferences?
- How can we build and maintain trusting business relationships with one another?

Cultural Knowledge

We must ground our cultural awareness in a comprehensive knowledge of other social and business cultures. Questions to be answered include:

- What general knowledge about a culture do I need to acquire?
- What specific business or industry knowledge do I need when conducting business in this context?

- How has the outlook on life in a given culture been shaped by history?
- How are conflicts resolved, decisions made, and problems solved in this culture?
- What motivates people in this culture, and how is performance rewarded?
- How are relationships established and maintained in this culture?
- Where does one get the necessary information about this culture, and what resources are at my disposal (e.g., Internet sites, books, CD-ROMs, films, videos, peers, magazines)?
- Are there people in my organization who can offer insights into other cultures, and how is that information stored and accessed?

Cross-Cultural Skills

Developing the skills needed to work effectively across cultures requires that the following questions be posed:

- How do I translate my awareness and knowledge into skills?
- How can I improve my ability to work in multicultural situations?
- How can I continue to refine and improve my skills?
- How do we adapt our business practices or management skills to a particular culture or situation?

Open, receptive attitudes built on curiosity and a willingness to undertake continuous learning are the foundation for developing cultural competence. These attitudes facilitate the development of self- and other-awareness. To become useful, however, this awareness needs to be grounded in a knowledge of culture (both general and specific), and that knowledge needs to be translated into specific cross-cultural skills and practices. By developing on all four levels, a manager builds the confidence and ability to integrate cultural differences into new and more rewarding ways of doing business. By making this an organizational competence, companies build their diversity into competitive advantage.

We have been successful in developing the hardware for increased globalization, such as transportation networks, computer and communications technologies, and flexible manufacturing systems. Where we have been weak has been in fostering in our managers and workers the flexibility and knowledge needed to maximize the value of the cultural capital available to the organization. As Edward T. Hall said about humanity in general, but which can also be applied to business specifically, "The future of the human race lies in maintaining its diversity and turning that diversity to its advantage."[1]

Cultural competence is no longer just a nice skill to have; it is fast becoming a key success factor. In our consulting practice, we have focused on developing practical and sound perspectives, approaches, tools, and practices that enable cultural competence. We have developed:

- A distinctive perspective on the phenomenon of culture that is conducive to building an open attitude

- A framework for understanding culture-based differences, the Cultural Orientations Model, that anchors the development of self-awareness, other-awareness, cultural knowledge, and cross-cultural skills

- A comprehensive learning and development system that links awareness from an individual cultural profile, the Cultural Orientations Indicator, to culture-specific knowledge and skill building

In the following pages, we do not just want to summarize our thinking and experience and introduce you to our approach and tools for building cultural competence; we want you to learn to use these tools to assist your own personal learning journey.

FINDING OUR FEET: UNDERSTANDING CULTURE

Success on this journey depends significantly on understanding culture and appreciating how profoundly our values, attitudes, and behaviors are shaped by it.

Unfortunately, culture is a complex phenomenon, the understanding of which is aided neither by the diffuse use of the term in everyday conversation nor by the wealth of definitions in current use. In 1952, Kroeber and Kluckhohn[2] identified 162 different definitions of the term *culture*. At the very outset, then, we face the challenge of developing an understanding of culture that both captures its essence and will serve as a practical guide to the broad spectrum of cultural diversity.

The philosopher Ludwig Wittgenstein captured the profound effect of culture when he wrote, "One human being can be a complete enigma to another. We learn this when we come into a strange country with entirely strange traditions; and what is more, even given a mastery of the country's language. We do not *understand* the people. (And not because of not knowing what they are saying to themselves.) We cannot find our feet with them."[3] An inability to find our feet is an apt description of the feeling of intense disorientation that can accompany contact with a new culture.

Wittgenstein implicitly captures three important insights: (1) Culture is a force that operates deep in the shadows of our interactions, (2) we are generally unaware of this force unless we experience an *ill-fit* in a different environment or context, and (3) obvious elements such as language are insufficient for understanding the true differences. Every expatriate manager, sojourner, or member of a global team will have this experience. An engineer from the United States may find herself working on a project team in Poland during April, troubleshooting problems in South Korea in May, and training engineers from India, Egypt, and Sweden in June, all the while staying in touch with her manager from Mexico and her peers from the Philippines and Canada via telephone, email, and voice mail. This engineer's ability to find her feet quickly with diverse people in a number of situations and contexts is critical to her success. For her, as for all of us in the multicultural, global environment, the ability to find her feet translates into her skill in establishing trust, credibility, and rapport.

We believe that most approaches to culture that are proposed today fall short and are not well matched to the types of cultural challenges typically faced by globalizing organizations and by global managers and leaders. To be useful, a perspective on culture needs to be of practical value in helping us to (1) navigate a broad spectrum of differences, (2) understand the fundamentals of various cultures and cross-cultural interactions, and (3) translate this understanding into personal behaviors and organizational expectations.

Roy D'Andrade is quoted as saying that studying culture in today's world is like studying snow in the middle of an avalanche.[4] To guide us in our endeavor, we have developed several axioms about culture.

Axiom 1: Cultural Boundaries Are Not National Boundaries

In the field of cross-cultural communication, the concept of cultural boundaries is often used interchangeably with those of geographical and political boundaries (i.e., the nation). This perspective delineates different values and belief systems largely on the basis of national boundaries.[5] This perspective nicely matches the contemporary understanding of the world, in which we have institutionalized the boundaries of sovereign nation-states as the universally recognized boundaries between peoples. It also has served well those businesses that divided the world into neat geographic regions and serviced them with a multinational organizational structure.

With the dynamic expansion of globalization, using geographical/political worldviews to represent cultural differences is no longer useful and in fact carries with it rather dangerous baggage. Erich Wolf most poignantly expresses the danger: "By endowing nations, societies or cultures with the qualities of internally homogeneous and externally distinctive and bounded objects, we create a model of the world as a global pool hall in which the entities spin off each other like so many hard and round billiard balls. Thus it becomes easy to sort the world into differently colored balls."[6] In this respect, we may say of the general thinking about culture, and the understanding of it that we foster in our organizations, what the renowned Spanish thinker José Ortega y Gasset said of notions of society in the 1940s and 1950s: "One of the most greatest misfortunes of our times is that the peoples of the West, coming up against the terrible public conflicts of today, have found themselves equipped with a wholly archaic set of notions on the meaning of society, collectivity, the individuals, customs, law. . . . Most of our statesmen, professors, distinguished physicists and novelists have opinions on these subjects worthy of a small-town barber."[7]

The simplistic habit of attributing characteristics to nationally defined groups is both unrealistic and unproductive in the global work environment. First, less than 10 percent of the world's nation-states can be considered homogeneous. In only half of these nation-states is there a single ethnic group that makes up 75 percent of the population.[8] *Multiculturalism is surely the norm and cultural homogeneity the exception.*

We do not have to resort to social scientists and philosophers to verify this axiom. We need only look into our own experience. Wouldn't we say that there are significant cultural variations within the nation to which we belong? Haven't many of our most profound experiences of difference taken place in the very country in which we were born? Doesn't this make dubious the utility and appropriateness of giving currency to differences based on nationality?

Ascribing characteristics on the basis of nationality can be an exercise in shorthand at best, an exercise based less on realism than on the need to develop a quick sketch of a different environment, mainly as an initial hypothesis to be qualified through careful verification and mindful engagement. What alternative understanding of culture do we need to cultivate?

Axiom 2: Culture Is a Shared Pattern of Ideas, Emotions, and Behaviors

Culture operates on both a conscious and an unconscious level; it both is a characteristic of groups and is carried by individuals. Many of the commonly used definitions of culture highlight these features. Geert Hofstede's definition, the "collective programming of the mind that distinguishes one group of people from another,"[9] emphasizes the shared aspect of a cognitive set of values, attitudes, and beliefs. Other definitions emphasize behavioral norms and rituals and/or institutions and products as key elements for the understanding of culture.[10]

We suggest that it is useful, in attempting to understand the programming language of culture, to think of it as an iceberg, as depicted in Fig. 2.1. The proverbial "tip of the iceberg" symbolizes the level of behavior and other

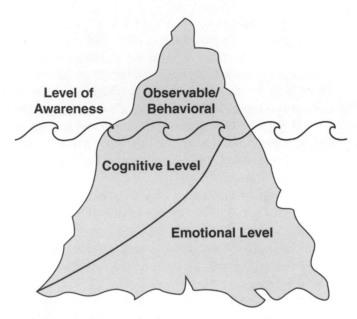

FIGURE 2.1 Culture—beyond the surface of awareness.

observables/tangibles—i.e., the world of manifestations. Beneath the level of our daily awareness, this behavior is linked to a world of values and meaning that is shared by a group. This internal world, which consists of ideas and their emotional value, is symbolically expressed as the "bottom of the iceberg."

You may, for example, observe an individual engage in a particular action upon greeting someone, such as a handshake, the folding of the hands in front of the chest area, or a bow. This individual has learned to associate this particular behavior with a key idea or notion, such as politeness and respect for others. In turn, the notions of politeness and respect are associated with a positive emotional disposition. Now, when the individual is engaged in shaking hands with or bowing to another, each is confirming to the other their shared notion of respect and politeness, and each instills in the other a positive disposition.

When two people have acquired different linkages between notion and behavior—when they greet each other with a bow on one side and an extended hand on the other—each fails to confirm the other's world of meaning, triggering momentary confusion and uncertainty.

In simplistic terms, the shared linkage between a behavioral expression (a handshake or a bow) and an idea or notion constitutes a *norm*. If we observe, for example, that a particular group of people tends to shake hands upon meeting, we may call this behavior the social norm for this group. The shared linkage between an idea/notion and an emotion can be considered a *value*.

Values and norms together constitute the programming language of cultural codes. These codes can differ on both the value and the norm level. While differences at the norm level are easy to bridge, those at the value level are much harder to reconcile. The example of greeting behaviors constitutes a clash of norms. However, the values of politeness and respect are shared. It is not that difficult for an individual entering a new group to substitute that group's behavior for his or her own when these behaviors express the same value.

However, consider the following: Two businessmen meeting for the first time are exchanging personal information. One asks the other about his children and proudly receives the following reply: "I have two sons; do you want to see pictures?" The first man answers yes and compliments the other on the good looks of his sons. After this exchange, the second man inquires about the first man's children. The first man takes out a picture of his three daughters. Upon seeing the picture, the second man exclaims: "Three daughters! Oh, I'm sorry!" In this scenario, two values are at odds. For the first man, children, regardless of gender, are of equally positive value; for the second, female children have a negative value, while male children have a positive value.

How do we acquire our patterns of norms and values? As human beings we are born into a social group whose "rules of engagement" we need to acquire. This process, known as *socialization* or *enculturation*, is a sort of cultural programming. Much of it takes place between birth and approximately 7 or 8 years of age, as it is during this period that each of us forms our sense of identity. Our parents and our immediate social environment play a dominant role in the process of acquiring these norms and values. Through intricate and, at most, semiconscious reinforcement and reward mechanisms, we acquire the deep dispositions, values, and norms that guide our behavior, provide our perspectives on the world, and profoundly define our sense of self and group affiliation.

These values and norms and the perspectives they engender are responsible for many social institutions, normative practices, and other systemic manifestations. The notion of *the equality of all human beings*, for example, became a dominant value in western industrialized societies, engendering a number of institutions, practices, and behavioral norms. It is at the foundation of the political system called *democracy* and its many institutions, such as parliaments, electoral systems, and legal systems. This value also finds expression in other areas of social life, such as the popularity of TV talk shows and the use of brainstorming as a problem-solving mode in businesses.

We may put forward the following definition of culture as a summary of the preceding discussion: *Culture is the complex pattern of ideas, emotions, and observable/symbolic manifestations (including behaviors, practices, institutions, and artifacts) that tends to be expected, reinforced, and rewarded by and within a particular group.*

Axiom 3: Cultures Reflect Distinctive Value Orientations at Various Levels

Axiom 1 rejects the simplistic popular understanding of culture as a static state or set of characteristics defining the population of a given country. Axiom 2 provides a framework for understanding the complex variables—the programming language—of any culture. The third axiom defines the scope and parameters of culture.

For our purposes, we may describe culture as holographic, i.e., as analogous to the structure of a holographic image. Holographic images are built in such a way that the smallest part contains the entirety of the image. The magnificence of the entire three-dimensional image that we behold is the result of the amplification and magnification of the totality of the smallest parts. Culture seems to work in much the same way, in that its smallest part—namely, the *individual*—contains within it the deep structure of values and norms. Both are amplified and reinforced in interpersonal interactions. The small group, or, in a business context, the team, further magnifies and reinforces cultural configurations. The same thing happens again at the larger societal level or, in a business context, at the organizational level.

The scope of culture is highly variable. It is an intrinsic aspect of any form of social organization, which leads us to the same conclusion as diplomat and anthropologist Carl Coon: "The parameters of a culture can be as varied as the human condition itself. The only requirement is that the people who share it sense that they are different from people who do not belong to their group."[11] Ultimately, the raison d'être of a culture seems to lie in the difference between *in*- and *out*-groups.[12]

Following this train of thought, it is useful for our purposes to distinguish four interrelated levels of culture:[13]

1. *The individual, interpersonal level.* This level is the primary building block of culture. It is at this level that we most significantly experience and create culture, namely through and in interactions with others. We may think of ourselves as reflections of a societal pattern of values and norms, a reflection that we exhibit through our actions and interactions. Through ourselves, we can both become aware of the larger societal patterns and also effect cultural changes through active shifts and changes in these patterns.

2. *The group or team level.* This level refers to social groupings of varying sizes as well as to functional/professional groups and teams. Each such group requires a set of values and norms if it is to be cohesive. As our interactions shape the dynamics of the group or team of which we are members, we as individuals directly affect the pattern of values and norms that define that group or team.

3. *The organizational level.* This level is a further amplification of basic cultural themes and configurations. It represents the deep patterns of values and norms that define societal institutions, including business organizations.

4. *The societal level.* This level involves the distinctive set of values, norms, practices, and institutions that define what it means to be a member of this society. It is the largest frame in which we feel membership, such as the *nation* or *modern society.*

Each distinguishable cultural group is characterized by a distinct set of behavioral norms, practices, and institutions that reflect a distinct set of value orientations. These value orientations critically define what it means to be a member of that group. Within each group, however, there will be significant variations around the dominant set of values, variations that are necessary if the group is to be able to adapt and change. As Florence Kluckhohn and Fred Strodtbeck point out, these value orientations have been variously defined as "systems of meaning," "unconscious canon of choice," "integrative themes," "ethos," and "configuration." Identifying the set of value orientations of a given group is akin to uncovering the grammar of a language; it entails identifying the threads of an inner logic that create, in Ruth Benedict's words "a more or less consistent pattern of thought and action."[14]

What do the three axioms presented above mean in practical terms? With regard to cultural competence, we reject the narrow focus on *national culture* as too simplistic for the social and organizational complexity of a global, multicultural environment. We seek to develop a more differentiated perspective on cultural phenomena that

- Defines culture as a pattern of values and norms that are expected, reinforced, and rewarded by a given group.
- Sees culture as a key element of group dynamics (axiom 3) at multiple levels—a highly useful perspective given the need for managers and leaders to apply the culture concept to complex teams and organizations.
- Focuses the mapping of cultures by identifying the inner set of value orientations that guides a culture's members. This focus overcomes the

reductionism of an approach that compares cultures only in terms of their behavioral norms or "tip of the iceberg" manifestations.

These axioms do not claim to be either complete or pure in an academic sense. They are meant to frame an understanding of culture that is meaningful in practical terms. They are designed to guide those who need to develop *cultural competence* as a key source of their own and their organization's success. The key to true cultural competence is our ability to create self- and other-awareness, leverage cultural knowledge (insights into institutions, practices, and behavioral norms), and build adaptive skills based on an internalized understanding of *value orientations*, or, as we prefer to call them, *cultural orientations*.

UNDERSTANDING CULTURAL VALUE ORIENTATIONS: THE GATEWAY TO CULTURAL COMPETENCE

Kluckhohn and Strodtbeck define a value orientation in very broad terms as "a generalized and organized principle concerning basic human problems which pervasively and profoundly influences man's behavior." These principles "give order and direction to the ever-flowing stream of human acts and thoughts as these relate to the solution of common human problems." Underlying Kluckhohn and Strodtbeck's work is a set of assumptions:

- There are a limited number of common human problems for which all people at all times must find workable solutions.
- While variations in these workable solutions certainly exist, they are neither limitless nor random, but rather fall within a limited range of possible solutions.
- All variants of recurring solutions are present in all cultures at all times, but particular variants receive varying degrees of emphasis from one society to another or one subculture to another.

This universalistic approach to the study of culture had been described earlier by Clyde Kluckhohn.[15] In his view, human biology and the human situation in general (including the need for food, shelter, and sex; differences in age and capabilities; and the dependency of the young) generate universal circumstances that must be addressed by every society. Every society, therefore, develops a "pattern for living" that is an internally approved and sanctioned solution to these common human problems. Each such solution is internally consistent, as it reflects a set of associated orientations regarding key dimensions of human existence. Kluckhohn and Strodtbeck identify these dimensions as follows:

- Relation to human nature (with the possible designations of Good, Good-and-Evil, Neutral, and Evil)
- Relation to nature and supernature (human-nature orientation, with the possible designations of humans' Mastery-over-Nature, Subjugation-to-Nature, and the Harmony-with-Nature)
- Positioning in the flow of time (with the possible designations of Past, Present, and Future)
- Relation to activity (with the possible designations of Being, Being-in-Becoming, and Doing)
- Relationships with other human beings (with the possible designations of Lineality, Individualism, and Collaterality)

In this view, culture is seen as an interlocking network of dominant (most preferred) value orientations and variant value orientations. While the theoretical notions of "common human problems" and "value orientations" are not uncontroversial in academia, we find that they give us a very useful platform on which to build a practical and operational approach to culture that is particularly useful for business and management.

Additional insights into the value orientations of cultures have been provided by numerous researchers, including Talcott Parsons and Edward Shils, Edward T. Hall, Geert Hofstede, Edward Stewart and Milton Bennett, Stephen Rhinesmith, Charles Hampden-Turner, and Alfons Trompenaars. Parsons , for example, demarcated five "pattern variables," or basic dilemmas that face human actors in any social situation. They argued that these pattern variables are key to understanding human action across societies—when we act, we emphasize one side or the other. A society, therefore, can be defined by the dominant choices made in relation to these dilemmas:[16]

- *Affectivity* (stressing feeling, emotion, and gratification) vs. *affective neutrality* (stressing practical or moral considerations)
- *Self-orientation* (stressing self-interests) vs. *collectivity-orientation* (stressing group goals and interests)
- *Universalism* (using common evaluative standards across situations and groups) vs. *particularism* (using different evaluative standards across situations and groups)
- *Ascription* (stressing who you are) vs. *achievement* (stressing what you do or have done)
- *Specificity* (stressing interaction for specific purposes) vs. *diffuseness* (stressing interaction across a wide range of activities)

While individuals may over time give preference to different sides of each dilemma in specific situations, overall the norms of a social group or society will tend to generally favor one side over the other. For example, how does mainstream U.S. American (Anglo-American) culture relate to the pattern variables? In general, it stresses

- *Affective neutrality*. Most social interactions are based on practical, instrumental concerns rather than on feelings and emotions.
- *Self-orientation*. Self-interest tends to predominate over broad social interests.
- *Universalism*. Standards embedded in such documents as the Constitution and the Bill of Rights are meant to be applied across different situations and groups.
- *Achievement*. While America is not a classless society, stress is placed on merit rather than on group membership.
- *Specificity*. Obligations to others tend to be narrow and restricted, and well defined in terms of role expectations, e.g., doctor, mechanic, salesperson.

Edward T. Hall has spent much of his career studying the implicit messages of different cultural value orientations concerning time, space, material possessions, friendship, and agreements. Differences in these matters present us with unspoken cultural languages that affect relationships, often quite profoundly. For example, Hall examines differences in relation to agreements:

> Few Americans will conduct any business nowadays without some written agreement or contract. . . . Americans consider that negotiations have more or less ceased when the contract is signed. With the Greeks, on the other hand, the contract is seen as a sort of a way station on the route to negotiation that will cease only when the work is completed. The contract is nothing more than a charter for serious negotiations. In the Arab world, once a man's word is given in a particular kind of way, it is just as binding, if not more so, than most of our written contracts. The written contract, therefore violates the Moslem's sensitivities and reflects on his honor.[17]

In Latin America also, many things get done because of relationships rather than because of formal agreements or laws. While friendships are not developed so quickly in many other cultures as they are in the United States, they tend to be much deeper and less casual, and to carry more extensive obligations.

Hall found that the languages of space and time are also meaningful. In terms of space, U.S. Americans like to be at least an arm's distance from others (as opposed to the 12 to 18 inches that is typical in Latin America), and they also use space to indicate status and privilege. To a U.S. American, a corner office with a window on a high floor indicates high status. The French or Japanese supervisor, on the other hand, may well be seated in the middle of his or her employees. To an Arab, the location or size of an office bears little relation to the importance of the person occupying it. Additionally, Western perceptions of time are not universal. Westerners tend to perceive time as something to be sliced into discrete bits—seconds, minutes, hours, etc.—and controlled through the use of detailed and precise schedules and plans. Furthermore, U.S. Americans, for example, focus on the immediate present and the short-term future rather than on the past or the long-term future. As Akio Morita, chairman of Sony Corporation, said, "America looks 10 minutes ahead; Japan looks 10 years."[18] U.S. Americans also tend to focus on one thing at a time. The U.S. system is alien to Arabic, southern European, and Latin American cultures, where people integrate the past into current decisions, have a less precise definition of punctuality, formulate less detailed plans, and tend to focus on multiple things at once.

Additional research in this area has been done by Geert Hofstede and is presented in his seminal work *Culture's Consequences*. Hofstede identified four major dimensions of culture and mapped their distribution among managers of one company across 66 countries between 1967 and 1973, furnishing the intercultural field with an important empirical foundation. Hofstede's four dimensions of culture are

- *Power distance.* The degree to which inequality is felt to be desirable or undesirable in a society, and the levels of dependence and interdependence. In countries with high power distance (such as Malaysia), the holding of power needs less legitimization than it does in countries with lower power distance (such as Austria).

- *Uncertainty avoidance.* The degree to which uncertainty is perceived as a threat, leading to anxiety about the future and the protection of society through technology, rules, and rituals. In places with high uncertainty avoidance (such as Japan, France, Russia, and Latin America), there is a need for comprehensive rules and regulations, a belief in the power of experts, and a search for absolute truths and values, whereas in places with low uncertainty avoidance (such as the United States, Indonesia, China, and northern Europe), there is less emphasis on rules and procedures, a greater reliance on relativism and empiricism, and more of a belief in generalists and common sense.

- *Individualism.* The degree to which individual interests are given priority over the interests of the group. In countries with high individualism (such as the United States), the emphasis is on the self or, at most, the nuclear family. Private life is valued, as are independence, individual initiative, and autonomy. Countries with low individualism (such as Guatemala) value collectivity, and personal identity is based on membership in a group.

- *Masculinity.* The degree to which achievement and success are given priority over caring for others and the quality of life. Countries that are high in masculinity (such as Japan) value performance and growth very highly, try to excel, and value work as an end in itself. Countries that are low in masculinity (such as Norway) have a people rather than a results orientation, see work as a means rather than an end, and focus heavily on the quality of life rather than on money and material objects.

Charles Hampden-Turner and Alfons Trompenaars investigated seven national cultures, those of the United States, Japan, Germany, France, Britain, Sweden, and the Netherlands, in relation to wealth creation.[19] In line with our own view, they argue that "a deep structure of beliefs is the invisible hand that regulates economic activity."[20] Hampden-Turner and Trompenaars identify seven basic valuing processes that are critical to the existence of wealth-creating organizations. As depicted in Table 2.1, for each valuing process they identify two complementary values existing in tension.

Hampden-Turner and Trompenaars maintain that the economic success of a culture depends on its ability to balance these values in tension. They also show how different cultures emphasize one value over another. They argue, for example, that the United States is being held back in developing a long-term approach to its economic difficulties by the following dominant cultural biases: universalism, analysis, individualism, inner-directedness, sequential time, achieved status, and equality.

Although they were not the first take this position, Hampden-Turner and Trompenaars are particularly helpful in focusing our attention on value preferences in patterns of thinking and their consequences for collective action. They refer to U.S. Americans as "Analyzers Extraordinary" who spend "more energy deconstructing than constructing." National cultures that tend to value more integrative approaches to thinking, such as Japan, France, Germany, and China, may have the edge as complex systems (those that are not easily reducible to parts) become increasingly important in establishing and maintaining a competitive advantage.

Stewart and Bennett provide further contributions by contrasting U.S. American patterns of thinking with Japanese and European patterns. As

TABLE 2.1 Capitalistic Cultures and Values in Tension

Process	Values in Tension
1. Making rules and discovering exceptions	Need to reconcile universalism (rules of wide generality) with particularism (special exceptions)
2. Constructing and deconstructing	Need to alternate the mental and physical processes of analysis (breaking down) and integration (putting together)
3. Managing communities of individuals	Need to reconcile the individualism of employees, shareholders, and customers with the communitarianism of the larger system
4. Internalizing the outside world	Need to reconcile inner-direction (those things invented here) with outer-direction (most things not invented here)
5. Synchronizing fast processes	Need to reconcile the speed of processes (sequential time) with the coordination of processes (synchronized time)
6. Choosing among achievers	Need to balance achieved status (based on performance and results) with ascribed status (based on, for example, age or seniority)
7. Sponsoring equal opportunities to excel	Need to balance equality (of input) with hierarchy (the structure for evaluating the input)

Source: From *The Seven Cultures of Capitalism* by Charles Hampden-Turner and Alfons Trompenaars. Copyright 1993 by Charles Hampden-Turner. Used by permission of Doubleday, a division of Bantam Doubleday Dell Publishing Group, Inc.

depicted in Table 2.2, they map different styles along a continuum.[21] At one end of the continuum, the focus is on the sensory aspect of perception, which favors thinking based on concrete description. At the other end, stress is placed on symbolic systems, which favor theoretical thinking.

How are such differences manifested? Stewart and Bennett give several examples. For example, the Japanese emphasis on concrete description underlies their practice of inspecting each item as part of their quality control initiative. In contrast, Americans, and to some extent Europeans, tend to rely on sampling, risk analyses, and probability studies. In an interesting brochure produced by the London Business School, a Japanese student discusses how

TABLE 2.2   Some Variations in Thinking Style

Perception-based	← ——————————————————→	Symbol-based
Japanese	**U.S. American**	**European**
Direct perception	Action orientation	Thought and action
Concrete description and intuition	Probability research (general principles)	Theoretical reasoning
Meaning attached to immediately perceived events	Inductive thinking (operation)	Deductive inquiry (concept development, rules of thumb)

Source: Adapted from Edward C. Stewart and Milton J. Bennett, *American Patterns: A Cross-Cultural Perspective,* rev. ed. (Yarmouth, Me.: Intercultural Press, 1991), pp. 28–30.

his experience at the school enabled him to understand the differences between the Japanese, European, and American ways of developing strategies for action. He points to the fact that American and European companies will invest a great deal of money in market research and product surveys. In contrast, in Japan a company is more likely to launch a new product based on informed intuition, then make product improvements and positioning enhancements based on actual consumer responses. For the Japanese, numbers are a commitment, not a measure of probability.

The thinking style that is valued in businesses in the United States is based on analysis and can be considered inductive, i.e., problems are broken down into small chunks that can be organized into linear cause-and-effect relationships, which are then developed into general principles of action. In contrast to this thinking preference, other cultures value deductive thought. In this mode, emphasis is placed on logically deriving principles from theoretical constructs rather than from raw data.

In addition to the contrasting thought patterns just described, Stewart and Bennett, Hampden-Turner and Trompenaars, and also Stephen Rhinesmith[22] draw attention to what is known as holistic, big picture, integrative, synthetic, or systems thinking (we will refer to it as systemic thinking). Cultures that value systemic thinking, like Japan, Singapore, France, and Germany, pay attention to integrated wholes and not just the parts. In such a view, the system has characteristics that cannot be found by looking only at the parts. Systemic thinking places value on the context and not just the data; it assumes that without understanding the context, we have no real understanding of what the data mean. Hampden-Turner and Trompenaars give the following powerful example:[23]

A steep rise in profits may be an 'unshakable fact," but it could be most unwise to rely on this as an unambiguous sign of virtue. Depending on the context, this could mean the company has switched to larger, gas-guzzling cars with higher margins, that less value is being given to consumers as compared with shareholders, that the volume auto business is being ceded to Japanese imports, and that the whole industry is headed for a precipice.

All the works mentioned in this section provide us with insights into different value orientations and help us discern the inner logic and organizing principles of a culture. However, there are important differences between what these authors have done and our own intent.

First, unlike Hampden-Turner and Trompenaars (and other cultural commentators such as Lawrence Harrison,[24] Joel Kotkin,[25] and Francis Fukuyama[26]), we are not trying to demonstrate how cultural values relate to economic success or the creation of wealth. Our goal is to provide managers with a framework, a vocabulary, for understanding, working with, and leveraging cultural differences, not to judge the economic utility of these differences. We believe that cultural value orientations are functional for the group or society that holds them, as they are key to that group or society's sense of identity (cohesion), material existence, reproduction, and continuing development. It is certainly clear that each configuration has consequences, of which economic performance is only one. It is far less clear, however, how cultural value patterns can be subsumed into a universal definition of *success* or *wealth*, economic or otherwise, if the very concepts, frameworks, and measurement have cultural biases embedded within them. Undoubtedly, though, globalization increases the speed and pressure with which cultural value orientations and their manifestations are imposed and reshuffled. Global organizations and the teams and individuals within them may find one particular set of value orientations better suited than another for achieving a particular goal. We have to be rather careful with our assumptions, though. Success is a highly relative notion, and to ascribe distinct and uniform cultural characteristics to it would not only be highly ethnocentric but add fuel to the fire of cross-cultural conflicts that permeate the headlines of the daily global news.

Second, many contributors to the field of intercultural communication discuss cultural differences by nationality, whereas we advocate a more differentiated perspective. Most writers on the topic state that equating cultural boundaries with geographical and/or political boundaries, though problematic, is the easiest and most intuitive way to differentiate distinct cultures.[27] We believe that we need to overcome this type of intellectual laziness in order to generate practical guidance for the leaders and managers that need them. We need to

1. Differentiate between our insights into the value dimensions of culture and their treatment on a national level as only one level of application.

2. Focus on the role that we as individuals play in the various cultural levels as well as the various ways in which cultural forces work through our own behavior.

In this sense, we find added value, both conceptually and practically, in the perspectives on culture offered by the structural functionalist[28] and dramaturgical[29] approaches to the study of culture. In our practice, we are dedicated to continually developing and honing an approach to culture that enables managers to "find their feet" on unfamiliar ground at any level of culture. To this end, we have synthesized the previously reviewed approaches to culture into the cultural orientations approach, consisting of a comprehensive model, and created a corresponding set of tools and knowledge base. The following chapters introduce this approach.

SUMMARY INSIGHTS

At this stage of globalization, we are only beginning to understand the impact of culture on the formation and maintenance of competitive advantage for our societies, economies, and organizations. Those who pay attention to culture are seeing the results and have understood the need to build cultural competence as the foundation for both individual and organizational effectiveness.

Cultural competence is about more than just understanding the intricacies of bowing in Japan or Korea, the inappropriateness of accepting food with the left hand in Saudi Arabia, or the propriety of using last names and titles in Germany. While this level of understanding is significant, reducing cultural learning to only this level unduly minimizes the importance of culture to our identities and the complex ways in which it affects our behavior, actions, and interactions.

Cultural competence is also about more than understanding how cultural value orientations drive assumptions and behavior in ourselves and in others and how they constitute the norms within various social groups across which we operate; it is about the ability to convert that understanding into improved relationships, alignment, and synergy. It involves going beneath the explicit components of a culture that are at the tip of the iceberg—as well as the simplistic definitions (often in terms of nationality)—and working with the implicit value orientations that shape and motivate behavior. Cultural competence is a continuous process that begins with an open attitude; this facilitates the development of self- and other-awareness, which need grounding in cultural knowledge for translation into cross-cultural skills. Numerous researchers have provided insights into the value orientations that underpin behavior. The complexity and increasing importance of culture requires us to internalize these insights into the various orientations and their effect on behavior.

3

THE CULTURAL ORIENTATIONS MODEL

The principle of contradiction must . . . be recognised
as being the universal and completely sufficient principle of all
analytic knowledge, but beyond the sphere of analytic
knowledge it has, as a sufficient criterion of truth,
no authority and no field of application.

IMMANUEL KANT, *CRITIQUE OF PURE REASON*

*T*o navigate through an unfamiliar culture, you need to be able to get
your bearings by relating yourself to specific features in the environ-
ment the way a sailor uses the sun, the moon, the stars, and the horizon. As
suggested by the material in Chap. 2, the Cultural Orientations Model, or
COM, is an important aid when we are trying to get our bearings with a
new culture. It identifies key features—the dominant value orientations of
the culture—and enables a general cultural positioning.

T he Cultural Orientations Model presents a framework for exploring and mapping the components of culture at any level. It is the cornerstone of the cultural orientations approach and provides a common language and comprehensive lens with which to analyze cultural phenomena and cross-cultural encounters. An understanding of this language can significantly assist in determining appropriate strategies for effective cross-cultural interaction, collaboration, and integration as well as personal and organizational adaptation. This model has become the central framework of our consulting, coaching, and research practice.

THE CULTURAL ORIENTATIONS MODEL

The salient notions in the field of cross-cultural communications, together with our own experiences in teaching cultural awareness and skill-building seminars to thousands of executives and managers throughout the world, form the basis of this model. We have identified ten cultural dimensions by applying three criteria:

1. Each dimension needs to recognize an important aspect of social life.
2. Each dimension needs to be something to which any sociocultural environment gives its members a basic orientation as the shared rationale for behavior.
3. Each dimension has practical value to managers, leaders, and anyone else who needs to reconcile, integrate, or transcend cultural difference in order to obtain a desired outcome.

These ten dimensions, shown in Fig. 3.1, are

1. *Environment:* How individuals view and relate to the people, objects, and issues in their sphere of influence
2. *Time:* How individuals perceive the nature of time and its use
3. *Action:* How individuals view actions and interactions
4. *Communication:* How individuals express themselves
5. *Space:* How individuals demarcate their physical and psychological space
6. *Power:* How individuals view differential power relationships
7. *Individualism:* How individuals define their identity
8. *Competitiveness:* How individuals are motivated
9. *Structure:* How individuals approach change, risk, ambiguity, and uncertainty
10. *Thinking:* How individuals conceptualize

FIGURE 3.1   Dimensions of culture.

Each of these dimensions contains at least one cultural continuum. Such a continuum is the "field of force" between cultural orientations. Figure 3.2 depicts one such continuum, or field of force, for the dimension of time. Each continuum allows us to identify the directionality of hidden values, expectations, and drivers of social phenomena and behavior patterns, including managerial styles and business practices.

Each dimension of culture consequently consists of one or more cultural continua. All together we can identify seventeen continua that comprehensively describe the cross-cultural challenges of global business and management. Figure 3.3 depicts the full model, identifying each dimension with its

FIGURE 3.2   Cultural continua—an example.

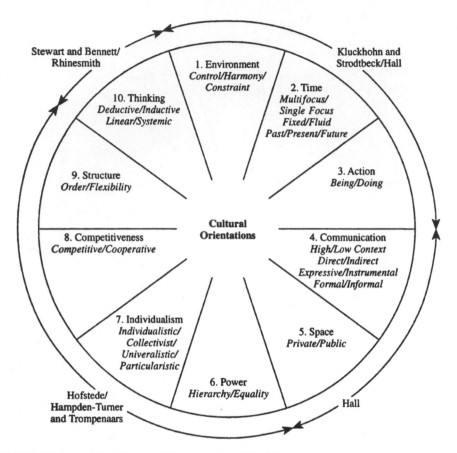

FIGURE 3.3   The Cultural Orientations Model

continua and giving the primary reference upon which our understanding is based.

When reviewing this model, it is important to keep the following things in mind:

1. By assigning particular cultural orientations to a society, group, organization, or team, we are creating a *generalization*, i.e., a general starting point for further inquiry. It is difficult to think of any field of inquiry that does not depend on generalizations. In the field of cross-cultural studies, generalizations become destructive when they degenerate into stereotypes. Generalizations about a culture are heuristic statements, subject to review and change, about what is expected, rewarded, and reinforced in a given social environment. They are initial hypotheses to be examined and

modified through active engagement. Stereotypes, in contrast, are closed systems of belief. No matter what new information is presented, the stereotype channels it into preexisting categories (either positive or negative). Figure 3.4 illustrates the difference between generalizations and stereotypes.

2. It is important to recognize that every culture contains each one of the orientations; the key differences among cultures are the emphasis and the expression given to one over the other depending on situations.[1] Always

STEREOTYPE	GENERALIZATION
A belief about a person or group considered to typify or conform to one pattern, lacking any individuality.	A principle, statement, or idea having general, not specific, application. When applied to individuals, a generalization serves as a hypothesis to be tested and observed.

INFORMATION

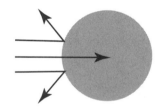

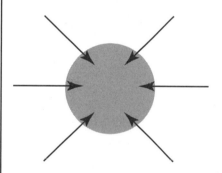

• Contradictory information is rejected	• All data are included and analyzed
• Contradictory information is amplified	• Hypotheses are constantly tested and refined
Based On Judgmental Attitude Biased Perception Refusal to Learn	**Based On** Open Attitude Insightful Perception Openness to Learn

FIGURE 3.4   Stereotypes and generalizations.

be open to new information that can offer you new insights and a richer and deeper understanding of inter- and intracultural nuances.

3. Many of the generalizations of social environments that we have provided as examples of cultural orientations in the following discussion involve the societal level of culture, as many of the examples given in the research in this field have used this perspective. For example, countries are often used as examples with the caveat that cultural boundaries are not the same as geographic boundaries. This is only a starting point and serves mainly to introduce the language and concepts of the Cultural Orientations Model. In subsequent chapters, we discuss the applications of this model for other levels of culture and implications for our own interpersonal skill base.

Now that you have an overall picture of the framework and its architecture and intent, it is time to consider each dimension and its constitutive continua in more detail.

ENVIRONMENT

The environment dimension recognizes a field of force among three distinct orientations, each giving us a way in which to view and relate to the people, objects, and issues in our sphere of influence. Through this dimension we can understand a basic relationship to the world at large.

Sue and Sue[2] draw attention to the fact that groups operate with dissimilar orientations concerning the locus of control in the world. Internal control defines a people's belief that individuals and groups can shape their own destiny, i.e., control their own environment. External control defines the belief that events are determined by chance, luck, or a supernatural force.

Control Orientation

In control-oriented cultures, you will hear people say things like "Go for it," "Life is what you make of it," "Don't let anything stand in your way," "Hard work and perseverance pay off," "You got a problem, fix it," or "God helps those who help themselves." In this view, the environment, including other people, can be molded to fit human needs. There is a driving belief that goals and desired transformations can be achieved if only the right tools are applied. The future can be planned for, and organizational structures and systems can be put in place and controlled in order to achieve objectives.

In business organizations, a control orientation leads to an emphasis on very detailed, precise, task-centered planning that is aimed at producing measurable and reproducible results. Risk analysis is routinely done and is based upon a forecast of forces to be overcome. Organizational thinking tends to be very analytic and linear, with problems broken down into small, manageable components and processes charted in sophisticated critical path and PERT diagrams. It is assumed that individual leaders can and should take charge and push through changes and that staff members will be evaluated on the basis of their ability to implement appropriate actions, achieve objectives, and overcome obstacles. Control-oriented cultures tend to view problems as opportunities just waiting for solutions. Ambitious visions can be implemented, problems should be attacked head on and proactively, any conflict arising from the effort should be dealt with, and the right tools and skills are all that is needed to overcome obstacles. High value is also placed on systematic organizing, monitoring, and control systems.

Harmony Orientation

In harmony-oriented cultures, you will hear sayings like "Don't make waves," "Don't rock the boat," "Go with the flow," or "We will need to adjust." In this view, people are an integral part (as opposed to masters) of nature and the social environment. Their actions and thoughts should reflect that awareness and facilitate harmonious relations with the world and with others. Cultures that emphasize harmony believe that plans should set challenging goals, but should have flexibility built into them to allow for changes in environmental conditions.

Decision making addresses the contexts that need to be in harmony with the plan if it is to be achieved, e.g., traditions and other organizations and business units. Risk forecasting is part of the planning process, but it is understood that not all risks can be controlled. Decision making may take longer in such a culture because of the need to involve many different parties. The practice of *Mitbestimmung* or codetermination in German organizations is a good example of an institutionalized harmony orientation. Labor unions are represented on company boards in order to guarantee the balance of viewpoints and positions in decision making.

In harmony-oriented environments, organizational thinking tends to be holistic (big picture) and cross-functional rather than strictly analytical and narrowly focused. Leaders will need to facilitate harmonious relationships and provide their staff with stability.

In such a culture, decision making, even product design, is aimed at facilitating harmonious relations with nature and with others. For example, a Japanese friend recently told us that the Walkman players sold in Japan have a built-in volume limitation; they are audible to the user but inaudible to someone standing next to the user. Another example comes from a recent multicultural sales training program we conducted in New York City. We were interested to hear from Chinese participants how difficult it can be to sell a house to the Chinese. Several stories were told of Chinese buyers refusing to buy houses in cul-de-sacs or on land with large trees. The Realtor was told that a cul-de-sac is a road that goes nowhere, and therefore living on such a street could harm the occupant's career. Big trees could also potentially block a person's career. These decisions are rooted in the Chinese concept of *feng shui,* which are earth forces whose balance or imbalance is considered to affect success or failure.

Constraint Orientation

In constraint-oriented cultures, people will say things like "It's a matter of luck," "It's fate," "*Insh'allah*" (Allah willing), "You take what life gives you," or "If God wishes it to be so." From this perspective, it is presumptuous to claim direct control over a business—or any other—environment. This orientation can be seen in societies that stress the influence of external forces, the cycles of time, and resource limitations rather than the impact of personal actions. In constraint-oriented cultures, planning will tend to be at the strategic rather than the detailed level, as there may be little perceived practical value in detailed execution plans.

The predominant orientations toward the environment dimension of culture of a given group or society are often related to that group's economic and material conditions, history, and religious belief systems. We can easily see that the history and colonial experience of the United States would ingrain a control-oriented outlook in the European American population, but not in the African American population. A history of social tension or warfare or the experience of having been colonized repeatedly makes a harmony orientation in a group or population critical to social stability. The experience of resource deprivation (as a result of natural or social restrictions) or unpredictable economic and political conditions, such as hyperinflation or a great depression, make a constraint orientation very functional, as it permits a group to survive psychologically and emotionally.

Religion is intricately tied to the environment dimension of culture. Religion, even to those who do not actively practice it, is an essential source of people's perspective on their relationship with the world and their actions within it. This perspective underlies the work of sociologist Max Weber, in *The Protestant Ethic and the Spirit of Capitalism.* He demonstrated a relationship between systems of religious and ethical belief and economic outcomes. He showed how such cultural *control* phenomena as saving, investment, and entrepreneurship have been nurtured by Protestant Calvinism, with its asceticism and its doctrines of calling and election, themes not unfamiliar to Judaism. Belief systems such as Confucianism, Taoism, and Buddhism, predominant in many Asian societies, stress harmonious relations with the world. Islam, Hinduism, and Catholicism, to varying degrees, exhibit, emphasize, and reinforce a constraint orientation.

Through their interpretation of the world and human life, and through the specific practices they command, religions are perhaps the single most important source of these core orientations in our formative social groups. It is a most powerful reinforcement and reward mechanism for the value systems and the behavioral expression that define a particular social group or cultural community.

TIME

Time is a key element of human existence, and groups have to devise a perspective on its nature and use. As Edward T. Hall says, "Time talks. It speaks more plainly than words."[3] The use and views of time that are expected, reinforced, and rewarded by social groups or within societies and organizations convey powerful messages about what we value and how we relate to one another and to the world around us.

Single-Focused Cultures

Single-focused cultural environments place a high value on doing one task at a time and meeting set deadlines. Sayings such as "Everything has its time and place," and "One after the other" are expressions of this orientation. The focus is on one particular issue, subject, or relationship. Step-by-step performance of tasks is the model for organizing work flow. Meetings will tend to be highly focused, with a set agenda, a time frame for each item, and little tolerance for injecting other topics or issues. Organizationally, this orientation is expressed in clearly demarcated functional or activity areas.

A single-focused orientation tends to be associated with industrialization and supports the compartmentalization of activity necessary for industrial production. It is therefore not surprising to find that this orientation is strong in manufacturing environments and the business organizations of industrialized societies.

Multifocused Cultures

In multifocused cultures, greater emphasis is placed on engaging in multiple tasks and/or relationships simultaneously. This orientation is very functional in both preindustrial and postindustrial environments (particularly global organizational matrix structures), as both the ability and the flexibility to satisfy multiple demands and rely on relationships are critical in these environments. In multifocused social environments, the completion of tasks and the accomplishment of goals tend to rely on strong relationships rather than on abstract plans.

Fixed-Time Cultures

Fixed-time cultural environments see time as the driver of activities. According to this perspective, the chronological passing of time structures the sequence of activity. These cultures rely on the measurement and tracking of time and regard good time management and punctuality as a key ingredient of propriety and, in a business context, professional behavior. Edward T. Hall explains, "People of the Western world tend to think of time as something fixed in nature, something around us from which we cannot escape."[4] Time is sliced into fixed increments, like seconds, minutes, and hours, and is scheduled and managed in great detail.

In such cultures, meetings are expected to begin on time, and deadlines and schedules are taken seriously. Like the single-focused orientation, a fixed-time orientation is critical for industrialization and capitalism, as the association of time and money (as in the saying "time is money") requires not only the careful management of money and investment, but also that of time. In such an environment, "wasting time" is considered unethical.

Fluid Time Cultural Orientation

Cultures with a fluid time orientation tend to see the requirements of relationships and their associated activities as driving their use of time. According to this perspective, a responsible person and good professional takes care of the requirements of a situation or an important relationship without making time the main consideration. It would be at best improper and at worst destructive not to tend to vital relationships or events as they need to be tended to.

Like a multifocused orientation, a fluid time orientation is particularly functional in agricultural environments, where the abstract tracking of time has little value. Rather than being divided into fixed categories, time is perceived to be an organic, flowing process that is related more to the prolonged agricultural seasons than to industrial seconds, minutes, and hours. In environments with a fluid time orientation, delays are expected, and deadlines and commitments on timing are endowed with a great deal of flexibility.

Nancy Adler tells the story of a U.S. American engineer working in Bahrain. The engineer was profusely apologetic when explaining that the opening of the plant under construction would be delayed by six months. To his surprise, the Bahrainian's response was, "We have lived for thousands of years without this plant; we can easily wait another six months or a year. This is no problem."[5]

Past/Present/Future

Past-oriented cultures tend to meet change—the unknown—with deep distrust, suspicion, and rejection. Maintaining historical continuity has a high value and is predominant in groups and societies whose identity is grounded in either long histories or collectively traumatizing historical events. For example, the peoples of today's China, India, and Europe, and Jews and Arabs, look back at thousands of years of civilization and tradition that critically define their collective identity in the present.

Practices such as ancestor worship and strong family traditions are related to this preference. The prevalent view in historical China was that nothing new could ever happen in the present or would happen in the future. Everything had happened before in the distant past. Florence Kluckhohn and Fred Strodtbeck tell the story of a Western visitor who thought he was showing some Chinese people a steamboat for the first time. The Chinese remarked, "Our ancestors had such a boat two thousand years ago."[6]

In this orientation, plans for change need to fit with what has happened previously, and long time frames are needed if the plan introduces a relatively significant change. Precedents guide decision making, organizing, and controlling, including the hiring of staff, who should fit well-established criteria and demonstrate loyalty and adherence to accepted norms, policies, and procedures. In such a culture, the leader is expected to carry the vision of the past into the future, for change for its own sake is not valued. The past is always the context for evaluating the present.

Present-oriented cultures aim for quick results and stress the here and now. This orientation can be seen in sayings like "Take care of today, and tomorrow will take care of itself" and "Don't look back." Organizations in such cultures will formulate short-term plans, divide and coordinate resources based on present demands, and select and train employees to meet current goals. The inherent logic of the stock market, for example, reinforces and

rewards a present orientation rather than a past orientation. As more companies in traditionally past-oriented environments list their securities on stock
exchanges, their time orientation is likely to shift.

Future-oriented cultures demonstrate a willingness to trade short-term
gains for long-term results and tend to be driven and motivated by a general
long-term vision. Organizations in such cultures will divide and coordinate
work and resources to meet longer-range goals and projections of the future.
Recruitment and professional development will be directed at future needs,
not just those of the present time.

ACTION

The action dimension focuses on the view of actions and interactions with
people and ideas that tends to be expected, reinforced, and rewarded in a given
cultural environment. We can distinguish two orientations, which we identify
as *doing* and *being*, respectively.

Doing

In doing-oriented cultures, emphasis is placed on external, measurable
accomplishments—achieving goals and completing tasks. In these cultures,
activity- or task-focusedness defines value, both social and professional. In
doing-oriented organizations, motivation is achievement-based, i.e., performance objectives are given, performance is measured against set standards, and
rewards such as bonuses, recognition, promotions, etc., are given on the basis
of goal achievement.

A British expatriate in the United States was annoyed by being frequently
asked, "What do you do?" He found the question not only rude and intrusive,
but also constraining. He didn't like the feeling of being defined by what he
did for a living, rather than who he was as a person. In cross-cultural training
seminars, we will often ask the participants, "Who are you?" not just once,
but several times. Invariably, many U.S. Americans will answer first with their
job titles, and only later with family information or personal interests. Latin
Americans, Africans, and those from the Middle East often answer with an
affiliation-type answer, such as their family, clan, or tribe name. Europeans,
by contrast, will often answer with a brief description of their humanistic,
political, or philosophical outlook.

Being

Being-oriented cultures value affiliations, character, and personal qualities.
Building affiliation, trust, rapport, and relationships is a key condition for an

effective and efficient focus on objectives and tasks. Therefore, in being-oriented cultures, socializing and "getting to know each other" are often embedded expectations and ritualized elements (i.e., they are associated with specific etiquette and protocol) of business social engagements. In such cultural environments, emphasis is placed on quality of life, on nurturing, caring, and relationships.

Job satisfaction is valued more highly than task accomplishment, and motivation is based less on the promise of future rewards and more on factors related to the quality of organizational life, such as relationships with superiors and peers, the work environment, and challenging, interesting work. In strong being-oriented cultures, business is awarded not simply on prior accomplishments and technical merit, but also on personal compatibility, trust, affiliations, and personal and organizational considerations. Being-oriented cultures also tend to value thorough reflection before taking or committing to actions.

It is important to recognize that both doing and being cultures can be active and business-minded; a being culture should not be thought of as passive. The difference tends to lie in whether activities are primarily task-driven or relationship-driven.

COMMUNICATION

The communication dimension recognizes the different formats for expression and information exchange—i.e., the sending and receiving of messages—that cultures expect, reinforce, and reward. This cultural process is often very subtle and complex. We can map major cultural differences on four continua: (1) high context–low context, (2) direct-indirect, (3) expressive-instrumental, and (4) formal-informal.

High Context

In high-context cultures, the successful exchange of information hinges on the ability to apply a shared and implicit framework of interpretation to a message. This framework is the product of the shared experience of groups or societies, which makes certain things understood without their needing to be stated explicitly. High-context communication is both the product of and contingent upon strong relationships between and deep knowledge and understanding on the part of the people involved in the communication. Meaning tends to be implicit and less literal, and making it explicit may be neither valued nor preferred.

In high-context cultures, the process of decoding meaning relies heavily on the group's understanding of voice tone, body language, facial expressions, eye contact, speech patterns, use of silence, past interactions, status, common friends/business partners, and other elements. A propensity for high-context communication is a main reason why among individuals from Asia, the Middle East, or Latin America, a spoken "yes" can mean "yes," "maybe," "I don't know," "if you say so," or "I hope I have said this unenthusiastically enough for you to understand that I mean no." The precise meaning depends on the context, not just the words.

High-context cultures also tend to require a great deal of contextual information about an individual or a company before business can be transacted. Business is personal, and trust is critical to the relationship; it is difficult to get things done without it. A significant amount of time may be spent on what Anglo-Saxons would consider to be small talk, e.g., family issues, food and drink, the weather. As a Japanese businessman said to one of the authors, "Every business relationship should begin with a *sake* party." Greeting rituals (such as business card exchange in Japan) may be quite elaborate and formal, with etiquette and protocol being important for sending the appropriate messages.

Also, information may not be provided in a linear form, i.e., it may not move directly to a conclusion through a series of logical steps. For the high-context speaker, it is more important to establish the broad context in which the conclusion makes sense. The order in which this contextual information is presented is secondary to the formation of the contextual whole. Repetition and the linking of already established points to other ideas may be a common element of conversations. In such cultures, as Edward C. Stewart and Milton J. Bennett point out, "Conclusions are often not stated explicitly; it is up to the listener to divine the conclusion implied by the context."[7]

For high-context communicators, particularly in an East Asian context, silence plays an important role; it is active, not passive. Silence in Asia designates thought, not disengagement. Rushing in to fill a silence may be considered pushy or impulsive, or even emotional. Silence can also be a strategy for helping others to save face, taking advantage of another's impatience, or leaving options open.

In conducting business in a high-context culture, therefore, it is important not only to communicate your own and your company's expertise, but also to provide your own and your company's contextual frame—education, work background, family, political and social connections, philosophical beliefs, affiliations, and experience. Contracts also tend to be fairly short and general in scope, as faith is placed in the spirit of the agreement rather than in numerous written clauses.

Low-Context Environments

Low-context cultural environments tend to expect, reinforce, and reward making meaning explicit, often in documentation. The focus is on deriving information from words and their literal meaning. Because of the idea that words are the most significant carriers of meaning, there is a propensity in low-context environments to block out potential interference from nonverbal or other contextual sources. Hence, documentation and a narrow interpretation of the written words are invested with great value. Specificity and accuracy in word usage are highly valued, and comprehensiveness in verbal and written communication is a hallmark of education, status, and also professionalism.

In low-context business cultures, trust and compatibility are assessed on the basis of documentation and abstract and explicit criteria. Job descriptions, authority relationships, monitoring and control procedures, and task and responsibility guidelines are communicated through detailed oral or, more likely, written instructions. Performance appraisals are likely to be impersonal and well documented. Good interpersonal relationships between the parties involved may be considered desirable, but are not deemed essential to the flow of information or to communication processes in general.

A low-context communicator is likely to be disturbed by too much contextual information, which is deemed unrelated or irrelevant, or frustrated when vital information or decisions are not put in writing. A high-context communicator, on the other hand, may find a low-context approach rude and disrespectful. This cultural continuum also significantly impinges on the usage and efficacy of communication technology and media in global communication processes. Email tends to rely on verbal and literal skills, favor a low-context communicator, and be a preferred form of communication in a low-context organization. A high-context communicator will favor opportunities for a face-to-face meeting or any medium that enables a more complete contextual reading of the situation.

Direct Cultures

Direct cultures value open handling and resolution of conflict and tension. They say things like "Let's deal with this right now," "Say what you mean, mean what you say," or "Give it to me straight." Cultures that value direct communication also tend to view many forms of conflict, tension, and frank feedback as constructive and important. Within such cultural environments, the ability to speak one's mind in a straightforward way tends to be valued and regarded as a sign of honesty and trustworthiness.

Direct approaches to conflict, tension, and feedback can be either one-way or two-way. In a one-way culture, information flows down the system in the form of orders and directives. Conflict is dealt with from the top by means of power and force. The emphasis is on following orders and instructions; there is little, if any, participative management or teamwork. In two-way cultures, information flows both up and down the system. Conflict is handled on an interpersonal basis through open discussion, debate, and negotiation in which employees feel relatively free to state their perspectives and voice their issues and disagreements with their superiors. There is often a high level of participation and teamwork, and time is taken to build consensus and agreement on the resolution.

Indirect Cultures

Indirect cultures value conflict avoidance in interpersonal communication and are careful not to bring contentious issues out into the open or to bring tensions into a relationship. This is particularly true when the relationship between the individuals involved is not well established or when others might witness the conflict or tension. Avoiding giving the impression of disrespect or causing embarrassment, avoiding shame (sometimes referred to as *loss of face*), and preserving honor and dignity can be prime drivers of communicative behavior by indirect communicators or within indirect cultural environments. Indirectness is maintained by a number of strategies; these are given in Table 3.1.

The direct manager who is working within an indirect culture must develop a high tolerance for ambiguity; he or she cannot take everything at face value. Richard Mead clearly summarizes the direct/indirect trade-off when he says, "There is a trade-off between directness, which gets your purpose across but can create resentment and hence be less persuasive, and indirectness, which maintains a cordial relationship but at the risk of misunderstanding."[8] On the other hand, an indirect communicator working within a direct culture perceives the direct style of communication (including direct eye contact) as highly aggressive, adversarial, and ill-mannered.

Expressive Cultures

For expressive cultures, the display and accentuation of emotions are key components of the communication process. Emotional alignment is a driving element of successful communication and the sensation of having *connected*. In expressive cultural environments, there is less concern with factual details and precision than with the establishment and maintenance of emotional

TABLE 3.1   Indirect Communication Strategies

Strategy	Description
Mediation	A third person is used as a go-between.
Refraction	Statements intended for person A are made to person B while person A is present.
Covert revelation	A person portrays himself or herself as a messenger for another in order to state his or her own opinions, or a person allows some kind of self-communication, such as notes or a diary, to fall into the hands of another party.
Correspondence	Communication occurs without the parties being actually present.
Anticipation	Understatement and unobtrusive behavior based on empathy allow accommodation to the unspoken needs of the other person.
Ritual	Rituals help maintain control of uncertain situations.

Source: Adapted from Edward C. Stewart and Milton J. Bennett, *American Cultural Patterns: A Cross-Cultural Perspective*, rev. ed. (Yarmouth, Me.: Intercultural Press, 1991), pp. 97–98.

connectedness. Those who hide their emotions may be perceived as unapproachable, cold, or even deceitful.

In an expressive workplace, both positive and negative emotions may run high. Voices may be raised in anger, joy, or another intense emotion. Body language is likely to be demonstrative, and touching or hugging may be considered an acceptable form of behavior among acquaintances. Expressiveness may be raised to the level of an art form, and eloquence in language usage and subtlety in expression, including the use of allegories, metaphors and similes, and storytelling, may be highly valued, as they allow a speaker to emotionally connect with a listener.

Instrumental Cultures

For instrumental cultures, communication is problem-centered, rational, pragmatic, and issue-oriented. Instrumental cultures value the reduction of emotion in conversation. Cognitive, rational alignment, not emotional alignment, is sought in communication. Attention to detail and accuracy and a dispassionate, objective style are expected, reinforced, and rewarded. *What* is said is placed above *how* something is said. Stress is placed on the accuracy of the communication rather than on its appropriateness or style.

In instrumental cultures, displays of emotion are perceived as a lack of professionalism or reason. Being "out of control" is frowned upon and causes embarrassment. The ideal in such cultures is to keep emotions hidden as much as possible, even under stress. The English refer to this as "keeping a stiff upper lip." In the workplace, many Japanese also shy away from being overly expressive. Outside of work, and among friends, they are likely to display a more expressive orientation.

The meeting of expressive and instrumental communicators in business situations can have mixed results. Individuals with an instrumental orientation may interpret expressive individuals as difficult, embarrassing, or irrational. As Lisa Adent Hoecklin points out, there is no reason to believe that emotions that are held in check will be less detrimental to reason than those that are expressed.[9]

Formal Cultures

In formal cultures, a high value is placed on etiquette, protocol, and ritualistic exchanges. People in these environments tend to believe that "There's a proper way to do things, and an improper way." Often, inferences concerning one's credibility, learnedness, and trustworthiness are made from the degree to which one knows and conforms to rules of etiquette, protocol, and customs. Such cultures tend to have a strong sense of history, culturedness, and tradition combined with a class or hierarchy consciousness. It is often the understanding of formal rules of conduct that set apart the upper and educated classes.

The businessperson shows sincerity and seriousness by observing appropriate customs and rituals in such matters as dress, greetings, business card exchange, forms of address, scheduling and conducting meetings, eating and drinking, entertaining, gift giving, choice of conversational topics, awareness of boundaries, etc. Relationships in formal cultures tend to form more slowly, but, once formed, they are deep and permanent.

In formal cultures, plans are developed through the "proper channels" and appropriate procedures are followed. Organizations in such cultures tend to be hierarchical, and communication with superiors tends to be more indirect and guided by protocol. When hiring new personnel, such organizations give a great deal of consideration to how the person will fit into, or adapt to, the system of rules and regulations. Managers establish trust by adhering to business and social customs and leading from within the established norms of behavior.

Informal Cultures

Informal cultures tend to value the absence of strict prescriptions for communicative behaviors and to view etiquette and protocol as a barrier to communication and relationship building. The absence of clear rules and guidelines for conduct is a key feature of informal environments. There is often a shared belief in "getting rid of the red tape" or "being oneself," indications that an informal communication style is associated with a sense of interpersonal authenticity. Such cultures tend to place a high value on change and give minimal significance to historical continuity or tradition. Progress is perceived as being of higher value than custom. Individuals from informal cultures tend to feel uncomfortable with social or power differences, want to be more direct and candid when communicating, and try to establish a friendly, relaxed atmosphere when doing business. They may also place more emphasis on accomplishing objectives than on the maintenance of image or status.

The extent to which a culture's formal-informal orientation is embedded in its language is noteworthy. English is really the only language that does not differentiate between formal and informal forms of address (for example *tu/vous* in French, *tu/usted* in Spanish, and *du/Sie* in German). In many non-European languages there are multiple forms of address with varying degrees of formality and contextual prescriptions for their usage.

SPACE

Cultures can be categorized according to the distinctions they make in their use and demarcation of space. While much attention has been paid to the use of physical space (e.g., the distance between individuals in conversations), this dimension also includes psychological space (i.e., the sphere of influence and authority that we claim as ours). This dimension is critically linked to information flow in a given group or society. This cultural continuum distinguishes between public and private orientations.

Public-Oriented Cultures

Public-oriented cultures value open access and accessibility. Close physical proximity is sought, relationship building is important, and information is shared on a "good to know" basis. Collaboration and connectedness tend to be supported by a public orientation. It is interesting to consider the implications of an open-space office environment in which there are large, open rooms with few partitions, and managers may be sitting in the midst of their employees.

Public-oriented organizational cultures tend to be relationship-centered. Location of office space is not necessarily an indicator of status, although in a traditional French office, the key person is the one in the middle, the one who "has his fingers on everything so that all runs smoothly."[10] On the one hand, a public space orientation allows more personal and informal interaction between managers and employees. On the other hand, it also facilitates centralized authority, more authoritarian monitoring and control systems, and line-of-sight management.

Private-Oriented Cultures

Cultural environments with a private orientation value the clear demarcation of boundaries and their respectful treatment. People value the maintenance of interpersonal distance from one another (both physically and socially). In such environments, information tends to be shared on a need-to-know basis. Discretion is valued highly in interpersonal and organizational relationships.

In terms of work space, private-oriented cultures are characterized by individual offices or rooms divided by partitions or cubicles. There is an increased emphasis on closed-door meetings with minimal interruptions. Permission tends to be required to enter a private workspace. In terms of personal space, cultures can be differentiated by the distance considered to be acceptable for conducting business. In the West, people tend to stand farther apart and tend not to touch during conversation. A comfortable social-business distance for Latin Americans or Arabs would be equivalent to a personal or intimate distance for most U.S. Americans, and touching would be frequent.

POWER
Hierarchy-Oriented Cultures

Hierarchy-oriented cultures value social stratification and accept differing degrees of power, status, and authority. Sayings such as "Know your place," "Don't go around the boss," and "Respect your betters" are common in such cultural environments. Power and authority are often centralized, and organizational structure (in terms of highly demarcated levels) is tightly controlled. Managers are expected to behave in ways that reinforce their standing.

An informal and equality-oriented manager from the Netherlands arrived in Mexico. When he brought all levels of his staff together for a meeting to get their input, he found himself with a severe credibility problem, as this behavior did not underscore his standing as "the boss." In hierarchy-oriented Mexico, as in other such environments, respect for position is seen as vital to the maintenance of company operations, and this manager had to learn the hard way that clear behavioral expectations are linked to position power.

Knud Christensen, human resources manager with BP, explains:

> We promote 360° feedback, a process in which managers comment on their bosses performance. That works well in Scandinavia, Britain and the Netherlands, where managers tend not to be overly intimi-dated by their superiors. But it is more difficult in France, Turkey and Greece, where tradition calls for showing more deference toward authorities. Managers in such countries might be less direct in pro-viding their feedback.[11]

Planning in hierarchy-oriented cultures tends to be autocratic and pater-nalistic. On the whole, managers make decisions without consulting people at lower levels. Work and information will not bypass the chain of command; employees tend to expect managers to take the initiative for the training and development of their subordinates, and plans are expected to be implemented according to the manager's wishes.

Equality-Oriented Cultures

Equality-oriented cultures value the absence or reduction of hierarchy. Inequality is thought to be an unsatisfactory condition, and attempts are made to minimize it through institutional means, including legislative and political action, as well as social practices, such as the disregard of professional or aca-demic titles or negative regard for status symbols.

Equality-oriented organizations tend to be flatter, with power decentral-ized; the organizational structure is aimed at encouraging individual auton-omy and responsibility. In general, employees in equality cultures don't accept the idea that a manager has an automatic right to more power and priv-ileges; rather, they believe that power and privileges must be earned—and to some extent shared. The manager is perceived as a consultant figure rather than simply an authority figure. Many employees in an equality culture pre-fer the impersonal authority of mutually agreed-upon goals and objectives rather than the arbitrary power of a superior.

To get things done, work often bypasses organizational levels, and employees are given a significant amount of leeway in how to implement plans and perform tasks. Delegation is an important means not only of getting things done, but also of developing employees so that they reach their poten-tial. Disagreeing with a manager is not uncommon, and employees are expected to take the initiative. Participation in decision making is often encouraged, as is consultation between levels in the organization.

The Global Competitiveness Report annually ranks national environments by their practice of delegating authority. The results of the 2000 survey, given in Fig. 3.5, are highly instructive for understanding worldwide variations in this practice, and illustrate the manifestation of differences along this dimension in managerial practices.

Concerning the hierarchy-equality continuum, it is important to point out the erosive powers of the Internet and enterprisewide resource and information management systems for hierarchy-oriented organization structures, particularly multinational ones. The deployment of SAP, Peoplesoft, Oracle, or other comparable systems challenges organizations deeply. Implementation managers, IT departments, and business leaders alike need to clearly understand the implications of this cultural dimension and develop strategies to ensure that the integration of the IT infrastructure is mirrored by the cultural integration of its worldwide users.

INDIVIDUALISM

The cultural dimension of individualism recognizes that cultural orientations significantly influence the way in which social identity is defined. Most com-

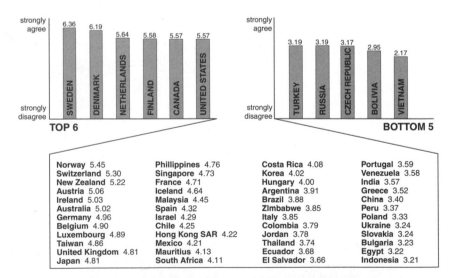

FIGURE 3.5 Delegation of authority—a national comparison. Key: 1 = strongly disagree, and 7 = strongly agree.
Source: The Global Competitveness Report, 1999

monly our sense of identity is entangled with our membership in or affiliation with a group, be it family, caste, clan, tribe, or class. However, cultures differ in their valuing of and perspective on identity based on affiliation as opposed to individual achievement. The *individualism-collectivism* and *particularism-universalism* continua emphasize different orientations toward identity.

Individualistic Cultures

Individualistic cultures tend to focus on the individual person and his or her achievements. In general, people in individualistic cultures place a high value on independence and reinforce beliefs such as "It's everyone for themselves." Often, people strive to minimize obligations to others (except for very close family members), and social bonds between people are relatively loose and flexible. Speaking one's mind is a sign of honesty and is respected. Social control is based on individual guilt, fear of losing self-respect, and an internalized sense of right and wrong. Motivation in individualistic cultures tends toward achievement and recognition for individual skills, contributions, and talent. Hiring and promotion are based largely on skill and merit. The employer-employee relationship is based on mutual advantage, and loyalty exists for as long as mutual benefits can be derived from it.

Value is placed on individual decisions rather than on those arrived at by a committee or other group. Individuals are expected to make their views known when plans are being developed and implemented, and impersonal standards of performance measurement will usually be used to distinguish among individuals. In such cultures, it is common to view conflict as inevitable and as something to be actively managed and not avoided. In individualistic organizations, task assignments, resource allocation, performance appraisals, and rewards are focused on the individual.

Collectivist Cultures

Collectivist cultures expect, reinforce, and reward the subordination of individual interests to those of the group. Cohesive groups protect their members in exchange for loyalty and obligation. Personal identity is grounded in the social network to which the individual belongs, and harmony rather than speaking one's mind is a key value. Social control is based upon fear of losing face and the possibility of shame. Publicly singling out an individual and praising his or her achievements in the midst of his or her work team might cause embarrassment.

In collectivistic business environments, putting coworkers in competition with one another to ascertain which one is best qualified for a promotion could be detrimental to morale. Motivation in a collectivistic culture tends toward affiliation and security, and relationships rather than tasks are of central concern. Hiring and promotions are not simply merit-based, but take into account group membership, loyalty, network obligations, and benefit. Employees expect organizations to protect their interests in terms of retaining, developing, and compensating them, and people generally are not fired unless they step outside of the group's moral and political boundaries. Promotion is often based on seniority (or ascriptive factors), and evaluations will take into account conformity to group norms and loyalty. Staffing policies and procedures may vary for different individuals, depending on their relationship to the decision makers. Compensation may take the form of special bonuses or "perks" outside of any prescribed system.

In a collectivist culture, group decisions take precedence over individual decisions. Not showing respect for or patience with a businessperson's need to consult with others before making a decision (even if that process is fairly lengthy) is considered offensive and pushy. It is expected that plans will be developed according to the shared values of the group and implemented through the strength of relationships in the group rather than by a simple assignment of tasks. Tasks and resources are likely to be allocated to groups of individuals, and these groups may be evaluated rather than each individual in them. Individual accountability is diffused into group accountability, and individual job descriptions may be vague or nonexistent. Conformity to group standards, policies, and procedures is expected.

Universalistic Cultures

Universalistic cultures stress the consistent application of rules, processes, procedures, and laws. Universalistic businesses tend toward the manufacture of universal products and services. From automobiles to fast food, the United States strongly exhibits this orientation. Product decisions consistently favor items that can be mass-produced in identical batches and sold to a mass audience through mass marketing. Perhaps no American product is more symbolic of this orientation than Coca-Cola.

In such cultures, the leader's role is to embody and implement universal principles in decision making. Reality in such cultures can be reduced to generalizable laws and widely applicable formulas and prescriptions. Behaviorism is an interesting product of U.S. American universalism, and its influence has been widely felt throughout U.S. culture. The search for the underlying laws and principles governing human behavior has led (especially in the field of training and development) to the creation of some simple models to explain and predict behavioral outcomes. One of the authors remembers a time when he was teaching a multicultural group in New York. Using a well-known model of behavioral types, he attempted to show how different combinations of these types in an interview situation may lead to very different results. The audience, many of whom were from outside the United States, soon reacted strongly to the use of the model. It was described as "too simplistic," "too American," and "too naive."

While predominantly U.S. audiences have found the model a useful tool, others have found it inappropriate to the reality they perceive, a reality that is more complicated, messy, and not reducible to simple models of universal intent. Overcoming this feature may be the single most important change required if globalization initiatives of U.S. companies are to be successful.

Universalism is often expressed in detailed contracts that are impersonal and meant to be enforced regardless of what situations may subsequently occur. While there may be some flexibility, the contract is an expression of universal agreement. Cultural environments that tend to share the United States's universalistic orientation include Germany, Sweden, the United Kingdom, and Switzerland.

Particularistic Cultures

Particularistic cultural environments emphasize difference, uniqueness, and exception. They see little value in the "one size fits all" approach that is at the heart of universalistic cultures. Particularistic cultures tend to emphasize the exceptions and the specific conditions that impede a universalistic process or approach. They tend to emphasize their own uniqueness and value standing apart from others. The specific needs of relationships or special situational requirements, not abstract rules, are the primary drivers for actions. The notions of universal principles and products and of services that are applicable in all situations, regardless of circumstances, are considered inappropriate.

Japanese businesses, for example, exhibit a strong particularistic tendency. Charles Hampden-Turner and Alfons Trompenaars point to "the extraordinary range of differences in its products, with its estimated 27,000 bookstores, 75 percent of its television presenting news and education, and dozens of products for every age group—for example, nine varieties of motor scooters for the female office worker between age eighteen and twenty-two."[12] This tendency is expressed in art and gardening. A dynamic harmony is created from a myriad of differences, with no tree, leaf, flower, or stone being like any other.

This particularistic or situational orientation builds principles for engagement from the ground up rather than imposing them in an abstract, institutional form. From this perspective, a contract is not set in stone, but functions as a framework of commitment, the specific manifestations of which are modified in the light of changing conditions and circumstances.

In particularistic cultures, extended family and friendship obligations are likely to predominate over larger social rules, government regulations, or international conventions. From this perspective, particularism and collectivism can be closely linked. Mobility may be reduced and power concentrated in social or ethnic groups and/or family networks. As a consequence, policies and procedures may be applied on the basis of relationships and affiliation, not common standards. The already important universal dynamic between in- and out-groups for extending trust, building rapport, collaboration, and decision making is further amplified by a particularistic orientation.

COMPETITIVENESS

The dimension of competitiveness addresses key cultural differences in motivation. This usage of the term is not to be confused with its relatively narrow usage in a business context. Motivation here concerns deeper drivers of actions, choices, decisions, and customs. The cultural continuum that defines this critical variation recognizes competitiveness and cooperativeness as opposing orientations.

Competitive Cultures

Cultures that are oriented toward competitiveness tend to be materialistic and emphasize the value of competition for resources and/or status recognition. The acquisition and development of wealth, property, goods, fame, expertise, etc., are accorded great importance on either a collective/group or an individual level. High value is placed on ambition, assertiveness, decisiveness, initiative, performance excellence, speed, and size; these may all be regarded as highly desirable and as justification for courses of action.

In competitive cultural environments, there is a desire "to be number one," 'to kick butt," or "to beat the pants off them." The ethos is "We live to acquire and attain." Success in competitive cultures tends to be measured in narrow terms, e.g., profits, degrees, or achievement of a specific goal. Plans are developed and implemented to attain the desired results, and, wherever possible, these results are measured and compared.

In organizational cultures that define competitiveness on the individual level, work is structured to permit and encourage individual achievement, recognition, and satisfaction and to feed into individual motivational factors such as high earnings, recognition, advancement, and challenge. People are hired and trained to take aggressive, independent action, to lead, to achieve, and to drive for success. Leaders expect employees to fulfill or exceed their responsibilities and to defend their own interests. The role of the leader is to track and reward achievement as well as to model success and encourage a strong work ethic.

In organizational cultures that define competitiveness on the group or collective level, internal collaboration and a collectivistic team spirit are nurtured. However, the group/collective is motivated by the desire to outperform rival groups/collectives.

Cooperative Cultures

Cultures that are oriented toward cooperativeness tend to focus on quality of life and to value sympathy, nurturing, and relationships. Material success is less motivational, and there is a higher concern with job satisfaction, work/life balance, quality of life, social interdependence, and actions that are socially responsible, fair, and just. The ethos is "We work to live." Success, therefore, is measured in broader terms than monetary ones, e.g., service. While task performance and achievement are important, they are only part of overall performance.

In cooperative cultures, stress is placed on consensual decision making. Work is structured to facilitate group integration and to satisfy such motivational factors as security, a positive working environment, and schedules that allow for a full personal and family life. In a cooperative cultural environment, quality leisure and recreation are important.

Highly cooperative cultures include those of the Scandinavian countries. In northern Europe, requests that an employee work after hours and on weekends are perceived as invasive and are often rejected. Highly cooperative cultures tend to believe that personal time and time spent with the family are very valuable, and that organizations should not interfere in one's private life. Vacation periods are often extensive and are guarded as "sacred."

The effects of the differences between competitiveness and cooperativeness are often felt in multicultural team situations. Highly competitive members may perceive cooperative members as lazy or uncommitted, while cooperative members may perceive their competitive coworkers as invasive, disrespectful, or having no sense of priorities. Divergent vacation policies, availability after hours, travel requirements, and other aspects of work life are frequent sources of dissatisfaction and frustration on global multicultural teams.

STRUCTURE

The cultural dimension of structure recognizes different perspectives and attitudes toward change, risk, ambiguity, and uncertainty. The degree of comfort or discomfort with change and uncertainty and the associated behavioral expectations are highly related to the cultural orientations operating in a given environment. We distinguish between order and flexibility orientations.

Order

Cultures that value order seek to reduce uncertainty, and they value security, predictability, and clarity. Change tends to be perceived as threatening, and there is a perceived need for rules, regulations, processes, and procedures—written and unwritten. In such cultural environments, stable employment and low job mobility are valued. There is a need for unambiguous descriptions of roles and responsibilities. Behaviors and decisions are guided by a desire to avoid failure. Hierarchical structures often support the order orientation.

Order-oriented cultures often leave planning to specialists or have formally defined planning roles and responsibilities. Individuals in order-oriented environments tend to experience high levels of stress in the face of uncertainty, emotional resistance to change, and less willingness to take risks. Loyalty and seniority tend to be major criteria for promotion.

A client of ours who works for a very large health care company was once told to oversee a business unit's activities in Japan; the unit was having some problems marketing and selling its product over there. He flew to Japan and asked to see samples of the Japanese managers' marketing plans. They were not able to produce any. He told them that they knew more than he did about the marketing environment, and he empowered them to develop a marketing plan. He gave them general guidelines and a month to come up with a plan for his review. After a month, no plan was forthcoming. Frustrated, he developed the plan himself and sent it over. On his next trip, he discovered the reason why no plan had been produced. The Japanese managers did not feel comfortable "being empowered" and felt uncomfortable about proceeding without detailed, clear instructions and development procedures. In the absence of such a structure, they were, in fact, disempowered.

Flexibility-Oriented Cultures

Flexibility-oriented cultures are more tolerant of unknown situations, people, and ideas. Deviation from established procedure tends to be tolerated—in fact, it is often expected and valued. Conflict and personal risk are considered natural rather than threatening. Such cultures value skill in improvising and often rely on it to get things done. Sayings such as "There's more than one way to skin a cat," "If it isn't broken, break it," and "It's what works that counts" underscore this value. Job mobility in flexibility-oriented cultures is higher, role and responsibility definitions are relatively loose, and there is a greater willingness to take calculated risks. Pragmatism is the dominant philosophy.

Flexibility-oriented cultures show a preference for broad planning guidelines rather than specific methodologies; they tolerate conflict and dissent and continually search for alternative ways of getting things done. Job and task descriptions are likely to be broadly interpreted, leaving room for the individual to make his or her own decisions. Formal relationships are less precisely defined, and organizational forms that accommodate conflict and competition are preferred. Loyalty to the employer is not considered to be a major factor in promotability, and managers select on the basis of merit rather than seniority. Achievement motivation is higher than in ordered cultures, and there is a greater reliance on individual ambition, leadership, and initiative for achieving results. The role of the leader in this type of culture is to provide the strategy and then let others determine how to carry it out.

THINKING

Thinking as a cultural dimension concerns the culture's propensities for conceptualization. Thinking patterns and perceptions of important criteria for cogent arguments, analysis, and planning are subject to cultural variations. The deductive-inductive and linear-systemic continua recognize key orientations that tend to be differentially expected, rewarded, and reinforced.

Deductive-Oriented Cultures

Deductive-oriented cultures emphasize abstract thinking and the reality of ideas, moral values, theories, and the principles that can be derived from them. Priority is given to the conceptual world and symbolic thinking rather than to the amassing of facts, i.e., generalizations are derived from other concepts by means of logic, rather than from facts. High value is placed on the powers of thought per se.

The influence of the past and future is greater in this type of thinking process. Appeal is made to theories, principles, or examples that have produced results in the past or are expected to produce results in the future. Problems—in the main—are classified and solutions discovered based on previous experiences and contextual circumstances.[13]

Highly deductive cultures tend to focus on the "whys" rather than on the "whats" and "hows." Negotiations between French and U.S. businesspeople can be very frustrating for both parties. Very often, the U.S. businesspeople, who tend to be inductive, want to begin with specific items for discussion— for example, price or distribution channels. The French, on the other hand, tend to be deductive, and want to establish agreement on general principles to guide the negotiation.

Inductive-Oriented Cultures

Inductive-oriented cultures derive principles and theories from the analysis of data. Models and hypotheses are based on empirical observation and experimentation, and the goal is verification through empirical proof. The amassing of facts and statistics is valued, and a good deal of faith is placed in methodologies and measurements.

Inductive decision making is guided less by the past or future than by the present. Surveys, one of the most popular methodologies, are usually set up to reflect a current condition, although results may be projected into the future. The focus tends to be on the costs and benefits associated with alternative courses of action, i.e., the operational impact. In this process, facts are given high priority and are assumed to be impersonal and reliable. U.S. American thinking, for example, tends to be very inductive.

Linear-Oriented Cultures

Linear-oriented cultures tend to dissect a problem or an issue into small chunks that can be linked in chains of cause and effect. The emphasis tends to be on detail, precision, and pragmatic results. Peter Senge comments on the U.S. thinking pattern as follows:

> From a very early age, we are taught to break apart problems, to fragment the world. This apparently makes complex tasks and subjects more manageable, but we pay a hidden, enormous price. We can no longer see the consequences of our actions; we lose our intrinsic sense of connection to a larger whole.[14]

Systemic-Oriented Cultures

When faced with a problem, systemic-oriented cultures stress an integrated approach, sometimes called *holistic* or *synthetic*. This integrated viewpoint focuses on the relationships and connections between parts. There is often a reliance on analogy, metaphor, and simile for explanations.

In contrast to the U.S. thinking style, many other cultures, such as the Japanese, Chinese, and Brazilian, are more systemic than analytical.[15]

Some companies—Toshiba America Consumer Products, for example—are seeking to leverage differences in thinking patterns to enhance their competitive advantage.[16] Toshiba found that American engineers think analytically and

follow a step-by-step approach to problem solving, whereas Japanese engi-
eers look at the whole and its relationships. To take advantage of the differ-
nces, Toshiba may have American engineers work on relatively
arrow-focus, complicated parts, while the Japanese engineers work on the
andardized parts and the whole design.

In the left margin, written vertically: Toshiba

PPLYING THE CULTURAL ORIENTATIONS MODEL

is evident that culture is as multidimensional and complex on the core value
vel as it is in terms of behavioral and institutional manifestations. The con-
pts and language of the Cultural Orientations Model may take time to internalize and apply. But once you have made this model an integral part of your
perspective, it becomes a powerful compass for navigating the social, organizational, economic, and political context of your actions and interactions. As a
global manager armed with this vocabulary, you can use it in a number of ways.

Identify Clusters of Related Values

We have discussed the ten cultural dimensions and seventeen continua of the
Cultural Orientations Model as though they were separate and distinct from
one another. This is, of course, not the case. Culture is fluid and immensely
complex; analytical boundaries like control orientation and doing orientation
are not as separate as our model portrays them. They relate to each other quite
closely and mutually reinforce each other.

What do those reinforcing relationships allow us to do? If we are engaging a foreign culture for the first time and all we know about it is that it is
highly collectivistic, what can we deduce that may help us to prepare ourselves? If we think through the other orientations in the model, we can say
with some degree of certainty that the culture is also likely to have a harmony
or constraint orientation to the environment, and that it may stress being over
doing and high context over low context. The likelihood is also high that more
value is placed on public rather than private space and on indirect/formal
communication rather than on direct communication.

An individualistic culture, on the other hand, is more likely to have a control orientation to the environment, a single-focus/fixed/present and future
orientation toward time, a doing orientation toward action, low context/direct/
instrumental/informal orientations toward communication, and a stress on
private space and equality.

Being a global manager is sometimes like playing detective. We always
need to search for—and recognize clues to—connections and meaning. The
Cultural Orientations Model is designed to expedite the detective work.

Relate Differing Management Practices and Workplace Behaviors to Cultural Differences

Being global managers also means selecting techniques that will be compatible with the cultures which our work spans. Take, for example, goal setting. Employee participation has been popular in Western management circles, but is it effective in every culture? A culture that places a high value on hierarchy is likely to reject it as inappropriate. A culture that places a high value on individualism may also find it difficult to implement, unless the individuals in the group feel that the process is contributing to their own personal needs and wants.

We can and need to leverage our insights into general cultural dimensions and dynamics in order to develop and calibrate the culture of our teams or organizations. Take, for example, the following email message written by a U.S. manager in the IT organization of a large New York–based financial institution, to her director:

As an employee of the Technology Organization, my colleagues and I are working with resources in India. We have been increasingly frustrated, as we are encountering significant obstacles in our working relationships. The differences between our Indian resources and our requirements as customers are putting quality, timeliness, and cost efficiencies—and ultimately our reputation—at risk. Below are some examples of where we need help in dealing with our partners from India.

Our partners seem to have a fear or reluctance to admit that they don't understand something or don't know something. Some of my on-site Indian colleagues have informed me that this could be due to a fear on the part of offshore or newly-arrived-in-the-USA partners of losing their jobs if they voice uncertainty or lack of knowledge. The result for us is work done incorrectly and having to be redone. How do we ensure that our partners understand what they are to do?

Our partners feel it is rude to challenge others and probe for information, especially with people of higher rank. The result is that they don't get the information they and we need. How do we make our partners feel comfortable with challenging others or probing for more information? How do we challenge our partners or probe them for more information without offending them?

Our partners spend much time analyzing before deciding or acting. We are used to making a decision and immediately acting on it, which seems abrupt to them. The result is that we appear to be rushing into things while they appear to be making no progress. How do we ensure they act on a timely basis?

Some of my on-site Indian colleagues have informed me that our partners may interpret words and situations differently than we do. The result is a misunderstanding. How do we ensure we and our partners are reaching the same interpretation?

Though intelligent and well educated, our partners seem reluctant to speak up with their ideas. My Indian colleagues say that in general, Indians are introverted and shy. Also, they may feel it to be presumptuous to make recommendations to someone of higher rank or to someone who is in charge. The result is that we miss out on good ideas and we may have the perception that our partners lack initiative. How do we make our partners comfortable with volunteering suggestions and recommendations?

Our partners seem to prefer to work on resolving issues without informing us that these exist. We, on the other hand, believe in raising flags early. The result is that issues may not become known at an appropriate time. In addition, when we do learn of an issue and raise a flag, it appears to our partners that we are panicking. How do we make our partners comfortable with raising issues?

How do we deal with our partners' perception that men are superior to women? My Indian colleagues have informed me that this perception is changing in India and that more women are becoming educated and holding jobs. However, they say, this perception still lingers. The result is a subtle disparity in how our partners interact with men and women.

Our partners are deeply and personally embarrassed when in error. The result is they become fearful of losing their job or being pulled out of projects. How do we help our partners save face when they are wrong?[17]

If you were able to relate the behavior patterns and differing assumptions and behavioral practices in this email message to differing cultural orientations, such as high context/low context, direct/indirect, harmony, hierarchy/equality etc., you have successfully used the language of the Cultural Orientations Model. Your application of the model illustrates how differences in management practices and workplace behaviors can be decoded and mapped. Viewing differences on the basis of this understanding gives you an improved vantage point from which to answer the "how to" questions this frustrated manager is asking. Viewing management and work practices through the lens of cultural orientations provides managers with the added perspective required for success in a multicultural, global environment.

Build Bridges, Not Barriers

Using the vocabulary of the Cultural Orientations Model to map differences and position oneself and others is a key step toward building bridges across cultures, not barriers between them. The model helps us to depersonalize our understanding of differences and to transcend the negative personal attributions of ignorance, incompetence, maliciousness, and/or lack of professionalism that too often erode human relations and create a downward spiral of distrust, blame, and lack of commitment. This perspective allows us to validate behavior patterns and our experiences of them and acknowledge their social context in value-free terms.

Where cultural differences amount to obstacles, as in the case given in the previous section, being able to see the heavy hand of culture in the behaviors and propensities of individuals is ultimately more constructive and realistic. When the language of the Cultural Orientations Model becomes a shared vocabulary for creating awareness of culture-based differences, we are laying the foundation for resolving them. In other words, when the U.S. manager and her Indian and U.S. colleagues start to frame their experience as the difficulties that collectivists and individualists or indirect and direct communicators face, they are demonstrating the respect and mindfulness required for an effective multicultural work environment.

Laying this foundation is increasingly the role of the global manager. We have worked with global managers in such companies as ICI, Royal Dutch Shell, Schering AG, Novartis, American Express, Citigroup, and IBM that face deep challenges in bridging cultural differences and creating cultural synergy to improve productivity, effectiveness, creativity, speed, and innovation. Figure 3.6 illustrates the process of cultural learning that is required. It shows that at the interface of business and culture, the most important criterion for choice of approach is not "correctness" or "superiority" but the generative process of creating added value.

We can increase our chances of global success by increasing cultural learning throughout the organization. We do this by

- Making cultural orientations patterns explicit and shared knowledge

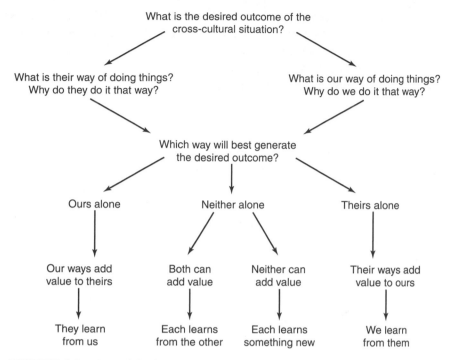

FIGURE 3.6   A model of cultural learning.
Source: Lisa Adent Hoecklin, *Managing Cultural Differences for Competitive Advantage,*
Special Report No. P656 (London: The Economist Intelligence Unit, 1993), p. 46.

- Agreeing on outcomes and the necessary cultural underpinnings—i.e., establishing the cultural ground rules for collective performance
- Operationally and behaviorally defining and modeling the approach(es) most likely to achieve the desired outcomes
- Reinforcing and encouraging sustained change on an individual, team, and organizational level
- Reviewing results and modifying approaches to find a better fit

SUMMARY INSIGHTS

The Cultural Orientations Model, or COM, is an important aid when we are trying to get our bearings in a new culture. It identifies key features—the dominant value orientations of the culture—and enables a general cultural positioning. Cultural orientations are value orientations that are the hidden drivers of behaviors, actions, and decisions; they indicate a preference for certain outcomes over others. The Cultural Orientations Model highlights ten dimensions of culture that are well researched and have practical implications: environment, time, action, communication, space, power, individualism, competitiveness, structure, and thinking.

Societal institutions, business practices, and workplace behaviors such as conflict management, feedback, decision making, planning, and staffing are expressions of a culture's primary set of orientations. It is the challenge of every global manager to create synergy out of cultural differences, and sometimes to devise creative new ways that are workable across cultures. The Cultural Orientations Model allows us to validate differing patterns and our experiences of them in a way that acknowledges their social context in value-free terms and enables a depersonalized understanding of barriers and obstacles so that they can be overcome and even leveraged.

4

A SURVEY OF CULTURAL PATTERNS

In culture, we must imagine a great arc on which are ranged the possible interests provided either by the human age-cycle or by environment, or by man's various activities. . . . Every human society everywhere has made a selection in its cultural institutions. Each from the point of view of another ignores fundamentals and exploits irrelevancies.

RUTH BENEDICT, *PATTERNS OF CULTURE*

In this chapter, we use the Cultural Orientations Model as a tool for organizing observations about human cultural diversity in and among the world's regions: the Middle East and North Africa, Asia, Western and Eastern Europe, North America, and Latin America. We focus on generalized cultural tendencies within and among these regions. Our descriptions are akin to a survey flight. From the vantage point of altitude, we can identify the main features of a vast cultural territory. The perspective is that of a surveyor, utilizing the cultural orientations approach to establish a rough map that can guide our subsequent movement, exploration, and refinement on the ground.

The description of each region provides a general overview followed by a discussion of the cultural orientations patterns found in common business and social interactions. For each dimension, the salient orientations are presented and explained. The treatment of each region concludes with a summary of the key insights and implications for successfully doing business in and with the region.

THE MIDDLE EAST AND NORTH AFRICA

At the outset, it is important to clarify the term *Middle East*. The region generally thought of as the Middle East is a large, diverse area extending from Morocco and the shores of the Atlantic across the Sahara Desert of North Africa to Egypt, and continuing eastward across the Sinai and Israel to the Fertile Crescent and the countries of Lebanon, Syria, and Iraq. Northward it includes Turkey, and southward it includes the vast region of the Arabian Gulf and Saudi Arabia, Kuwait, Bahrain, and Yemen. Farther east is Iran, which is also part of the Middle East.

Most of the countries in the Middle East are Arab, although Israel, Turkey, and Iran are not. Certainly, Turkey and Iran share many cultural norms with the Arab Middle East. However, it is important to recognize the differences and diversity within the region. To the people in the region, of course, the differences are obvious. It may take some time for an outsider to notice them; still, it should be recognized that doing business with a Saudi will be different from doing business with an Algerian.

Perhaps the idea of the "Middle East" is best used as a point of departure for acquiring a deeper understanding of the country in which you will be working. There is no single Middle Eastern or Arab culture, but there are shared patterns that can serve as an entry point to successfully doing business in the region. Remember, though, that many Middle Easterners do not consider themselves "Middle Eastern." To them, the term is an outgrowth of the British Empire. The people of the Middle East strongly identify with their national, ethnic, religious, and family identity before they identify with any geographic location known as the "Middle East." It might be helpful to think of the region as being composed of the following countries: the Arabian Gulf states of Saudi Arabia, Yemen, Kuwait, Qatar, Bahrain, Oman, and the United Arab Emirates.

Note: You may encounter differences in conducting business based on the generational cohort of the person—from the older, more conservative decision makers who formed the nations we know today, to the middle-aged "risers" who were educated in the West, to the youngest, who are most comfortable with a balance between their own culture and Western culture and have frequent interaction with technology and with outsiders. The young and the middle-aged are knowledgeable in the ways of conducting business internationally. They know how to communicate with foreigners and what to expect from them. However, along with their older counterparts, they still embrace a strong sense of the importance of relationships and the necessity of building trust with people before they feel they can work with them.

- *Fertile Crescent (Lebanon, Syria, Jordan, Palestine).* In these countries, the business mindset is aligned more closely with the West. Business exchanges may move faster, since the focus may be less on building long-term relationships than on immediate, feasible, and affordable outcomes.

- *North Africa (Morocco, Tunisia, Algeria, Libya, Egypt).* These countries are accustomed to doing business with Europe and the United States. Morocco, Algeria, and Tunisia (referred to collectively as the Maghreb), as former colonies of France, are accustomed to the European way of business—for example, the use of metric measurements and fluency in French. Therefore, there are greater barriers between these countries and non-European countries. Egypt, on the other hand, was under the control of the British; thus, English is the second language there today. As a result of the 1979 Camp David peace accords with Israel, Egypt has a close relationship with the United States. It is the second largest recipient of USAID funds, which has led to strong business ties with the United States. In addition, Egypt, with a population of 67 million, is the largest country in the region.

- *Turkey, Iran, Israel.* These countries are distinct in history, politics, and ethnicity. Their most significant common bond with the other Middle Eastern countries is their geography; beyond this, it is essential to study the culture and history of each individual country carefully. These three nations are not Arab. Turkey and Iran share some cultural, religious, and work-style patterns with the other Middle Eastern countries, but Israel is distinctly different.

Cultural Orientation Patterns

ENVIRONMENT OF CONSTRAINT

A sense of destiny, along with a belief rooted in Islamic theology that nothing happens unless it is the will of God (Allah, to Muslims), gives many in the region a conditional, constrained view of their environment. Whereas control-oriented cultures have a strong attitude of personal control over the environment and one's own life, the Middle Eastern belief is firmly rooted at the constraint end of this continuum. Life's circumstances, particularly those outside the ethical realm, are viewed as ultimately beyond all individual control. Fatalism is a way of life in the Middle East. One expression that sums up this mindset is the ubiquitous *Insh'allah* ("God willing"). Even a cheery parting, "See you tomorrow," may be answered with *"Insh'allah."* This expression and the attitudes behind it, which may also arise in business exchanges, can be disconcerting to people who are used to more definitive statements about the future. Success and failure may also be viewed differently. Middle Easterners may not feel comfortable taking pride in a successful endeavor, nor do they regard a failure as an unmitigated loss. In keeping with their belief in Islam and their deeply ingrained cultural values, both success and failure are seen as deriving from God, and for purposes more important than worldly business outcomes. As one saying goes, "God gives, God takes away, and God compensates." This compensation is the opportunity to achieve spiritual growth when confronting life's vicissitudes.

The Muslim perspective is that a higher authority controls and changes life's circumstances. God is the ultimate higher authority, but the concept of authority also extends to human society, where the authority of political, social, or corporate leaders is rarely questioned. As a result, Middle Easterners tend to be more prepared to accept situations in which change as well as authority and guidance come from above. For someone with a control orientation, the emphasis on constraint and on destiny and fate can be disconcerting and at times challenging. It can also be viewed as an indication of uncertainty and a lack of ability to "get the job done."

The following scene between engineers with a constraint orientation and trainers with a control orientation toward the environment illustrates the type of misunderstanding that can occur. A team had trained several engineers to run a power plant. At the end of the training, the trainers expressed confidence that the operation would run smoothly. The engineers replied, *"Insh'allah."* The trainers were baffled. What did *Insh'allah* mean? Could it be that the engineers were not confident enough? Could they be trusted to do what they had been trained to do? Concerned, the trainers wondered if more training was needed if they were to avoid a disaster in the future. What they did not know was that the engineers, by force of habit and belief, were merely acknowledging that, ultimately, God would determine whether the plant would run smoothly. Yes, they would be running the plant, but only if it were the will of God would smooth operation be guaranteed.

A SENSE OF TIME

Multifocused orientation.   Middle Easterners tend to conduct several conversations and do multiple tasks at the same time when they are engaged in discussions and meetings. They are more likely to be working at several levels at the same time than in a linear, step-by-step manner. This also means that the exchanges between people at personal and professional levels are interwoven, not separated. A Dutch businessman describes the confusion he felt during a phone conversation with an Arab. Throughout the conversation, the businessman could hear a strange smacking sound, something like the sound of kissing, that came and went. Not until he saw his contact in his office did the Dutch businessman realize what the sounds were. While the Arab was on the phone, friends would walk into his office, whereupon he would greet them with the customary embrace and kisses on each cheek, all the while holding the phone up to his ear. In a multifocus-oriented culture, to keep someone waiting until one has finished a phone conversation is considered rude and insincere, putting on hold one's acknowledgment of another.

Fluid orientation.   According to an Arab proverb, "There is something good in every delay." Patience is a critical asset for communicating, managing, working, and negotiating successfully in the Middle East. The concept of time in the Middle East is that it is fluid and flexible; it cannot be controlled, wasted, or managed. Interaction with people is considered more important than schedules or deadlines. Therefore, timelines that are set are assumed to be approximate—there is an elasticity of time. One often hears, "We will meet in the morning (or afternoon)," with no exact or precise time indicated. However, if a precise time is set, do not be late. Be there on time, but be prepared to wait, sometimes for what you may consider a long time. Exercising flexibility regarding deadlines is essential and a reality to which one must adjust.

For those with constraint and multifocus orientations, deadlines are presumed not to be final or definitive. Also, there is no distinct separation between "work time" and "play time." As a result, you will find that socializing and conducting business can occur any day or night of the week, not just on the weekend. A Jordanian who had attended training in Switzerland was surprised at the way towns and businesses shut down at a precise time, much earlier than he was accustomed to. He also considered his hosts inhospitable and believed that they did not like him because they did not extend invitations to gather and socialize at their homes after work hours. Given his fluid orientation toward time, the Jordanian found the fixed orientation toward time to be cold, impersonal, and lonely.

An orientation in the past.   "Modernization, yes; Westernization, no." This expression is heard principally in Saudi Arabia, although it reverberates throughout the Middle East. In its best meaning, it reflects the notion of acquiring Western technology without importing Western culture and thought.

This issue has vexed Middle Eastern intellectuals and leaders for years and suggests that while they want to modernize, they remain worried about their subordinate status vis-à-vis the West. Specifically, traditionalists believe in the necessity of maintaining an Arab heritage that is rooted in Islam and the teachings of the Prophet Muhammad. In particular, they are opposed to Western cultural influences, seeing them as corrupting and debasing and as potentially undermining their religious, ethnic, and tribal heritage. A more moderate goal is to borrow from the West what is needed to allow the country to develop and modernize, while not abandoning the values and norms that have shaped this region over the years.

Many Middle Easterners have already adopted Western imports. At the same time, with the mounting pressures from globalization and market economies, Middle Easterners are beginning to pursue policies of economic liberalization and privatization. Seeking a prosperous future and global competitiveness, the Middle East is changing. At the same time, these trends represent an attempt to maintain a balance between modernization and Westernization.

ACTION: BEING RATHER THAN DOING

"We are peaceful people; we want to maintain the relationship," says Sulaiman Olayan, a top Saudi businessman and industrialist. "You have what we need and we have what you need." These words sum up his view of how business relationships between the Middle East and the rest of the world should proceed. Relationships, critical elements of doing business—and, thus, of survival—show virtually no separation between the personal and the professional. A considerable investment has already been made via the establishment and maintenance of relationships. The process of relationship building rests on being seen, being present at both professional and social events, and accepting and reciprocating invitations.

"Conspicuous hospitality" is a major plus in a society where hospitality is a time-honored tradition and a major feature. "Your personal image and status will be affected by people's perceptions of your hospitality."[1] In the Middle East, hospitality is an art form with its own set of rules and practices that is essential for social and professional interaction. It includes meeting and greeting upon arrival, coffee and tea in the office, food served at lavish receptions and dinners, gift giving, and being there to drink tea or coffee, for conversation, or just to be around. All of these reflect how serious Middle Easterners are about hospitality, as well as its importance to them in conducting business. For someone with a doing orientation, this can be difficult, since the actions of a being-oriented person can seem like a waste of time.

A businessman arrived in the Middle East, hoping to promote night vision binoculars for the military. He spent a great deal of time sitting in offices and meeting rooms, in restaurants and homes, waiting to discuss or conduct his mission. It was interesting while it lasted, but, in his mind, nothing happened; after a week, he assumed that there was no interest in his binoculars, so he packed up and went home. A week later, a high-ranking military official with whom he had spoken while he was there asked to see him. The official was planning a hunting trip and wanted to try out the binoculars. The general should have passed a message to the businessman (although the businessman might have been constrained by the need to get approval from higher up), but the businessman should have known that the "waiting game" is common practice. His failure to do so cost him a lucrative deal. And since physical presence shows your commitment and seriousness, and not just an interest in a quick deal, he was not called back. For this reason, serious investors looking for business opportunities in Middle Eastern markets are well advised to set up an office with a local representative. Had the businessman in this case set up an office or appointed a local representative, he would have had more success.

In the Middle East, many prominent businesspeople have studied in the West and today are doing business with college friends and colleagues. Canada found that after it had started recruiting people from the region to study in its universities, Canadian companies began to experience an increase in business, particularly from the Arabian Gulf. This illustrates how the shared college experience of the Arabs and the Canadians developed into long-lasting relationships that extended into the professional arena. Having learned about each other through living together, studying together, and socializing together, Canadians and Arabs later began to trade together and to establish prosperous business exchanges based on a foundation of friendship.

COMMUNICATION

High-context communication.   Communication in high-context cultures such as the Middle East can be far more implicit and subtle than that in low-context cultures. To fully understand the import or sincerity of a message, there must be greater reliance on nonverbal communication—for example, eye contact, personal space, the tone and inflection of the voice, the repetition of certain words and phrases with emphasis, and head and hand movements. All of these are important ways to communicate.

Egyptian visitors once arrived at the home of their host after a long drive. It was midafternoon. The host asked if they would like something to drink, and they politely declined. The host then engaged them in conversation. A few hours later, the host took them to dinner. In the eyes of the Egyptians, the host had not been very hospitable; he had given them neither food nor drink when they first arrived despite the fact that they would be thirsty and hungry after such a long trip. What they experienced was the same bewilderment that someone in a low-context culture might feel if, after the question "Would you like something to drink?" the person answered, "I don't want to put you to any trouble," and the host did not follow up by repeating the offer. In most cases, Middle Easterners will politely decline an invitation, with an assumption that the invitation will be repeated and pressed on the guest.

One businessperson became so experienced in reading Middle Easterners' messages that he could detect the actual intention and degree of seriousness behind the response of "*Insh'allah*" based on body language and tone—when it meant yes, no, or maybe. When it meant yes, he paid attention to the inflection of the speaker's voice and the degree of body and eyebrow movement and direct eye contact. This is very important for those who are low-context-oriented, where the emphasis is on the words alone. A statement commonly heard from someone with a low-context orientation is something like, "Well, they said yes, that they would get the papers to me next week. But now two weeks have passed, and there are no papers." The businessman who expressed his frustration started to feel distrustful as a result of relying on the words, unaware of the full situational context of how the message was being conveyed. Often the person you are communicating with will respond in agreeable or pleasant ways when direct or factual answers might prove embarrassing or distressing.[2]

"*Insh'allah*" is a common response to all invitations and agreements. The response "Yes, *insh'allah*" is one way to gauge the seriousness and affirmative intention behind an agreement. Without a yes, the response more likely means "maybe" or "no" or "probably not." However, one never responds, "No, *insh'allah*." To directly respond with "no" is offensive. It does not convey sincerity and could cause too much ill will.

Directness and indirectness. Saving face and maintaining harmony are most important in the Middle East, as are honor, respect, and reputation. Depending on the country and the individual, this dimension of communication can be either more direct or more indirect.

Although indirection usually drives interactions, directness may be more apparent in Egypt and the other countries of North Africa. The degree of directness and indirectness varies, based on the context of the communication and one's relationship to the person. "Avoidance of [direct] confrontation is a precondition of successful business of any kind. Once he [an Arab] is angered and his pride is aroused, he becomes immovable."[3] There is no doubt that a loss of temper or display of annoyance is a serious mistake when dealing with the Arabs. A major oil company was almost thrown out of a country because the locals did not like the on-site company manager, who had lost his temper a few times with a high-level national. It took a year to rebuild the relationship, including the appointment of a new country manager, and the relationship still is not as strong as it should be.

An expatriate who had worked for a few years in Algeria found that, in general, the people there are approachable and open, but that, when it comes to expressing personal needs or wants, they prefer indirection. A German businessman in Algeria was riding in a car with his Algerian counterpart. As they drove, the German said, "My wife would love something like that beautiful necklace your wife was wearing last night. It was so beautiful." The next day, the Algerian gave his colleague a box, inside which was the necklace from his wife. The German was embarrassed, but it was too late, and he had to accept the gift. For the Algerian, the compliment paid his wife's necklace was not simply a nicety but an indirect way of indicating a desire or need to have something like this. It is recommended that you refrain from complimenting a specific item or possession. Keep compliments general. For example, in this situation, the German could have said: "The gold here is beautiful. Where would you recommend my buying something for my wife?"

Here is another example of how misunderstandings can occur between people with direct and indirect orientations. A newly arrived U.S. American worker left some articles on his supervisor's desk when the latter (a Middle Easterner) was out of his office, along with a note stating that the articles had to do with the industry and the field of work they specialized in. The next day, the supervisor told his midlevel manager that he wanted this new worker to be moved to another office, accusing the U.S. American of shaming him by placing the articles on his desk. The manager's perception was that this new worker thought that he knew more than the manager and that the manager needed to be more knowledgeable. The U.S. American was shocked and explained to the midlevel manager that all he meant was just what he had said: Here's some information that might be of interest. The U.S. American wanted to directly explain his intention but was told that the supervisor did not have time to speak with him and that it would be best if he just did his work. The U.S. American almost returned home because of this incident. It took many months to strengthen the relationship and rebuild the trust.

There are numerous dynamics at play here. First, the hierarchy orientation to power dictates protocol based on one's position. Roles are clearly defined and stated, and boundaries should not be overstepped. Second, when the subordinate left the articles without any personal or expressive content, the manager, whose orientation to communication was indirect and high-context, assumed that there was much more behind the action. Finally, if this employee had been attuned to the needs of a being-oriented manager and had established a trusting relationship with him, this exchange would have been very different and much more productive and positive.

Expressiveness.   Middle Easterners are very expressive. Usually, the use of language is accompanied by a strong display of emotion. This display (for example, hand gestures and a loud tone of voice) reflects the genuine conviction behind one's words. North Africans may be even more expressive and louder than those in the Gulf region, who tend to be formal, reserved, and soft-spoken.[4] The expression of emotion is seen as indicating strength and sincerity and is as important as the words themselves. A display of emotion and expressiveness shows "deep and sincere concern for the substance of the discussion."[5] The expression "It's not what you say, but how you say it" is especially true in the Middle East.

Formality.   Ceremony, protocol, and social etiquette are essential to making a good impression and creating a positive image in formal-oriented cultures. In the Middle East, formality indicates status, respect, reputation, education, class, and professionalism. A more formal tone is maintained when communicating with a higher-ranking official or at a public event. The degree of formality varies depending on the country and the position of the individual, but formality is always expected when communicating. Being aware of the formal protocol for meeting and greeting is imperative—for instance, acknowledging the eldest member first, standing when someone enters or leaves a room, and using a title and full family name. More formal dress is appropriate for business and social occasions, as is wearing a business suit, regardless of how warm it might be. Ceremonies and formal gatherings are abundant. For instance, depending on the level and status of an individual or group of people, in circumstances that may seem ordinary—for instance, one's arrival in the country or the completion of a training program—one may expect a reception or special ceremony with speeches, gift giving, and lavish meals.

A SENSE OF SPACE: PUBLIC AND PRIVATE

While Middle Easterners may be quite private regarding their personal lives, in business and friendships they maintain a far greater public orientation to space. Because business depends heavily on relationships, there is no distinct separation between private and professional life. "Westerners who have Arab friends sometimes feel overwhelmed by the frequent contact and wonder if they will ever have privacy. There is no concept of privacy among Arabs. In translation, the Arabic word that comes closest to the English word privacy means 'loneliness.'"[6] It is common for friends, neighbors, and family to visit without a formal invitation. Wanting to be alone communicates that something is wrong. Once a visiting consultant was in the region and suddenly wasn't feeling well. He asked to be taken back to the hotel and to "have some time alone." The host, knowing that this person was without family, felt that it was his obligation to care for him; he insisted on taking the consultant to his home, having his wife make some special food for him, and allowing him to rest and not be alone.

Among people of the same gender, there is a closer, more public orientation toward space in all relationships. Between members of the opposite sex, however, the physical distance between individuals is quite large. A businessman stated that he knew he was "in" or accepted when his host held his hand as they walked. As uncomfortable as he was with this, he knew that it was a demonstration of trust and friendship. From that day forward, business flowed with ease.

As a result of this closer proximity of space, one will notice more tolerance for crowding, pushing in public, and the sharing of space between workers, e.g., many desks in one room in an office.

With regard to the sharing of information, the tendency is to be more private and to withhold information from those at a lower level. At a peer level, communication and information are shared quite freely once trust is established. The degree of sharing depends on the status of and relationship with the individual. Generally, business is male-dominated, but one may have business interactions with women, particularly in North Africa and the Fertile Crescent, where women have a significant presence.

THE POWER HIERARCHY

Acknowledgment of rank and status is important in Middle Eastern cultures. When you enter a company, you should be able to immediately determine the corporate rank of the people who work there. This can usually be done by observing who is allocated what amount of work space, who asks questions and who replies, and whom people look to for their cues when they speak. Respect for age and experience is important.

People with a strong hierarchy orientation can clash significantly with those with an equality orientation because of their opposing perspectives on status and appropriate behavior. For example, a foreign employee was working on a short-term assignment at a firm in North Africa. From the beginning, she had difficulty with the idea of pushing the buzzer on her desk to call someone merely to bring her something to eat or drink. Many of the kitchen workers were men twice her age, and besides, she felt that she could get what she wanted by herself. So one day she went into the kitchen, talked to the workers, and left with a cup of coffee. Before she knew it, she had been summoned to the director's office. He immediately asked her why she was in the office kitchen. Was something wrong with the service? She replied, "Nothing is wrong. I just thought I could get what I needed without any assistance." The director then said, "You must understand two things. First, going into the kitchen diminishes your credibility and mine as well. I have been speaking to the staff of your credentials since before you arrived. Second, entering the kitchen indicates to the staff that they are not doing their job well, that they are not needed." Though the foreigner thought she was doing something positive and was well intentioned, she damaged both her relationship with the kitchen workers and that of the person who hired her. Breaches of hierarchy nearly always have such far-reaching ramifications.

In a hierarchy-oriented culture, certain behaviors are expected of each person, depending on that person's class, age, education, and position. "No upper-class (or higher rank) person engages in manual labor in front of others. A white-collar or desk job in an office is much desired because of the status it confers. An Arab in a white-collar job will resent being asked to do something which they consider beneath their status."[7] If, in an office situation, you make requests that are not carried out, you may find that you have been asking a person to do something that is demeaning or threatening to his or her dignity.[8] Because of the indirect orientation toward communication, the person being asked will most likely hesitate to say anything. This complicates the situation even further. Observe your counterparts carefully. Take your cues from them. Once you have established a closer relationship with one of them, ask questions delicately to indicate your willingness to learn and adapt to your new environment.

INDIVIDUALISM

Collectivist orientation.   The previous example on the use of the office kitchen can be further understood through the collectivist orientation. Even though the employee could get what she needed by herself, in a collectivistic culture there is tacit acknowledgment of one's responsibility to others. Interdependence is cultivated and acknowledged. What is commonly seen in shops and workplaces throughout the Middle East is that more workers are employed than are needed. This is due partly to the culture's sense of responsibility, the feeling that as many people as possible should be employed.

In the Arabian Gulf, one frequently hears about *majlis* (literally, a "sitting"), which serves as a vehicle for exchanges, learning, and sharing as well as questions about business matters. It is a way to consult (in Arabic, *shura*) and seek consensus, placing value on others' input even though the highest-ranking or oldest person present will make the final decision. As a result, decision making tends to take longer than in cultures that are more individualistic. A businessman in the Gulf region once said, "The *majlis* after 11:00 P.M. is the best place to do business, exchange ideas, and gain information."

In business, you will find that an invitation from one person does not necessarily mean that you will be meeting only with that individual. You are likely to find that there are others present. In collectivistic cultures, unaccompanied people are thought to lack status.[9] To be yourself is to be a part of the group. "I am a mother, a daughter, a sister, worker, friend, cousin, aunt, grandmother" was the response by an Arab woman to the question "Who are you?" Membership in a country club or the local chamber of commerce, for example, will be essential for building connections.

In the Middle Eastern and North African cultures, there is also an emphasis on caring for others. One often hears a reference to someone else, even a stranger, as a brother or sister. This stems from a feeling of connection and responsibility toward the other person. "[The] concept of collectivism extends beyond the biogenetic relative."[10]

Particularistic orientation. In the Middle East, everything in business is negotiable. This is obvious even when you are shopping for souvenirs. Prices may be stated, or even written, but they are never fixed. They are always open, and the shopkeeper expects to negotiate the final price. During personal and business exchanges, one often hears, "For my sake." This means "for my sake, give me a good price or make a special exception for me"; this illustrates the attitude that one must sustain, protect, and take into consideration the relationships that currently exist. Contracts are the area where the contrast between universalistic and particularistic cultures is most obvious. In a universalistic culture, a contract is an agreement to be followed precisely; in a particularistic culture, relationships "may involve more than the contract requires . . . and businesspeople may expect contracts to be qualified where circumstances have changed."[11]

The following is an example of how the perception of a contract by a person with a universalistic orientation and that by a person with a particularistic orientation can lead to a clash of understanding regarding the terms of an agreement.

In a ten-year contract between a Canadian ball-bearing producer and an Arab machine manufacturer, a minimum annual quantity of ball bearings was agreed upon. After about six years, the orders from the Middle East stopped coming in. The Canadians' first reaction was that this was illegal. A visit to the customer only increased their confusion. The Arabs had apparently canceled the contract unilaterally because the Canadian who had signed it had left the company. The contract that the Canadians saw as universally applicable was not considered relevant any more in the eyes of the Arabs. What could the Canadians say against this logic, especially when they discovered that the ball bearings were never even used? It turned out that the product was purchased solely out of the Arabs' loyalty to the Canadian contract-signer, not because of a felt legal obligation.[12]

Usually, when people from the same village, country, tribe, or group interact, there is an expectation that favors will be granted and special considerations will be given. The same expectation often extends to a joint venture, merger, or commitment to work together, which is expected to be mutually beneficial.

Avoid presenting contracts that are or appear to be rigid and inflexible. Universalistic cultures must master the art and skill of being creative while at the same time addressing the special requests that will inevitably be made in particularistic cultures.

COMPETITIVENESS VERSUS COOPERATION

Trade and business have existed for centuries in the Middle East, and long-standing traditions accompany them. Success is often based on the cultivation of relationships and the maintenance of a cooperative spirit. However, although cooperation is valued, competition remains strong. The Middle Eastern organization will be moderately competitive with other organizations at times. A sort of "cooperative competition" prevails. As a result of the emphasis on collectivism and this cooperative competition, Middle Easterners tend to build alliances and to avoid direct competition with companies, colleagues, or individuals with whom they have a relationship. Therefore, competition is greater with people outside one's family, tribe, village, or country. However, with the economic boom and privatization has come an increase in competition. Overall, the tendency is to pursue joint ventures and opportunities collaboratively. One example of cooperative competition is found in marketing. There, competition with rival products is downplayed. Advertisements focus on the attributes and assets of the product, not on criticism of its competitors.

ORDER-ORIENTED STRUCTURE

Most Middle Eastern cultures are quite order-oriented. Middle Easterners, in general, make spoken and unspoken assumptions about each person's role and responsibilities. Jobs and expectations are clearly defined in indirect and high-context ways. For example, a North African delegation arrived in a less order-oriented country for an intensive training program. Following the training, members of the delegation confided in an Arab American about their unfulfilled expectations. They felt that there was much too much free time during the training. This information was relayed to the host government agency. The agency staff was surprised and defensively said, "We thought they would be happy with some free time to do what they wanted without us telling them what to do every minute of the day." The Middle Eastern delegation, on the other hand, felt that the agency's staff was in charge and should have stated what was expected of them during the open time. Many expatriates have learned not to overextend themselves in their jobs in ways that can be perceived as threatening to the status quo or noncompliant with the management.

WAYS OF THINKING

Deductive versus inductive thinking.   Middle Easterners tend to be deductive thinkers, making decisions and assessments through both theoretical and empirical prisms, which are supplemented with doses of abstract logic or pure sentiment and, in many cases, religious connotations. The role of fate is a constant factor in their thinking, largely as a manifestation of some divine intent, while a heritage of superstition is never far away, along with a kind of cultural memory that continually drives their thinking.

The patterns of thinking are changing, however, as outside influences gain momentum. By its very nature, the business sector seems to respond to change well ahead of others, except perhaps for a segment of the foreign-educated intellectual class.

Systemic thinking.   Middle Easterners tend to approach matters from a large perspective (often called in the West "the big picture") that tries to take into account both the matter at hand and other factors that might seem to be unrelated—including, for example, cultural and social sensitivities. All these factors are connected to the way a Middle Eastern businessperson generally looks at business prospects.

Thinking patterns in the Middle East are heavily influenced by cultural codes of conduct that seek to ensure that adapting to foreign (mainly Western) ways in business—or in anything else, for that matter—will not compromise or undermine recognized values. A prominent Egyptian thinker once lamented that Arab society in particular suffers from "many dualisms," including that of "importing" modern Western products while "rejecting the thought" behind the products—adding, tongue-in-cheek, that most Arabs believe that this is "doable." This mindset continues to reflect Middle Eastern thinking, but efforts to adapt to Western technology and its cultural underpinnings are slowly becoming the norm.

If, in the United States, "all politics is local," in the Middle East all business is local. The profit motive is not the sole determinant of a business deal, though.

People have to know that their business ventures will make a difference to others—to their society, to their city or village, and to their extended family.

"Losing face" is as strongly felt in the Middle East as it is in many Asian countries. This encourages a cautious approach to thinking out business projects.

Key Insights for Effectiveness

The Middle Eastern constraint orientation means that you must be patient when conducting business negotiations. Middle Easterners value consensus building, a time-consuming pursuit. If you come from a control-oriented culture, business will probably take longer than you are used to. Be prepared to invest and spend time in the region. Time spent on socializing and entertaining is important and can enhance a business relationship. Keep your schedule open and flexible.

Remember that Middle Easterners value relationships and believe that it is necessary to establish trust before beginning negotiations and making commitments. Understand that this aspect of the being orientation is of paramount importance in all exchanges, personal and professional.

Be ready to address the specific needs of your Middle Eastern customer or future partner and to tailor a given product or service to those needs. Their deductive and systemic orientations mean that Middle Easterners will want to understand both the conceptual and the analytical details of the entire venture.

Their multifocused orientation means that Middle Easterners are accustomed to having multiple conversations, interruptions, and diversions during any given session. Remain focused and prepared to pick up the discussion from where it was interrupted.

Middle Easterners are master negotiators and will want to learn a great deal about the company and the negotiators they are dealing with. Do not try to speed up or force the resolution of an issue or the closing of a deal by claiming time constraints or schedule pressures. That approach will not work. Expect delays and a slower pace during the negotiation process.

Because Middle Easterners are expressive in their mode of communication, it is recommended that you always try to communicate enthusiasm and passion for your project, but at the same time maintain a respectful and courteous tone and approach. Insincerity can easily be detected.

The formal and hierarchy orientations play an important role in Middle Eastern business situations. If your culture has an equality and informal orientation, try to bear this in mind and act accordingly. Be extremely polite and formal in your speech. Know the exact position, status, and appropriate title for each person and the pronunciation of his or her name before a meeting.

Be up-to-date on political and social issues concerning the host country and the Middle East in general. Being consensus-driven, Middle Easterners who believe that a given cause is right will seek agreement from others. Unless you are willing to say what they want to hear, avoid discussing politics by offering innocuous statements. Since religion is such a large part of their lifestyle and worldview, Middle Easterners will want others to know it. Show appreciation and respect, but try to steer clear of religious discussions unless you are well versed in their belief systems. Otherwise, you run the risk of damaging your credibility and the business relationship.

The key to successful communication while conducting business in the Middle East is to build trust and credibility through sustained interpersonal contact and to demonstrate respect for local customs and ways of thinking.

Many Middle Easterners have traveled and studied in the West; even so, they sometimes flinch at attempts by foreign businesspeople and investors to have it their own way. In many cases, how a person conducts business outweighs the financial considerations involved. The Middle East is a status-conscious society, where rank matters and formal behavior is expected. Middle Easterners also tend to adopt a leisurely pace in conducting meetings and negotiations. In this regard, process can be more important than content: "The how often matters more than the what."[13] In a culture in which, as a general rule, directness is avoided, nuance and nonverbal communication play significant roles. This is why well-connected local intermediaries can be of great assistance to foreign business concerns. Even when you are communicating with someone who appears direct and quick to negotiate, remember that this does not mean that you can dismiss the importance of the relationship.

ASIA

Its enormous cultural diversity is perhaps the most striking feature of this region. The dominant culture varies significantly from country to country, with many countries being heavily influenced by their dominant religion and by their colonial past. As a result of colonization, your firm may have to deal with cultural influences other than those that are traditionally characteristic of the country in question.

Adding to the importance of recognizing the diversity of the region is the latent antagonism between some Asian countries. For example, in China and Korea there is lingering resentment over Japan's past behavior, which translates into apprehension over Japan's success in marketing consumer products. Both China and Korea have benefited from Japanese business, but these benefits have been offset by fear of Japanese domination. In terms of conducting business in Asia, this means, for example, that using a Japanese agent to conduct business with a South Korean firm may jeopardize a foreign company's chances of success in that market. Many foreigners are also unaware of the distinction between regime and nationhood. While China and Korea have rival Communist and non-Communist governments, the Chinese on Taiwan and on the mainland and the Koreans on both sides of the Demilitarized Zone are united in their belief that there is only one China and only one Korea. These perceptions go beyond merely theoretical contemplation of rivalry and legitimacy. For example, while South Korea would like to have extensive commercial relations with the People's Republic of China (PRC), the PRC has moved slowly to avoid offending North Korea. Similarly, although many businesspeople in Taiwan profit from trade with the PRC, the Taiwanese government does not want to appear too approving of such trade in order to avoid the appearance of legitimizing the mainland regime. All of these are very sensitive issues and must be handled delicately and with tact.

In order to prepare yourself for your work in Asia, it is best to do some reading on the history of Asian countries and their current political and economic situation.

Cultural Orientation Patterns

ENVIRONMENT

Harmony.   Balance, harmony, order, and the establishment of relationships are all values that are of deep significance in Asia. The high value that Asians place on the preservation of harmony dictates that they avoid confrontation. When differences do occur, they try to find a mutually acceptable way to handle them. Decision making may take longer in such a culture because of the need to involve the many different parties and to build consensus. Leaders will need to facilitate harmonious relationships and provide staff with stability.

Harmony-oriented Asians are willing to spend a great deal of time and money fostering cooperative relationships with suppliers and customers. Relationships will be built on copious exchanges of information, frequent face-to-face meetings (both official and social), and exchanges of favors.

In a speech about Japan's change of government in 1993, Lee Kuan Yew, Singapore's former prime minister, attempted to identify how Asia's harmony orientation differentiates Asian cultures from cultures that do not share this orientation:

> I do not see them becoming a fractious, contentious society like America, always debating and knocking each other down. That is not their culture. . . . Americans believe that out of contention, out of the clash of different ideas and ideals, you get good government. That view is not shared in Asia.

He goes on:

> If we follow the West in our social relations and family structures, we will be in deep trouble. In the West the Christian religion used to instill fear of punishment in hell or reward in heaven. Science and technology have eliminated that fear. So the controlling mechanism has gone awry. I am hoping that because Asian moral control is based on what is good in a secular this-world, not a spiritual after-world, we will not lose our moral bearings.[14]

Asian cultures with such embedded belief systems as the Confucian, Taoist, and Buddhist religions stress harmonious relations with the world. As the *Tao Te Ching*, written in China in the sixth century B.C., says:

Attain the highest openness,

Maintain the deepest harmony.

Become a part of all things;

In this way I perceive the cycles.[15]

To foster harmony in the workplace, subordinates never openly contradict their superiors. Reciprocally, managers attempt to correct or criticize their subordinates in an indirect fashion, rather than openly. Such reciprocity fosters a respectful, harmonious environment. Harmony is also demonstrated in the widespread formation and use of teams throughout Asian companies. The value placed on harmony means that the group becomes more important than the individual; relationships and obligations are placed above individual welfare.

Constraint.   The presence and practice of the Confucian, Buddhist, Taoist, and Hindu religions have instilled a constraint orientation in Asians. As a result, Asians stress the influence of external forces rather than attempting to change their environment to fit their needs. For instance, astrologers are an influential part of Indian culture; many people in India believe that nothing is accidental, that the universe and all living creatures in it have a fundamental order.

Throughout Asia, folk beliefs, customs, and the idea of fate will often affect business activities and attitudes toward work. For example, the Pakistani belief in spiritual powers and in God (*Allah*) may influence their perception of a business situation. Pakistanis believe that all things come from Allah, and success is usually attributed to Allah's mercy. The term *Insh'allah* (God willing) is commonly used to express hope for success on a project, for one's family, or for a positive outcome of events. Thus, a Pakistani businessperson may make frequent use of the term. Asians' constraint orientation is also a result of the ever-present economic and political instability in their societies. For example, politics is a controversial topic in Pakistan and a major constraint on Pakistani business. A Pakistani businessperson might easily feel discouraged by the political barriers within his society and, as a consequence, withdraw from a business venture. Another example of the influence of the constraint orientation on Asian business practices is that Malaysians will always negotiate for an escape clause in their formal and written contracts. Such institutionalized business practices can be seen as reflecting a mindset that acknowledges that there is every possibility that things will not work out. The Westerner who believes that he or she has made an agreement with an Asian counterpart may be shocked to discover that, because of altered circumstances, the agreement has been modified or ignored.

As part of their constraint orientation, Asians believe that they cannot control all repercussions, that the environment is responsible for many outcomes. At a multicultural sales training program in New York, several Chinese participants described how difficult it can be to sell a house to the Chinese, e.g., Chinese buyers refusing to buy houses in cul-de-sacs or on land with large trees. The realtor was told that a cul-de-sac is a road that goes nowhere, and therefore that living on such a street could harm the occupant's career. Big trees can also potentially block a person's career. These decisions are rooted in the Chinese concept of *feng shui*, which are earth forces that affect success or failure.

THE SENSE OF TIME

Single- and multifocus aspects.   As a result of a single-focus orientation in Asia, not only is emphasis placed on punctuality, but the work style is highly regimented. Asians have a high commitment to schedules, which is characteristic of a society with a single-focus orientation. It is not unusual for a company to schedule deskside calisthenics, singing of the national anthem at 5:00 P.M., and regular after-hours drinking sessions with coworkers (to show loyalty to the company). This commitment to schedules is a consequence of the effort to achieve efficacy and to do a superior job.

As a culture that also contains a multifocus orientation, however, Asians are highly flexible even while maintaining a commitment to schedules. Their perception of time is multifaceted. Asians' multifocus orientation facilitates parallel processing and flexible manufacturing. Productive Asian companies are masters of synchronizing several alternating sequences.

Asians' multifocus orientation is also a result of their emphasis on teamwork; they place great importance on knowing what other members of their team are doing. The multifocus orientation allows members of the team to step in and assist their colleagues whenever it is necessary to do so.

In parts of Asia (particularly Southeast Asia), frequent interruptions during a business meeting are not unusual. It may also be acceptable for participants to come in and out of a conference room, either to answer a telephone call from a family member or a colleague or to respond to a superior's query or request. These interruptions reflect the importance Asians place on relationships as a result of their multifocus orientation. It is a good idea to maintain a sense of humor throughout a series of interruptions.

Fixed and fluid time orientations.   As a result of their fixed time orientation, Asians place great value on punctuality. Being punctual for appointments and keeping to schedules are very important to them. Punctuality is seen as a sign of respect for the other person. But, while they value punctuality, Asians do not place much emphasis on getting tasks accomplished quickly and within a limited time frame, because they also have a fluid time orientation. They value the building of trust and compatibility between business partners, which takes time. In other words, the needs of a business relationship take precedence over a schedule of tasks to be completed. Asians thus create a network of business ties based on obligation and reciprocity. As a result, a business agreement is a formalized, ongoing, dynamic relationship.

Negotiators with a more fixed time orientation often find themselves at a disadvantage because of their impatience and because of self-imposed time pressures. Asians can use time as an indirect negotiating tool when doing business with companies that place a great emphasis on accomplishing tasks quickly. The Taoist concept of *wu wei* (nonassertion) is applied to business negotiation: State a position and wait, hoping that your opponents, in order to close the deal, will make concessions. Once a deal has been signed, however, Asians will initiate delaying tactics, pushing for more and more concessions in the gray areas of the contract.

The past and the future.   Throughout Asia, there is a strong orientation both to the past and to the long-term future. That is, current decisions are related to the past and to the future.

Asians conceptualize time differently from most Westerners. Eastern philosophies conceive of a cycle of eternal return. The Asian perception of time as being cyclical influences this past/future orientation. The future is not distant. To the decision maker, if time revolves, past, present, and future are all now.

Because of their strong connection with the past, Asians have a highly developed sense of personal identification with national and family histories. There is great respect for the past; value is placed on what worked in the past. When confronted with a situation requiring action, Asians will often look to the past for a precedent. The expectation is that what was successful in the past will prove so again.

As a result of their past orientation, Asians are also sometimes resistant to change. They may not like sudden changes or changes made simply for the sake of change. They are more comfortable with knowing that the status quo will remain at approximately the same level. It is common to hear something like "This is the way things have always been done." Once a group has agreed to make a change, however, the change will be carried through.

Because of their orientation to the future, Asians are particularly interested in getting to know you and your company before they invest in a long-term relationship with you. As a consequence, negotiations can take a fairly long time. Asians are also far more likely than cultures with a present orientation to invest in ventures that will yield profit in the far-off future. This is true of both public and private business ventures. For example, it is not uncommon in Japan to have multigenerational (that is, 100 or more years long) mortgages for houses. Asian nations also save a larger portion of their gross domestic product than other nations and invest this in the future of their nations. On the other hand, long-term planning (and assumptions) has contributed to the Asian economic crisis, as countries prepared budgets and accumulated debts on the assumption that there would be continued, vigorous growth.

MODES OF ACTION: BEING AND DOING

Asian cultures display both a being and a doing orientation. There is emphasis both on working hard and achieving success and on developing trust in relationships.

Because Asians are being-oriented, they believe that it is important to build and maintain solid relationships. They believe that this provides a stronger guarantee that agreements will be followed. For Asians, a firmly established relationship means more than a written contract.

People from doing-oriented cultures may not be accustomed to building relationships with their business associates. They must do so, however, before they embark on a business venture in Asia; otherwise, they risk failure of the business deal. In Asia, little business is conducted around the negotiating table. Instead, it is done in a more relaxed, even social, setting. It is highly unlikely that Asians will proceed with a business venture if they have been unable to build a relationship with their foreign counterparts.

Entertaining is a vital part of doing business in Asia and is critical to building and maintaining relationships. However, entertainment and other relationship-building activities should not be considered as necessarily leading to a deep relationship. If circumstances change, the relationship is likely to change along with it.

Closely tied to their being orientation is the value Asians place on reciprocal obligation. The process of building and maintaining relationships leads to reciprocal obligations. These obligations are incurred in both business and social situations. For example, a third party who introduces two potential business partners incurs the obligation to mediate future conflicts or issues. This means that Asians will not act in haste to incur such obligations. To them, failure to follow through on one's obligations can result in loss of face and the end of a business relationship.

Asians need to know who you are, as well as your company's reputation and position in the business world. It is important that you take time to develop a relationship through personal contact and do not rush to discuss price, delivery dates, and so forth. Who you are is as important as what you are selling.

While there is a strong being orientation throughout most of Asia, many Asians, particularly East Asians, also display a strong doing orientation, with some of them being willing to exchange leisure activities for long working hours. This, in turn, is also related to the Asian desire to save face. An inability to complete tasks, to assist your corporation in gaining competitive advantage, could result in loss of face. David Rearwin describes one Asian businessperson's reaction to the difference between the work ethos of the Japanese and U.S. Americans:

> If the American makes a major mistake on Friday, he will start to correct it on Monday, while the Japanese—like many other Asians—will take care of it over the weekend. Over the course of a year, it is only natural that the American should fall behind, and that the farther back he falls, the less respect he deserves. . . . For these reasons, many Asians (Japanese or not) find it absurd that American government officials have seriously suggested that one solution for the U.S. trade imbalance with Japan is for the Japanese to work less, save less and spend more.[16]

Many Asians will perceive a person who does not work hard as being undisciplined and self-indulgent, willing to put pleasure above family and corporation.

COMMUNICATION

Formal orientation. Formal communication and adherence to protocol facilitate communication and business in Asia. Formalities are important throughout Asia (for example, the Japanese tea ceremony), and they extend to all aspects of doing business—greetings, business card exchange, gift giving, terms of address, negotiation protocol, and dining and entertaining. Formality with those outside one's immediate group is especially important; this involves following protocol and social customs.

Some Asian languages allow speakers to switch easily between formal and informal speech. Part of the Japanese language, for example, is referred to as *keigo*. This is the language that people use with their superiors or those to whom they wish to show respect. The grammatical rules that apply to *keigo* are different from those for ordinary speech. The degree of formality used in speech allows individuals to gauge the type of relationship that exists between the speakers. More formal language can show either respect or the absence of a relationship between the parties involved.

The forms of address used between people are a further indication of the formal orientation of Asian communication. Outside one's family or close friends, first names are rarely used. The proper form of address is usually the person's last name, with the appropriate honorific attached.

Another culture's tendency toward informality can result in confusion in business dealings with Asians. For example, a U.S.-American trainer opened a training session for a group of Asian managers by sharing some jokes. Her goal was to loosen up the group and make everyone comfortable in preparation for the hard work that was to come. The Asian audience, however, saw the trainer's behavior as a signal that they need not take the training seriously. When they continued joking and talking to each other after the trainer got down to business, she became angry. She could not understand why they did not take the training seriously, and she concluded that they did not respect her. Her failure to take into account Asians' formal orientation had resulted in a serious misunderstanding.

An indirect communication style. On the whole, Asians are indirect and self-controlled in their communication style. They avoid open conflict and the expression of anger. When disputes arise, an intermediary known to both parties may be asked to help resolve the conflict. In Bangladesh, for example, the tradition of parents acting as intermediaries in arranged marriages reflects and reinforces the indirect patterns of communication and decision making found in business organizations.

The Asian tendency toward an indirect communication style is a result of the importance Asians place on saving face. The Asian concept of "face" represents an individual's entire being—body, soul, and spirit. Saving face is important not just for the individual concerned, but also for his family, tribe, or clan and the entire community to which he belongs. Asians' indirect orientation is therefore linked to the importance they place on preserving harmony and hierarchy. Direct communication can rupture relationships. Direct criticism may give the appearance that a person does not respect and honor the other person's status and rank. For example, Indonesians view direct questions, particularly when posed to one's superior, as particularly embarrassing. *Sembah* or *hormah* is the art of paying respect to one's superiors. One way to display *sembah* or *hormah* is not to question one's superiors.

Indirect communication is also important in preserving harmony in a region where many countries are vulnerable to ethnic and religious conflicts. Indirect communication is further necessitated by the tendency not to differentiate between what is personal and what is not. A comment made about someone's work is taken as a comment on the person himself. Everything has personal significance. Therefore, any criticism is construed as personal criticism. Rejection of someone's work or proposal may be considered a rejection of the person.

Therefore, it is considered rude to confront differences directly. Asians will not disagree publicly or reply to a question with a direct "no." Instead, they will give an affirmative answer peppered with exceptions or suggestions. Asking direct, probing questions should be avoided, since these usually result in embarrassment for Asians. Similarly, any rejection of a proposal or any suggestion or criticism should be made indirectly.

Asians' indirect orientation can generate conflict and embarrassment when they work with more direct communicators. At a meeting held in an Asian capital that was attended by division managers for a U.S. multinational company, two supervisors, one U.S. American and one Asian, were asked to present proposals for meeting their yearly sales forecast. When the U.S. manager presented his proposal, there was little comment from the boss or from other attendees. After the Asian manager's presentation, however, his U.S. colleague suggested some ways in which the Asian manager's plan could be improved. His intention was to help, to come up with the best possible marketing plan for the company, but the result was that the Asian manager felt embarrassed. The U.S. manager viewed the conversation after the proposal as an opportunity to generate a better proposal together. The Asian viewed it as disapproval.

A high-context orientation.   Asians' high-context orientation is another reason that Asia is relationship-centered. Asians need a great deal of contextual information about an individual or a company before they can transact business. Thus, a significant time may be spent on what U.S. Americans might consider small talk—family issues, food and drink, the weather. As one Japanese businessman noted to the author, "every business relationship should begin with a *sake* party."

As high-context communicators, Asians place great emphasis on implicit communication. They often assume that their addressees have a complete knowledge of the context and background of the subject matter that they are discussing. They assume that much communication can be implied, that it need not be stated explicitly. Communication between people can rely on body movements, facial expressions, eye contact, and other nonverbal signals to get the point across.

To be polite and to avoid conflict, Asians will often say "yes" when they mean "no," but as high-context communicators, they assume that the person they are addressing will understand them through their body language and the context in which they are speaking.

The challenge for low-context communicators is to recognize when "yes" is a polite "yes" that actually means "no." It is thus important to pay attention to qualifiers, facial expressions, and body language. If you are unsure, probe the opposite point. If that elicits a different sort of "yes"—with affirmative nonverbal indicators—the first "yes" probably meant "no."

Silence can also play an important role in high-context cultures. In Asian cultures, silence is active, not passive; it designates thought, not disengagement. A U.S. American dealing with, for example, a Singaporean may become anxious to fill silences. Rushing in to fill a silence may be considered pushy or impulsive, or even emotional. Silence can also be a strategy for helping others to save face, taking advantage of another's impatience, or simply leaving options open.

An instrumental orientation.   Asians tend to display an instrumental orientation. The Asian approach to communication stresses self-discipline and emotional control. Emotional outbursts and extreme anger or frustration in a business environment are not respected. Restraining one's emotions is considered evidence of good character, demonstrating maturity and respect for the individuals with whom one is communicating.

Asians' instrumental orientation toward communication is reflected in their preference for restraint in body movements and words. They prefer to display no emotions when communicating. Especially in negative circumstances, a face that is devoid of expression is considered desirable. A smile is often used to cover embarrassment or discomfort. Reactions to something positive will be restrained and concealed. As a result of their instrumental orientation, Asians are more impressed with content than with expressive style or eloquence.

THE SENSE OF SPACE: PUBLIC AND PRIVATE

Asians often display a mixture of a private and a public orientation toward space. In business interactions, they have a more private space orientation, preferring considerable space between themselves and the person with whom they are communicating (they usually stand at least 24 inches from the other person). Physical contact of any kind is limited; even tapping someone on the shoulder to demonstrate a point is highly unusual. In many Asian countries, the culture's private orientation extends to the delineation of property boundaries, with stone or wooden fences often used to mark these boundaries. It also is rare for Asians to conduct business in their homes. Private and professional spaces are kept separate.

On the other hand, office spaces tend to be public, with private offices rare. For example, in many Japanese offices, the desks for a section or department are positioned in a single open area in clusters by work group. The desks face one another, with no space or divider between them. Several people often share one phone. This office setup allows for the free flow of information among members of the same work group. On the other hand, it also facilitates centralized authority and a more authoritarian monitoring and control of systems.

It is important to keep in mind that while office spaces in Asia are generally public, Asians still need to have their personal space respected. In South Korea, for example, if someone approaches another person's desk, he will cough to announce his arrival, since he cannot knock. The visitor will not be acknowledged until the person he has come to visit rises. This allows Asian businesspeople to prepare themselves for an impending interruption.

Adding to the complexity of spatial usage in Asia is the language of space, which is intricate. Seating positions are sometimes a clue to power relationships. For example, in Japan the seat farthest from the door is likely to be the "power seat." In a car, the seat directly behind the driver is considered the most prestigious.

A HIERARCHY OF POWER

The Asian orientation to power tends toward hierarchy, or *soft authoritarianism* and *authoritarian pluralism*, as the power structure is sometimes called. Deference to older family members, particularly males, is widespread, and the observance of rank and status is very important. Differences in age, sex, and status are commonly acknowledged through deferential and honorific speech and through one's behavior. In India, for instance, the Hindu religion influences a woman's position in the societal hierarchy. Although the legal position of Hindu women has improved in recent years, a woman is still bound by ancient traditions that stress her dedication and obedience to her husband and his wishes. Paternalistic authority is often the norm in Asian countries. In China, management by committee is widely used. In the large South Korean industrial complexes (known as *chaebol*), orders flow from top to bottom, and loyalty and obedience are prized. In many Southeast Asian cultures, there is usually a large difference in power levels between managers and subordinates. For example, in Thailand, it is appropriate for a businessperson to ask a secretary to get coffee or run an errand. On the other hand, it is unacceptable to try to bypass a step of the ladder of authority when working on a project. Most Asians will feel slighted and confused if their status is ignored.

Motivated by an orientation that places emphasis on hierarchy, Asians are unlikely to seek personal prestige or individual recognition for their accomplishments; group recognition, however, is a powerful motivator (see the discussion of individualism). Concern for reputation means that Asians are not likely to seek personal credit for achievements. Asians feel that they must abide by certain unwritten rules of conduct pertaining to status. The hierarchical structure of Asian society ensures that traditions are passed on to future generations.

INDIVIDUALISM

Collectivist orientation.   In Asia, the group, rather than the individual, is honored. Individualism, in general, is not highly valued in Asia. As a result of their collectivist orientation, Asians tend to identify themselves as part of a larger whole. They subordinate their interests to the interests of the group, and they usually do not like being set apart from the group for either praise or criticism. In many Asian countries, a famous American fast-food restaurant recognizes its outstanding performers by posting, where all employees and patrons can see it, a picture of "The Crew of the Month." This same company follows the same method of employee recognition in the United States, but with just one difference: the picture is of "The Employee of the Month."

Outside one's working team, however, individual success may be stressed. In Taiwan, mainland China, and Hong Kong, for example, there is a strong entrepreneurial spirit. This has been evident in Taiwan and Hong Kong for some time, but is only just beginning to appear in China. It has been a very strong trait in Chinese emigrant groups overseas.

Where a U.S.-American mother may say to her 2-year-old son who is misbehaving in public, "Don't act like that. Good boys should behave in public. Where are your manners?" an Asian mother, equally concerned, might say, "Don't act like that. People will say you are a naughty boy. What will they think of our family?" The U.S.-American mother appeals to manners, a set of rules or standards that her youngster should follow; the Asian mother appeals to the embarrassment that might come to the family as a result of the youngster's poor behavior in public.

This collectivist orientation results in tighter teamwork, more consensual (and therefore lengthier) decision making, more obedience, and more widespread information sharing than are generally found in North American and northern European countries. This orientation, however, should not be overemphasized. The Chinese and Koreans tend to put personal and family concerns before organizational and societal concerns. Japan stresses organizational and societal ties. As part of the collectivist orientation, government and nationalistic pressures tend to play a large role in economic life. The government—which is authoritative and sometimes authoritarian—defines the needs of the community and determines the country's general direction.

Particularistic orientation.   Asian cultures have a particularistic orientation. Although a culture (or particularly a community) may be guided by many rules, Asians are comfortable making exceptions to these rules. Bending rules is a way of life, particularly if the rules are bent out of loyalty to friends, family, or colleagues. Asians focus on the unique circumstances of a particular situation and adapt rules to fit that situation. For example, an office might have a policy that workers stay from 8:15 A.M. until 5:00 P.M. Everyone will acknowledge that this is an important rule, but workers will also think nothing of signing Mr. Sutthorn in at 8:15 A.M., even though he does not arrive until 9:00 A.M. They all know that he is taking his daughter to school in the morning and cannot get to work earlier.

This particularistic orientation is also demonstrated in the approach to contracts. As David Rearwin writes:

> Abstract concepts like right and wrong, or truth and untruth, depend on the circumstances, rather than being absolute. Behavior that is acceptable in one situation may be unacceptable in another. Both morally and legally, individuals and governments have no compunctions about changing the rules at any time to fit a new set of circumstances (including newly discovered needs or newly defined objectives on the part of the Asian in question).[17]

Asians also view contracts in a more flexible manner than many other people; in their view, it is appropriate not to adhere to the terms of a contract if the circumstances under which the contract was originally negotiated change. Often contracts establish the general spirit of the business venture but do not spell out the procedures to be followed in every contingency. It is understood implicitly that the contract can be modified if necessary. Similarly, while many

Asian nations are governed by large bureaucracies, this does not mean that government regulations are never changed. Regulations are created by the government for its own use and are subject to change whenever it suits the government's purposes. A bureaucracy may tell a company that there are no rules but use unidentified regulations to justify a negative decision.

A COOPERATIVE RATHER THAN COMPETITIVE VIEW

As a result of the emphasis on relationships, Asian culture has a cooperative orientation. Rather than working in competition with one another, Asians prefer to work as a group, sharing information or breaking up a task. This way, each person performs a certain part of a task and contributes to the project—which, in turn, ensures that no one stands out as having made a particular decision or completed a certain task alone. Rewards and blame are equally shared among all the members of the team. Someone who is competitive within his or her own workplace may seem selfish, overly aggressive, or uncaring in the eyes of coworkers. The cooperative orientation may be linked to the fact that most Asian companies promote workers on the basis of seniority rather than merit; this encourages workers not to compete against one another because each feels that promotion will come eventually.

However, while Asians are cooperative within their own group, organizations usually display a competitive orientation in their dealings with other organizations. By early childhood, a competitive attitude and a strong drive to succeed have been instilled. For example, many Asian children, while still very young, are placed in competitive classes to prepare them for entrance to prestigious universities. Japan is considered one of the most competitive cultures in the world, which can be seen in the long workweeks put in by many Japanese managers.

The result of the competitive environment in which many Asian children are raised is that many of them become highly adaptable players who may use indirect or manipulative means when the competitor appears stronger.

STRUCTURE

As a result of an order orientation, Asian culture places a high value on structure and control. The Confucian religion values roles, obligations, and the correct way of doing things. Asians generally prefer their roles and responsibilities to be delineated in a straightforward manner. Employees like the parameters of their superiors' expectations to be clearly defined. This order orientation stems, in part, from the importance of saving face. Generally, Asians do not appreciate situations for which they are not prepared because they risk embarrassing themselves, and the maintenance of order protects them from such situations. For example, an American businessman who works for a large health-care company was once told to oversee a business unit's activities in Japan; the unit was having some problems marketing and selling its product there. He flew to Japan and asked to see samples of the Japanese managers' marketing plans, but they were unable to produce any. He told them that they knew more about the marketing environment in Japan than he did, and he asked (or empowered) them to develop a marketing plan. He gave them general guidelines and a month to come up with a plan for his review. After a month, no plan was forthcoming. Frustrated, he developed the plan himself and sent it to Japan. On his next trip to Japan, he discovered the reason why no plan had been produced. The Japanese managers did not feel comfortable being "empowered." They felt uncomfortable proceeding without clear, detailed instructions and procedures. In the absence of such a structure, they were, in fact, disempowered.

THINKING

Deductive and inductive orientations. Because of their inductive orientation, Asians generally wish to have as much data on a project as possible. They are detail-oriented and prefer precise information and data for the analysis of a situation or proposal. Reliance on data minimizes risk and thus reduces the chance that someone will lose face. When there is no precedent for the business venture under negotiation, Asians are likely to want to discuss a variety of possible business arrangements and their probable outcomes. This approach may lead to extensive negotiations, prolonged by the tendency to negotiate each issue separately while assembling all the details and information available. When there is no concrete model to follow, each issue becomes important in its own right.

However, Asians are not limited by an inductive orientation; on occasion, their approach is also deductive. Conclusions are not reached solely on the basis of the data collected; usually there are other factors to consider, such as situation and hierarchy. Asians recognize that, because of the particular qualities of each situation, concrete data must be adapted by reconciling facts with logic and theory. This may lead to confusion in business negotiations with people from cultures that are either solely deductive or solely inductive, as the data considered and the conclusions reached may appear contradictory.

A systemic orientation. As a result of Asians' systemic orientation, their thinking patterns are difficult for foreigners to comprehend. David Rearwin has one of the best descriptions of this pattern:

> You will encounter refusals with no apparent reason, leaps of logic (or illogic) that lead to totally impossible conclusions, willingness to

follow a course that already leads nowhere, cheerful acceptance of mutually contradictory statements, and a literal-mindedness that forces you to ask exactly the right question in order to get useful information (remember that Asian thinking tends to reach a given target by moving in a spiral or by generating a holistic image centered on general, and often rather amorphous concepts) rather than a clearly discernible line of thought.[18]

These thinking patterns will require adjustment for individuals who are accustomed to a linear orientation. The key for such a person is to concentrate on the information received, rather than on the information anticipated.

Asians emphasize that specific issues are intricately interwoven with more complex ideas. As a result of their systemic tendency, it is important for them to see how a decision affects not only immediate issues but those outside the matter at hand. Learning and knowledge acquisition are important aspects of the ventures undertaken. Thus, a deal might be undertaken for "intellectual profitability," rather than for simple monetary gain. The reason many Asian businesses are highly successful is that they are able to think systemically while also identifying important specifics: knowledge that is also profitable.

Some companies—Toshiba America Consumer Products, for example—are seeking to leverage differences in thinking patterns between linear- and systemic-oriented thinkers in order to enhance their competitive advantage. Toshiba found that American engineers think analytically and follow a step-by-step approach to problem solving, whereas Japanese engineers look at the whole and the relationship of the parts. To take advantage of the differences, Toshiba may have American engineers work on relatively narrow-focus, complicated parts, while the Japanese engineers work on the standardized parts and the whole design.

Key Insights for Effectiveness

The Asian harmony and constraint orientations mean that you must be patient when conducting business negotiations. Asians value consensus building, which takes time. If your culture is control-oriented, doing business will probably take longer than you are used to. Be prepared to spend time in Asia. Make your departure date flexible.

Remember that harmony is not the same thing as passivity. Asians are competitive. If you are not assertive, they will take advantage of this. Make sure that, in the course of negotiations, your Asian counterparts do not acquire proprietary information.

Be ready to address the technical needs of your Asian customer and to tailor a technical product to those needs. Their systemic orientation means that Asians want to understand both the conceptual and the analytical details of the venture.

Asians' multifocus orientation means that, for them, a business agreement is an ongoing relationship. Be prepared to spend time establishing a relationship outside the business setting.

Asians attempt to reach an agreement in which there are neither winners nor losers, rather than to negotiate a deal in which one side or both sides make concessions and compromises. If you are from a culture that expects a competitive orientation not balanced by a cooperative orientation, you may perceive this type of cooperative bargaining as a form of collusion between buyer and seller. Asians see this type of bargaining as a chance to reduce serious altercation between negotiating parties. Direct conflict is thereby avoided.

The formal and hierarchy orientations play an important role in Asian business situations. If you come from an equality and informal orientation, be sure to bear this in mind and act accordingly. Be extremely polite and formal in your speech.

Expect involved discussions at business meetings, as well as on social occasions. Be up to date on political and social issues in your host country and Asia, and be prepared to indicate your knowledge of them in a nonconfrontational way.

Asian communication style is influenced by an indirect orientation, a result of the need to preserve and protect face. To avoid direct confrontation, which can cause loss of face, Asians often use gestures and euphemisms to indicate disagreement instead of making direct statements. People who are too direct and assertive usually are considered risky business partners. Their indirect orientation also leads Asians to avoid open debate. Instead, an individual will present an idea and then allow others to do the same. Then the parties will seek common ground on which to base a compromise without having to reject anyone's ideas openly. Asians will rarely answer a direct question with "no." Instead, they will express themselves indirectly. Christopher Engholm elaborates on the problems that can result from this behavioral gap between Asians and Westerners:

> One of the biggest conflicts in communication style between Japanese and people from EuroAmerican cultures is that of confrontational debate as a vehicle of discussion. When, for example, our Japanese participant sets forth a set of ideas and is suddenly attacked by some American members of the online discussion group, he is put

into a defensive position. The American members may not actually disagree with him, but may merely be taking opposing positions for the sake of discussion, engaging in an intellectual sport typical of Western communication style. However, [the Japanese person] may feel that his personhood is being attacked, as he is not used to separating his ideas from his personality. . . . Why should he waste his time when the rules of the game are such that one side wins and the other loses, rather than both sides learning and moving together to some middle ground, especially when it appears that those he is talking with have already made up their minds and that they are, in fact, correct and he is wrong?[19]

In short, if one takes issue with an Asian's personal ideas, it is likely to be interpreted as a personal affront.

Asians attempt to assess their listeners' reactions in order to avoid saying something that their listeners may not agree with. To protect their listeners' feelings, they may go so far as to conceal negative reports, manufacturing mishaps, and similar bad news. This may also be done to protect themselves from criticism or to influence the way they are viewed by a superior. The Asian habit is to use an intermediary to communicate disconcerting news.

In your business dealings in Asia, the problem of communication may be exacerbated because, as high-context communicators, Asians often use nonverbal cues and signals, but they do not always agree on their meanings. In the Philippines, for example, a jerk of the chin downward means "no" and a jerk upward means "yes." But when Indians mean "yes," they use a head gesture that is the same as the one Westerners use for saying "no." In Asia, a smile or a laugh can mean embarrassment or disapproval as well as happiness and approval. Direct eye contact, which is used by Westerners to demonstrate undivided attention and honesty, may be considered an intimidation tactic.

WESTERN EUROPE

Western Europe is a highly dynamic region, and vast economic, social, and political changes are sweeping through it. Since 1957, member nations of the evolving entity now known as the European Union (EU) have been striving to increase cooperation and foster closer integration among themselves. A formal agreement that has been in force since 1993 allows goods, people, services, information, and capital to move freely from one EU country to another. The recent switch to a single European currency, the Euro, is a milestone in the integration of key European economies.

Efforts toward European integration and standardization may eventually lead to greater unification of political systems. As the countries of Europe move from rigid national borders toward regional cooperation, barriers to the exchange of people, information, and trade will be lowered yet further, yielding a new European identity. However, increasing economic interdependence and integration does not translate into cultural integration or homogenization. The cultural and linguistic diversity within and among the countries of the region is highly significant. Many countries have several dialects, and some have more than one official language—Switzerland, for example, has four.

When we reflect on the wars and disruptions in Europe in just the past century, we can understand why Europeans, in sharp contrast to their U.S. cousins, feel that tragedy is never far away. Historically, in developing their country, U.S. Americans were motivated to "conquer" nature, whereas Europeans engaged in warfare among themselves, something that has taught them much about surviving as a region. They perceive U.S. Americans as naïve, partly because they give the impression of believing everything that they hear and say. Furthermore, because of their long history, Western Europeans think in terms of many generations, whereas U.S. Americans think in terms of only a few decades.

To prepare yourself for doing business in Western Europe, it is important that you read up on the history, geography, and current political and economic situations of the region.

Cultural Orientation Patterns

ENVIRONMENT: CONTROL AND HARMONY

In the area of human relations, Western Europeans share the urge to achieve control. In business, this urge often leads to the creation of tools and procedures designed to provide solutions to problems. The control and harmony orientations are manifested in the use of slow, methodical decision-making processes that are intended to merge the new with the old. Although Western Europeans strive to shape their environment, at the same time, they are capable of adjusting as circumstances require.

The Scandinavian countries exhibit the harmony orientation most clearly in that they see cooperating with one another and living in harmony with nature as the only viable way to survive. On the interpersonal level—for instance, when making decisions—they seek harmony by avoiding direct confrontation and by building consensus. This is demonstrated, for example, by the predominance in Norway of labor unions that work with management in a cooperative, rather than an adversarial, fashion. As a result of this cooperation, the distinctions between employees and managers are fewer; for example, salaries paid to management and nonmanagement employees in Norway do not differ greatly from one another the way they do in many other countries.

It is not only the Scandinavian countries, however, that exhibit a harmony orientation. The Dutch, for example, try not to stand out among others in either their private or their public lives. Using "I" too much in a business negotiation may be interpreted as an individual's desire for control or a lack of wider support or respect. This desire to appear as if one is not seeking control or respect and to maintain the appearance of equality with one's peers is indicative of a harmony orientation.

Most Western Europeans appreciate products that fit with their own culture, which exemplifies their orientation toward their environment. For the most part, Western Europeans combine a strong drive to shape their environment with an equally strong desire to maintain harmonious relations with their environment and with other people. Throughout much of the region, compliance with and placing trust in the decisions of superiors is a valued attribute. In other words, once a plan has been decided on, subordinates rarely disagree with their managers about it.

THE SENSE OF TIME

Single- and multifocus aspects.   As a result of their single-focus orientation, most Western Europeans emphasize the importance of concentrating on one task at a time, subscribing to the adage "There's a time and a place for everything." To them, a linear, structured approach signifies efficiency and quality. Reflected in meetings where a detailed agenda is presented, this single-focus approach is a tool for the logical monitoring of an item's progress. For instance, time is viewed as existing in a fixed quantity and is devoted to specific activities or tasks. No disruptions are allowed.

The Swiss and Germans, for example, exhibit a strong single-focus orientation. In order to complete tasks in an orderly and timely fashion, they count on establishing and following schedules and try to avoid any deviation from these schedules. The Germans put an emphasis on a single-focus approach, as well as on promptness and linearity. To Germans, focusing on only one issue at a time is most efficient. Whatever business task is at hand supersedes any other demands.

As a culture that includes a multifocus orientation, however, Western Europeans are quite flexible, even while maintaining a commitment to schedules. The French are among those who prefer to do several things simultaneously. They can tolerate numerous interruptions. While a foreign visitor is in a manager's office talking over a project, the manager might also be talking on the phone and signing something for his secretary. Spain, Italy, Portugal, Greece, and Ireland are other Western European countries that also exhibit a multifocus orientation; in these countries, it is not unusual for a business meeting to be interrupted frequently. It may also be acceptable for participants to go in and out of a conference room, either to answer a personal phone call or a phone call from a colleague in another part of the company or to respond to a manager's request.

A fixed time orientation.   As a result of their fixed time orientation, most Western Europeans value punctuality highly. To them, being punctual for appointments and keeping to a schedule is important and is viewed as a sign of respect for the other party. However, although in general Western Europeans tend to have a fixed time orientation, this is more true for some nations than for others. While Swiss and Germans are very interested in punctuality, people in Mediterranean nations, such as Greece, Spain, Italy, and Portugal, are much less so; businesspersons there may even arrive several minutes late for an appointment.

Business appointments should be made several days in advance. That way, you give the other party a chance to coordinate his or her schedule with colleagues and any others who may be involved. Most Western Europeans expect a meeting to begin and end as scheduled. Always be on guard against the tendency to emphasize simply meeting the deadline, at the expense of failing to do quality work.

The best suggestion for foreign businesspeople conducting business in the region is to be on time for an appointment.

The meaning of time and punctuality varies not only from culture to culture but also within a particular culture, depending on the social context. In Portugal, a person of high status should never be kept waiting by a person of lesser status; a woman may keep a man waiting, but it would be considered very bad for a man to keep a woman waiting; an older person can be late for an appointment with a younger person, but the reverse is not true. It is better to wait a few minutes than to be late, especially when dealing with cultures that have a fixed time orientation. In this context, lateness will be looked upon as a weakness and a sign that one should not be trusted. Punctuality is also considered a sign of courtesy.

The past and the future.   Western Europe has a long history. Countries value their past and, to varying degrees, are proud of both their country's history and its heritage. In fields as varied as music, architecture, literature, philosophy, art, and science, Western Europeans continue to look to tried-and-true traditions as a way of establishing a solid foundation for the future.

The region has a skilled workforce. With the advent of the EU, changes are continually occurring, with precedents and past successes helping to determine long-term strategies. The guiding rule, which fits with the past orientation toward time, is that what was successful in the past will continue to be successful. If forced to make a choice, companies in most countries will forgo short-term results in the hope of achieving long-term gain (future time orientation). When undertaking a new project, they like to look ahead to the future and try to determine a project's long-term benefits. A new venture that provides only short-term results probably will not be viewed favorably. Therefore, a foreign company hoping to do business in the region will likely face skepticism, at least initially. Once Western Europeans sense that the project is viable, though, they usually will set aside whatever reservations they may have.

For example, the French, who exhibit a past/future orientation toward time, are sometimes suspicious of new ventures and new business acquaintances. Their past orientation toward time leads to a reliance on tradition and an emphasis on continuing with the status quo. In keeping with this orientation, the French feel that if something has worked in the past, it will continue to work. A foreign businessperson should not take offense at the skepticism he or she might first encounter. Credibility in this culture is, in part, established through a testing process. Once this process is complete and trust has been established, the French are willing to interact freely with a new business partner. On the other hand, the way the French embrace new technology and adventurous architecture is testimony to a future orientation toward time.

In a similar fashion, Germans, who also demonstrate a past/future orientation, are suspicious of new ventures, especially those that promise short-term results. Because of their future orientation, Germans favor long-term goals and benefits. Thus, a new venture that promises short-term results (present time orientation) will not be taken seriously by a German businessperson.

While all Western European countries exhibit a past orientation to some degree as a result of their long histories, Greece, Spain, Portugal, and France seem to hold to it most firmly. In contrast, the Scandinavian countries, Germany, Austria, and Switzerland demonstrate the future orientation more clearly.

MODES OF ACTION: BEING AND DOING

Western European cultures are oriented toward both being and doing. While members of a doing-oriented culture stress task and achievement, those in a being-oriented culture stress affiliation, character, and personal qualities. For instance, *benessere*, or "well-being," is important to Italians in both the personal and the business sphere. Tasks and achievements, though considered important, are secondary to the establishment of relationships that make these tasks and achievements possible. Examples of being-oriented cultures are those of Belgium, France, Greece, Ireland, Italy, Malta, Monaco, Portugal, and Spain.

The being orientation of Western European countries is reflected in their emphasis on quality of life. Members of a being-oriented culture "work to live" rather than "live to work." In dealing with a new business partner, especially a foreign one, members of a being culture expect to have time to establish rapport with the new partner. Occasionally, this may mean that during the early stages of negotiations, there will be long lunches and dinners at which little business gets discussed. The French have a saying *"entre la poire et le fromage,"* or "between the pear and the cheese"—meaning that business usually is not discussed until dessert time or later after the meal.

In a doing-oriented culture, the emphasis is on achieving external, measurable accomplishments, reaching goals, and improving standards of living. "Work first, pleasure second" is an expression that is often heard. In the business context, relationships often are approached pragmatically. At times, people from this type of culture will be perceived as abrupt, even cold. As friendships are often developed over a long period of time, people frequently devote more time and energy to developing a friendship that is already begun than to establishing a new one. At the same time, people place great emphasis on end results attained by a logical series of steps. Thus, the primary objective is to go through these steps as quickly and efficiently as possible. Trust, though important, is established by everyone adhering to commitments. Gender and age are not important—only the ability to perform. A professional demeanor is required, which means setting aside one's feelings and staying focused on the business at hand.

Doing-oriented cultures include Switzerland, Germany, Austria, the Netherlands, and the Scandinavian countries. Consider the Dutch doing orientation. A Dutch businessperson is impressed by someone's achievement, ability to take risks, drive, and charisma rather than by that person's social or hierarchical status. In many being-oriented cultures, it is common to give preferential treatment to relatives and close friends. The following example demonstrates how the Dutch react to such actions:

A Dutch delegation was shocked and surprised when the Brazilian owner of a large manufacturing company introduced his relatively junior accountant as the key coordinator of a $15 million joint venture. The Dutch were puzzled as to why a recently qualified accountant had been given such weighty responsibilities, including the receipt of their own money. The Brazilians pointed out that he was the best possible choice among employees since he was the nephew of the owner. Who could be more trustworthy than that?[20]

To the Dutch, an individual who is given a significant task should have experience and education that matches the job. Although the Dutch believe that knowing the right people is important, they often look down on those who have achieved positions without a merit-backed history with their company. While those in cultures with a being orientation would view the Brazilian company's choice as the proper one and the one that would most benefit the company, the owner, and the owner's family, those in doing-oriented cultures, such as the Dutch, would view this choice simply as bad business.

COMMUNICATION

Low- and high-context cultures.   Most of Western Europe's cultures, including those of Greece, Spain, Portugal, Italy, Ireland, Monaco, Malta, France, and Belgium, are high-context. Low-context cultures include those of Germany, Britain, Austria, Switzerland, the Scandinavian nations, and the Netherlands; these cultures are primarily task-centered, with business tending to be impersonal. Communication in these low-context cultures is based on the premise that, no matter how complex the content, it still needs to be communicated through succinct, explicit language. When a business meeting is conducted in a low-context culture, there is little contextual information shared by the participants, so the small talk is quickly exhausted. People from low-context cultures prefer to discuss concrete details, interpreting statements literally and not trying to "read between the lines" for hidden meaning. For example, in some cultures, saying "yes" means "I hear you" or "I understand what you are saying," but in Dutch culture, "yes" means "yes, this or that will take place." Even if a "yes" is mumbled under your breath in order to avoid saying "no," the Dutch will understand this as definitive and will not hear the clues in your voice that you may associate with reluctance to carry out the task.

As a result of their need for impersonal, succinct, and explicit communication, low-context communicators are often perceived by foreign businesspeople who are high-context as abrupt, or even cold and indifferent.

High-context cultures are relationship-centered. In such cultures, a great deal of contextual information is needed about an individual or company before business can be transacted. Business is personal, and trust is critical to the relationship; without it, little gets done. This means that much is left unsaid. High-context communicators expect a great deal to be understood implicitly during a conversation. Also, when they speak, they place much emphasis on the nonverbal cues being given. This high-context orientation is expressed in the care with which they approach written forms of communication, both when sending and then receiving. When writing letters, high-context communicators tend to use circuitous, veiled language that communicates as much between the lines as directly. They will carefully read communications for nonverbal, symbolic, and situational cues that modify what is explicitly stated. In keeping with this high-context orientation, members of such a culture tend to prefer meeting in person to communicating by telephone or fax, because such face-to-face contact maximizes their ability to read the context in the communication of others.

Direct and indirect orientations.   Both a direct and an indirect orientation to communication are found among Western Europeans. People in direct cultures, such as those of Germany, Switzerland, Austria, the Netherlands, and some of the Scandinavian nations, tend to meet conflict head on. They say such things as "Let's deal with this right now!" For instance, Germans appreciate directness and openness in verbal interaction. Even in the face of criticism, a German businessperson prefers straightforwardness to an attempt to "save face." The Dutch prefer a direct orientation as well. Consider how one Dutch businesswoman, working in more indirect Britain, had to change her communication styles:

> I had to learn how to bite my tongue and to become more tactful. I slowed down and I'm not as vocal as I was before, for example, in taking charge of a group. I also learned to listen more. In a way, I have become quite Anglicized in that I find the more energetic discussions at home in the Netherlands a bit stressful.[21]

In contrast, the French, who exhibit a direct/indirect orientation, emphasize subtlety and tact in speaking and in writing. Consistent with both their indirect and formal orientations, the French highly value courtesy and diplomacy; yet, in keeping with the direct aspect of their orientation, they do not shy away from voicing their opinions and engaging in lively debate. Other countries that exhibit the direct/indirect orientation include Belgium, Malta, and Monaco, while Greece, Spain, Portugal, Italy, and Ireland tend to have a decidedly more indirect orientation.

Expressive and instrumental orientations.   The region demonstrates both the expressive and the instrumental orientations toward communication. Cultures that demonstrate an expressive orientation are those of Spain, Ireland, Portugal, Italy, and France. People from these cultures eagerly display their emotions. They consider themselves eloquent communicators and place a high priority on aesthetics and style.

Demonstrating verbal fluency is an important way to establish your credibility with a counterpart from an expressive culture. The Irish, for instance, are more easily persuaded by someone who can communicate expressively and humorously and will quickly come to like such a person. A sense of humor and a facility with language are important assets in doing business with the Irish. In France, the expressive orientation is demonstrated in the great emphasis the French place on the purity and beauty of the French language. It is useful to have a working knowledge of French and its many conversational nuances. The French love of debate and their belief that people should be actively engaged in ideas and issues means that they expect others not to shy away from expressing and defending their opinions. French businesspeople expect others to disagree and argue with them, although they do expect discussion to be tactful and diplomatic.

On the other end of the spectrum are the instrumental communicators. These include individuals in Switzerland, Germany, Austria, the United Kingdom, and the Scandinavian countries. Switzerland offers an illustration. When conducting business, the Swiss are firm believers in *Sachlichkeit*, the conviction that the facts, if interpreted correctly, speak for themselves and will lead all parties to the same, mutually beneficial conclusion. The Swiss will therefore distrust any means of communication that does not directly serve to present, illustrate, or interpret these facts. Having to deal with charm or excessive small talk in a business context makes the Swiss feel that they are about to be manipulated—what other reason could there be for introducing such unrelated elements into what should be a very straightforward situation?

Instrumental communicators value disciplined, content-based disclosure. Stress is placed on the accuracy of the communication rather than on its appropriateness or style. Their primary objective is to reach a factual, objective, unemotional conclusion that leads to action. To establish credibility, a businessperson should introduce his or her points in meetings or presentations in a precise, measured manner.

A German businessperson views interactions between colleagues simply as occasions for the exchange of information and ideas concerning specific problems or issues, not for the development of interpersonal relationships. In business situations with Germans or other instrumental communicators, business-specific content is proper.

Formality. Formal communication and adherence to protocol facilitate communication and business in Western Europe. Business is conducted on the basis of formality, courtesy, respect, and good manners. Formality extends to forms of address, which start with the title "Mr." or "Mrs." Traditionally, professional titles are used as well in some areas—for example, "Herr Professor Schmidt."

With the exception of English, where there is no formal "you," languages in the region provide a formal way of addressing business partners. Some examples are:

- In French, *tu*, the informal "you," is used among friends, whereas *vous* is a formal way of addressing someone at a meeting or a dinner party.

- In Spanish, *tú* is the informal "you"; *usted* is formal address.

- In Italian, *tu*, the informal "you," is never used in business; *lei* is the formal way of addressing business partners.

- In German, *du* is the informal "you"; *Sie* is the formal "you" and is always capitalized, which emphasizes the formality.

Formality and politeness go hand in hand. In fact, the emphasis on formality in French culture is so strong that formal expression appears even in situations in which most other cultures would not expect politeness. Take for example, the following robbery report that appeared in *Le Parisien* on September 24, 1993: "Beretta in hand, a thief robbing a gas station in Paris began his hold-up with this indispensable code: *Excusez-moi de vous déranger, mais j'ai besoin de fric.* ('Excuse me for bothering you, but I need some dough')."[22] In this example, even a thief making a request makes sure to use the five magic words, "Excuse me for bothering you." The French value courtesy above all else in their use of language, whether on the street, in a restaurant, at a business meeting, or at a social gathering. Such conditional phrases as "could I" or "would you" are the norm in asking questions, and the frequent use of "thank you" and "please" is expected.

THE SENSE OF SPACE: PRIVATE AND PUBLIC

Western Europeans generally have a private space orientation, but they also display a public space orientation, depending on the social context. People in most cultures of the region prefer considerable space between themselves and the person they are talking to—on average, about 20 inches. The distance varies from culture to culture, however. For instance, in the United Kingdom, the distance may be greater—up to 30 inches. In Greece, however, it may be as little as 12 inches.

Here is an example of how Britons view their private space. Two businessmen with common interests, a Briton and an Egyptian, were introduced at a reception. As their conversation began, the Egyptian stood close to the Briton, who moved to the side so that they stood about four feet apart. The

Egyptian continually tried to close the gap, and the Briton continued to move away. As this dance continued, each man became increasingly uncomfortable. They both went home feeling that they could not trust each other, and no deal was concluded.

In dealing with most organizations in the region, it is important not to "drop in," as this is considered to be invading the private space of others. You will gain credibility by contacting the other party as far in advance as possible to let her or him know that you are coming or to set up a meeting.

In the business world, the physical workplace is divided into distinct private and public areas. Private areas are clearly demarcated to create a physical barrier between people and their coworkers. Depending on their position in the company, most employees have their own cubicle or office. The office of an executive is considered private space, and it is considered bad form to enter such an office without permission. When an office door is closed, you should knock on the door and wait for permission to enter.

The public areas in the office include meeting rooms, cafeterias, restrooms, and in-house libraries. The public orientation is also exhibited in such public places as the metro, buses, trains, and even bars, where people usually crowd together more than in a culture with a private orientation toward space. The French, who exhibit a private/public orientation, provide an interesting example of this dual orientation. After experiencing French culture, one U.S.-American businessperson (an individual from a country with a private orientation toward space) was surprised at the nearness of strangers on the street: "'Why are people always trying to bump me off the sidewalk? Why do they crowd me so in lines?' asks a baffled and somewhat annoyed systems engineer from Philadelphia, very recently after being transferred to Paris."[23]

The answer is fairly simple: the French notion of acceptable physical distance differs considerably from that of a North American or northern European. In a formal situation, the French stand at a distance of 12 inches or less, whereas a U.S. American, Briton, or German may maintain a distance anywhere between 18 to 30 inches. The French will often crowd close together in public places, such as a bar, the post office, a supermarket, or the metro.

In contrast to this public space orientation, cubicles are rare in a French company. Most employees have their own offices arranged along a corridor, and the doors are kept closed. An employee who needs to speak with a colleague will go to that colleague's office and knock before entering. In this respect, the French are extremely private in their use of space. Respecting this need for privacy in the office and adhering to proper office etiquette concerning space will greatly assist you in establishing your credibility among your French colleagues.

THE HIERARCHY OF POWER

Throughout most of the region, authority plays an important role. Differences in position and power are emphasized. There are those who decide what is to be done, and there are those who implement these decisions. In France, for example, this orientation leads businesses to resemble a monarchy or military system. In fact, the French word for manager—*cadre*—also means "officer." A French businessman explains the system this way.

> There is no skipping levels up or down, and each boss is not only careful of his power, but behaves as much like the autocratic CEO [PDG in French] at the top as he can. He passes on every decision on the way down as if it comes from him only—he would lose face if he were seen to be only a mere cog in the machine. Every cadre is a Napoleon unto himself.[24]

The hierarchical structure of most companies in Western Europe is evident in their chains of command, where decisions are made by upper management, then handed down to the lower ranks in the form of detailed directives. A title—whether in politics, social situations, or business—is important. Employees with expertise in a certain field are included in the decision-making process, though at the discretion of management. These employees are given enough information to enable them to apply their expertise to solving a specific problem, but they may not be given the broader context. In making decisions, managers rarely consult members of their support staff, even when their decisions have direct impact on those staff members.

The hierarchy orientation is strong in the German-speaking countries (Germany, Switzerland, and Austria) but is also evident in Spain, Greece, Portugal, the United Kingdom, and France. This orientation exists to a lesser extent in Italy, Belgium, Malta, Monaco, and Ireland. Like most other aspects of culture in Western Europe, the corporate culture differs from country to country. However, there are certain attitudes that apply in a general way to most companies in the region:

- A clear hierarchy exists; the boss is the leader, and everyone knows where he or she fits in and acts accordingly.
- The organizational structure is generally vertical, with all important decisions being made at the top.
- Top-to-bottom communication is generally poor.
- Top managers dislike sharing information with subordinates.

Germany provides an example of the strong hierarchy orientation evident in many Western European countries. Rank there is not only designated but clearly signaled. In German businesses, managers have remarkable authority. They are in charge of their departments, and interference from outsiders is neither common nor easily accepted. Employees generally accept the authority of managers and do not argue. As long as the law is followed, Germans are often willing to do as they are told. Those from equality-oriented cultures, such as the English, may become very uncomfortable in the face of such an assumption of authority.

Exceptions to this rule are the Netherlands and the countries of Scandinavia, where one of the most clearly defined cultural characteristics is a strong equality orientation. The Dutch have a saying, "You are born naked and will die naked as well." Holding a higher level in a firm does not confer authority over others. The equality orientation has an important effect on businesses and their structure. Companies in these countries are relatively egalitarian, with a more horizontal organizational structure, shared responsibilities, relatively open communication, and a willingness to share information readily. Most decisions are made by consensus.

INDIVIDUALISM

Individualistic and particularistic orientations. Most Western European cultures highly value individualism. Speaking one's mind, for example, is a sign of honesty and is respected. Motivation in an individualistic culture tends toward achievement and power. Tasks are valued over relationships, and hiring and promotions are based largely on skill and achievement. France, for example, is a highly individualistic culture. Richard Hill sums up an example of French individualism in this way: "Getting a group of French people to work together virtually defies the laws of dynamics: each of them runs his or her own little fiefdom and the operating principle (from the top down, which is the only way French business works) appears to be 'management by retention.' "[25]

The French are great admirers of independent thought and action and do not like working in teams. In contrast, German organizations are geared toward utilizing teams as a result of the collectivist orientation that emphasizes group cooperation. Although each department of a German company enjoys considerable independence and autonomy and each carries considerable responsibility, members of different departments often work on related projects directed toward the same goals—all the while feeling an obligation toward the success of their own department.

On a continuum of individualistic to collectivistic, the French demonstrate the greatest preference for individualism. In addition to Germany, the Scandinavian countries, Spain, Portugal, and Greece tend to be more collectivistic.

Universalistic and particularistic orientations.   Western Europe exhibits both universalistic and particularistic orientations. Along with the production of standard products and services, universalistic cultures stress the consistent application of generalizations, rules, and procedures. As exemplified by contracts in Germany, for example, the universalistic orientation requires everyone to comply with all rules, with no option for considering particular cases subjectively. In Germany, everyone involved will be held to the letter of the contract with no exception.

The standardization process that is taking place in most of Western Europe can be especially difficult for particularistic societies, which prefer to consider situations and their circumstances individually and to act according to the unique conditions present in the particular case rather than expecting all situations to fall tidily under the same set of rules. An example of this type of process is illustrated by the International Organization for Standardization, which has been successful in developing global standards in business practices and product quality. To become certified, a company must demonstrate the reliability and soundness of all business procedures that affect the quality of the company's products. Many companies also seek certification because of the quality message such certification sends to prospective customers. Naturally, this poses more problems for particularistic cultures, which see each circumstance as unique and defying categorization.

In business, Italians express this particularistic orientation as they find creative ways to get around their infamous amounts of bureaucracy and red tape. Common in Italian business is paying the *bustarella*, or "envelope," to politicians or civil servants for contracts, the installation of utilities, or completing bureaucratic procedures quickly, especially at the local level. While recent legislation has tried to end this practice (reflecting a shift to a universalistic preference) and other aspects of government corruption, the long-term results of these efforts remain to be seen.

COMPETITIVENESS

Although Western European culture has a competitive orientation, its cultures are quite different from that of the United States. The United States thrives on the friction resulting from rivalry among individuals, teams, and organizations, whereas Western European competitiveness is a function of a widely held desire to improve products. The competitiveness of the region is driven by both a highly competitive educational system and the individualism characteristic of Western European cultures.

Although Western Europe has a growing entrepreneurial culture, most people do not cultivate the mentality of an entrepreneur. In fact, in many

Western European cultures, corporate careers are not respected nearly as much as most other occupations. Surveys show a preference among young people for jobs in government service, teaching, and law. Their moderately competitive orientation is seen more clearly in the private sphere. Most managers in private enterprise tend to work longer hours and expect financial gain and other material perquisites for their efforts. This attitude toward competition is common in Italy, yet competition among coworkers is undesirable, as demonstrated in the following example:

> [The] Italian representative, Mr. Gialli, began describing his experience with the system. In his country, the pay-for-performance experiment did much better than he had expected during the first three months. But the following three months were disastrous. Sales were dramatically lower for the salesperson who had performed the best during the previous period. "After many discussions," he continued, "I finally discovered what was happening. The salesperson who received the bonus for the previous period felt guilty in front of the others and tried extremely hard the next quarter not to earn a bonus."[26]

The results of this experiment illustrate the importance of the cooperative orientation in Italy. The successful salesperson could not afford to continue being successful when he felt that it would be to the detriment of his coworkers.

STRUCTURE: ORDER AND FLEXIBILITY

As a result of an order orientation, Western European culture places a fairly high value on structure, order, and control. Job or task descriptions are likely to be detailed, if only to avoid conflict or ambiguity. Standardization and long-term planning are favored, as is adherence to established rules and procedures. Among the countries exhibiting strong order orientations are Germany, Switzerland, Austria, Greece, Portugal, the United Kingdom, and France.

Both security and risk aversion are important considerations for individuals in order-oriented cultures. In consonance with the being orientation toward action, relationship development plays an important role in maintaining this order orientation. Keeping well-known business contacts and using proven methods will help avoid risk. As a result, many firms and individual businesspeople may be slow to change. In planning, they tend to be preventive rather than corrective. In an effort to avoid risk, they seek to prevent or remove obstacles and to solve problems from the outset, instead of testing a plan through trial-and-error implementation.

This preference for the order orientation is illustrated by the following quote regarding German behavior: "In discussing the German temperament, one seems to keep on coming back to what I call the 'con words': conservatism, conformity, consensus, continuity, condoning."[27] Hill's list of "con words" alludes to the German respect for tradition, predictability, and stability. Transposed to the business setting, this means that Germans look for security, well-defined work procedures, company rules, established approaches, and clearly defined individual assignments. In short, the German business environment is highly structured. *Ordnung* (order) is the backbone of company life.

At the other end of the spectrum, the Scandinavian countries, Spain, Italy, and the Netherlands exhibit some tendencies toward flexibility as well as order. In Spain, the flexibility orientation deemphasizes detailed planning and strict guidelines and schedules. The Spanish view timelines for projects as rough guidelines. They expect changes to take place during the negotiation process, and they believe that it is important to adapt to these changes in order to complete a deal successfully.

The flexibility orientation toward structure indicates a more open approach to risk taking. This is evidenced in Italy, as Italians thrive on ambiguity and risk and are adept at on-the-spot, creative problem solving. They place a high value on *opportunismo*, or opportunism, adapt well to changing circumstances, and have a great facility for—and take enjoyment in—improvisation.

This flexibility orientation is also expressed in the way the structure of companies and organizations is designed. Businesses from flexibility-oriented cultures generally do not develop detailed business plans but instead work out continuously changing strategies as different players come onto the scene, various goals are set, and new crises arise.

MODES OF THINKING

Deductive and inductive thinking.   In Western Europe, both the deductive and the inductive orientation toward thinking are exhibited. Switzerland, Sweden, and Ireland have cultures that are inclined to be inductive in their orientation toward thinking. Conversely, Germany, France, the United Kingdom, Portugal, Greece, and Norway exhibit the deductive orientation. There are some countries in which a mix of these two orientations is present, such as Spain, Italy, and the Netherlands.

The inductive orientation calls for acquiring as much data as possible. Individuals from such cultures are detail-oriented and prefer large amounts of information and precise data for a given project. Inductive Western Europeans believe that it is difficult to make assumptions and predictions about the future;

therefore, they seek more details, with which they make intermediate decisions. The inductive thinker is most concerned with the "how" and the "what" and will consider the "why" to be unnecessary. When preparing a business plan for the upcoming financial year, for instance, such thinkers may look at past perform-ance and combine that information with data on current market trends.

The inductive model is prevalent in Switzerland, where the following process is carried out when a project is being set up or a new product is being launched. The Swiss project team will be focused on implementation (how and what), not conceptual issues (why). They will be frustrated and feel that nothing tangible has been accomplished if a great deal of time is spent discussing ideas and general principles that are not directly related to hard data. The Swiss sar-castically refer to a debate of this nature as *a Diskussion aus dem hohlen Bauch*, which is literally translated as "a discussion with an empty stomach," that is, a discussion with no substance. Even a logically brilliant argument will fail to impress your Swiss counterparts if it cannot be readily substantiated by data.

As mentioned previously, certain Western European countries approach thinking from a deductive orientation. Personal experience and experimenta-tion coupled with established theory are used to build a foundation from which general concepts and conclusions can emerge. These concepts, in turn, become the basis for understanding specific situations.

For example, French thinking tends to be highly deductive, focusing on "why" rather than on "what" and "how." A logical argument based on proven theory will gain the most respect in French circles.

The deductive orientation is also strong in Germany; the following quote exemplifies this orientation: "Power can be financial, political, entrepreneur-ial, managerial, or intellectual. Of the five, intellectual power seems to rank highest in Germany."[28] The capacity for theoretical understanding, deep analysis, and logical reasoning is valued, not only in the abstract sense, but also as the essential foundation of any concrete project, plan, or decision. For Germans, empirical data and experience have little significance unless they fit into a greater conceptual framework.

As a result of these different approaches, negotiations between deductive thinkers and counterparts with an inductive orientation can be highly frustrat-ing for both parties. Very often, the inductive thinkers want to begin a discus-sion with specific items—for example, price or distribution. Those with a deductive orientation, on the other hand, are likely to demand a thorough presentation of theories and principles and to want to establish agreement on general principles to guide the negotiation. The pace of the deductive style, which can be slower, may also be frustrating to the inductive thinker.

Linear and systemic reasoning. When faced with a problem, linear cultures break it down into small pieces, which can then be linked in chains of cause and effect. It may be surprising to learn that Germans, who favor logic and deductive reasoning, are also linear thinkers. They tend to focus on a specific issue and want to analyze and understand every aspect of that issue before moving on to the next. Other examples of linear-thinking cultures are those of the United Kingdom and Scandinavia.

It can be helpful to remember the potential differences between these two orientations when business relations cross these cultural borders. For example, in the opinion of one visiting negotiator from a systemic society, his British counterpart's proposal lacked clarity, giving too much detail about the individual components to the exclusion of the larger goal. He felt that priority was given to in-depth analysis rather than the global view. He was clearly more systemic in his thinking. On the other hand, the British businessperson, being more linear, would be disappointed at a perceived lack of attention to detail on his associate's part.

Most Mediterranean countries, plus Ireland and France, have a systemic orientation toward thinking. People from these countries prefer to understand a project or issue as a whole before moving on to individual details. Their thinking is holistic or synthetic, focusing on the relationship and interconnectedness of the various parts. Systemic thinkers first want to understand how all the pieces fit together to form a whole; only then do they move on to discuss individual parts.

Forming a "big picture" view is not a matter of reducing knowledge to a small number of general principles; rather, it is one of developing a large and probably complicated conceptual scheme into which all the information can be fit. Italy exhibits this systemic orientation toward thinking. Italians generally value drawing analogies and using metaphors and similes for explanations, rather than thinking in terms of cause and effect. When arguing a point in international business, an Italian might try to persuade a counterpart by drawing analogies between the two countries' systems of government, emphasizing the interrelatedness of markets, or linking the issues that businesspeople in both countries face.

Italians, like other systemic individuals, are very contextual thinkers who tend to consider the ways in which their projects fit into a larger system or whole. In a business context, this translates into an expectation that their foreign counterparts will be very knowledgeable about products or services and will be able to talk about how a business proposal fits into the larger scheme of things.

Some companies, in order to enhance their competitive advantage, seek to leverage differences in thinking by assigning individuals with particular orientations to those projects for which they are best suited. For example, to take advantage of these differences, some U.S. telecommunications companies working in France may have their engineers (who have a linear orientation) focus on a narrow area—complex parts—while their French counterparts (who have a systemic orientation) work on standardized parts and the overall design.

Key Insights for Effectiveness

Perhaps the most important thing to remember is that no single cultural orientation within any of the cultural dimensions applies equally to all the countries discussed here. Each time you cross the border from one country to next, the rules (and often the language) change. The most successful businessperson, therefore, will be the one who is the most flexible in adapting to the demands of each individual business environment.

An important difference to which businesspersons should be sensitive is the respect for protocol and formality that is prevalent throughout Western Europe. In general, you should address foreign colleagues by their surnames. Irish, British, Dutch and Scandinavian managers tend to be less formal than other Western Europeans, however, and the use of first names is widely accepted in these cultures.

Keeping the space dimension in mind, note that the standard physical distance between you and the person with whom you are communicating varies from country to country.

Since the being-doing continuum varies throughout the entire region, be prepared to adjust your style (and expectations) accordingly. When you are conducting business with the members of being-oriented cultures, expect to spend a considerable amount of time socializing and getting to know your counterparts before discussing business. In doing-oriented cultures, however, expect to focus on business immediately after the introductions.

It is important to arrive punctually for all appointments and to adhere to the deadlines set. Although many cultures in the region have a more fluid time orientation, it is still advisable for the foreign businessperson to arrive on time. This demonstrates respect and the formality expected, and will be appreciated by your host.

Adjust your presentations and business proposals to match the expectations of your clients. Remember that the region has a long history and that most countries in the region value their past and are proud of their heritage.

Both the formal and the hierarchy orientations play a major role in Western European business. Authority in the region manifests itself through a chain of command; therefore, it is best to be formal and polite and to acknowledge differences in title and rank among your counterparts.

Observe the information-sharing tendencies of your Western European counterparts. The order orientation toward structure in many Western European cultures leads to a reluctance to share information vertically. If you are used to sharing information in a different way and you do so in your counterpart's firm, you will endanger the business relationship, not to mention the business venture.

Communication styles vary throughout Western Europe, from low- to high-context cultures. For example, the British tend to be indirect, whereas the French can be direct and confrontational. Building credibility in France requires a willingness to engage in intellectual argument, whereas wit and subtlety are important in the United Kingdom.

Italy, Spain, Portugal, Ireland, France, and Greece are all, to varying degrees, high-context cultures. In these cultures, the first business meeting will be a session in which the participants get acquainted. This meeting will be required because of your counterpart's need to build trust in personal relations, so that the participants can decide whether to continue contact and, thus, the negotiations. At the same time, the formal orientation of these cultures toward communication, as well as their hierarchy orientation toward power, means that business communication is quite formal. As far as the business context goes, these cultures tend to remain formal in their speech and writing. Further, protocol and manners are crucial to building and maintaining a business relationship.

In contrast, Germanic, Nordic, and English cultures are low-context. In these cultures, communication is focused more on content than on relationships. Emphasis is placed on explicit statements, and words are expected to be understood more or less literally. In the business context, formality in speech and writing must be strictly observed, taking into consideration exact wording, structure of the text, and flow of argument.

EASTERN EUROPE

This section discusses the countries of the former Soviet bloc. Loosely referred to as Central and Eastern Europe, these countries actually constitute several regions, usually broken down in the following manner:

Central Europe: Czech Republic, Hungary, Poland, and Slovakia

The Baltic states: Estonia, Latvia, and Lithuania

The Balkans: Albania, Bulgaria, Romania, and all the countries of the former Yugoslavia (Bosnia-Herzegovina, Croatia, Macedonia, Slovenia, and Yugoslavia—which today consists of only Serbia and Montenegro)

Russia and the Commonwealth of Independent States (CIS): Belarus, Moldova, Russia, Ukraine, and the Central Asian republics (Armenia, Azerbaijan, Georgia, Kazakhstan, Kyrgyz Republic, Tajikistan, Turkmenistan, and Uzbekistan)

It is important to note that the concept of Central Europe is a politically charged one, as it has had at least 16 different definitions over the past century. Rival definitions have been made on the basis of geography, history, culture, religion, economics, and politics, and the perspective and agenda of the speaker play a part in determining which definition is used. Belonging to Central Europe has often carried overtones of being called "civilized, democratic, cooperative."[29] Today, whether these overtones persist depends on the context; however, within the context of this book, "Central Europe" is intended purely as a geographic designation.

A cultural fault line can be drawn through the former Soviet bloc, and cultural differences in the region can be grouped around this line. The line provides an interesting tool for understanding regional differences; at the same time, it must be treated sensitively. First, however, let us consider some of the historical and cultural features that unite the region of Central and Eastern Europe, or the CEE.

The first feature shared by all the countries in the CEE, more or less, is a common history over the past two centuries. The Baltic states were all part of the Russian Empire during the nineteenth century, and, after very brief periods of independence following World War I, all three were invaded by the Soviet Union. The Central Asian republics shared a similar fate. In addition, Ukraine, Belarus, and Moldova were ruled either partly or completely by Russia and subsequently by the Soviet Union over the past two centuries. Thus, the Baltic states and the states of the CIS were part of either Russia or the Soviet Union for most of the nineteenth and twentieth centuries.

Most of Central Europe and the Balkans was divided up among the Ottoman Empire, the Hapsburgs, and the Hungarians for several centuries before the region came under the Soviet sphere of influence in the midtwentieth century. Following World War I and the breakup of the Austro-Hungarian Empire, the countries of Central Europe and the Balkans all declared their independence. Many of them became prosperous, democratic republics. After World War II, however, they all became Soviet satellites with authoritarian, Communist-controlled governments and strictly regulated economies.

Thus, by the midtwentieth century, all the countries of the CEE had come to share very similar political and economic systems, and to either be part of the Soviet Union or fall under its political and economic control. These countries were governed by repressive regimes that severely curtailed freedom of expression and punished open dissent through various means, including exile and death. Their economies were command economies in which the state owned the means of production and tried to control all economic activity by setting production goals, allotting raw materials, and fixing prices.

Another significant feature common to the Soviet regime and its imitators was an attempt to rapidly industrialize production and modernize the workforce. Some countries, such as the former Czechoslovakia and Hungary, had already achieved a degree of industrialization very much on a par with that of their Western European neighbors prior to the Communist era. For them, the transition was not particularly difficult, although pollution became a severe problem. Many areas of the former Soviet Union, however, had largely agrarian economies that had only recently ended serfdom. The forced industrialization and collectivization of farms in these areas was devastating to both the people and the environment.

Another feature uniting the countries of the region is that a good portion of the population of Eastern Europe is ethnically Slavic. The Czechs, Slovaks, Poles, Slovenians, Serbs, Croats, Macedonians, Bulgarians, Ukrainians, Belarussians, and Russians are all Slavic peoples who speak Slavic languages and share cultural roots. Yet this is where the commonalties among Eastern Europeans begin to break down. The Latvians, Lithuanians, and Georgians are all non-Slavic peoples, and the Hungarians and Estonians belong to a linguistic group that isn't even Indo-European. The Romanians claim descent from the Romans, although they do have a large Slavic component to their background. The peoples of the Central Asian republics, also non-Slavic, display a large ethnic mix, with at least 110 ethnicities and 112 recognized languages.

As the countries of the CEE emerge from the shadow of Soviet political and economic domination, they can all be said to be going through a period of self-redefinition in which they are reasserting their cultural and ethnic roots. Politically, this has had some drastic consequences, as in the former Yugoslavia. In subtler ways, however, it has had an impact on all areas of culture, including a redirecting of local business cultures to meet the demands of the new free market economy.

Economically speaking, the CEE countries have had different degrees of success in making the transition to a free market system. The ones that have made the most progress are those that are geographically closest to the

European Union: Poland, the Czech Republic, Hungary, Slovenia, Slovakia, and the Baltic states.

The economies of Russia and the CIS, by contrast, are ailing greatly, and the transition to democracy has proved difficult. The former Yugoslavia has been in bloody turmoil over the past decade, leaving its economy in bad shape and contributing to the continued depression in the economies of Romania, Bulgaria, and Albania. It is important to mention these differences at the outset, because they play an important role in the business culture and business prospects.

As these countries make the transition to free market economies, they are looking to the West for business models. Today, their business cultures consist of a mix of imported Western models, holdover practices from the Soviet era, and local customs.

Cultural Orientation Patterns

AN ENVIRONMENT OF CONSTRAINT

An old Hungarian saying claims that "An average day is worse than yesterday but better than tomorrow," while in a similar vein, a Romanian saying asks, "What is small, dark and knocking at the door? The future."[30]

Eastern European pessimism is legendary. The prevalence of oppressive regimes and foreign domination, as well as the wars and cataclysmic turnovers that have marked the region's changing political and economic fortunes for centuries, have served to make Eastern Europeans pessimistic about the future. Their experience has given them little hope that human beings can control their own fate or their environment.

This pessimism translates into a strong constraint orientation. As one Russian professor explains: "Our main concern, that which determines all our actions and feelings, is *strakh* (fear). The world is dangerous, and we must be careful."[31] While people from control-oriented cultures such as the United States believe that things will turn out well and that they can control their environment to effect good results, Eastern Europeans expect things to turn out poorly and prepare themselves to live with misfortune. More recently, the Russian prime minister, Viktor Chernomyrdin, put it this way: "We did the best we could, but it turned out as usual."[32]

Prime Minister Chernomyrdin's statement can be used to sum up the way the Eastern European constraint orientation expresses itself in the business context. Although an Eastern European businessman may actively—even enthusiastically—embark on a new business venture in the new economy, he will easily be inclined to give it up entirely if conditions change or the business does not prove successful within a few months. This contrasts sharply with what a businessperson from a control-oriented society would do.

An important factor keeping the constraint orientation going in today's Eastern Europe is the persistence of constant and unexpected changes in the political and economic conditions of the region. Another concrete constraint to doing business in the region is the persistence of government control. Government regulations dating back to the Communist era still play a large role both in controlling businesses and in doing business in general. The state also exercises a great deal of control through the granting of licenses. Foreign investors should be aware that in many CEE countries, every aspect of a business, even waste management, requires a license or permit from the state. For example, a company may have a license to manufacture a particular product, but not have a license to export it—or it may have permission to do research but no license to develop products once the research is completed.

In certain Eastern European cultures, such as Russia, this constraint orientation may translate into a degree of fatalism or passivity that becomes frustrating to those from control-oriented cultures. Yet, given the many hardships and numerous waves of change this region has endured, there is also a clear control-oriented edge to the CEE constraint orientation. After all, it was Eastern Europe that experimented with a radically new form of government and economic system. In order to do so, many countries in the region radically changed their work environment and the structure of their workforces, all within a few decades. In the Soviet Union, this involved a complete overhaul of farming through forced collectivization and the rapid and often brutal industrialization of a largely agrarian economy. The massive Soviet space program and other pushes for scientific and technological advancement within the region are expressions of a stubborn insistence on control.

CEE ingenuity in dealing with hardship permitted Central and Eastern Europeans to circumvent the many repressive rules and regulations imposed by the Communists. Many firms found ways to get around government controls and thus encourage real productivity and compensate workers adequately.

A SENSE OF TIME

Single- and multifocus aspects.   "You try to have a meeting with them and two phones on their desk are ringing constantly, plus their mobile. And on top of that every few minutes somebody comes barging in with an urgent paper that needs signing."[33]

This comment was made by a Western investment banker working in Warsaw. The years spent under Communism, in which efficiency was completely undervalued, has produced a haphazard working pattern among CEE employees. Since there was little incentive to get work done and since wages were extremely low, many employees adopted the habit of doing several jobs at once while they were at their official place of employment. If one were to add up the numbers of hours per week an average employee reported to his various jobs, the total would frequently equal more time than there could be in seven days.

The habit of doing various tasks simultaneously and switching from one thing to another persists in CEE businesses. Eastern Europeans are not accustomed to singling out tasks and attending to them in a sequential order. Part of this multifocus orientation also comes from the fact that business under Communism could be accomplished only through unofficial channels. Thus, one of the most important tasks of successful businesspeople was to maintain their contacts. Being multifocused did not just mean doing several things at once; it also meant tending to interpersonal relations at the same time as business. Today, as unofficial channels of business and the ability to stay on good terms with local government officials are still important, this multifocus orientation persists.

Yet Eastern Europeans are also known for a certain single-focus orientation. For one thing, as one moves west and north into Central Europe and the Baltic states, the single-focus approach to tasks is in greater evidence. More important, however, all Central and Eastern Europeans demonstrate a single-focus orientation in their desire to keep their private lives distinctly separate from their professional lives.

Given the highly repressive regimes under Communism, businesspeople in the region developed a strong preference for secrecy. This secrecy included an attempt to keep matters of private concern from intruding into their work lives. Information about family and friends was not quickly shared with coworkers, and interaction with coworkers during business hours was conducted in a limited, if not secretive, manner.

Fixed and fluid orientations.   In Russia, patience, not punctuality, is considered a virtue. This is true throughout the CIS, and in Poland and Bulgaria as well. In these countries, time is not considered an economic commodity that needs to be broken up into discrete units and used sparingly. Instead, time is seen in terms of the flux of the changing seasons, in keeping with the agricultural heritage of the region. These cultures thus demonstrate a fluid orientation to time.

The historical volatility of the area has made planning and timeliness traditionally difficult. Communism only strengthened this orientation, as, under this system, employees could not be fired, had little control over their own work, and were not rewarded for efficiency. Thus, they had little incentive to be punctual or get work done on time. Since their work was often unrewarding, they looked to fill up their time by avoiding work.

This orientation persists today in both the business and the social context. It is acceptable to arrive well after set appointment times or to miss deadlines. Since the region's economic fortunes remain unstable, even an individual businessperson who has a fixed time orientation often misses deadlines.

What distinguishes the fluid time orientation of the CEE from the same orientation in other regions is the emphasis on contemplation and reflection. Central and Eastern Europeans very much enjoy sitting with coworkers or friends and reflecting and philosophizing on everything from the particular business venture to the state of the world. They would consider not taking the time to do this as rude and disrespectful.

Czechs, Slovaks, Hungarians, Estonians, Latvians, and Lithuanians, by contrast, have more of a fixed time orientation. Perhaps because they look west, as opposed to east, for a model of business culture and other aspects of general culture, individuals from these countries have developed a fixed time orientation that resembles that of their Western European neighbors.

Central and Eastern Europeans from cultures with a fixed time orientation regard time as a fixed quantity to be divided up into discrete units. Appointment times are considered set, and punctuality is expected. Czechs, Hungarians, and Romanians will often be several minutes early for an appointment to make sure they are on time. Deliveries and payments are also expected on time. The one impediment to the fixed time orientation in these CEE countries is the persistence of unpredictable and changeable conditions, a factor that may cause unexpected and unavoidable delays.

The past versus the future. In the CEE, the future looms large. Individuals from this region are concerned with what will happen in the future and how future events may be kept under control. This coincides, in part, with the CEE constraint orientation, which assumes that all future events are potentially threatening and harmful. Next in importance is the past, which dominates the region's consciousness through Central and Eastern Europeans' strong awareness of history and the influence of past events. Least important is the present. The three time frames—past, present, and future—are viewed as disconnected rather than as a coherent whole in CEE cultures.

Because of their future orientation, CEE businesses are looking for plans and proposals that will guarantee their future prosperity. Prospects and potential and future achievement are important to CEE partners. Often, CEE firms are especially interested in how a particular project proposal will give them a technological advantage or make them leaders in their field. Planning is generally done with much enthusiasm, even if the means for carrying out the plan are uncertain. The sense of a limitless future feeds into the CEE fluid time orientation, as CEE businesspeople draw up grandiose plans that, in the end, may not all be carried out.

In those areas of the CEE where the economy is most stable and prosperous, the present and short-term results have come to play a larger role in business decisions and planning. In these areas, shorter-term results may also sway a potential business partner. Nevertheless, because of their order orientation to structure, cultures in the CEE will not find change particularly appealing. The past orientation comes into play here, as they look to the past as a guide for ways to conduct business. Although new ventures may be enthusiastically taken up, new management models, new production methods, or new products may be much more difficult to introduce, especially in Russia and the CIS.

Traditional Marxist planning focused all business efforts on production and production quotas. The resource inputs, the quality of the good or service, and questions of customer service were, for the most part, ignored. The particular challenge for foreign managers going into the CEE is to address this lopsided focus.

ACTIONS: BEING AND DOING

During the Soviet era, the CEE developed something known as a "kitchen culture." This was the common custom of friends gathering in the kitchen of one of their homes over dinner or tea and philosophizing about politics, art, life, or anything and everything until far into the night. It gave them a space where they could speak their minds and show their art, free of the fear of reprisal.

In addition, since work usually was unrewarding and possibilities for advancement were few, Central and Eastern Europeans came to prize the time spent with friends and family. This gave them a strong being orientation—something that was true of these traditional societies before Communism as well. Even today, as the material quality of life is improving in some CEE countries, money and possessions are not highly esteemed. In fact, a common lament heard among citizens of the region is that life was better under Communism because, although they lacked the material possessions they now have, people spent more time with one another and cared more for one another.

Unofficial channels were crucial to business under Communism. It was often impossible to accomplish anything—from obtaining raw materials to establishing work incentives to getting out sufficient quantities of a desired product—without first circumventing official channels. Conducting business in this way made it extremely important for you to first establish whether your partner was a trustworthy person, one who would not purposely or inadvertently give you away to the authorities. Unofficial channels and unofficial sites for doing business continue to play a crucial role today. In writing on Russian-U.S. business relations, Vladimir Kvint, a professor of international business who managed a company in Siberia, put it this way:

> To make a good impression, Americans should spend time socializing with potential Russian partners. Many deals have been hatched in a sauna between discussions of life, family, and philosophy. But politics, a sensitive subject that is becoming more sensitive every day, should be avoided at all costs.[34]

Taking the time to socialize with business partners is crucial to establishing a relationship of trust. Contrary to the view of most doing cultures, this time is not considered to be "wasted"; rather, it is as integral to doing business as are the business discussions themselves.

As one moves west and north, however, a stronger doing orientation emerges. Because of the heavy influence of northern European culture in countries such as the Czech Republic, Slovenia, Latvia, and Estonia, some strong doing tendencies in conducting business become evident in these countries. Although most businesspeople in Central Europe and the Baltic states seek to develop a long-term relationship with partners, business trust is developed through doing business together, as well as through some socializing. Some time will be devoted to social exchanges and encounters, but not as much as is the custom farther to the east and south. Initial interactions may be restricted primarily to a discussion of business matters; however, as time goes on, more and more social interaction will take place, and a lasting business partnership characterized by loyalty will become possible.

COMMUNICATION

High-context communication.   Central and Eastern Europeans are high-context communicators. Under Communism, the formal channels for communication were extremely inefficient. They had a high risk of failure and provided little incentive for managers. Official information was completely governed by ideological considerations. Today businesspeople in the region thus have come to rely on unofficial and informal channels for conducting business and transmitting information.

Christopher Earley and Miriam Erez offer the following anecdote about a large Czech firm, emphasizing how most important business arrangements are made through informal means:

[A] finance manager had learned about a new way of assessing the quality of engine housing. Rather than using the formal chain-of-command in the company, he contacted a family friend in production and met with him over drinks and dinner. The manager in production did not have enough authority to implement a manufacturing change, so he called a friend who was several organizational levels above himself in production. . . . The net result was that the finance manager's idea was implemented for a substantial cost savings for the company.[35]

Important business information is transmitted via personal contacts. Official business communications are sparse and relatively uninformative. Individuals prefer to convey information in face-to-face meetings with people they know well. Important business deals are rarely concluded over the phone or through email. In some instances, reliable intermediaries are used to convey important data.

Direct and indirect styles.   Central and Eastern Europeans do not hesitate to voice their opinion, whether it be on politics, the arts, or matters of personal interest; in this respect, they are fairly direct communicators. Often they will be openly critical of their own country, government, or countrymen, yet they generally do not take well to criticism of their country or countrymen from foreigners.

In fact, most Central and Eastern Europeans, especially in professional contexts, will seek to avoid open criticism and conflict. In this respect, they are indirect communicators. Because saving face is important in most CEE cultures, business interactions are conducted as diplomatically as possible. Criticism and challenges are always phrased indirectly.

The only Central and Eastern Europeans who are known for a more direct style of communication are the Russians and Ukrainians. In Soviet times, Russian managers used threats and coercion to make employees fulfill the production quotas required by socialist planning. Today, a Russian businessperson will not hesitate to voice disapproval of something or to openly criticize an employee's poor performance. The belief, in this case, is that forthright feedback demonstrates honesty and trust.

Yet, in today's business climate, Russians and Ukrainians are highly indirect when it comes to providing factual information on their firm or the actual possibilities of carrying out a business plan. As Kvint notes, "I've seen Russian companies claim to earn [U.S.] $100 million in profits when they have absolutely nothing."[36] Businesspeople in the CIS are known for saying "yes" to proposals that either they do not have the authority to carry out or for which they do not yet possess the necessary licenses or means. They make various promises simply so that they can continue their contact with foreigners.

In CEE countries that are doing better economically, empty promises and the presentation of false data are much rarer.

Instrumental and expressive communicators.   Hungarians, Romanians, Poles, Russians, Ukrainians, and Belarussians are expressive communicators. This means that they will not hesitate to show their emotions openly or to use emotional appeals as persuasive tactics during negotiations with business partners. As one moves west and north, however, the instrumental orientation becomes considerably stronger. Czech, Slovenian, Lithuanian, Latvian, and Estonian businesspeople, in particular, tend to be reserved in their communication styles. They find emotional appeals and the open expression of emotion inappropriate in a professional setting.

In one sense, however, all Central and Eastern Europeans are instrumental communicators. Businesspeople in the region do not have much of their personal style vested in business communications. They view written and spoken communication as a way to convey information, not as a means of expressing themselves personally through a particular style. Thus, while eloquence is valued, business presentations, letters, speeches, and so forth will be judged primarily on their content. Little emphasis will be placed on form per se.

Formality.   All Central and Eastern Europeans are formal in their use of language in professional settings. Individuals are addressed by their last names, preceded by "Mr.," "Miss," or "Mrs." in the language of the country. If the individual has a professional title, it too is used. First names are not used until a genuine friendship has developed between two individuals.

All languages of the region have a formal second person singular, and this should be used in professional situations. The informal second person singular is used when a friendship has developed.

In their written communications, Central and Eastern Europeans maintain a formal orientation. Business letters are written in a reserved style, rather than in a chatty or intimate manner. In their comportment, however, most Central and Eastern Europeans—with the exception, perhaps, of the Czechs and Estonians—are not as reserved. Humor, for example, plays a large role in all cultures of the region. It is considered acceptable to weave humor, personal anecdotes, and a bit of small talk into presentations and speeches. Meetings tend to be lively rather than somber events, although dress, as well as forms of address, remains formal.

SPACE: PRIVATE AND PUBLIC

Central and Eastern European workers are known for their secretive ways. This was an inevitable response to the years spent under repressive regimes.

Because of the intrusive presence of the government in all areas of life under Communism, Central and Eastern Europeans became more and more reticent about sharing information about themselves with others. This reticence extended to the workplace, where one could never be sure who was a government informant and where one might be circumventing official regulations rather than adhering to them. Office doors were kept closed whenever possible, and workspaces filled with cubicles did not exist.

Today, this type of office arrangement persists. Every employee, even if he or she is sharing office space, has a desk in a discrete room off a large hallway. The offices have no windows or glass doors opening onto the hallway, and doors are usually kept closed. People in the CEE thus have a very private side to their orientation to space.

Central and Eastern Europeans are, however, public-oriented when it comes to how they use public spaces. When conversing, they stand in closer proximity than do North Americans and other individuals from private-oriented cultures. Similarly, when sitting in public places, such as subways, trains, or park benches, they sit closer together than do individuals from private-oriented cultures. Even if the car is nearly empty, when an Eastern European gets into a subway car, he or she usually takes a seat or spot next to someone else, rather than in a seat with several empty seats around it.

The extent to which physical contact in the CEE is part of interacting with others varies from country to country. Accustomed to physical contact with strangers, the Russian businessman thinks nothing of embracing his colleague as he tells him his favorite joke. His Polish or Czech or Latvian counterpart, however, would be embarrassed by the physical intimacy, as well as by the loud laughter; he is used to maintaining a much greater reserve.

POWER: EQUALITY AND HIERARCHY

Central and Eastern Europeans display a strongly split orientation to power. On the one hand, the communal style of living that has marked so many areas of the region emphasizes equality; on the other, a history of highly bureaucratic systems and authoritarian regimes emphasizes hierarchy.

The peoples of Eastern Europe have been accustomed to living in societies where the ultimate power lay with distant, often foreign, rulers who governed in an autocratic manner. Whereas Western Europe was already experimenting with democracy in the nineteenth century, much of Central and Eastern Europe was only then freeing its serfs. And Communism, despite its philosophy of egalitarianism, turned out to be merely another authoritarian system.

This history has produced a strong hierarchy element in the Central and Eastern European orientation to power, with authority being vested in a single charismatic leader. This strong hierarchy orientation applied to businesses as well. Under the Communists, there was a large power distance between subordinates and superiors. Decision-making authority was reserved for the few managers at the top, and they, in turn, made sure that company policy complied with party regulations.

Today, this hierarchy orientation continues to manifest itself in companies. Many older managers try to maintain the same power distance that existed under the Communists, and subordinates feel that they have to continually check with their superiors for approval. Furthermore, many employees are not accustomed to taking responsibility for their own work, preferring instead to place the responsibility on their managers.

Yet, despite—and, indeed, because of—this history of authoritarian rule, Central and Eastern Europeans also display a strong equality orientation. After all, in the past authority was imposed from higher up, and almost always from the outside. Most people, therefore, resented those in power and viewed them with much suspicion. The centuries of oppressive monarchical rule and the last century of repressive Communist regimes has bred a great distrust of authority and authority figures. This distrust of authority is crucial to any consideration of what business organization might be best in today's emerging Central and Eastern European markets.

In many countries, the presence of a foreign ruling elite meant that the domestic population did not develop its own aristocracy or any other leadership class. Instead, the social structure was focused on the local community, where the hierarchy was flat or nonexistent. Even in Russia, which did not come under foreign domination, the village commune was the main political organization with which most people had experience. The commune made collective decisions in which all local heads of households shared equally. Historically, then, most Central and Eastern Europeans were accustomed to an egalitarian situation on the immediate local level, one in which they shared power fairly equally with neighbors and fellow workers.

Many new enterprises that have been successful in today's CEE nations have achieved their success by giving employees a much greater say in the operation of the business. Managers who wish to establish their authority cannot simply rely on their position within the company hierarchy. To win the regard of employees, they must also have the appropriate technical expertise. Thus, one important area in which the hierarchy orientation continues to play a role in today's business is that of knowledge and training. The CEE has a highly educated workforce, and educational credentials and titles remain important. Managers and executives are expected to be experts in their field and are accorded considerable respect and responsibility because of these attributes.

INDIVIDUALISM

Collectivist orientation.   Those who are familiar with the Russian space program will recall the word *mir*, often translated into English as "peace." *Mir* does mean "peace," but it also means both "village commune" and "world." To the Russian mind, therefore, the village commune has traditionally been the world, and it is this kind of world that was thought able to maintain peace. Russia and all of the CEE have a strong collectivist orientation.

The centuries of foreign rule experienced by most of the countries of the region other than Russia led to a sense of group solidarity that united villages and towns against their foreign occupiers. Also, the harsh physical environment could be overcome only through a collective effort. A tradition of mutual assistance developed in which there was little room for individual struggle; instead, individuals focused their energy on acquiring skills that would allow them to contribute effectively to the collective.

Although Russians have usually been the ruler rather than the ruled, their harsh physical environment along with the constant threat of invasion bred a strong group affinity. Russians have a special term for their collectivism: *sorbonost*, which means "communal spirit" or "togetherness." Over the centuries, tribal communes gave way to the *mir*, which survived into the twentieth century—and when Russians moved to the cities, they continued the tradition with the workers' cooperatives or *artel*.

Thus, Russians and their Central and Eastern European neighbors take their identity from the group to which they belong, be it family, local community, or ethnic group. Loyalty to these units is more important than individual fulfillment.

In many cultures, such a strong collectivist orientation translates into a strong identification with, and loyalty to, the company. In the CEE, the opposite is the case. Since company policies were always instituted from the top down and employees had little say in them, employees have felt extremely alienated from their work.

As many foreign investors have discovered, when it comes to work, employees feel neither a sense of responsibility to the organization nor a sense of pride in their own accomplishments. Rather, they have come to view work as a necessary evil. Under Communism, they had no incentive to work productively or carefully; ironically, the concept of teamwork was all but eliminated by the forced collectivization.

The collectivist orientation in this region operates in other ways as well. Any enterprise is seen as being integrally linked to the surrounding local community. A foreign business will be much more successful if it demonstrates a long term interest in the well-being of the entire locality, not just in its own prosperity. Furthermore, a foreign manager will garner much more respect and cooperation if she cultivates good relations with local and regional leaders. There are numerous examples of big Western companies whose business ventures in the CEE failed not because of a lack of resources, but because those involved refused to first consult with the leaders of the local community.

As the business cultures in the region make the transition to free market systems, some of these cultures, specifically those of Central Europe and the Baltic, have been displaying occasional individualistic tendencies. Individualistic-oriented employee incentives such as bonuses and benefits have worked well to bolster productivity in these areas, but it remains to be seen whether or not an individualistic orientation will emerge. Most Central and Eastern Europeans still prefer team-based work with equality among members.

Particularistic orientation.   A survey of Central and Eastern Europeans with regard to the particularistic/universalistic continuum will show that most, if not all, are particularistic in their orientation. Under Communism, official policy dictated a universalistic orientation. The law was considered to be above any particular case or individual circumstance—but, in fact, the only way for people to accomplish anything under these repressive regimes was to find ways to circumvent laws and regulations.

A foreign businessperson will discover that in many countries of the CEE, the wording of regulations and laws is scrutinized in order to establish the narrowest definitions possible. Then, whatever was not expressly forbidden will be considered to be permitted. Much corruption within the former Soviet bloc is, in fact, fostered in this way.

COMPETITIVENESS AND COOPERATION

For many Russians, engaging in business and earning a profit, especially if it is at the expense of others, is still considered selfish and unethical. Coming from a country with a largely peasant population, Russians respect superiors who go out into the field and work alongside their workers. They suspect that great wealth and success have been achieved through dishonest means and through other people's labor. This gives them a cooperative orientation to competitiveness. The other citizens of the CIS and those of the Balkans share this orientation with Russians—as do, to a lesser degree, all other Central and Eastern Europeans.

Communism, which made competition for business success meaningless, only reinforced this orientation. Under Communism, any incentive for competition between companies was squelched by a planned economy that operated through state-run monopolies. Competition among workers was also meaningless, since everyone was paid essentially the same salary and advancement depended on other factors that had nothing to do with productivity.

Outright competition with one's neighbors and colleagues at work is still considered unethical in the CEE. Although some in the new wealthy class flaunt their riches by driving ostentatious cars or wearing fur coats, doing so is considered vulgar. As Karl Topp, president and CEO of Die Welt Development Company, Inc., explains, "working with local people, staying in fourth-class hotels, and bringing my own food and water" brought him more success than if he had separated himself from the population by staying in expensive hotels and eating in Western-style restaurants.[37]

Competitiveness has increased in this region over the past decade, as the walls of Communism have crumbled and businesses in the CEE have had to compete with one another for foreign investors and scarce resources. This is particularly true of Central Europe, Slovenia, and the Baltic states, where the swiftest and most drastic economic changes have taken place. In Poland and Hungary, for example, the aggressive practices of newly reformed managers have been met with applause, as they have contributed greatly to an improvement in the economy. In many companies in the region, higher pay and increased benefits for better work have boosted productivity.

STRUCTURE: A SENSE OF ORDER

Caution and conservatism characterize the Russian approach to the new. This gives Russians a strong order orientation to structure, something that they share with their neighbors in Central Asia and the rest of the CIS. According to a Russian proverb, "The slower you go, the further you'll get."[38] Individuals from this region value stability, security, and the persistence of social order. They fear and resist change. Given the harsh physical environment in which they live and the numerous human-made disasters that have been visited upon them, this caution is understandable.

In business, this order orientation translates into a strong aversion to changing the way business is done. As Russia and the CIS try to make the transition to free market economies, government and business are hesitant to make the many changes needed to do this successfully. Those who benefited from the old Communist way of doing business do not wish to give up their privileged positions within their firm or within the government bureaucracy, and those who were less fortunate are afraid that a new system will only prove worse than the one they already know. A strong order orientation means that changing the system is going to be an extremely slow process. Therefore, Western businesspeople from more flexibility-oriented cultures who have gone to the CIS to help institute local reforms have felt frustrated.

As is demonstrated, in part, by their greater success in making the transition to free market economies, the Baltic states, the countries of Central Europe, and Slovenia are less risk-averse and thus less strongly order-oriented. Their orientation to structure can be described as a mixed order/flexibility orientation. Although traditional in some respects, these countries have experienced more genuine change in both the political and the economic sphere over the past century than Russia and the CIS have. For one thing, each enjoyed a period of capitalism and democracy prior to Soviet domination. Consequently, they have found the current changes easier than have their neighbors to the east.

State subsidies were cut and privatization instituted, a process that has been termed *shock therapy*. This process has been much more effective in Central Europe and the Baltic than in the CIS, where it was applied badly and inconsistently. Such quick and substantial changes would not have been possible had these cultures been only order-oriented. Management at many firms in these countries has proved to be capable of thoroughly overhauling the firms' approach.

WAYS OF THINKING

Deductive and inductive thinking.   The Central and Eastern European orientation to thinking is partly deductive. Businesspeople in the region spend considerable time on the conceptualization phase of project development before launching into actual implementation. This is especially true in Poland, Hungary, the Czech Republic, Ukraine, Slovenia, and the Baltic states, where the educational system emphasizes the theoretical over the practical. Individuals from these countries prefer to have the general principles behind a project or business venture explained before specific examples are introduced. They will find logical arguments more persuasive than anecdotal experiences.

Because of the inductive side to their orientation to thinking, however, Central and Eastern Europeans also spend time on the practical details of a business plan. This is especially the case among Russians, Belarussians, Slovaks, and Romanians, whose educational systems emphasizes learning by analyzing concrete data and actual experience. Businesspeople from these countries like to understand abstract ideas by way of example and experience.

They prefer to push through with the implementation of a new business plan before laying the groundwork. For them, trial-and-error testing in the marketplace seems the best way to determine the viability of a new product or production method.

Linear and systemic thinking. Soviet-style management encouraged a focus on action rather than on goals. Manual labor was valued over intellectual labor. Holistic thinking was not rewarded, whereas the accomplishment of tasks was. Workers were encouraged to do their bit of the project exactly as they were told to do it and were discouraged from considering the overall plan. The latter was the domain of someone in government, who had a central plan for the entire economy.

In today's CEE business culture, this focus on particular details rather than the entire whole persists, giving Central and Eastern European businesses a partly linear orientation to thinking.

When making a decision, Central and Eastern Europeans prefer to consider the historical and philosophical issues surrounding the particular topic, whereas people from linear-oriented cultures, such as the United States, will focus on the practical aspects of getting from one point to the next.

Key Insights for Effectiveness

When confronted with Eastern European pessimism, it is best to reply with sympathy and understanding. Responding to this attitude with an insistent, cheery optimism and saying that everything will turn out all right in the end is likely to backfire. Most Eastern Europeans find such a view of the world unrealistic and will regard it with much suspicion.

If you are from a culture with a fixed time orientation, respond to the fluid time orientation in Central and Eastern Europe with patience. Becoming visibly frustrated or annoyed will only cause further delays. It is best to demonstrate understanding of your client's need for a flexible time schedule. Then, if a critical deadline arrives and you state clearly that it must not be missed, your Central and Eastern European counterparts will find the time and energy needed to meet it.

Show up punctually for all business appointments, regardless of whether your Central or Eastern European counterpart is on time. The fact that you are on time demonstrates to the Central or Eastern European that you are serious about doing business.

Remember to use the appropriate professional and educational titles when addressing others. This demonstrates the proper formality and respect for internal company hierarchies.

Take the necessary time to achieve a good personal rapport with your CEE counterpart. This will go a long way toward ensuring cooperation and success. Once negotiations have been concluded, make sure that you maintain contact to check up on the progress the firm is making.

Make sure to investigate whether the company with which you are doing business has the necessary documents and licenses from the government to carry out all parts of the agreed-upon business venture. Entire deals have collapsed because of one bureaucratic omission.

Cultivate good relations with local and regional officials, as well as with the local community. This will satisfy both the being side of the CEE orientation to action and the collectivist orientation. It will convince your colleagues that you are genuinely interested in the welfare of the community and in the successful development of the CEE, not just in your company's gain.

Never assume that your counterparts will not understand the technical or technological details of a particular project. Although Central and Eastern Europe had a restrictive political and economic system, this did not prevent advances in technology or science. Individuals from this region are highly educated, and many managers are experts in their field of work. Insinuations to the contrary will only insult your associates.

Business communication in Central and Eastern Europe is governed by a strong mistrust of official statements and reports. Any businessperson coming to the region will have to overcome this mistrust, as well as a lingering suspicion of foreigners. In the Soviet era, official statements were vehicles for propaganda or misinformation, and contact with foreigners was severely restricted. Central and Eastern Europeans were therefore accustomed to conducting business through unofficial, private channels. Today, much business continues to be conducted through these channels, and Central and Eastern Europeans remain wary of official data and documents, such as those commonly presented at a company meeting or in an annual report. While they are known for their generous hospitality, individuals from the region remain reserved and cautious with strangers.

The orientations that play the greatest role in communication in the CEE are the being orientation to action, the high-context and indirect orientations to communication, and the private orientation to space.

Given their high-context and being orientations, Central and Eastern Europeans prefer to conduct business face to face. Initial contact is often made through a trusted intermediary who introduces the foreign businessperson to the local firm. Once this contact has been established and preliminary introductory letters have been sent, business will proceed best through face-to-face encounters, during which a relationship of personal trust can be established. It is important, as well, to set up meetings with local and regional officials and whoever else in the community may be affected by the new venture. This is particularly the case in Russia and the CIS.

Much of what passes between business partners in the CEE may be through spoken rather than written communication. Because of the private orientation to space in the CEE, there is also a certain degree of secrecy in communications. The concept of public disclosure of company earnings and expenditures is still foreign to many companies, and internal company records may be spotty or nonexistent.

The indirect orientation to communication in the CEE partly finds expression in an unwillingness to say "no" to business proposals that would bring Western investment. Companies that do not have the means or the proper authority to carry out a project will agree to it anyway in order to get Western business. It is thus advisable not to restrict oneself to oral sources of information and communication, even though oral communication is important. A foreign businessperson should always request company records, official documents, and licenses. If the CEE firm does not possess them, it is best to patiently wait until the necessary documentation is put together. Going ahead with a project when some of these documents are missing will usually prove fruitless, as the missing documents will become a problem later on.

Although much business is conducted through unofficial channels, Central and Eastern Europeans like to get all agreements, official and unofficial, down in writing. This is to the advantage of both sides, since it allows everyone to refer back to a common document if disputes arise down the line.

NORTH AMERICA

For the purposes of this book we restrict our discussion to the three largest political and economic powers in this region: Canada, the United States, and Mexico.

On January 1, 1994, these three countries entered into a trade agreement called the North American Free Trade Agreement (NAFTA) whose aim was to drastically reduce all barriers between these countries over a 15-year period and thus unite them commercially and economically.

There are several factors to keep in mind when considering the business cultures of these three nations. The first is that, despite NAFTA and similar economic ties, there are significant cultural differences, and these differences have a strong impact on business practices. Although the cultural and political foundations of both Canada and the United States are strongly in English or Anglo-Saxon culture, the Canadian cultural outlook and manner are closer to those of Great Britain than to those of the United States. Canada, after all, never completely broke with the mother country; despite its independence in 1867, it remains part of the British Commonwealth, and Canada's chief of state is the British monarch. This is not to say that Canadian culture merely reflects English culture, as Canada has the greatest proportion of immigrants of any country in the world. Yet, at its roots, Canadian culture has been shaped more by English than by U.S. American culture.

The United States, in contrast, is largely defined by its rebellion against the mother country. It gained its independence from Great Britain a century earlier than did Canada, and it did so through a revolution. Many U.S. political and cultural institutions, while heavily influenced by English culture, have also been formed in direct opposition to these roots. The stereotype that Canadians are basically U.S. Americans who simply inhabit a country that is a bit farther north is, therefore, misguided and widely resented by Canadians.

A further difference between Canada and the United States is that Canada officially and explicitly recognizes two cultures and two languages within its borders: French and English. In many ways, French Canada differs significantly from English Canada; thus, it is important to keep in mind that cultural differences between the two will affect cultural orientations and business practices. In fact, the French Canadian cultural orientation is often similar to the Mexican cultural orientation, the third culture in our triad of North American countries. The reason for this has a lot to do with religious views and practices. While English Canada and the United States are, to a large extent, Protestant countries with strong cultural roots in the attitudes and practices deriving from Protestant religions, Mexico and French Canada are Catholic. French Canada was once a colony of Catholic France, and its culture reflects its roots in that country.

Because Mexico was once a colony of Catholic Spain, its culture has numerous similarities to the cultures of Central and South America. In fact, the Mexican social and business cultures are often closer to those of Central and South America than to those of Mexico's North American neighbors. Thus, while differences between Canada and the United States can be said to originate in their differing relationship with Great Britain, differences between these two countries, on the one hand, and Mexico, on the other, can be said to derive in large part from differences in religion and religious culture.

Another factor that greatly influences differences in the business climate across Canada, the United States, and Mexico is the marked contrast in economic conditions and trade patterns. By land mass, Canada is the second largest country in the world, yet it has a relatively small population. Its vast resources and high productivity, coupled with low domestic consumption, have led it to a high dependence on foreign trade. The United States, by contrast, has a large population and the highest per capita consumption of goods in the world; thus it has a large internal market on which it depends heavily, although external trade has increased since World War II and now represents one-quarter of all U.S. trade. Finally, many Mexicans still live at subsistence level, producing little more than goods for local trade. Recently, however, Mexican foreign trade in certain metals, oil, and tropical crops has expanded.

While Mexico and Canada may differ considerably in culture and economics, in their historical relationship to the United States the two countries have much in common. Both have experienced economic and cultural penetration by the United States as well as losing territory to that country. As the United States has become the world's only superpower, Canada and Mexico have found themselves culturally and economically in the shadow of their sometimes parochially minded neighbor, a situation that makes both countries sensitive to assumptions that global business practices essentially mean U.S.-American business practices applied to the global marketplace. Many Mexicans may be offended, in fact, when people assume that the term *American* applies only to people of the United States, as they too inhabit the North American continent. It is important that the foreign business traveler be aware of these sensitivities.

Given the diversity of cultures and cultural orientations within North America, it cannot be said that there is a single way of conducting business that applies equally across this region. Which cultural orientations and business practices prevail in a given situation depends entirely on context. A U.S. manager who is overseeing a wholly or largely Mexican workforce in Mexico will find it both productive and expedient to adapt her management style to fit the Mexican understanding of work. However, a Mexican team that is coming to the United States to negotiate a deal might try to accommodate itself to U.S.-American business habits during the negotiations. Similarly, a U.S. businessperson who is concluding a deal with a Canadian firm usually will pay careful attention to the more formal, ordered ways of doing business in Canada.

Cultural Orientation Patterns

ENVIRONMENT: CONTROL, HARMONY, AND CONSTRAINT

Canada, Mexico, and the United States span the spectrum of orientations on the environment dimension. The United States has a strong control orientation to the environment, whereas Canada has a control orientation tempered by leanings toward harmony. Mexico straddles the line between the harmony and constraint orientations.

The control orientation in the United States expresses itself as a can-do attitude in which the environment is viewed as something to be controlled and shaped in accordance with human needs and concerns. Problems are seen as a challenge and as an opportunity to try something new. In the U.S.-American mindset, there is no problem without a solution. Consequently, U.S.-American business professionals are often perceived as assertive, ambitious, and eager to take the initiative.

U.S. Americans place great value on setting and working toward goals. Unforeseen delays or complications are rarely considered acceptable excuses. When obstacles arise, attempts are made to deal with them in such a way that predetermined results can be achieved and deadlines met with as little adjustment as possible.

Canadians, too, view their surroundings as something over which human beings have and ought to have control. In particular, Canadians feel that technology plays a large role in shaping the environment so that it is safer and more comfortable. Yet, while U.S. Americans might be said to approach the environment as an adversary to be conquered, Canadians are much more likely to view it as a partner that, while adversarial at times, is to be handled through a process of give-and-take—the harmony aspect of the Canadian orientation to the environment.

Canadians are highly aware of and concerned about technology's potential to harm the physical environment. They believe that there should be a balance between satisfying human needs and preserving the physical world that we inhabit. They are likely to favor projects and goals that help to maintain the status quo over projects with more radical consequences. In consonance with their strong equality orientation, Canadians' harmony orientation finds strong expression in the need to build consensus before coming to a business decision.

Although Mexicans share a harmony orientation with Canadians, among Mexicans this orientation is expressed more as a desire to maintain a harmonious balance within the environment of human interaction than as a desire to maintain a balance with the physical environment. Mexicans feel that it is important to maintain a positive balance with all aspects of their environment, but they focus much more on human interactions and on human custom and tradition. Thus, within the business context, maintaining good interpersonal relations and adhering to company policy and established ways of doing business all influence work performance. Mexicans are hesitant to engage in a project that might upset established human networks and traditions.

With regard to the physical environment and areas outside the business realm that might nevertheless have an impact on business concerns such as the economy, Mexicans display the constraint side of their orientation to the environment. Concerns such as bad weather, traffic jams, an illness, a dip in the economy, or an upheaval on the political front may be viewed as something over which the individual has no control and something that must be accepted as a given constraint in conducting one's life and doing business.

The following anecdote illustrates the consequences of these different orientations to the environment within the business context:

Three different teams from three different companies, one each from Mexico, Canada, and the United States, are set to meet in New York during the second week in February to negotiate a contract. Several days before the meeting is to take place, a large snowstorm is predicted. The Mexican team immediately phones the U.S. team to request a month's postponement of the meeting. Their U.S. counterparts are greatly surprised and insist that the weather should pose no obstacle to their plans. As the U.S. team manager explains it, all parties involved should keep to their original plans, but simply expect that some delays might occur. The project cannot wait another month. The Mexican team remains hesitant, however. When the U.S. Americans and Mexicans then phone their Canadian colleagues, the Canadians suggest that the meeting be moved to a different location with better weather and that those faced with the snowstorm consider leaving a day earlier.

None of the three is right, of course. Each solution can be said to have its merits. What emerges clearly from this example, however, is how different orientations to the environment affect each team's reaction to the impending bad weather and the possibility that business might be delayed.

A SENSE OF TIME

Single- and multifocus orientations.   Both the Canadian and the U.S. business cultures display a single-focus orientation to time. This orientation is expressed both in a businessperson's approach to accomplishing various tasks and in the interplay of personal relations and the business setting.

From beginning to end, U.S. and Canadian employees are rewarded for accomplishing tasks and for scheduling their time efficiently and effectively. Managers are expected to set up detailed project plans and agendas and to follow them. Individuals and teams are recognized (and rewarded) for compartmentalizing their tasks and following guidelines to handle each segment of their agenda. Any interruptions or deviations from these guidelines are usually unwelcome. At meetings, for example, individuals who stray from the business at hand or who interrupt while others are speaking are considered rude.

When competing interests do arise and multiple priorities demand attention, the U.S. or Canadian businessperson will respond by considering who is responsible for what and in what time frame. The main objective is to establish priorities by considering timelines and objectives. Items that are considered to have a lower priority will either be delegated to others or postponed until a later time.

Because of their single-focus orientation toward time, Canadian and U.S. business professionals tend to separate business matters from interpersonal relations. The latter are generally regarded as something that should not interfere with business in the workplace. Except in extreme situations, such things as taking a personal phone call during a meeting, letting personal likes or dislikes impede a business deal, or spending time at work attending to personal affairs are deemed inappropriate.

This is not equally true in Mexico. Mexican businesspeople display a multifocus orientation toward time, meaning that their sense of the interconnectedness of everything overcomes the need to break down the surrounding world into manageable units. Thus, the Mexican businessperson will not compartmentalize the personal and business realms to the extent that a Canadian or U.S. American would. A Mexican businessperson would consider it rude not to attend to interpersonal relations, whether in the workplace or outside it, at the same time he is engaged in business. He would not think it inappropriate, therefore, to interrupt a meeting to take a phone call from another client. Similarly, while speaking to an office colleague, he might also be planning next week's agenda.

A multiplicity of tasks is handled in a similar manner in the Mexican business context. Mexicans' multifocus orientation means that they will be comfortable working on several things at once, with no strong sense that a particular task must be completed first.

Fixed and fluid time orientations. U.S. Americans and Canadians, particularly English-speaking Canadians, have a highly structured view of time, which gives them a fixed time orientation. Although there are numerous similarities between the two business cultures on this orientation, there are also some distinct differences in the way the fixed time orientation finds expression in each culture.

"Time is money" is perhaps the most widely heard statement of the U.S. practical view of time. U.S. Americans see time as a rigid, precise concept, a commodity to be saved and spent wisely, not "wasted" or "lost." The U.S. lifestyle and business culture reflect this in the value they place on efficiency and effectiveness. Squeezing more tasks or errands into a day is a desirable goal, and U.S. Americans often feel a sense of triumph when they accomplish more than they expected to in a given period of time, and despair when they accomplish less. They eagerly share information about timesaving techniques and equipment.

By contrast, the Canadian fixed orientation to time is motivated some-what less by the idea that "time is money" and more by the notion that being punctual and adhering to schedules displays good manners, respect, and/or a proper attitude toward doing good work. Thus, Canadians also value effi-ciency and effectiveness, but with dual motives: profit and courtesy. Furthermore, once a schedule has been set, Canadians are reluctant to change it. This is strongly connected to the Canadian past orientation, which tends to support the status quo.

Both business cultures often make reference to time when planning activ-ities, scheduling appointments, traveling from one point to another, meeting deadlines, and fulfilling commitments. Canadians and U.S. Americans expect business professionals to adhere to schedules and to arrive promptly for appointments and meetings. Delays or postponements cause them to express their irritation, both verbally and nonverbally, and they quickly take action to get things back on schedule.

Punctuality is defined precisely in both countries, but here too Canadians and U.S. Americans display variation. A U.S. American will allow a person's tar-diness to extend to five or perhaps six minutes without requiring an explanation or becoming irritated. For a Canadian, however, even three minutes past the appointed time may be considered inexcusably late in a business context.

Among French Canadians, the interpretation of time is more fluid than among either English Canadians or U.S. Americans. French Canadians do not adhere to precise schedules in the same way that English Canadians do. As a foreign businessperson, you should be aware of this variation.

Mexicans also have a fairly fluid rather than a fixed interpretation of time. Their fluid orientation to time is derived primarily from a sense that commit-ments to individuals and to the particulars of a situation take precedence over time commitments. Thus, when a colleague or a project needs more time, they will make greater allowance for changes to a schedule than either Canadian or U.S. businesspeople will.

Business meetings in Mexico seldom start on time and may run hours longer than planned if necessary to finish discussing the matter at hand. Schedules and delivery dates are not always adhered to, nor are last-minute changes and cancellations considered unacceptable. As a general rule, morn-ing meetings are more likely to start on time, but as the day progresses and unexpected situations arise, the meetings planned for later on get pushed back as people fall further behind schedule.

The past, present, and future.   Mexico, Canada, and the United States run the gamut of time orientations. Grounded in a tradition of pioneering—indeed, of breaking with tradition and the past—the United States is strongly oriented toward the present time. Unlike the United States, however, Canada has maintained the political, cultural, and institutional ties it inherited from its former European colonizer, Great Britain. This is reflected in the Canadian business culture, which displays both a past and a future orientation to time, like that of Great Britain. And Mexico, like many Latin American countries with which it shares portions of its culture, has a past/present orientation to time.

Within the U.S. business setting, there is little fear of making changes or breaking with established custom. Great value is placed on innovative approaches and on progress, with U.S. businesses focusing much of their energy on developing "new and improved" products and services. Immediate results, quick turnarounds, and short-term planning characterize the mindset of the U.S. manager. While long-term planning and long-term goals are always kept in mind, actions or strategies favoring the present and the near term are usually the ones acted upon.

Rather than concentrating on the immediate present, Canadians usually take a long-term view of history when making business plans and entertaining the idea of new projects. Thus, they often emphasize long-term consequences and continuity with past actions over short-term results. This makes them somewhat more risk-averse and cautious in their business planning than U.S. Americans. It will take a businessperson longer to convince a Canadian firm of the merits of a new undertaking; however, once the Canadian firm has committed to the project, it will be committed to the project for a long time. A U.S. firm, by contrast, may be quick to renegotiate the agreed-upon plans if it believes that things would be done better if they were done differently.

Mexico shares Canada's past orientation to time, yet the emphasis across the two cultures differs slightly. While both cultures favor continuity with tradition and long business relationships, the Mexican past orientation derives more strongly from the high priority Mexicans place on established interpersonal ties. Because of their need to build trust, whether in private friendships or in business, Mexicans require a long time to get to know their partners. This is strongly linked to the Mexicans' being orientation to action. Once these ties have been established, Mexicans think it crucial to maintain them and to conduct business in the manner that best supports them.

In Mexico, this past orientation is coupled with a present orientation. Because the Mexican political and economic environments are quite unstable, Mexicans have to rely on short-term planning. As a result, they are skilled in crisis management and able to take good advantage of rapidly changing situations.

MODES OF ACTION: BEING AND DOING

A U.S. businessman reported the following after a business trip to a being-oriented culture:

> In every city I went to, I was taken on a tour of the local sights and to good restaurants. My potential customers asked many questions about the history of my company and who our other customers were. They also asked me about my background and commitment to the company and our product line. They also told me a lot about their company and customers. Every time I tried to turn the conversation back to my proposal, they directed the conversation to other topics. After three days I realized I [had] enjoyed my time with my hosts, but [that] I was also frustrated to have to leave without a signed deal. They did invite me back to talk again, though. I guess that means I met with their approval.[39]

In this account, one clearly sees the difference between a being- and a doing-oriented business culture. The U.S. American, who comes from a highly doing-oriented culture, assumes that the primary focus of a business trip is business. Other than a bit of small talk before meetings or perhaps a lunch or dinner unconnected to business, he does not expect much in the way of social events. Therefore, he is surprised that during his first visit to the country, most of the time is spent not on doing business but on getting acquainted. Spending time on establishing a good rapport is central to a being-oriented culture's way of conducting business.

The United States, as we have seen, is a highly doing-oriented culture. Canada straddles this continuum and is both doing- and being-oriented. Mexico is a being-oriented culture.

In Mexico, building a solid relationship takes precedence over accomplishing a task quickly. Mexicans believe that it is more important to "be" in a good relationship with their physical and human environment than it is to "do" many things. The Mexican emphasis is on "working to live" rather than "living to work." In the business context, this being orientation is expressed in various ways. Mexicans spend considerable time getting to know their business partners before beginning a discussion of the deal under consideration. An individual's character is considered more important than that person's professional expertise. Mexicans will look for traits that they admire in potential partners: dignity, patience, respect, flexibility, and seriousness combined with a sense of humor. Whom you know and what you know are key in conducting business in Mexico.

In the United States, by contrast, businesspeople take little, if any, time to get personally acquainted with their negotiating partners; instead, they go straight to the business at hand. U.S. Americans focus on results that are measurable by objective standards and emphasize the accomplishment of tasks over relationship building. For example, if a businessperson comes to the United States for three days to negotiate a deal, most of that time will be spent discussing the deal and attempting to close it. Little time will be devoted to socializing or dining out.

Canada's orientation to the action dimension lies somewhere between those of the United States and Mexico. Canadian businesspeople, especially those outside Quebec, are generally task-oriented when it comes to business. Business relationships are often formed on the basis of the work that has to be done. Canadians do not spend much time getting to know their business partners as individuals first. At the same time, they do not regard these business relationships purely as a means to an end. Although a relationship might be established because of a need to do business, once a good rapport exists, Canadians will often try to maintain this relationship even after the business relationship has ended. Furthermore, even if collaboration with the same partner on a future project may not be most advantageous in terms of making a profit, a Canadian businessperson will often draw on an already established business relationship rather than seeking a new one. This mixture of business approaches gives Canada a being/doing orientation to action.

COMMUNICATION
Low- and high-context orientations. Mexicans leave a lot unsaid in their communications. Although they select their words carefully, there is much they will express through nonverbal cues, such as tone of voice or gestures. In fact, when Mexicans speak with or write to someone else, they rely heavily on a web of interpersonal associations and a large context of previously communicated information. This makes them high-context communicators. The Mexican high-context orientation is closely associated with the being orientation, which assumes that important contextual information will be passed through informal interpersonal channels.

A high-context communicator may say "yes" to something, but indicate by her tone of voice, her body posture, or the statements with which she surrounds the "yes" that she actually means "maybe" or even "no." A low-context communicator, however, will assume that whatever is not explicitly stated is not part of the communication. As would be expected given their doing orientation, U.S. Americans are low-context communicators. Since they do not emphasize informal interpersonal channels for doing business, they do not assume a high-context environment for the exchange of information. A U.S. American will greatly prefer explicit, detailed communication to ambiguous or brief messages. A low-context communicator will also rely on getting everything in writing, as spoken communication, which relies more on personal trust, will seem insufficient. U.S. Americans place little emphasis on nonverbal cues contained within a communication, such as body language or visual cues. For them, a "no" or "yes" means exactly that.

Because Canadians have a partial being orientation to action, they also have only a medium- to low-context orientation to communication. Generally, Canadians rely on explicit statements to convey meaning rather than on statements with implicit meaning. Thus, like U.S. Americans, they prefer to get things in writing, preferring detailed, unambiguous communication to brief messages. Yet, since Canadians also rely on long-term business relations more than U.S. Americans do, they will sometimes display a higher-context style of communication. In the context of long-established business partnerships, a Canadian may feel that he need not be as comprehensive or explicit as he is when he is communicating with someone he does not know. In addition, French Canadians display a more high-context style of communication than do English Canadians.

Direct and indirect communications.   Both Canadian and U.S.-American businesspeople favor a direct orientation to communication. They feel that it is beneficial to express their thoughts and feelings directly and impersonally when sharing information, reaching agreements, or resolving conflicts, and they encourage frank dialogue to create consensus. As direct communicators, they feel that it is appropriate and important to give open, honest feedback to employees and colleagues, regardless of whether this feedback is critical or complimentary. The Canadian and U.S.-American preference for direct communication does not, of course, mean that personal attacks or disrespectful language or behavior is considered appropriate; feedback should be confined to professional matters. U.S. Americans, in particular, view open discussion and resolution of conflict as signs of honesty and trust. They soon become suspicious of behavior or speech that seems hesitant or reticent, especially if they suspect that someone is trying to hide something (even though that person may simply have an indirect style of communication).

It should be noted that French Canadians display a much more indirect style of communication than their English-speaking counterparts. Unlike English-speaking Canadians, French Canadians think it inappropriate to openly challenge an opinion or to directly point out another person's error.

Mexicans resemble French Canadians in their style of communication. That is, they are indirect communicators. In the Mexican business culture, discussion and feedback are governed by the need to save face. Preventing public embarrassment and loss of personal dignity are considered more important than correcting others' mistakes or critiquing their performance. Mexicans seek to avoid or minimize conflict and direct confrontation. In the business context, this means that Mexicans will not openly disagree with or challenge superiors. Conversely, superiors, when giving constructive criticism, are extremely careful not to embarrass their employees. For example, in conveying to a member of the sales force that his performance during the first quarter was inadequate, a superior may say that she appreciates the salesperson's tremendous effort during the first quarter but would be happy to see even higher sales during the second quarter.

Instrumental and expressive styles. Mexicans feel that emotion and expression of a personal style are not only acceptable aspects of communicating but necessary ones as well. This makes them expressive communicators. Mexicans value the style in which something is communicated as much as they do the content. In the business context, eloquence is considered important; professionals are expected to be capable of making articulate, well-informed presentations that are put together well.

Displays of emotion and passion are considered acceptable in a professional situation. Mexicans believe that "to be without passion, in sadness or joy, is to be less than complete as a human being."[40] It should be noted, however, that despite the Mexican expressive orientation, Mexicans are more reserved than people in most other Latin American cultures.

French Canadians also display a relatively expressive mode of communication. Although generally more reserved than most Mexicans, French-speaking Canadians accept the use of emotional appeals as a legitimate way to do business. Elegance in speech and writing is valued as much as the content being conveyed.

By contrast, English-speaking Canadians and U.S. Americans are instrumental communicators. Both groups value the content of a communication more than the style of the delivery. In the business context, they prefer messages and presentations that present facts in a relatively unadorned manner. Correspondence tends to be direct and to the point, with the focus being on the conveyance of as much relevant content as possible. Displays of emotion and emotional appeals in a business setting are generally considered unprofessional.

Formal and informal communications. Mexicans are extremely formal communicators. Protocol is followed at all times and in all situations. It is considered common courtesy always to show deference to and respect for others through the appropriate use of language. *Tú*, the informal form of "you," is used only in addressing family members and close friends. Anyone else, especially those in business situations, is addressed with *usted*, the formal version of "you." Professional titles are extremely important. Colleagues will use first names if they hold the same rank in a company; otherwise, they generally use last names. However, when colleagues of only slightly different ranks get to know each other well, they may use first names.

Even in situations where foreign business colleagues might act with a certain degree of informality, in Mexico formality is the norm. For example, one Mexican professional explained that she was insulted when her U.S.-American colleague left her a quick note asking that she do something for him. She felt that her colleague should have written a formal interoffice memo.

U.S. Americans are informal communicators. They often feel uncomfortable in situations in which it is necessary to follow prescribed etiquette and decorum. They are quick to dispense with ceremony and protocol, and they seek to establish informal relations, which, they believe, allow for a freer flow of information and ideas. U.S. Americans believe that an informal, casual style of communication demonstrates sincerity and credibility.

This difference between Mexicans and U.S. Americans in their orientation to communication can be seen in their different managerial styles. A U.S. manager will treat superiors and subordinates alike, with a certain degree of informality and familiarity. He may take off his jacket at a company meeting, use first names, or think nothing of telling a joke. In Mexico, these are considered out of place, if not downright rude.

The orientation of Canadians has both formal and informal elements. Communication with Canadian businesspeople usually does not involve set protocol. In this sense, Canadians display an informal orientation to communication. At the same time, however, they tend to be extremely polite and fairly reserved. Although they will not disguise what they think about matters relevant to the business at hand, they are less comfortable than their U.S.-American counterparts in talking about personal matters (such as family or their private lives). French-speaking Canadians are somewhat more formal than other Canadians; this is reinforced by the existence of a formal "you," or *vous*, and an informal "you," or *tu*, in the French language.

SPACE: PRIVATE AND PUBLIC

Despite having an open, casual, friendly attitude toward most people, U.S. Americans value their privacy and "personal space" immensely. Permission is always requested before entering another person's office or room; when conversing, people stand at least at arm's length. In the workplace, U.S. Americans exhibit a private orientation to space, favoring private offices and partitioned cubicles. Meetings and phone calls are conducted behind closed doors. If someone needs to interrupt, that person will first knock and excuse himself. Other than a handshake, physical contact when greeting another person in a professional setting is rare.

As part of their private orientation, U.S. Americans assume that people "need time to themselves"—or "time alone," as they might put it—to recover their emotional energy. A foreign businessperson from a culture with a relatively public orientation may occasionally be surprised at being left alone to dine on her own. Her U.S. partners are not trying to ignore her, however; they are simply giving her the "personal space" they think she might need and are thereby demonstrating respect.

The U.S. private orientation to space is thus true in both an emotional and a physical sense. Canadians share this private orientation to space with U.S. Americans. Like U.S. Americans, they tend to keep their personal and business lives separate. Canadians maintain a physical distance from other people as well. There are few common areas, and each employee has his or her own clearly defined space in the form of an office or cubicle. As in the United States, permission is requested before entering someone else's work area.

Mexicans have a split public-private orientation to space. Like Canadians and U.S. Americans, Mexicans maintain an emotional distance, preferring to keep their private lives well separated from their professional lives. They also take their time getting acquainted with and "opening up" to a new person. In this sense, they have a private orientation to space.

However, Mexicans maintain considerably less physical distance from others than do U.S. Americans or Canadians. They tend to stand close together in both social and business situations. When speaking with someone, they maintain only about a foot of distance between them. Colleagues of the same rank may share space in an open office area, although managers will have private offices and sometimes keep the door closed. Individuals are less hesitant to simply enter through an open office door than they are in the United States or Canada.

POWER: EQUALITY AND HIERARCHY

Of the three countries discussed in this section, Canada has the strongest equality orientation to power. Canadian businesses tend to be organized in a way that minimizes, rather than emphasizes, differences between managers and subordinates in terms of authority. Instead of being given a specific job description with a list of responsibilities, employees often are expected to understand the overall company structure and define their place within it.

Employees at all levels are encouraged to take part in decision making, to suggest solutions to problems, and to devise innovative ideas to help their company succeed. Decisions are usually made by a committee or group, not by individuals, but a good idea will be heard and considered regardless of who proposes it. Some of the larger Canadian firms are more hierarchical in their distribution of power, however, because they are owned and operated by an elite group of historically wealthy families that keep company positions within the family.

U.S. Americans exhibit a mixed equality and hierarchy orientation to power. The hierarchy in most companies is relatively flat, and subordinates have easy access to their superiors all the way up to the top of the company hierarchy. It is not uncommon for a top-level executive to come down to the warehouse floor, take off his jacket, and talk to the workers there or to encourage them to come upstairs and stop by his office. Formal titles are infrequently used, with superiors not expecting to be shown deference.

Yet despite the relatively informal and open interaction between subordinates and their superiors, U.S.-American businesspeople also display a hierarchy orientation. They are tacitly aware of the differences in rank between themselves and others in their company. Job descriptions tend to be circumscribed, and employees are usually expected to perform the tasks most pertinent to their position. Decision making takes place from the top down. Although a manager may ask her employees for their input, she has the final say over what is done or not done, even if this goes against the employees' preference.

Mexican businesses display a clear hierarchy orientation. As we have seen, Mexican society is extremely hierarchical. There is a clear power structure in almost all areas of life: business, politics, family, and religion. The way individuals are treated differs in accordance with their age, sex, and rank or role. Therefore, Mexicans are accustomed to work environments in which the division between ranks is clear. Work is performed according to the directions of senior executives; subordinates never expect managers to work alongside them on a project. Decisions made at the top are imposed on subordinates. In many companies, managers do not pass on knowledge to subordinates in a detailed, organized fashion. In fact, the demarcation between ranks is so strong that top executives would consider it inappropriate to dine with subordinates.

Given their strong hierarchy orientation, however, Mexicans are taken aback by the idea that their managers might ask them for advice on professional matters. They think it inappropriate for managers to turn to their subordinates for input, and managers would lose credibility in their eyes. They would perceive them as weak managers and would question whether the business would survive.

INDIVIDUALISM

Individualistic and collectivistic orientations. A U.S.-American writer aptly describes the difference between the Canadian and U.S.-American orientations to individualism:

One of the predominant differences between Americans and Canadians is that, while Americans pride themselves on and rejoice in being individuals per se, Canadians see themselves more as individuals within a group setting. Also the group has more permanence than it seems to have for Americans—Canadians see themselves as a less transient people, and more rooted to whatever community they adopt.[41]

The individualism/collectivism continuum specifies the primary derivation of an individual's identity in a culture. In their orientation to this dimension, U.S. Americans are highly individualistic, whereas Canadians display a mixture of individualism and collectivism, and Mexicans exhibit a collectivist orientation.

From an early age, U.S. Americans are taught that they must make their own choices and solve their own problems. Independence, self-sufficiency, and individual initiative are highly valued in U.S.-American culture, far more than allegiance to a greater collective. In the business context, therefore, U.S. Americans identify most with their own individual achievements and successes, rather than with those of the firm that employs them. Although many U.S. companies have recently been promoting teamwork, a U.S. American still tends to view a team or a firm as a collection of individuals and individual interests.

The Canadian sense of identity is split much more between loyalty to the collective and attachment to personal interests and achievement. Everyone at a Canadian firm expects to do his or her own work and be rewarded for it, and Canadians do view the firm as being composed of independent individuals with independent goals. At the same time, they feel strong bonds of loyalty to their fellow workers and to the company and its success—more so than do U.S. Americans. Thus, Canadian businesses are more likely to use teams to represent a company in business exchanges than are U.S. companies. In general, Canadians feel a greater sense of loyalty to and rootedness in their families, communities, and nation.

For a Mexican, the primary sense of identity is found in the group. Family, community, social networks, and organizations are all seen as essential to defining oneself. Close interdependence among individuals is highly regarded. Individuals feel most comfortable in situations where they can maintain contact with an established network of relations. In the workplace, Mexicans identify strongly with their colleagues and the firm they are working for; in exchange for their loyalty, they expect a certain security. Mexican workers will base their decisions and actions on what they consider most beneficial to the group.

Universalistic and particularistic orientations. Both Canadians and U.S. Americans have a universalistic orientation. Both within and outside the business setting of both cultures, great emphasis is placed on the equal application of rules and procedures. What applies to one is believed to apply to all, and vice versa. Both countries have laws in place prohibiting discrimination in the workplace on the basis of age, sex, creed, ethnic origin, physical handicap, and other personally distinguishing characteristics. In company settings, this means that both nepotism and favoritism based on personal connections are regarded as highly unprofessional. All employees are expected to adhere to the same set of rules and procedures. Individual exceptions based on personal circumstance are rarely made.

Mexicans display a mixed orientation to this continuum. In the workplace, formal rules and procedures are treated with great respect. Individual exceptions based on personal circumstance are rare. In this sense, Mexicans are universalistic. However, in hiring practices, personal connections play a greater role than they do in the United States or Canada. More important, within the general culture, Mexicans are particularists; societal rules are viewed as guidelines or expressions of intent, not as strict regulations for conduct.

COMPETITIVENESS

Mexicans, Canadians, and U.S. Americans each demonstrate a particular orientation to the cultural continuum of competitiveness. U.S. Americans are competitive, whereas Canadians are only moderately competitive, and Mexican businesspeople are cooperative within their own companies and cultural settings but highly competitive with foreign firms.

The U.S.-American business culture is centered on the idea of competition. This competitive orientation can be summed up by the Olympic motto: "faster, higher, farther." Both firms and individual employees are motivated by a strong desire to win or gain advantages, to acquire money or material goods. This fosters the belief that individuals can always achieve more and do better, that a product or service can always be improved.

Each company seeks competitive advantage over other companies in the marketplace. Employees also are rewarded for their own personal achievements and therefore seek to shine. U.S. professionals thus frequently act in a self-assured, outspoken, assertive manner, which often causes outsiders to view them as aggressive, inconsiderate, or worse. This strong competitive orientation is the reason U.S. Americans have one of the longest workweeks in the world. In fact, they often seem to "live to work."

While competitive advantage and personal gain are strong motivators in the Canadian business culture, the Canadian competitive orientation is tempered by the fact that, for Canadian employees, considerations other than monetary gain and professional promotion come into play. Canadians will seek to perform the best they can on the job, but they are less willing than U.S. Americans to sacrifice their personal lives for work.

Salary and the possibility of advancement are not the only things that determine a Canadian's sense of job satisfaction; personal loyalties and job security also play a role. This moderate orientation toward competitiveness in the Canadian business culture arises in part out of the Canadian split being-doing orientation to action and an individualistic-collectivist orientation to individualism.

Mexicans also display a split orientation to competitiveness. Within Mexico, Mexicans are, for the most part, cooperative in the business setting. They strongly value interdependence and seek harmonious, mutually support-ive relations with their colleagues. Therefore, they avoid open competition with their fellow workers for professional success. There is some competition among Mexicans, however, in the form of company politics. Employees have been known to maneuver for positions of favor with superiors.

Mexicans are also motivated more by the desire to maintain the general quality of their lives away from work than they are by the opportunity for financial gain and professional advancement. Yet, driven by strong nationalist sentiments, Mexicans are highly competitive with foreign firms and foreign countries in general. The Mexican saying *"Como Mexico no hay dos"* ("Mexico has no equal") expresses this sentiment well.

STRUCTURE: FLEXIBILITY VERSUS ORDER

Mexicans have a dual orientation to structure. In the areas of company organ-ization and employee responsibility, they display an order orientation. However, their adherence to authority and tradition, and the importance they place on personal ties, may prompt resistance to company procedures. For instance, they are less likely to undertake a new, risky project just for the sake of embarking on a new venture. Nevertheless, because of the severe and unpredictable economic difficulties that affect their country periodically, Mexicans need to be able to make appropriate adjustments. Companies that are not flexible enough to respond swiftly and effectively to the flux in Mexican markets risk failure. Therefore, when it comes to responding to these changes, Mexican business culture exhibits a flexibility orientation.

Canadian and U.S.-American businesses, by contrast, predominantly dis-play a flexibility orientation to structure. As highly industrialized countries, both Canada and the United States have had ample time to adjust their busi-ness cultures to the ever-faster global economy. Indeed, they have played a significant role in setting the pace of that economy. The United States, in particular, has led the way in developing a global marketplace marked by innovation and frequent change. It therefore exhibits a business culture that not only tolerates flexibility and risk but also encourages it.

U.S. Americans place a high value on being able to adapt to new circumstances and respond to new needs. In both their professional and personal environments, they exhibit a lower need for stability than do most other peoples. Consequently, U.S. firms are quite open to taking risks, in the belief that only those who adapt to and take advantage of market trends will survive and thrive. They are willing to experiment both with new products and with new ways of doing business. Employees are rewarded for being innovative and resourceful as well as for operating easily in unstructured environments.

Canadians, too, have a flexibility orientation to structure. Canadian businesses value the ability to adapt to changed circumstances and to take business risks. Especially in technology, Canadian firms value employees who can be innovative and come up with novel solutions to problems. Canada's flexibility orientation is tempered, however, by its strong past orientation to time. Canadians take greater care to consider past traditions when making changes in business practices, and therefore take longer to decide to go forward with a new plan or project. They are thus slightly more risk-averse than are U.S. Americans.

MODES OF THINKING

Deductive and inductive orientations.   Canadians exhibit both a deductive and an inductive orientation to thinking. They have a commitment to theoretical thinking that expresses itself as an interest in the general principles and theories that lie behind the details of a situation. Yet, at the same time, they are interested in those very details. When considering a new business venture, they often will discuss its conceptual framework first, but then go into considerable detail concerning its practical applications. When introducing a new product, they will spend time on both preliminary analysis and actual implementation, as well as on testing in the marketplace.

One cross-cultural guide to doing business illustrates the combined deductive/inductive orientation to thinking this way:

> A Canadian company was considering erecting a late-night entertainment center in a middle-class suburb. When plans were discussed in a board meeting, a fierce dispute broke out over whether much resistance could be expected from local residents. Figures produced by a marketing analyst could be interpreted ambiguously. Eventually an

American board member described the history of the Chicago Cubs' move to introduce late play to the Wrigley Field ballpark and the unexpected opposition. This use of narration rescued the argument from the logical cul de sac where it was stuck. The analogy did not fit precisely, as supporters of the scheme pointed out; but it threw the whole problem into a different light; the sense of nose to nose conflict lifted, and the board reached a decision.[42]

In this example, when the deductive approach of statistical analysis and general predictions proved inconclusive, a switch to an inductive approach—drawing an analogy with a particular case—broke the deadlock.

It is no coincidence that the businessperson presenting the analogy in this example is a U.S. American. U.S. Americans are heavily inductive thinkers; they prefer to go from the particular to the general. In reports or presentations, the collection, analysis, and interpretation of actual data help to create confidence in the resulting recommendations and decisions. Little time is spent considering how a business plan fits into a company's or project's larger, more abstract goals and principles. U.S. firms also spend much more time on market testing than on prior conceptualization of a product or service.

Mexicans, on the other hand, are decidedly deductive thinkers. "Mexicans are by nature theorists, that is, they enjoy the intellectual pursuit of abstract concepts," comments one observer.[43] Mexican businesses will spend a long time conceptualizing a project or product, and will be slow to reach the stage of implementation and testing. Similarly, when they argue a point or discuss an issue, Mexicans use logical thinking and abstract reasoning. They will find analogies and actual data less convincing.

Linear and systemic thinking. Mexicans are also systemic thinkers. They display a holistic way of thinking, preferring to understand how the overall picture fits together before getting into specific details. When presenting a proposal, for example, they will discuss all the issues involved and how they are interrelated and integrated with one another.

U.S. Americans and Canadians, however, are linear thinkers. They tend to approach problems by breaking them down into separate components, then dealing with one component at a time. When developing a plan or proposal, they begin with the details, then eventually form a larger picture by assembling and analyzing the details and seeing how they fit together.

For Canadians and U.S. Americans, the sharing of information, development of project plans, and even discussions proceed in a sequential fashion. An analysis of the benefits and consequences of any business deal is considered crucial to the negotiating and decision-making process. The following

English idioms shared by both cultures reveal their linear way of thinking. When a Canadian or U.S. American tries to clarify something someone has said, he will often say, "Let me get this straight." When beginning a discussion of something controversial, she may say, "I'll get straight to the point." When there is a disagreement or something has gone awry, he might say, "I'll straighten it out." The repeated use of the word *straight* is not accidental; it reveals a preference for regarding matters in a linear, sequential fashion.

Key Insights for Effectiveness

Never assume that the U.S.-American way of doing business applies equally to Mexico and Canada. Both Mexicans and Canadians, and also U.S. Americans, for that matter, will be most likely to trust those individuals who show respect for and knowledge of the business practices prevailing in their own country.

Bear in mind that a culture's orientation to the action dimension is a foundational orientation, one that underlies many other cultural orientations in other dimensions. Since Mexicans are primarily being-oriented, Canadians are being/doing-oriented, and U.S. Americans are doing-oriented, be prepared to adjust your style and expectations accordingly. In Mexico, expect to spend considerable time socializing with your counterparts before discussing business. In French Canada, expect a similar approach. It is advisable, in fact, to suggest social engagements yourself. In the United States and English-speaking Canada, however, expect to focus on business immediately. If you are from a being-oriented culture, do not be surprised or offended if there are few or no social engagements scheduled. This does not indicate a lack of interest in or concern for your needs, nor should it be viewed as a way of pushing you into a deal.

Given the Canadian and U.S.-American fixed orientation to time, it is important to arrive punctually for all appointments with colleagues in these countries and to adhere to set deadlines. Although Mexicans have a much more fluid time orientation, it is still advisable for foreign businesspeople to arrive on time. This demonstrates the formality and attentiveness that Mexicans interpret as respect for their cultural integrity.

In Mexico, it is important to take time to socialize with colleagues and to demonstrate an interest in the individual outside the business context. This means participating in, or even initiating, social engagements. You should expect initial business trips to include quite a few non-business-related activities. These activities should not, however, be confused with becoming close friends. It usually takes time for Mexicans to develop personal friendships.

Their being orientation is offset by their hierarchy and formal orientations, which dictate that, while one needs to get to know one's colleagues, getting personal is something that is done only over a considerable period of time. Questions about family and private life are not considered appropriate. On the other hand, the Mexican public orientation to space means that touching is part of communication. This, too, should not be taken as an indication of intimacy. It is common for Mexicans to linger over a handshake or to touch the forearm of the other person; if you pull back, your Mexican counterpart may interpret this as displaying a lack of trust.

Related to the Mexican being orientation is the Mexican high-context orientation. Mexicans choose their words carefully, considering both what is said and what is left unsaid. They see business communication as not only a means of accomplishing tasks but as an indicator of the degree of trust between business partners. Because Mexicans place heavy emphasis on a continuing relationship with specific individuals, they will assume that one communication builds on another, and they will leave many things unsaid that a low-context communicator might feel bear repeating.

The combination of Mexicans' formal and hierarchy orientations means that business communication, especially written communication, will be highly formal. To Mexicans, formal, polite language and the use of appropriate titles are key expressions of respect for one's business colleagues. Decorous language is also seen as an expression of respect for the person being addressed; this derives from the Mexican expressive orientation. It is important that all written and oral communication adhere to these indicators of respect and courtesy to establish trust with your Mexican business counterparts.

Indirect communication is another central component of expressing respect in Mexico. Negative opinions or feelings are usually concealed. Direct confrontation is to be avoided at all costs in order to maintain relationships. Saving face is always important in Mexico's business context.

Given the Mexican high-context and being orientations, both written and oral agreements will be seen as binding, although an oral agreement is usually backed up by a written communication.

In the United States, little time is taken up by socializing with business colleagues. Prior to the beginning of a meeting, there will be several minutes of "small talk" about such matters as the weather or one's trip, and a business trip might end with a lunch or dinner that is not related to business. Aside from such occasions, however, little socializing takes place. This derives from the United States's doing orientation. To establish trust with one's business colleagues in the United States, it is important that you be ready to focus on business immediately upon meeting them, and that you show a dedication to the task at hand.

U.S. Americans will develop an interpersonal rapport with their business colleagues through other channels of communication, relying heavily on their informal orientation to lend an air of ease and comfort to business encounters. Smiling and other facial expressions and the use of humor during face-to-face encounters are signals used by U.S. Americans to indicate that they feel a sense of rapport with their business colleagues. The equality side of the U.S. orientation to power also comes into play here, as U.S. Americans downplay the use of formal titles. Their strong private orientation, however, dictates that touching is not appropriate, nor are questions concerning one's family and private life.

In written communication, U.S. Americans will focus primarily on conveying relevant business information. This is connected to their doing, low-context, and instrumental orientations. Oral and written communications about business are seen primarily as opportunities to convey information. They are generally taken at face value and are not examined for possible hidden meanings or for what they might convey about the extent of trust between business colleagues.

U.S. Americans gauge the trustworthiness of communication by the directness of their colleagues' statements, how willing those colleagues are to share all relevant information, and their colleagues' ability to make good on their word and remain on schedule. This is derived from the U.S.-American direct and low-context orientations to communication and from their fixed time orientation.

Business communication in Canada, especially English-speaking Canada, has many features in common with business communication in the United States, but there are certain notable exceptions. Canadians have a slightly different balance between the being and doing orientations and the informal and formal orientations. As their dual orientations in these areas suggest, they are more formal communicators than U.S. Americans, and they rely heavily on the continuity of business contacts with the same specific individuals over time. Although Canadians also use humor in their communications, they do so less than U.S. Americans. In general, their use of language and titles is more formal than that of U.S. Americans.

The Canadian moderate low-context, instrumental, and direct orientations to communication, as well as their fixed orientation to time and their private orientation to space, all mean that many of the ways in which Canadians establish trust through communications bear a resemblance to those of U.S.

Americans. Canadians will be frank about their opinions and rely primarily on detailed written communications to establish agreement.

French Canadian business communications are somewhere between the English Canadian and Mexican orientations in the way trust is established. French Canadians are certainly formal communicators, they have a stronger being and high context orientation than their English-speaking counterparts, and they place greater emphasis on saving face. Nevertheless, the expression of these orientations generally is not as strong as that of Mexicans.

LATIN AMERICA

In speaking about Latin America, it must be kept in mind that the region is made up of many diverse, independent nations whose differences greatly outweigh their similarities. Since nearly all the countries in the region were colonized by the Spanish, who introduced their language and the Catholic religion, it is tempting to believe that Latin America is one homogeneous area projecting the image of siestas, fiestas, mañana, and hot, spicy foods. This belief irritates the Brazilians, who were colonized by the Portuguese, speak Portuguese, and account for about half the territory and one-third of the population of Latin America. It also provokes the people of other Latin American countries, who resent having their individuality deprecated.

Geographically, there are Mexico (part of North America), Central America, South America, and the Caribbean. Culturally and linguistically, there are Spanish-speaking America (most of the countries), Portuguese-speaking America (Brazil), and French Guiana, as well as some Caribbean islands whose inhabitants speak French. There are also various regional groupings, such as the Andean countries of Bolivia, Chile, Ecuador, and Peru and the highly European Argentina and Uruguay.

On the other hand, there are some similarities that bear mentioning. First, most professionals traveling to Latin America will go to Spanish-speaking countries or to Brazil (where Portuguese is spoken). Second, Catholicism, with all its cultural implications, remains the dominant religion. And third, the Spanish and Portuguese colonizers transplanted to the Americas a hierarchical society based on relationships and courtesy that persists to this day.

Among the regional rivalries, Colombia–Venezuela, Argentina–Brazil, and Argentina–Chile are three of the more active "competitions" for world status, economic development, and trade. In addition, there are ongoing, but relatively minor, skirmishes over borders and offshore fishing rights. Visitors should never make comparisons among these countries in front of people from one of the countries.

The importance of the hierarchical societies that Spanish and Portuguese colonizers transplanted to the Americas cannot be overstated. Strong pyramidal organizational structures exist in all the major institutions: family, Catholic church, government, and work environment. Latin Americans accept the idea of these different levels. They show deference and respect to those above them while expecting deference and respect from those below. This ordering also generates a variety of relationships that are cultivated and protected and that inspire a complex weaving of obligations and favors.

In the business world, relationships are the key to everything. To put it differently, it is not what you know but who you know that counts. Fortunately, it is relatively easy to make contacts in Latin America, especially if one uses appropriate referrals and introductions. Relationships also generate loyalty, which in turn inspires its own obligations, one of which is nepotism. In addition, in Latin America, being known can be as important as knowing. To be seen hobnobbing with highly visible, powerful, and famous people is a way to signal one's influence. Foreign executives who bury themselves in their work and their company's internal operations will be perceived as isolated and lacking in true power.

It is imperative not to mistake the warm, courteous demeanor of Latin American professionals toward foreign visitors or acquaintances for instant friendship. It is also true that a successful business relationship does not always translate into a personal relationship. The Latin American's apparent charm covers a social and professional stance that is formal and hierarchical. Friendship in Latin America comes only after sufficient time has elapsed and the person has shown himself or herself worthy of the privilege through deeds and gestures. A noticeable change from a solely professional relationship to a personal one occurs when a person proves to be *buena gente* (literally, "good people"), or someone who is worthy of trust and confidence. Since this demarcation does exist, it is always prudent to err on the side of conservative behavior, to expect to move slowly in your business dealings, and to take cues on the progress of the relationship from your hosts.

Foreign professionals who visit their Latin American counterparts with the intention of cultivating long-term, mutually beneficial relationships will ultimately be more successful than those who merely offer proposals for quick results and make no lasting personal commitment. Those who take the time to research each country individually and who tailor their proposals to the needs and conditions of that country will enjoy more successful dealings. Latin Americans prefer to do business with people they like and trust; if they have any suspicions about their foreign counterparts, even those with an apparently good business proposal, they are unlikely to come to a satisfactory agreement.

Cultural Orientation Patterns

AN ENVIRONMENT OF CONSTRAINT

Among Latin Americans, there is a sense that certain things, or certain outcomes, are beyond the control of humans. Catholic fatalism—the idea that God determines and decides most important events—may influence individuals to relinquish responsibility for their actions. While most Latin Americans value work and progress, at times they may leave the end results in God's hands. In Mexico, this attitude can be described this way:

> Many Mexicans feel that their lives are controlled by a Higher Power, so that they can fatalistically accept success or failure, happiness or tragedy, wealth or poverty. While such an attitude provides them with resilience in bad times, it also, particularly in the lower echelons of society, inclines them to accept whatever is, discouraging effort and initiative. In work situations, U.S. executives often interpret this as laziness.[44]

With their belief in the wisdom of God's guiding hand, Mexicans can give the impression of lacking initiative and drive, when in reality they have chosen to follow the directions of God.

A SENSE OF TIME

A multifocused orientation.   The Latin American cultures are generally multifocused in their orientation toward time. Latin American managers are renowned for simultaneously paying attention to several people while engaging in multiple tasks. A U.S.-American manager visiting Mexico City recounts a meeting in which his Mexican host was conversing with him, answering a phone call from his son, and getting a haircut, all at the same time.

To professionals from single-focus cultures, Latin Americans, because of their multifocus orientation, seem unable to focus on one topic for a long time. However, this ability to handle several tasks simultaneously is beneficial for managers and employees, as they are often generalists and need to keep their eyes on overall processes at work as well as on three or four specific issues.

A fluid orientation.   With some notable exceptions (such as the business centers of Santiago, Chile, and São Paulo, Brazil), the social and business cultures of Latin America display a fluid orientation toward time.

The Latin American concept of time is important for visitors to understand and begin to adapt to. One author describes it this way:

> Many North Americans, Europeans and Asians view someone being late as showing a lack of respect and having sloppy, undisciplined

personal habits—even potentially being unreliable as a partner or supplier.

Being "on time" is very different in South America. What's late in North America may well be early in South America. Lateness isn't considered rude or disrespectful. If you become angry or upset with your South American colleagues because they are late for an appointment, they probably won't expect or understand your anger and they will not feel guilty or apologize.[45]

Bosrock advises visitors that, when dealing with their Latin American counterparts, they should adopt a more fluid orientation toward time.

In social situations, time is measured imprecisely, regardless of whether a family celebration or a meeting with colleagues is involved. If, for instance, an invitation calls for a starting time of 8:00 P.M., most of the guests will arrive around 8:30 P.M. Most Latin Americans would consider it impolite to arrive on time, since they might catch their hosts before they were prepared. Written invitations do not indicate an ending time, since that would be rude. Many social occasions go past midnight.

In business situations, the time framework is tighter, although anywhere from 10 to 30 minutes of lateness is still allowed for face-to-face meetings or conferences, and perhaps up to several days between the initial due date of a project and actual delivery. Planning sessions and negotiations can take longer than they do in cultures with a fixed-time orientation, since time restrictions are looser and adhering to schedules is secondary to building a solid relationship and reaching a satisfactory agreement.

An orientation to the present. Latin American professionals, in general, are present-oriented. They prefer, or are obligated by economic, political, or social conditions, to take a short-term perspective when planning and executing tasks and projects. Longer-term plans can be thwarted by volatile circumstances and thus can prove disappointing.

Another indicator of the present orientation of Latin Americans is their rapid adoption of communications technology. First faxes and now email are replacing traditional mailed letters between colleagues, a sign of the urgent need and desire for action in the fast-paced world of business.

Socially, Latin Americans enjoy life. They revel in the pleasures of the day, leaving the worries of tomorrow for later. This is not to say that Latin Americans cannot be serious and dedicated to their work; on the contrary, they are loyal and hardworking employees who focus on the needs of the moment.

A BEING ORIENTATION TO ACTION

Latin Americans display a being orientation to action. They depend heavily on relationships to accomplish tasks, win favors, and, in general, make their lives more pleasant. They cultivate long-term relationships in which mutual trust, benefit, and enjoyment are developed through sustained contact and interaction. Latin Americans tend to do business with people they like and trust, as well as with those who present interesting proposals. Therefore, it is important that companies send representatives to Latin America who have both excellent interpersonal skills and superior subject matter knowledge of their field.

In the professional world, managers and employees often value relationships over job opportunities or the accomplishment of certain tasks. For example, some Latin Americans might refuse a promotion at work if it meant moving to another city where they would be far from their families. As another example, an employee may refuse to identify the person who makes a mistake because of the employee's relationship with that person.

The work lives and private lives of Latin Americans are closely integrated. This integration of two important parts of their lives illustrates the attitude of Latin Americans toward finding enjoyment and fulfillment in life and not taking things too seriously. This approach to life often causes managers from doing-oriented cultures to view their Latin American counterparts as lazy or slow. Latin Americans, for their part, view their doing-oriented counterparts as working nonstop without giving much thought to their actions. These negative evaluations amount to little more than viewing a situation from two perspectives: work to live, or live to work. Interestingly, both sides are moving toward the opposite end of the continuum. Many Latin Americans—especially those from large or industrial cities such as São Paulo, Santiago, Mexico City, and Buenos Aires—are moving toward a doing orientation as they compete in the international marketplace. At the same time, many U.S. workers, for example, are becoming tired of being "workaholics" and are seeking more balance between their work and personal lives and trying to regain their connection to their families and communities.

In terms of personal relationships, association with the extended family is the norm in Latin America. Children often do not leave home until they marry, and then the married couple frequently establishes a home near one or both sets of parents. Grandparents, aunts, uncles, and cousins play important roles in people's lives and command their first loyalties. Close friends come to resemble members of the family, with many of the same rights and responsibilities. All these relationships provide a strong sense of identity and belonging.

COMMUNICATION

A high-context orientation. People from Latin American cultures have a high-context orientation to communication. This means that they send implicit messages rather than make direct statements. They convey and receive the subtleties of messages through tone of voice, eye contact, and physical gestures. Members of high-context cultures have learned to "read between the lines"; they gather hidden meaning by carefully listening to how something is said as well as what is said. People from low-context cultures, who are used to having everything stated explicitly, are often confused or misguided by high-context communicators, sometimes accusing the latter of deliberately being evasive or of outright lying.

In the business environment, both employees and managers will often utilize a high-context communication style, especially when saying "no," imparting negative information or feedback, requesting a favor, or giving advice. They expect the receiver of these messages to intuitively understand the message that is being sent and respond accordingly.

Indirect communications. On the whole, Latin Americans are indirect communicators. This is especially true in circumstances where they need to express negative information, deal with their superiors, or try to avoid conflict. Bad news, such as an unmet deadline, a poor performance appraisal, or disappointing results of a project, is often communicated by suggestion and innuendo. In the high-context orientation, the recipient of the information is expected to understand the true underlying message. Consistent with the hierarchical orientation, conveying messages to one's superiors needs to be done tactfully. You should never seek to embarrass the other person or put her or him on the defensive. Further, when managers speak to their subordinates, they should avoid direct criticism, instead making statements that are intended to encourage and motivate those subordinates. In trying to avoid open conflict, and in accord with the being orientation, the introduction of "another possibility," as opposed to "my idea," will often come across as collaborative rather than confrontational.

In a negotiation or planning session, indirect communication is often useful in maintaining harmony between opposing groups. Given the overriding desire to maintain a relationship, key players may address critical disagreements in a separate session, apart from the group discussion. This arrangement allows both sides to save face while at the same time resolving the dispute.

Expressive style. Latin Americans are known for their expressive communication style, which uses flowery language, colorful expressions, and innuendo to elevate written and spoken language to the level of art. Their compliments are effusive, their praise lavish, and their descriptions detailed enough to create an accurate mental picture. Language becomes a tool for educated professionals to use to project intelligence and self-assurance in an elegant way. Therefore, they may be judged by their superiors and competitors on their eloquence in both everyday conversations and formal presentations.

Politeness and good manners are indicative of an expressive orientation. Mexicans, for example, are among the most courteous people in the world. Courtesy, protocol, and ritual are as much a tradition to Mexicans as they were to the Aztecs, who valued diplomacy along with valor. The Spanish Conquistadors added another dimension to this—the "grand gesture," which today is an essential part of every Mexican's makeup. It is a form of "courtesy one-upmanship" or "I can be more generous than you." In essence, the grander the gesture, the more points for the expressive person.

Formal orientation. Consonant with their hierarchy orientation, Latin Americans are formal communicators. Venezuelans, for example, focus on the differences between social classes, following predictable patterns of behavior at work and in social situations. They observe the organizational hierarchy by respecting their superiors and using more formal speech with them. It is unusual for individuals with different social status to fraternize. High-ranking managers and business leaders receive special deference. They are friendly with employees but keep them at a distance, and never consider them part of the manager's family, close or extended.

Formality is communicated in Latin America through the use of the formal "you," *usted* in Spanish and *o senhor* (for men) or *a senhora* (for women) in Portuguese. These forms are always used with elders and superiors unless those being addressed give the speaker permission to use the more informal term for "you," *tú* in Spanish and *tu* or *você* in Portuguese.

A SENSE OF SPACE: PUBLIC AND PRIVATE

Latin Americans display a mixture of public and private orientations toward space. As an example of the public orientation, Latin Americans touch each other more than U.S.-Americans, Britons, or Germans do, both in social and in professional situations. They also stand closer to each other when conversing. In the office setting, employees often work in a common room or a space divided by low-walled cubicles. This arrangement is meant to foster open communication and facilitate centralized control by managers.

In their home life, Latin Americans tend to have a private orientation. Homes are often sheltered behind walls or fences, as much for security as for privacy. Latin Americans do not casually invite people into their homes until

a certain degree of familiarity and trust has been established. In business settings, privacy often accompanies hierarchy; upper-level managers usually
work in separate offices and are not in close physical contact with their colleagues.

A HIERARCHY OF POWER

Latin American culture often exhibits a strong tendency to hierarchical organization, from the dominant father figures in families to the *patrón* (boss) to
the history of dictators and *caudillos* (strongmen) who have led these
countries.

In both personal and professional settings, one of the tools Latin
Americans use to take advantage of, or circumvent, the existing hierarchy is
palanca, which translates literally as "lever" but which means "leverage or
influence due to a personal connection." One researcher of Latin American
culture describes *palanca* this way:

> *Palanca* provides a means by which individuals can transcend general
> rules, procedures, and the effects of scarcity by interacting with pow-
> erful others to gain what they need. The idea of *palanca* is rooted in
> a more fundamental notion that a person's identity is largely consti-
> tuted by relationships with others. It is also tied to the notion of hier-
> archy and power distance because it is the more powerful persons who
> can help others.[46]

Individuals will use their *palanca* as either a favor to a friend or an obligation to a family member, for example, and some sort of reciprocation, either
a simple "thank you" or a favor returned, is expected.

INDIVIDUALISM

Collectivist orientation.   Latin American cultures primarily have a collectivist orientation to individualism. In these cultures, what is good for the
group is protected and promoted over what is good for the individual.
Individuality, or the recognition of individual uniqueness, however, is highly
valued in Latin American cultures. One should not confuse individuality with
individualism, in which the primary focus of the individual is himself or
herself.

Hofstede, in addition to studying hierarchy, looked at the levels of individualism, and by default collectivism, among the members of various
cultures. He defines individualism as having an "I" orientation, where the
individual is concerned primarily with himself and his immediate family,
rather than a "we" orientation, where people are concerned more with their

extended family and other important reference groups, with whom they maneuver, exchanging expressions of loyalty. The higher the score, the more individualistic the culture.[47]

While the United States and Canada rank as the first and fourth most individualistic cultures, respectively, of those surveyed, the Latin American cultures are much more collectivistic, with five of the lowest rankings of all fifty-three countries included in the survey attributed to Latin American countries.

What this means for behavior in the workplace is that employees are more likely to cooperate with their colleagues than to compete with them, to place high value on being identified with a certain work group or company, and to disdain overt self-promotion. They are also more likely to hire former colleagues, friends, and relatives—in other words, people whom they know, who have similar values, and who can be counted on to be loyal. While this may be viewed negatively in the United States, where nepotism is frowned upon, in Latin America it is the method by which a trusted and responsible workforce is recruited.

A key element of the individuality of Latin American males is the concept of *machismo*. Researchers in Colombia describe the image that U.S. Americans and Europeans have of this male identity, as opposed to how Latin Americans themselves view it:

> For many North Americans and Europeans machismo conjures up the image of aggressive males showing off, competing with each other, and dominating women. A more accurate interpretation . . . is that Latin men behave in accordance with their image of what a man should be: strong, respected, and capable of protecting and providing for women and his family.[48]

Thus, it could be said that to Latin American men *machismo* represents traditional male behavior, not exaggerated displays of superiority and control.

Women traditionally have exercised their individuality through their husbands and children, although this is changing as women are gaining their own voice through increased participation in the workforce, shrinking family size, and newly passed legislation in the areas of divorce, maternity leave, and equality in the family.

Particularistic orientation. Latin Americans seem to prefer individual attention to being treated the same way as everyone else. They enjoy special consideration based on age, professional position, social class, or membership in a group. They view their obligations as being first to family and friends and then to business. In practice, this does not mean that when faced with an important business deadline, a Latin American professional will decide to have lunch with a family member. It does mean that in cases of emergency, they will always make an exception for people in their inner circle.

One cross-cultural expert contrasted particularistic cultures with universalistic ones:

> Business people from both societies will tend to think each other corrupt. A universalist will say of particularists, "They cannot be trusted because they will always help their friends"; a particularist, conversely, will say of universalists, "You cannot trust them; they would not even help a friend."[49]

This example illustrates possible attitudes that Latin American particularists and U.S. universalists might hold toward each other, as well as giving an idea why building a trusting relationship between people from these two cultures can be challenging.

The particularistic orientation is exhibited through various business practices. Managers in Latin America widely consider nepotism the preferred method of filling available positions. When awarding a contract, for instance, a bidder with a better relationship or a more generous offer of special considerations is likely to get the job over a bidder who offers a lower price or faster delivery. One manager in the United States observed that his Brazilian colleagues continued to negotiate the terms of their contracts even after the contracts were signed—a demonstration of the need to adapt to changing circumstances and develop a relationship of trust.

COMPETITIVENESS: COOPERATION AND COMPETITION

Latin Americans display both a cooperative and a competitive orientation toward working with others. In keeping with their collectivist orientation, they are cooperative, placing emphasis on relationships and interdependence with people and agreeing to help and support one another in business and social situations.

On the other hand, to achieve a higher quality of life, Latin Americans must work hard to achieve larger salaries and the material goods that represent higher business and social status. This introduces a great sense of competitiveness into the workplace. With the privatization of many state-owned industries and the opening of foreign markets in such countries as Argentina, Brazil, and Chile, businesses have seen an incentive to compete more aggressively. Individual employees who have never had any reason to fear losing their jobs have suddenly realized they have to make themselves valuable to their employers.

Competition Latin American style takes subtle and indirect forms. Open rivalry is discouraged, since it can harm relationships that have taken time and effort to build. For example, because Mexican managers define themselves by their family situation first and do not attach undue importance to their success on the job, they do not openly attempt to outperform their colleagues. Instead, they might engage in maneuvering within their companies, seeking special favor in the eyes of their superiors. Employees and managers alike see university and graduate degrees, bilingual skills, and relationships with influential people as other, indirect ways to be viewed favorably.

An interesting illustration of this dichotomy between cooperation and competition can be found on the soccer field. Soccer is the single most played and watched sport in Latin America. Players consider it an honor to be chosen to play on local or national teams. They know that they have to work together to dominate their opponents. However, both on and off the field, they often engage in the most flamboyant behavior in order to generate publicity for themselves as individual stars.

STRUCTURE: ORDER AND FLEXIBILITY

Latin Americans exhibit a strong orientation toward both order and flexibility. A tradition of hierarchy and fluctuating economic, political, and social conditions leads many managers to seek order and, in general, to be averse to risk while also wishing to follow established lines of control. However, precisely because of these dynamic market situations, managers have had to learn to be flexible in order to take advantage of new opportunities or to avoid potential pitfalls.

Chile may well be the most order-oriented country in Latin America. Managers there tend to minimize uncertainty, change, and risk. When these challenges do appear, decision makers try to bring the work environment back into balance. Chileans believe that laws and regulations exist for the benefit of business development; they usually adhere to recommended social and business norms.

Most other Latin American nations exhibit a flexibility orientation to structure. For example, consistent with their particularistic orientation, Argentines and Brazilians often operate under the belief that rules and regulations are meant to be broken, redefined, or even ignored, according to their needs. Venezuelans have experienced so many changes since 1994 that they are becoming accustomed to working in an unstable environment. On a broader scale, managers in most Latin American nations practice leadership styles that shift with the economic conditions, often taking small risks and spontaneously making whatever changes they view as beneficial.

One U.S. manager with several decades of consulting experience in Latin America spoke of the Latin American duality of order and flexibility:

> In my experience, one way to describe the struggle between order and flexibility is along generational lines. The older managers view their success as built upon adherence to hierarchical relationships, more cautious investments, and following established ways to do business. The younger managers, many of them educated in the U.S. or Europe, are more willing to take risks and challenge the traditional ways in order to capture new opportunities.[50]

This duality can also be seen in various industries, with the more traditional ones, such as utilities, being more likely to exhibit an order orientation and newer businesses, such as computer and Internet companies, showing a flexibility orientation. Privatization and the opening of foreign markets have contributed to the creation of a business climate that is favorable to flexibility, creativity, and new ventures.

WAYS OF THINKING

Deductive thinking.   Traditionally, Latin Americans of the upper classes have received a liberal arts education that focused on the works of the great European thinkers. Because managers have usually come from these classes, they generally think in broad terms and thus concentrate less on details or the practical application of their knowledge. Thus, it is not uncommon for them to place ideal outcomes before realistic goals, since they are focusing on principles rather than on the pragmatic realization of those principles.

Because of Latin American managers' need to see the bigger picture first, when you present proposals to them, you should start with the general and then move to the specific. In your introduction, which should present the conceptual framework, you should address the broad benefits to all concerned, then deal with the details, then, after that, plan for the execution of the strategy.

Because they work in such a deductive fashion, Latin American managers can pay less attention to implementing new projects than to planning and developing them. Mexicans, for example, give priority to the more abstract concept of a project over its execution. This can be frustrating to people from cultures with an inductive orientation, who prefer to deal with the specifics of a project and are more concerned with its successful implementation.

Systemic thinking.   Latin Americans seem to enjoy the complexity of systemic thinking, often commenting that the linear approach seems too simplistic to be of use. Their deductive orientation provides them with a large conceptual framework, to which they like to add all the interrelated elements and thus create a complex, unified picture.

Argentine managers, for example, often begin the planning process by trying to understand the conceptual framework of a project before focusing on specific details. Until they learn how this framework emerged and how the different pieces are connected, they have no interest in a detailed description. They will also weigh the image of the project and try to gauge its impact on other areas of the organization.

Brazilian managers also exhibit a systemic orientation toward thinking. They take an inclusive, integrated view of workplace activities; they analyze the connections among various processes and then establish controls that protect the performance of the system, rather than merely protecting the individual parts. They prefer organizational procedures that enhance complex relationships to processes that focus on discrete, isolated parts.

One Canadian vice president described how the Latin American deductive and systemic thinking orientations influenced her financial planning sessions with her Latin American regional managers:

> I arrived at the meeting with an agenda containing time slots and topics for each of the seven regional managers. We had agreed via email that each manager in turn would present his or her concerns, and then we would look at the regional implications and implementation schedule. As soon as the first manager started presenting his thoughts, I saw that he was still at a theoretical stage and had not yet devised an implementation plan. He also felt it necessary to include the input from several other departments. Soon other managers began to raise issues of internal competition. In short, he took a superficial and integrated approach which was helpful in many ways, but which was very different from the finance-focused implementation plan for which I had asked. By the time he finished, he had taken more than twice his allotted time.[51]

This example illustrates how theoretical and integrated thinking patterns influence the planning process.

Key Insights for Effectiveness

Because of the Latin American harmony and constraint orientations, you should pay great attention to building and maintaining relationships, and you should also recognize that a certain degree of fatalism may influence the attitude toward or outcome of large decisions or changes. If you really want to cement the deal, do not quibble over less important details.

Latin Americans move at a different pace and rhythm. Because of their multifocused, fluid, and present orientations, time seems more circular and more intensely related to people and events. Therefore, Latin Americans move at a more leisurely pace. Pushing or rushing your hosts will have negative consequences. Be prepared to allow time for accomplishing your tasks, reaching agreements, and executing plans.

The Latin American being orientation focuses more on relationships and a work to live attitude. However, Latin American managers are dedicated professionals and will often go beyond what is expected of them in order to finalize an agreement and meet a goal. Try to cultivate long-term relationships that will bear fruit over many years and many deals.

Latin Americans communicate in high-context, indirect, expressive, and formal ways. Their conversations are filled with courtesy, respectful forms of address, subtle evaluations and suggestions, and eloquent phrasing. If you are dealing with a negative issue or a disagreement or if you want to obtain more details than are forthcoming, proceed slowly and diplomatically, requesting small bits of information. Avoid aggressive, direct, or casual approaches. If you don't, Latin Americans may view you as pushy, egotistical, and interested only in short-term results.

Hierarchy is paramount in understanding relationships and influence in Latin America, both in business and in social settings. Always try to deal with the highest levels when negotiating and making decisions.

Given the collectivist and cooperative orientations of Latin Americans, employees and managers may work cooperatively, but when it comes to enforcing rules and making special considerations, Latin Americans treat each person in a particularistic fashion, as a special individual. Be prepared to offer concessions to "sweeten" the deal and thus gain favor with your hosts.

Latin Americans operate with both an order and a flexibility orientation. While hierarchical and somewhat authoritarian organizations seek to maintain predictable environments, outside market factors often bring change and uncertainty, both of which require a flexible approach. Your Latin American counterparts will view favorably your own willingness to adapt to changing circumstances.

In high-context Latin America, communication is much more than language alone. There are many ways in which speakers can strengthen or weaken the impact of their message, such as sentence structure, vocabulary, tone of voice, pacing, body language, facial expressions, personal appearance, and the ability to listen well and respond accordingly. Since it is assumed that much information is already known, communication can be cryptic and filled with insinuations and suggestions. Latin American professionals are often judged by their peers and superiors on their ability to communicate with others, especially on contentious topics or during stressful situations. Additionally, one achieves status through one's credentials and affiliations, which are often subtly inserted into a conversation or presentation. Remember the phrase "Sir, what you are speaks so loudly that I cannot hear what you say!"

Latin Americans value an indirect orientation toward communication, especially when conveying negative information. This allows speakers to avoid offending or hurting the feelings of their listeners. It also allows them to be less precise, thus providing latitude in meeting deadlines or assigning responsibility. The indirect approach can be used to avoid personal responsibility and eliminate the tendency to "punish the messenger," a common reaction to bad news in Latin America's authoritarian, hierarchical organizations. This indirect orientation is demonstrated as well in the general Latin American desire to avoid conflict and to find more subtle means of conveying disagreement or critical evaluations. However, Latin American cultures have differing degrees of tolerance for confrontation. The Andean peoples (those from Bolivia, Chile, Ecuador, and Peru) tend to be averse to confrontation. Argentine executives, because of their schooling and the European influence of their culture, are less averse to confrontation, since it usually appears in the guise of intellectual debate rather than personal challenge. Peoples of the tropical areas (the Caribbean, the northern coast of South America, and parts of Central America) seem not to have as much of a problem with confrontation, although they still tend to avoid it.

SUMMARY INSIGHTS

How can we summarize this broad cultural survey of the world? We should, perhaps, focus on the most important principles. In your dealings with individuals from other cultures, (1) seek to minimize actions that you regret, (2) take nothing for granted, (3) prepare for a cross-cultural encounter with purpose and thoroughness, and (4) ensure that your actions take into account the underlying perspectives, beliefs, and value orientations.

Don't:

- Assume similarity; it's safer to assume differences and find out that there are similarities than vice versa.
- Try to adopt another culture. Remember, adaptation does not mean adoption!
- Keep comparing and contrasting the other culture with your own.

- Keep evaluating the other culture in terms of its being "good" or "bad."
- Assume that just being yourself will be enough to bring you cross-cultural success.

Do:

- Set realistic expectations for yourself and others.
- Factor cultural orientations patterns into your planning and approach.
- Accept the fact that you will make mistakes, but remain confident.
- Be patient with yourself and your counterparts.
- Slow down. Aim to build relationships, not just make deals.
- Keep your sense of humor.
- Keep your integrity. Know what you stand for and know your limits.
- Stay objective and minimize blame.
- Most important, hone your cultural self- and other-awareness, continuously gather cultural knowledge, and actively acquire skills and practices that enable you to transcend cultural barriers.

Our survey flight has given us a general grounding, a surface introduction to the intricate variability that exists around us and that constitutes the global, multicultural environment. Increasingly we are challenged with developing common ground out of this diversity, whether in multicultural virtual teams, through global management processes, or through global approaches to the solution of problems that face all of humanity.

Understanding the driving societal value orientations and their variations is only the beginning. It is the start of a learning journey that ultimately leads to ourselves and our own approach to communication and interaction. Hopefully, it will challenge our own consciousness of differences and increase our willingness to translate insights into actions.

We have identified three key skills and practice areas as the hallmarks of the successful traveler on this learning journey: (1) style switching, (2) cultural due diligence, and (3) cultural dialogue. In Chap. 5, we investigate the elements of these skills and their power in cross-cultural communication.

5

CULTURAL ORIENTATIONS IN COMMUNICATION

All persons are puzzles until at last we find in some word or act the key to the man, to the woman; straightaway all their past words and actions lie in light before us.

RALPH WALDO EMERSON

You can be totally rational with a machine. But if you work with people, sometimes logic often has to take a backseat to understanding.

AKIO MORITA

Our exploration of culture has yielded a differentiated understanding and general framework, the Cultural Orientations Model. We have applied this framework to high-level generalizations about societal differences. These generalized characteristics can help us to understand and explore the cultural contexts of organizations and individuals alike. However, they do not predict individuals' behavior, nor do they apply to all groups or segments within a given society. As Derald Wing Sue points out, "there are more differences within groups than between groups."[1]

The societal patterns of cultural orientations identified in Chap. 4 along with their organizational corollaries constitute a macro level of culture that acts like gravity[2] upon individuals. Through interpersonal interactions and their tangible products, either we reproduce and reinforce these patterns *or* we change them. The micro level of interpersonal and group interaction is, after all, both the building block of culture at large and the agency of cultural change. The micro and macro levels exist in a dialectical relationship with each other, so that it would be utterly misleading to think of individuals, including ourselves, as merely passive "victims" of societal culture. Culture may help to form our identity, but it does not determine our behavior.

As soon as we become aware of these macro-level forces and their connection to our own behavior, values, and practices, they become changeable as well. Understanding ourselves as active agents of culture moves culture itself into our spheres of influence. In a business context, this sphere is primarily that of the work group or team and, by extension, the organization.

It is therefore the individual and interpersonal level that we are concerned with in this chapter, as it is at that level that we define our responsibility for, effect on, and influence on culture. Building and cementing a global organizational culture, as well as transcending and leveraging cultural differences in small work groups and teams, is first and foremost the task of individuals. This can be accomplished only through the development and exercise of specific awareness, mindsets, and skill sets, and this development ultimately amounts to a very personal journey.

This chapter introduces specific tools, insights, and approaches gleaned from our consulting practice in which the terminology of the Cultural Orientations Model provides a common vocabulary. With this vocabulary, we can refer to and categorize cultural differences in an appropriate, differentiated, and ultimately practical way. Our understanding of cultural variation changes substantially once we distinguish between, for example, a low-context and instrumental environment (or expectations) and a high-context and expressive environment (or expectations), rather than between Germany and Spain. We can truly transcend stereotyping and turn awareness into active ways of fostering understanding and cultural synergy.

MYTHS ABOUT INTERCULTURAL INTERACTIONS

Before we can investigate the details of intercultural communication and interaction processes, we need to look at some pervasive myths that this investigation will further dispel.

Myth 1: We're Really All the Same

The differences in value orientations outlined in the previous chapters make a convincing case for the contrary. And although we certainly share a common human nature, culture channels our common needs, energies, and desires into specific patterns that provide individuals with fundamentally different ways of perceiving themselves, the world at large, and their actions within it. While there certainly are many similarities, assuming that these similarities predominate when engaging in an interaction carries a great risk. Nancy Adler provides a practical guideline: "Assume difference until similarity is proven."[3] Implicit in this guideline is our obligation to probe for similarities and differences in the course of our interactions.

Myth 2: I Just Need to Be Myself in Order to Really Connect

Cultural differences can run deep. Being a naïve stranger who is intelligent and charming may carry you for a time. Pretty soon, however, that will wear thin and be insufficient. As your intercultural relationships develop, not understanding or attempting to understand differences will be increasingly detrimental. While it is important that you maintain your sense of identity and integrity, naïvely assuming that because you have good intentions, people will somehow understand frequently leads to rude awakenings. You may need to change your behavior, going outside of your comfort zone in order to truly communicate your intent and keep your integrity intact.

Myth 3: I Have to Adopt the Practices of the Other Culture in Order to Succeed

You need to *adapt* rather than *adopt* the other culture's practices. Being successful in intercultural communications and interactions does not require you to "go native" and change your fundamental perspective. In fact, trying to do so may not earn you respect from members of the culture you are adopting, as imitation can easily be understood as disrespectful mockery. Adoption can also alienate you from those in your native environment. Of course, you can and should adopt some practices of the other culture if they seem to be useful, desirable, comfortable, or satisfying. This decision, however, should be based on thorough engagement with the culture, and with a good sense of your own cultural background and identity. Generally, striving to understand the underpinnings and cultural conditions and factoring them into your consideration, your course of action, and your decisions is sufficient.

Myth 4: It's Really All about Personality

For mapping and understanding differences in communication and interaction styles, the Myers-Briggs Type Indicator and/or DISK profile, both of which are roughly based on Jungian psychology, are tools that are frequently employed to bring about interpersonal self- and other-awareness in managers and leaders. It may be too simplistic to assume that these approaches are sufficient for understanding and explaining differences.

We may think of culture as a force for evaluating and selecting among personality types and characteristics. While the same range of personality types may exist within any given population, a culture's value orientations provide an overall framework for favoring one particular trait over another. For example, we may assume that, in any population, there are roughly the same number of introverts and extroverts. However, in a public- and expressive-oriented cultural environment, behaviors that are commonly associated with extroversion are more favorably viewed, i.e., more ideal, than introverted behaviors.

Applying this cultural vantage point, it is easily seen why a bias toward individual, psychological-based approaches to self- and other-awareness persists in many Western organizations: Culture is a feature of groups, and the organizational bias reflects the focus on individual merits and performance. Such a view of differences based on group affiliation runs counter to the individualistic core belief and value set of these organizations.

UNDERSTANDING THE INTERCULTURAL COMMUNICATION AND INTERACTION PROCESS

Communication is simply the exchange of meaning between individuals. Culture is an integral part of this exchange. This perspective corresponds to Edward T. Hall's definition of culture as a "system for creating, sending, storing and processing information."[4] If this exchange is successful, it involves little loss of meaning, establishes or maintains a relationship, and leaves open the possibility for further exchanges. The most basic goal of communication is transmitting *meaning* as closely as possible to the way it was conceived. The ultimate goal is the creation of synergy,[5] i.e., *the creative output of a whole that is greater than the sum of the individual contributions.*

The intercultural communication and interaction process is most easily conceptualized using the simplified sender-receiver model, in which culture functions as a filter through which we code and decode messages. In the ideal communication process, as depicted in Fig. 5.1, information flows between the sender and the receiver, and the intended message is identical, or very close, to the received message. There is no interference (noise) in the message flow from sender to receiver or in the confirmation flow of feedback from the receiver to the sender. However, all of us know only too well that this communication process is far from what we see in reality, even when no cultural differences exist. When we factor cultural differences into the already difficult communication and interaction process, we become aware of a potentially powerful source of distortion to our interactions. Consider this simple example:

A well-respected arbitrator from India was visiting a U.S. telecommunications company that was involved in an international dispute. The purpose of his visit was to discuss a proposed resolution to the dispute on behalf of his client, the Indian Ministry of Telecommunications. The U.S. company was interested in hearing the proposal, although it wondered why the Indian Ministry did not send a member of its own staff. When lunchtime neared, the arbitrator's host asked him whether he was hungry and said that he would treat him to lunch. The arbitrator declined and subsequently watched his host eat. When he returned to his hotel in the evening, he was both hungry and furious at the disrespect that had been shown him. After all, it was only polite, from his perspective, to decline the first couple of times when food is offered. He had expected his host to offer several times, after which he would hesitatingly

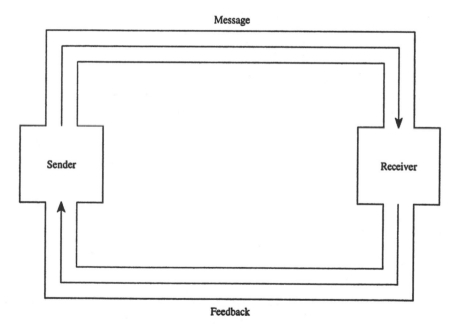

FIGURE 5.1   The ideal communication and interaction process.

accept. When his host did not even offer a second time, he was infuriated. He subsequently had little interest in and motivation for engaging with his host.

Both the arbitrator and his host are exhibiting behavior that rests on a configuration of cultural orientations through which they read, interpret, and react to each other and the situation in which they find themselves. At lunchtime, the arbitrator's *indirectness*, sense of formality, and high-context orientation was mismatched with his host's directness, informality, and pragmatism concerning lunch.

Each person's cultural orientations can be considered to be his or her cultural frames. A *cultural frame* is the perceptual window through which an individual defines him- or herself, others, and the world. The perceptions filtered through the cultural frame are highly selective because each frame contains those classifications, categories, values, and expectations the culture determines to be necessary, relevant, and appropriate. Glass windows can differ in terms of the amount and type of light they let in and the means by which they transform the light into patterns and colors. Our cultural frames perform a similar function. Our physical senses flood us with information, and we can make meaningful sense of it all only by passing it through the selective filters derived from our value orientations embedded in our cultural frame. From birth, we are socialized by parents, schools, church, friends, etc., into supposedly "normal" patterns of thinking, feeling, and behaving.

Mismatched frames can be a significant source of mismatched expectations even before an additional layer of corollaries to cultural frames add "noise" and have an additional distorting effect: They are the contextual and situational components that make the decoding of messages even more difficult (see Fig. 5.2).

In this more realistic formulation of the communication and interaction process, the sender formulates the message in terms of a cultural frame. The receiver interprets the message in light of another cultural frame, then creates feedback based on that frame. The original sender now interprets that feedback from within his or her original frame.

This process is messy, is full of cultural static, and easily leads to a rapid decay of communication. This decay is accelerated by a variety of communication barriers that create "noise" and increase the possibility of further distortion and misunderstanding. With the exception of language, they are not inherently as much a part of the communication and interaction process as the cultural frames. We have some degree of control over them, and their interfering effect can be minimized.

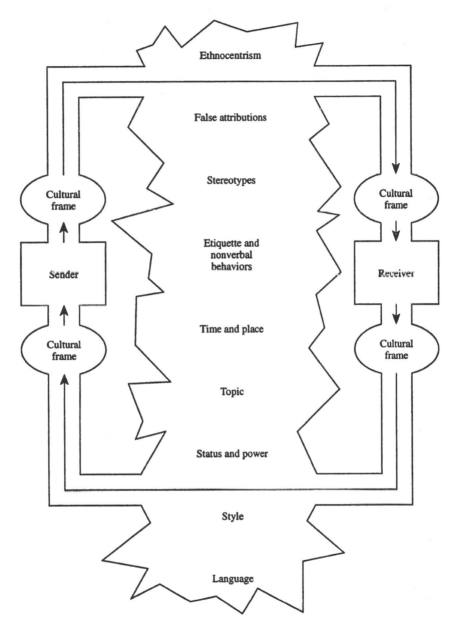

FIGURE 5.2 The real communication and interaction process.

Ethnocentrism

The intense positive and negative feelings—from enchantment and excitement to confusion, fear, and even hate—that many experiences with a different culture can generate often reflect an ethnocentric perspective. *Ethnocentrism* is the evaluation of another culture according to the norms, standards, practices, and expectations of our own culture. Negative ethnocentrism is the belief in the inherent superiority and naturalness of one's own culture and the inferiority of another. Positive ethnocentrism is the opposite, namely the elevation of another culture because of a perception that one's own is inferior or in some way lacking. Either form of ethnocentrism clouds our ability to truly understand and evaluate another culture or its individual members. As our societies become more complex and complicated and as groups from different cultures increasingly come into contact with one another, ethnocentrism becomes a destabilizing element.

We need to continuously reflect on our own emotions, attitudes, and views by asking ourselves, "Why do I feel and think this way? How would I see things if I were in their shoes? What is interesting and valuable in the way they see and do things?" Such questions slow down the judgmental process and provide a breathing space for thought and reflection. The following practices can also help avoid the destructive consequences of ethnocentrism. When experiencing a different culture:

1. Monitor your own emotional reactions. Both positive and negative reactions can give you important insights into your own values.
2. Be curious. Seek to learn all you can about the new culture, and probe into statements, viewpoints, and behaviors.
3. Remember that most people behave rationally; you may have to find the rationale.
4. Try to look at problems and experiences from the other person's point of view. Seeing both sides does not mean you have to agree with, like, or prefer the one that is not yours.
5. Beware of value judgments; they can block understanding.
6. Be forgiving. Accept the fact that you and the others are going to make mistakes and are going to have ethnocentric perspectives.

False Attributions and Inferences

When we witness behavior that differs from our expectations, we try to make sense of it by attributing a cause to it and/or inferring meaning to it. For example, when talking to a report, a manager may evaluate that person as weak and dishonest. This inference may come about because the manager has experienced an unexpected lack of eye contact by the report. If the manager was raised in an environment where parents and teachers often say, "Look at me when I'm talking to you," he or she would have learned to associate eye contact with attention, honesty, and assertiveness. Averted eyes would signal shame, guilt, and subordination. However, such an association would miss the mark if the report associates eye contact with aggressiveness and disrespect.

A manager from Switzerland was sent to South India to present a new performance management system to a group of local managers. He was flustered by the degree of what he took to be disagreement and rejection in the form of side-to-side head shakes that he experienced. In South India, this type of head shake is generally a sign of agreement, encouragement, and engagement. However, since this manager did not know the local significance of this behavior, he could explain it only in terms of his own environment, where a side-to-side head shake carries a negative connotation. This false attribution caused him to become defensive and upset.

Usually such attributions result from our having only a little knowledge about the other culture. We fill in the blanks by inserting our own meanings rather than pursuing additional information. Often, like the Swiss manager, we are not in a situation where we either (1) could pursue the information or (2) would be open to it.

Stereotypes

Often our attributions may be based on stereotypes that we hold about other groups. We talked earlier about how our cultural frame contains specific classifications and categories that organize our experience. Stereotypes are closed categories that leave no room for individual differences or exceptions. Any new information is channeled into the existing category and thus strengthens the category and confirms our existing viewpoint. Sikkema and Niyekawa offer good advice: "Each observation must be kept separate. Labeling and categorizing must be suspended. When certain things are observed repeatedly, when a recurrent pattern is noted, then one may tentatively create a category . . . until one has had enough exposure to and contact with the people of a new culture, no generalizations should be made."[6]

We need to add that our generalizations should be free of value judgments. All too often, stereotypes have their origin in ethnocentric perceptions and explanations of experiences. Stereotypes are resistant relics of ethnocentrism that make cross-cultural understanding difficult. For example, when conducting workshops in the United States, one of the authors often encounters well-intentioned people who comment, "You are not very German!" This statement, if left unchallenged, essentially protects a stereotype. Rather than saying, "I had one image of Germans, but I have to revise it based on my experience with you," they protect their image by defining the actual behavior outside of it.

We need to be aware that we hold stereotypes of others and that others hold stereotypes of us. We also need to understand how cultural orientation patterns and our experience of them may reinforce these stereotypes when we interpret these patterns from an ethnocentric perspective.

Etiquette and Nonverbal Behaviors

The U.S. American gesture for "okay" (touching the index finger to the thumb and making a circle) is an obscene gesture to the Greeks, the Brazilians, and the Turks. Japanese and Indians may point with their middle finger, which is close to an obscene gesture to others. Showing the soles of your feet to a Saudi is a insult, and passing anything with your left hand in some countries is a taboo, as that hand is reserved for personal cleanliness.

Business and social etiquette is a vast topic, and no other area of cross-cultural understanding has been more talked or written about. Understanding the meanings associated with particular gestures, facial expressions, and body positions requires specific knowledge of a culture. It can be a particular problem when the participants in a cross-cultural interaction are of different sexes. For example, the physical closeness of Hispanic or Arab men might be misconstrued as a sexual advance.

There is no substitute for preparing oneself for the vast differences in nonverbal behaviors and forms of social and business etiquette. A number of books and resources that deal with the do's and don'ts for specific countries and regions are available.[7] The following list gives some general guidelines that you may want to integrate into your business practice.

1. Be more polite and formal in a foreign culture than you would be in your own. Stay formal until you are invited to use more familiar terms. It is better to err on the side of formality.
2. Take time to learn names and titles, and their correct pronunciations.
3. If another language is involved, pay attention to your pronunciation; small differences can have dramatic results.
4. Learn the culture's customs regarding the giving of gifts (also know your company's policy toward gift giving as well as any legal restrictions of your own or your host's country).

5. Respect holidays and time-zone differences when scheduling your communication and interactions.

6. Provide appropriate down time for people traveling across time zones and communicating in a language other than their native language.

7. Observe status and power differences. In most cultures it is very important to show deference to and respect for those of higher rank and to recognize hierarchical levels.

8. When entertaining, understand customs in relation to alcohol and appropriate foods. For example, Muslims don't drink alcohol or eat pork, and Hindus don't eat beef.

9. Gauge appropriate conversational topics. In general, avoid voicing strong opinions on a topic that may be internal to a particular culture. Ask for clarification and explanation, and use open-ended questions.

Language

Language is perhaps the greatest barrier of all, even when all the participants in a cross-cultural encounter supposedly speak the same language. For example, in a meeting between British and U.S. American managers, one of the British managers may say, "And I'd like to *table* another item." The Americans think that she wants to postpone talking about that issue or put it aside altogether. Instead, she wants to bring it to their attention.

Many U.S. and European companies readily assume that English is the language of global business and have declared it their official language. However, if the 350 million native speakers of English sometimes experience their shared language as a barrier, for the estimated 1.5 billion people worldwide who are everyday users of English although it is not their first language, the barrier is even more complicated. For one thing, speakers of English as a foreign language, or "offshore English," often superimpose the grammar, syntax, and vocabulary of English onto their native language. In many cases, English words are used in an entirely different context. For example, in continental Europe, the word *benefits* is often used for profit and the word *cost* for expenses, and Germans know their mobile phone as a "handy." The filtering of English through the native language entails more than the use of different words: The native language thus modified remains the capsule for a worldview and the source and vehicle for humor and the expression of attitude, disposition, and emotion.

In a business world in which English is increasingly becoming the lingua franca, both native and nonnative speakers share responsibility for minimizing the barriers that language can pose. The following list summarizes some of the practices associated with this responsibility:

- Avoid jargon, slang, idiomatic expressions, contractions, and colloquialisms.
- Avoid long sentences, double negatives, and negative wording.
- Seek clarification and definition when you do not understand something.
- Assist others to acquire and improve their language skills.
- Actively build goodwill and survival skills in a variety of languages.
- Be aware of your accent and pronunciation and, if necessary, make an effort to enhance your understandability by enunciating more clearly, speaking more slowly, or reducing your accent.
- Invite feedback on the clarity of your speech.
- When using an interpreter:

  Prepare the interpreter in advance. Make sure that he or she understands the subject matter and your objectives.

  Speak in a clear, slow voice and be concise.

  Avoid obscure or difficult words.

  Repeat key ideas in different ways.

  Divide what you have to say into small chunks.

  Allow ample time for the interpreter to clarify points.

  Never interrupt the interpreter.

- Use spoken and written media to communicate, reinforce, and clarify your message.

We have briefly identified some of the barriers to effective communication and interaction that may create significant "noise" and make it difficult to transmit our message, even when our cultural frames are congruent. We now turn to the fundamental problem of understanding the dynamics of incongruent cultural frames.

UNDERSTANDING CULTURAL FRAMES

Cultural orientations configure powerful *frames* through which a sender and receiver interpret and filter signs, symbols, and data. If these cultural filters are partially or fully incongruent, the received message will almost certainly be different from the intended one, setting in motion a communication or interaction process in which each party is often highly dissatisfied. We call incongruence between frames a *culture gap*.[8] We may call the dissatisfaction and discomfort that is created by culture gaps and that is amplified by ethnocentrism, false attribution, language, or other barriers *social distance*.[9] If left unattended, cultural gaps lead to the escalation or widening of social distance and missed opportunities for understanding and synergy. Figure 5.3 expresses this dynamic.

Social distance is an experience on the behavioral, cognitive, and/or emotional level that we either externalize or internalize. The incident involving the U.S. host and the Indian arbitrator is a good illustration. The experience of social distance was probably entirely on the arbitrator's side, as he did not externalize—i.e., show or articulate to his host—his emotional (anger) and cognitive (judgment of impoliteness and disrespect) reaction. This is a highly

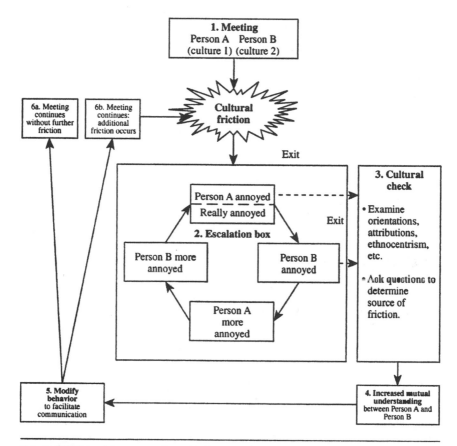

Source: © Training Management Corp. (TMC), *Doing Business Internationally: The Cross-Cultural Challenges,* Seminar Coursebook (Princeton, NJ, 1992).

FIGURE 5.3   Escalation box.

significant aspect of intercultural communication and interaction processes—we are not aware of the full extent to which social distance is a factor in our interactions. Out of a sense of politeness, propriety, and professionalism, the arbitrator would not even communicate a hint of his reaction. From the host's perspective, no cultural gap or social distance may have been apparent, so that this important dimension of their interaction was entirely hidden and inaccessible.

In our experience, these internalized experiences of social distance are the most common results of cultural gaps and products of the hidden consequences of culture. Too often, our repeated experiences lead us to dispositions and judgments that reinforce stereotypes and are erosive to building good relationships, effective collaboration, and desired outcomes.

Sales situations provide a good venue for studying the effects of social distance. Let us imagine two people from two different cultures: A is a salesperson, and B is a customer. The differences in cultural frames may manifest themselves as follows:

A: "And what's more, this little device will cut through that mountain like a knife through butter."

B: "But I don't want to build a road through the mountain. I want a road that blends in with the natural landscape and doesn't disrupt the animal sanctuary. To cut through this mountain would be very wrong."

In this scenario, the salesperson assumes a control orientation; the potential customer, however, has a harmony orientation. If this harmony orientation is articulated (externalized), as in this example, and if the salesperson is astute enough to understand it, he or she may adjust the presentation so that it is more appropriate.

A: "Boy, I wish I could get his attention. I've never known such a rude person. Why doesn't he tell his father to call back after the meeting?"

B: "Why is he looking so upset? Interruptions are a fact of life. And I must see to my father's needs before anyone else's."

Here the mismatch between the customer's multifocused orientation and the single-focused expectation of the salesperson creates the experience of social distance for both, making each less positively disposed to the other.

A: "When I set up this sales meeting to begin at 10 o'clock, I assumed that it would begin at 10 o'clock, not 10:55. I've got other appointments to get to. Unbelievable!"

B: "Typical! Always in a hurry to get somewhere else. Does he think I'm just another customer who will make do with 'Hello. Buy this. Goodbye'? I've lived without this gadget all my life; what's the rush now? Please take the time necessary to do this properly.'"

In this scenario, there is a mismatch between the salesperson's fixed time orientation and universalistic approach and the customer's fluid time orientation and particularistic approach. Again, if the customer's orientation is articulated or expressed, the salesperson, if skilled, may be able to adjust his or her approach. If the customer's response is internalized, an inability to close the sale will be a direct consequence. And the salesperson is likely to attribute the missed sale to a "difficult customer" rather than to his or her inability to adjust to the customer's cultural frame.

We have mentioned several times that it is critical to develop culture-based self- and other-awareness and to understand how to convert this awareness into a specific set of skills. This will enable us not only to understand the intricate dynamics of reducing ethnocentrism, but also to navigate the many challenges associated with intercultural communication and interactions.

EXPLORING YOUR CULTURAL FRAME

To explore your personal cultural frame and its effect on your business and management environment, you need to identify and analyze the pattern of cultural orientations that characterizes your interactions. To enable this type of *cultural positioning*, we have developed the Cultural Orientations Indicator (COI).[10] The COI is a tool for assessing your workplace preferences along the continua of the Cultural Orientations Model. It is available to you in its Web-based format.

With this profile, you are ready to engage in self-validation, impact analysis, and identification of the origin of your cultural orientations. We have summarized here the most salient features of our findings on cultural orientations in interactions.

For each cultural orientation, we have provided a general description of the behavior of people with that orientation. We also list common behavioral identifiers that we have been able to associate with a given orientation. Acquiring the ability to link these identifiers with cultural orientations provides you with a framework for observing a counterpart's behavior and forming hypotheses about that counterpart's cultural frame.

Read through the following summaries, indicate which ones you think apply to you, and note your thoughts and reflections. When you engage in this activity, please keep the following in mind:

1. Your COI profile is a cultural profile, not a personality profile. This means that the results are not meant to describe you in general terms. The profile seeks to identify your tendencies, i.e., the cultural underpinnings of your behavior in business and management contexts. Your profile may be entirely different in a social and/or family context.

2. The profile is a way of personalizing cultural dimensions and revealing how your preferences may match those of others and also match what is expected, reinforced, and rewarded in your organization and work environment. It is not uncommon for people to observe that several of their preferences run counter to the behaviors that make them successful in their organization. By comparing your preferences with those of your social group, organization, team, etc., you may be able to determine your degree of cultural fit with your environment. As a result of this analysis, many managers have been able to explain their subjective experiences of stress, tension, anxiety, and performance problems as well as their successes.

3. Recognizing the importance of understanding the individual in interaction as the agency of culture, the COI allows you to investigate the underpinnings of your own behavior and analyze the culture that you are likely to create and reinforce within your sphere of influence. This is particularly important for leadership of people, teams, and departments.

4. You should pay particular attention to those orientations that you see as being strong or very strong. They may exert a particularly powerful influence on your behavior, especially when you are under stress, tension, and performance pressure. Cultural differences may appear insignificant as long as people do not work together under pressure. Only when you are under pressure are your cultural orientations likely to emerge, and conflicts may then unexpectedly erupt.

Dimension: Environment; Orientation: Control

You are a strong believer in the saying "Where there's a will, there's a way," and you believe that your destiny is primarily in your own hands. When you encounter a problem, you immediately look for a solution. You approach the world with a natural sense of empowerment. You view very few problems as insurmountable. You have a need for individual ownership of tasks and problems in your immediate environment.

You often assume that the objects and people surrounding you should conform to your preferred approach, methods, and processes. You tend to be proactive, self-driven, and assertive, and you find that you naturally take initiative. You want to take charge of situations and do not shy away from conflict and risk. You get frustrated with people who do not seem actively engaged in problem solving, do not share your sense of priorities, or seem to lack initiative.

People with this orientation frequently

- Are among the first ones in a group of equals to assume a leadership role.
- Display a high degree of optimism when confronting a problem.
- Trust in, value, and emphasize pragmatic tools and techniques.
- Advocate personal accountability and risk taking.
- Use declarative statements and closed (yes or no) questions with high frequency when speaking.
- Display impatience with intangible and vague statements, assessments, and evaluations.

Dimension: Environment; Orientation: Harmony

Maintaining a balanced relationship with your social, natural, and physical environment is important to you. You adjust your style and approach to the expectations and conditions of your surroundings in order to bring about balance.

Decision making and consensus building with all parties involved in an interaction are key values that drive your behavior in social as well as business environments. Establishing and maintaining positive relationships is of key importance to you. You tend to avoid conflict and direct confrontation. You value flexibility and diplomacy, and you expect others to do the same. When you propose a new idea or make plans, you readily assume that a compromise will be required. You dislike radical change and champion the careful contemplation and testing of innovative solutions.

People with this orientation may be identified by

- A frequent use of qualifiers and open-ended questions when speaking.
- Very gradual self-disclosure as relationships become more firmly established.
- A high degree of (visible) distress in confrontational situations.
- A frequently expressed need to assume the role of facilitator and mediator.

Dimension: Environment; Orientation: Constraint

You feel that you must live and act within the given limits of your environment. You see the world as immutable and trust that, in the larger scheme of things, situations will generally work out. You see it as presumptuous, even naïve, to claim direct control over organizational and/or business environments.

You often perceive problems or resistance to your ideas or goals as obstacles that cannot be overcome. You generally accept the status quo and adjust your own behavior and expectations to the limits that are presented to you. You do not feel naturally empowered to alter those limits in any way.

Your approach to problems and situations is often reactive and risk-averse. You prefer to behave cautiously and/or to have clear instructions and guidelines. You expect superiors or people in power to make decisions on your behalf.

People with this orientation may be identified by

- Their frequent references to and caution with respect to problems, obstacles, and risks.
- Their frequent requests for clear instructions and guidance.
- Their use of passives and negative sentence structures.
- Their references to preestablished procedures, processes, and guidelines as binding and immutable.

Dimension: Time; Orientation: Single Focus

You prefer to work on one thing at a time, and so you break down your work into a series of tasks and handle them sequentially. You tend to have a high commitment to schedules, which you see as effective tools for ordering tasks. You are generally analytical in your approach to problem solving. You consider it impolite or unprofessional to talk to several people simultaneously about different things.

People with this orientation may

- Become irritated when they are required to focus on multiple things and interactions at the same time.
- Make an effort to sequence and structure tasks and work flow.
- Compartmentalize and organize their work and personal space.
- Display frustration when plans and projects have to be disrupted at the last minute.

Dimension: Time; Orientation: Multifocus

You prefer to work on a variety of tasks and/or relationships at the same time. You are not likely to be disturbed by unpredictable and unscheduled events.

You seek dynamism in your environment, and you welcome change. You tend to be easily bored when you are asked to concentrate on one issue exclusively. People with this orientation may

- Frequently engage in multiple activities at the same time, e.g., write letters while conducting a telephone conversation.
- Bring up issues that are not related to the main topic.
- Become visibly irritated when they are forced to pay exclusive attention to one person, issue, or question for an extended period of time.
- Express feelings of boredom when they have to devote themselves to only one person, issue, or question.

Dimension: Time; Orientation: Fixed

For you, events are critically determined and affected by time. You value time highly and feel that it needs to be controlled and managed. You think of time as consisting of precisely defined and discrete chunks. Punctuality is important to you. Good time management defines much of your behavior, and you tend to view this as a critical professional attribute. To your way of thinking, planning and preparation are intricately connected to time. You take schedules, deadlines, and commitments very seriously.

People with this orientation may be identified by

- Their frequent mention of and reference to time and time constraints.
- A propensity for planning and scheduling.
- The need to structure events precisely.
- Their irritability when planned activities and priorities take longer than expected.

Dimension: Time; Orientation: Fluid

You recognize time as an important framework for life's events, but you do not feel the need to control and manage it precisely. You do not believe that time can or should be tightly defined and tracked. You generally see time lines and deadlines as expressions of intent, but you do not feel bound by them during work processes and events.

You focus on what happens within a period of time, and you let situations and events rather than schedules determine your course of action. You focus on the people with whom you are interacting and/or the tasks with which you are involved, and you feel that it is imperative to deal with them or meet their needs before you focus on other issues. You have an open-ended approach to planning.

People with this orientation frequently

- Emphasize the requirements of situations and relationships in determining business processes.
- Treat schedules and time lines as approximate.
- Show up late to meetings and turn in work later than expected.
- Fail to understand the frustration experienced by individuals with more of a fixed time orientation.
- Express a preference for spontaneity and a resistance to long-term planning.

Dimension: Time; Orientation: Past

You look to the past as a guide and model for your present and future behavior. You tend to judge plans and changes according to whether or not they adhere to tradition. Continuity with the past is of great concern to you, and your behavior is guided by the need to preserve consistency. You have an intuitive sense of the importance of history, and you value the achievements of previous generations. You may experience change as threatening. You are not easily intrigued by novelties, and you require a relatively long period of time to assess and evaluate situations and opportunities. You see precedents and past successes as important in solving problems and making decisions.

People with this orientation frequently

- Exude a sense of stability.
- Allude to past models and traditions.
- Voice concern over a lack of stability and continuity with the past.
- Display skepticism in the face of novel ideas, novel concepts, and proposed changes.

Dimension: Time; Orientation: Present

You are guided by concerns about the present and the short-term future. You are motivated by promises of quick results and returns. You prefer handling immediate day-to-day problems or crises. Your planning is based on the demands of the moment, and you tend to have a keen sense of the requirements that affect your business today. You are a skilled crisis manager and a good tactician.

People with this orientation may frequently

- Emphasize present opportunities.
- Seem rushed.
- Emphasize immediate results and short-term profits and payoffs to the exclusion of long-term benefits.
- Seem irritated with or critical of requests for long-term plans and projections.

Dimension: Time; Orientation: Future

You are guided by concern for the long-term future. You tend to base planning and problem solving on long-term projections. You evaluate the present in terms of its potential effect on the future and judge ideas based on their benefits over the long term.

You have little problem envisioning a future that is radically different from both the past and the present. Indeed, your actions in the present are often motivated by the desire to attain this different future. You welcome and frequently champion change, but only if you are confident that it will be profitable and beneficial in the long run.

People with this orientation frequently

- Voice concerns about the long-term impact of decisions.
- Are preoccupied with the future and articulate a long-range vision.
- Exhibit high tolerance for frustration and are not thrown off course by setbacks.

Dimension: Action; Orientation: Being

In your interactions, you are guided by a concern for building and maintaining good relationships with those around you. You are motivated by good, trusting interpersonal relations, and you expect that building such relationships is a function of time, experience with the other person, and incremental self-disclosure. For you, relationship building often takes precedence over accomplishing tasks quickly.

You may have a need to surround yourself with a circle of trusted individuals. When you meet new people in business, you require a relatively long "warmup" period. You are careful not to extend your trust too quickly. You consider it important that individuals establish their credibility and reliability. Before taking action, you need time to contemplate and reflect. You tend to scrutinize issues carefully. You do not jump to conclusions or take action quickly or lightly, and you feel that it is important that decisions be well founded and well grounded.

People with this orientation frequently

- Invest considerable time and effort in building relationships.
- Are skeptical of unfamiliar people.
- Approach new social and/or business situations cautiously.
- Prepare their activities well and do not jump into action.
- Require a lot of information and consultation before making a decision.

Dimension: Action; Orientation: Doing

In interactions, you focus on accomplishing tasks quickly and tend to empha-size measurable achievements. You are pragmatic in your approach to com-pleting tasks, making decisions, and building relationships. You view business relationships as functional; they exist to get a task done. Once your counter-parts have signaled their interest in doing business with you, you extend trust readily in order to focus on the speedy accomplishment of tasks. You may not expect relationships to last beyond the particular task to be accomplished.

When contemplating actions and activities, you seek the quickest and shortest path to accomplishing particular tasks and achieving preconceived goals. You often feel that any action is better than inaction. You are generally comfortable with making a decision or mapping a course of action even when detailed information is not available. You locate required resources easily, and you tend to be a pragmatic, quick, and effective problem solver.

People with this orientation frequently

- Focus exclusively on "getting the job done" rather than on furthering a relationship with the people who are performing a given task.
- End relationships with others once the task that led to the relationship is completed.
- Make decisions swiftly and focus on the speedy implementation of a plan.
- Get impatient when asked to contemplate and consider issues at length and in detail.

Dimension: Communication; Orientation: High Context

As a high-context communicator, you hold symbolism and propriety in high esteem and value behavior more than words. You are very sensitive to a wide array of situational components and tend to extract meaning from a wide variety of sources. You rely on nonverbal, symbolic, and situational cues more than on spoken and written cues. You value the indirect and artful use of language, and you tend to imply rather than state what you mean. In order to get work done, you require a lot of contextual information about those with whom you are communicating and/or conducting business.

Individuals with this orientation frequently

- Distinguish themselves by excellent observational and listening skills.
- Have well-developed interactional acuity and astuteness.
- Are concerned with how others may interpret situations and often ask for others' interpretations of a given situation.
- Communicate in a detail-oriented manner and attach great significance to nonverbal elements of communication.
- Are conscientious and sensitive to the total effect of all aspects of situations and interactions.

Dimension: Communication; Orientation: Low Context

As a low-context communicator, you value words and documentation. You explicitly state what you mean, and you tend to view language pragmatically and use it with precision. For you, successful communication is directly tied to the literal meaning of the words used. You tend to value the processes of choosing and interpreting words. You see written messages and detailed documentation as having more value and significance than information that is conveyed orally or personally. You need little contextual information about those with whom you communicate and/or conduct business. You place great value on good and precise oral and written communication skills and the maintenance of records.

Individuals with this orientation frequently

- Require that meaningful and significant information be recorded meticulously.
- Are good record keepers.
- Are prolific writers.
- Ask for and provide explicit confirmation of their understanding of interactions and situations.
- Show little appreciation for symbolism and metaphors.

Dimension: Communication; Orientation: Direct

You tend to handle conflict in a direct and explicit manner. You generally see conflict situations as impersonal issues that need to be addressed openly and face to face in order to reach resolution. You believe that conflicts can be positive and constructive and that most of them can be resolved quickly. In general, you are not deeply disturbed when tensions run high. You appreciate the benefits of bringing contentious issues out into the open. For you, direct conflict management is intricately tied to the notion of honesty and trustworthiness.

Individuals with this orientation frequently

- Address problems and conflicts explicitly and immediately.
- Use words to identify and address problems or contentious issues.
- Evaluate indirect methods of managing conflict negatively.

Dimension: Communication; Orientation: Indirect

You tend to handle conflict in an implicit way by avoiding direct confrontations. Minimizing the surface appearance of conflict and criticism is important to you. Generally, you see conflictual situations as threats to your personal integrity, dignity, and/or "face."

Preserving and saving face, personal dignity, and integrity so as to prevent possible embarrassments are overriding concerns for you in interactions. You may prefer passive resistance or the use of formal or informal mediators (lawyers, arbitrators, colleagues, friends, etc.) to address, manage, and resolve contentious issues for you. You believe that open conflicts are not beneficial to the parties involved. Openly displayed tensions can disturb you deeply.

Individuals with this orientation frequently

- Avoid making and addressing critical comments and challenging remarks in public situations.
- Express their true thoughts and feelings about issues and people only to trusted colleagues and friends.
- Implicitly or explicitly expect others to facilitate conflict resolution on their behalf.
- Use implicit, nonverbal, and/or contextual ways to communicate disagreement, frustration, and/or anger.

Dimension: Communication; Orientation: Expressive

As an expressive communicator, you value demonstrative expression in the workplace. In fact, work is an emotional experience for you. Emotional expression and expressiveness play an integral role in convincing and persuading the people with whom you work to adopt a particular point of view. It is important for you to see emotional responses to work issues from your counterparts, subordinates, and superiors.

You expect both positive and negative emotions to run high in the work environment. You may even require a constant ebb and flow of emotions in order to remain motivated. You tend to be quite animated in your use of words and body language, and you may even seek and expect physical contact with others. You evaluate the credibility and trustworthiness of coworkers and business partners on the basis of their display of human qualities, which you associate primarily with an open display and expression of emotions and passions.

Style and eloquence may also be critically important to you. You may feel that the display of your personal and professional competence significantly depends on your ability to express ideas and opinions artfully through the use of similes, metaphors, and allegories. Your favorable evaluation of others may be linked to your impression of their stylistic sophistication.

Individuals with this orientation frequently

- Display positive and negative emotions openly.
- Distinguish themselves through a high degree of empathy.
- Make emotional appeals in order to convince and persuade colleagues and clients that their point of view is correct.
- Appear spontaneous when it is not warranted.
- Use rather complex sentence structures.
- Respond well to metaphors and similes and use them in presentations and/or speeches.

Dimension: Communication; Orientation: Instrumental

As an instrumental communicator, you value factual, objective, and pragmatic exchanges of information. You see communication as problem- or issue-centered, impersonal, and goal-oriented. You prefer an emotionally detached way of presenting information in order to persuade your coworkers and clients to share your perspective on a given matter. You tend to have limited tolerance for displays of emotion in the workplace. Emotional expressiveness in others may lead you to doubt their professionalism, credibility, and trustworthiness. You often see work relationships as qualitatively different from social relationships, and you evaluate individuals at work on the basis of their direct and measurable contributions to business.

Individuals with this orientation frequently

- Use a relatively pragmatic and "dry" vocabulary.
- Limit body language in business interactions.
- Become visibly irritated and/or impatient with emotional displays in the workplace.
- Show little appreciation for eloquence of style.

Dimension: Communication; Orientation: Formal

Observing specific rules of etiquette and protocol in the workplace and in business situations is important to you. This need is particularly strong in your interactions with superiors. You also expect subordinates to be mindful of etiquette when they interact with you. You feel that observing decorum establishes credibility, respect, and sincerity.

Overall, you see formalities, social conventions, and customs as conducive to communication as well as to the development of business and social relationships. You feel uncomfortable in informal business environments, and you may perceive informality as communicating a lack of respect for you, your position, and your endeavors. You see a lack of formality in others as indicative of a lack of professionalism, education, and social graces. You tend to be keenly aware of the social structures within which you operate. You value respectful interactions.

Individuals with this orientation frequently

- Carry an aura of seriousness into the workplace and business interactions.
- Dress according to formal, conservative, or traditional conventions of the social environment.
- Refrain from using colloquial language and adhere to rules of grammar.
- Are sensitive to proper forms of address.

Dimension: Communication; Orientation: Informal

You value casual, relaxed, and friendly conduct in the workplace and business situations. You feel that etiquette, decorum, and tradition establish an undesirable distance between people. For you, credibility, trustworthiness, and sincerity are intimately tied to a friendly, casual, and jovial style.

You see formalities, social conventions, and social customs as unnecessary and as insurmountable barriers to good communication and solving problems. You are uncomfortable in formal situations, and you feel alienated and excluded when others maintain social distance from you through the use of rules and decorum. You may feel uncomfortable participating in traditional customs and rituals.

You tend to value a free, open, and uncensored flow of opinions and thoughts. You emphasize flexibility and spontaneity and an appearance of basic equality between the people in a business relationship.

Individuals with this orientation frequently

- Are clearly unconcerned with protocol and etiquette.
- Appear uncomfortable in situations that require the heeding of rules of decorum and protocol.
- Exhibit a desire to feel comfortable and relaxed in business situations.

Dimension: Space; Orientation: Private

Cultures with a private orientation to space may place distance between people through separate offices, seating arrangements, or the size of the room. Such cultures place an emphasis on closed-door meetings with minimal interruptions. People prefer to stand farther apart and tend not to touch during conversation. People with a private orientation to space prefer a task-oriented approach to communicating with others and select locations that enhance their ability to solve problems and reach agreement. The use of technology for communications may be expected and emphasized for sharing information across long distances. These cultures may require more decentralization and empowerment of individuals because managers cannot supervise the daily activities of subordinates who are separated by location, distance, or geography.

The difference between private and public orientations to space can also lead to a difference in what information will be shared or not shared among members of a group. People with a private space orientation tend to share information on a "need to know" basis. Office arrangements that separate people and job tasks may lead to less information sharing, even if everyone is connected through communications technology (email, voice mail, groupware, etc.).

Individuals with this orientation frequently

- Spend time by themselves and seek seclusion.
- Avoid close proximity to and physical contact with others.
- Clearly establish and define physical boundaries in the work environment.
- Apologize when they intrude on the space of another (e.g., "I am sorry to disturb you").

- Feel a need to schedule appointments with people who work in their immediate vicinity in order to avoid disturbing them unexpectedly.
- Reject participation in or appear visibly uncomfortable at public events.

Dimension: Space; Orientation: Public

Office space in cultures with a public orientation to space may seem overly small, crowded, and noisy. Such cultures place an emphasis on open-door meetings with frequent interruptions. People prefer to stand closer together and tend to touch when communicating. People with a public orientation to space prefer a relationship-oriented approach to communicating with others and select locations that enhance the development of trust and rapport. While technology is utilized for communications, it may not replace the need for face-to-face meetings or the informal exchange of information among people. These cultures may establish control over larger office spaces through the centralization of work activities and decision making, which ensures that performance and progress can be monitored.

The difference between private and public orientations to space can also lead to a difference in what information will be shared or not shared among members of a group. People with a public space orientation tend to share information on a "nice to know" basis with those members who belong to their work or social group. Office spaces that group people together in one large room and require daily interaction and a sharing of resources can lead to more information being shared among group members on a personal and informal basis. While communications technology is available to everyone, it may not be the preferred method of sharing information between a boss and subordinates.

Individuals with this orientation frequently

- Engage in physical contact (touching, embracing, etc.).
- Seek out public social environments.
- Stand close to others when interacting with them.

Dimension: Power; Orientation: Hierarchy

You assume that society and organizations must be socially stratified in order to function properly. As a result, you assume that different people have qualitatively different values, as well as different rights and responsibilities. Titles, ranks, position, and/or age bestow authority and status on individuals, and these individuals must be respected by people at lower ranks.

You may feel that it is important to show respect and deference openly and to acknowledge "power distance" by using appropriate forms of address that reinforce hierarchical structures and social status. For you, it is not acceptable to bypass formal lines of authority in order to complete a task.

You prefer to work in organizations that maintain demarcated lines of power and authority, and in which work is performed according to the specifications of superiors. You require clear job descriptions that indicate detailed job expectations.

Individuals with this orientation frequently

- Surround themselves with objects that connote status and power.
- Tell a superior what he or she wants to hear, not what they really think.
- Emphasize and display evidence of their educational achievements.
- Use declarative or imperative expressions.
- Do not contradict a superior publicly or privately.
- Refrain from offering personal opinions to a superior about key decisions.
- Express outrage when coworkers behave in ways that show disrespect for people with higher status or position.

Dimension: Power; Orientation: Equality

You assume that everyone has the same essential value, rights, responsibilities, and social status. You tend to downplay, minimize, or even hide economic and social differences, both at work and in your personal life. It is important to you that everyone is included and has the same opportunities. You tend to be sensitive to the needs of everyone in a situation.

You feel that it is acceptable to bypass formal lines of authority in order to get things done. You may also feel uneasy with and irritated by official titles and forms of address that reinforce hierarchical structures. You generally prefer to work within a "flat" organizational structure.

Individuals with this orientation frequently

- Use open-ended questions when making requests of subordinates.
- Downplay their own formal title and ignore others'.
- Start relationships informally.
- Stress that everyone's opinion is valued.
- Display irritation or even outrage when they observe deferential or status-conscious behavior.
- Feel comfortable contradicting their superiors, both publicly and privately.
- Offer personal opinions to a superior about key decisions.

Dimension: Individualism; Orientation: Individualistic

You are driven and motivated primarily by your own personal interests, accomplishments, and potential. You make decisions and take action on the basis of what is best for you, following your own wishes and judgment. You require and expect your environment to provide you with a great degree of personal choice.

You expect every individual to be primarily responsible for him- or herself. You embrace conflict between individuals as the natural way in which people assert their personal interests, reach their goals, and meet their needs.

You value personal independence, prize individual achievements, and expect to be recognized and rewarded for your contributions and achievements. You value and admire self-driven, determined, and self-motivated individuals.

Individuals with this orientation frequently

- Discuss themselves and their motivation and interests.
- Emphasize the first person singular when proposing ideas (e.g., "I think . . .").
- Act and make decisions without informing or preparing others.
- Decrease their interest in and contribution to activities when the personal benefits become less obvious to them.
- Do not appear to consider the impact of their decisions and actions on others.
- View teams as a temporary collection of individuals.
- Object to and resist predetermined structures and processes.
- Maintain a loose relationship with others in their larger social environment.

Dimension: Individualism; Orientation: Collectivistic

You are driven and motivated primarily by your affiliation to groups and/or organizations. You make decisions on the basis of what is best for your organization and determine your actions on the basis of what the organization expects of you. You prefer to make decisions by building group consensus, and you expect groups and organizations to take care of their constituents. You tend to consider open conflict to be negative and disruptive to group functioning, and so you avoid it or minimize any potential for its occurrence. You value close interdependence and prize the accomplishment of groups. You are uncomfortable in situations in which you are isolated from the group, are individually rewarded for your efforts, or have to make decisions by yourself. You have a strong sense of loyalty to your chosen organizations. You assimilate corporate/organizational goals and characteristics as your own, and you have a strong sense of social responsibility and obligation.

Individuals with this orientation frequently

- Require meetings to process information and make decisions.
- Do not decide on an action quickly or by themselves.
- Seek feedback from others.
- Feel personally offended when the group or organization is criticized.
- Show great concern for the impact of decisions and events on the group or organization.
- Use the first person plural when referring to business processes, accomplishments, and goals.
- Defend decisions made by their group, even if they had no role in the decisions.
- View themselves as a permanent extension of a group or organization and expect security from the organization, while offering loyalty in return.

Dimension: Individualism; Orientation: Universalistic

Your judgments and actions are guided by an abstract sense of fairness and of right and wrong. You value the equal application of standard rules, principles, and processes. You believe that everyone has essentially the same rights and responsibilities, regardless of his or her particular circumstances. Your sense of obligation is primarily tied to rules and not to individuals.

You dislike favoritism and view fairness as an essential component of integrity and professionalism. You expect people to submit to general guidelines.

Individuals with this orientation frequently

- Refer to universally applicable rules, standards, and principles when assessing situations.
- Seek to establish rules and processes when solving problems.
- Resort to formalized methods of problem resolution (e.g., lawsuits).
- Expect consistent behavior from others in a wide range of situations.
- Strongly believe that there is one "truth" and/or one "right way."

Dimension: Individualism; Orientation: Particularistic

Your sense of obligation centers primarily around your family and your social network. You have a strong sense of your own uniqueness. Trust in and obligations to those in your network tend to determine your decisions. You are very loyal to the people in your network, and you expect loyalty from them in return.

You may respect formal rules and procedures for conduct, but you tend to think that they do not apply to you. You value and encourage uniqueness and the careful consideration of particular circumstances. You tend to view norms, rules, and procedures as expressions of intent and loose guidelines, not as binding regulations. You value the ability to adapt your behavior and approach to the requirements of the situation.

Individuals with this orientation frequently

- Emphasize the unique and particular circumstances of a given situation.
- Make exceptions to norms, rules, or procedures.
- Assume that rules and norms do not apply to them.
- Accentuate their uniqueness through unconventional behaviors and/or accessories.
- Visibly display their membership in a particular group.
- Believe that there are multiple truths and a variety of acceptable ways of doing things.

Dimension: Competitiveness; Orientation: Competitive

You generally assume that employees compete with one another for recognition and rewards. You value achievement and results. Personal ambition and assertiveness are important to you. Harmonious teamwork, consensus building, and the development of mutually beneficial interdependencies are not powerful motivators for your behavior and actions.

Individuals with this orientation frequently

- Assert their opinions and desires.
- Emphasize achievement, results, and goals.
- Display and underscore their achievement through material possessions and personal accessories.

Dimension: Competitiveness; Orientation: Cooperative

You seek harmonious and mutually supportive, even familial, relationships with colleagues and coworkers. You expect to build strong and trusting relationships with work associates. Maintaining and nurturing long-term relationships built on trust is important to you. You tend to be strongly team- and group-oriented, and you place great value on conforming with established norms, patterns, and procedures.

Individuals with this orientation frequently

- Emphasize the importance of process and balance.
- Spend a lot of time building and maintaining relationships.
- Avoid behaviors that make them conspicuous or that call attention to them in any way.
- Seek consensus in decision making.

Dimension: Structure; Orientation: Order

You tend to feel comfortable with clearly defined parameters and guidelines for actions and work activities. You prefer to have a precisely defined job description that explicitly states what is expected of you. You expect the work environment to be stable. You value rules, regulations, and systematic procedures that are consistently applied. Predictability and security are appealing to you. You tend to feel threatened by irregularity, uncertainty, and change. Your need to avoid risk and seek predictability and stability guides your decision making and problem solving.

Individuals with this orientation frequently

- Emphasize the need for stability, consistency, predictability, and the containment of risk.
- Require a lot of information, data, and time for contemplation in order to make decisions.
- Create elaborate contingency plans.
- Create and look to rules, systems, and structures as solutions to problems.
- Are irritated, insecure, and frustrated in situations that are unpredictable or ambiguous, or that require improvisation and spontaneity.
- Resist and avoid change.

Dimension: Structure; Orientation: Flexibility

You expect the conditions of your work to change, and you are willing to adjust your behavior, activities, and priorities accordingly. You value innovative and unconventional ways of doing things and are open to new behavior patterns. You tend to view change and risk as an opportunity for growth. You are not threatened by shifting parameters or by unpredictable and ambiguous situations. You are comfortable in situations that require you to take risks, improvise, or be spontaneous. You tend to value and strive for innovation and adaptability.

Individuals with this orientation frequently

- Deemphasize the need for detailed preparation before meetings, presentations, and negotiations.
- Trust their ability to "make things work" without preparation.
- Emphasize the positive nature of risk and change.
- Seek out innovation and new, unconventional ways of doing things.
- Challenge the status quo.

Dimension: Thinking; Orientation: Inductive

You are interested in the details and particular components of situations and circumstances. In other words, you emphasize the specific over the general. You expect patterns and principles to emerge from situations, and you readily assume that these patterns and principles will serve as rough guides for planning actions and activities. You are generally detail-oriented, and you emphasize the careful analysis and interpretation of data. Abstract theories and principles mean relatively little to you if they do not emerge from individual circumstances and do not support a pragmatic approach to handling issues.

Individuals with this orientation frequently

- Focus and comment on the details of a situation.
- Are interested in discussing case studies rather than theories.
- Emphasize application.
- Are impatient with discussions of abstract theories and principles.
- Ask for examples to illustrate a given idea.

Dimension: Thinking; Orientation: Deductive

You focus primarily on theories, abstract concepts, and principles rather than on the details of a situation. In other words, your thinking moves from the general to the specific. You tend to evaluate the quality and soundness of a presentation or proposal on the basis of the concepts upon which it rests. You become frustrated when the conceptual foundation is not readily apparent or sufficiently developed. You tend to scrutinize and debate conceptual frameworks and key principles before applying them to individual situations. In addition, you frequently introduce new ideas by outlining and discussing the underlying principles and theories rather than by focusing on their application to particular scenarios.

Individuals with this orientation frequently

- Comment on, critique, and question the soundness of theories on an abstract level.
- Present theories, concepts, and models before describing particular cases.
- Deemphasize application and implementation.
- Become impatient and frustrated with case studies and anecdotes.

Dimension: Thinking; Orientation: Linear

You prefer to approach issues and problems from an analytical perspective. A holistic, systemic presentation of problems and issues can be very frustrating for you. You tend to look for ways to identify discrete components and map primary cause-and-effect relationships. You prefer to convert issues into causal chains of events, each of which can be handled as an individual entity. You tend to articulate ideas, present proposals, and convince others by taking each variable individually and in a logically determined sequence. You assess the ideas of others on the basis of their analytical and logical soundness and become frustrated when these criteria are not met.

Individuals with this orientation frequently

- Find the arguments of systemic thinkers lacking in focus and clarity.
- Structure presentations by outlining discrete components and sequentially treating each one.

Dimension: Thinking; Orientation: Systemic

You prefer to approach questions and problems from a broad, "big picture" perspective. You tend to focus on relationships between concepts or between components of a situation. In order to persuade others to accept a proposition or argument, you point out the likely impact and effect on related variables. You prefer a synthetic pattern of thinking. Being mindful of the complexity and interrelatedness of issues is a hallmark of realism for you. You tend to find a linear orientation to thinking reductionistic and naïve.

Individuals with this orientation frequently

- Focus and comment on the interrelatedness of issues.
- Emphasize the complexity of issues and their theoretical ramifications.

- Find linear approaches overly simplistic.
- Structure presentations in a synthetic way by emphasizing complex inter-connections among issues.

Having identified your own propensities and tendencies, you may want to consider the following questions in order to intensify your cultural self-awareness:

1. What is the origin of these cultural orientations? How did you learn and acquire them? What were some of the formative experiences in their development (childhood, school, peer group, experiences, etc.)?
2. How are you experiencing this cultural orientation in your workplace? How do you tend to exhibit these orientations in your work behavior?
3. What are the negative and positive consequences of this orientation? How might others perceive them?
4. Is there a gap between your preference and what is expected, rewarded, and reinforced in your team or organization? How are you bridging this gap?

Once you have completed this analysis and reflection, you have taken an important step, namely to understand yourself and your identity as a unique reflection of a multitude of social and cultural influences that have shaped your perceptions, attitudes, and expectations and are expressed through your behavior patterns. These patterns, in turn, affect and significantly shape the culture in your work environment as well as its tangible outputs. You have also started to use a different framework for mapping cultural differences and understanding yourself as a cultural vector. By understanding cultural environments as either low- or high-context, for example, and yourself as a particularist or a universalist, you are not only overcoming the limitations and dangers of stereotyping, but also depersonalizing the stresses, strains, and conflicts in your working environment, thus rendering them more solvable. This cultural orientations approach can be a powerful way to generate culture-based self- and other-awareness, and a useful way of organizing culturally specific information. With this foundation, we can turn to the specific skill set that helps you convert your insights into actions.

DEVELOPING YOUR CULTURAL SKILL SET

The power of cultural orientations to affect our communication and interactions should be readily apparent. Congruent—i.e., shared—cultural orientations are the hidden dimension of and precondition for the efficient and effective exchange of meaning, as well as for the building of trust, credibility, and rapport.

By becoming conscious of the cultural frames, their constituent cultural orientations, and the role of these orientations in the encoding and decoding of messages, we provide an opportunity to

- Reduce culture-based distortions in our interactions and communication.
- Avoid the escalation of social distance and culture-based misunderstandings.
- Create a shared system for encoding and decoding that can enable efficient interaction and collaboration.

To bring about these results, awareness and knowledge need to be translated into a specific skill set.

Consider the following scene, which one of the authors observed at a party in honor of a Japanese visitor to Mexico. The food served at the party was rather spicy. When the Japanese guest had almost finished her water, she remarked to the host, "This is very spicy." The host took this remark as a welcome invitation to discuss Mexican cuisine and explained the different types of peppers that are used in various Mexican dishes. After these explanations, the guest thanked her host politely and repeated, "This is very spicy." At this point, the author poured the Japanese guest more water from the carafe and inquired whether her comment was really a request for water. She nodded appreciatively and laughed with a mixture of embarrassment and amusement. The host, also embarrassed about his oversight, asked, "Why didn't you simply ask for water?" When she replied that it would have been impolite, the author used this situation to build a dialogue about high and low context and indirect and direct communication styles. By the end of the evening, both guest and host not only understood each other better, but they had actually practiced each other's behavioral style, which all present found greatly amusing. The better understanding and relationship built in this way were very useful during the meetings scheduled for the subsequent days, as both felt comfortable exploring their experience with each other and the Mexican host could explain key features of Mexican business and management practices.

This scenario involves three interrelated skills that we have identified as critical for overcoming cultural barriers in communication and interaction:

- The ability to exercise *cultural due diligence*
- The ability to exhibit *style switching*
- The ability to engage in *cultural dialogue*

Cultural Due Diligence

In line with the principle that one should assume difference until similarity is proven, cultural due diligence is the ability *to adequately assess and plan for the possible effects of culture in interactions.* This is essentially a research and preparatory activity that involves (1) investigating and determining the cultural backgrounds and orientations of one's colleagues, counterparts, partners, clients, etc., (2) evaluating potential and actual culture gaps, and (3) developing a strategy for minimizing any resulting negative effects. It is a skill that is best exercised in preparation for serious business and management interactions.

In this process, one strives to understand the history, backgrounds, and experiences that have shaped the perspective, outlook, and value system of specific individuals and/or groups with whom you are communicating and interacting. This information can be gleaned from a variety of sources.

MEDIA AND PUBLICATIONS

Media and publications can be good sources of cultural information. Some of the information may be very explicit; however, most of it is focused on the national level of culture. You can glean highly valuable information if you focus on the implicit information contained in media and publications in order to assess the discourse that exists within a given cultural environment. You need to have the skill to scan such sources and distill patterns from them that give you cues as to what is expected, reinforced, and rewarded in a given environment.

INFORMANTS

Individuals who have experience in a particular cultural environment or who have been immersed in it have particularly valuable insights and make astute observations. When using informants to engage in cultural due diligence, you need to be aware of the following:

- Although these individuals have experience with the cultural environment, they may not be able to give you an explicit cultural debriefing. You will have to probe for good information.
- Assessments of culture can be highly subjective. Therefore, do not rely on the opinions and insights of only one informant. Always check the information with others.
- Informants are often not free from stereotypes and ethnocentrism, as even being immersed in a different culture does not in and of itself guarantee increased tolerance or open-mindedness. You will have to filter the information accordingly.

DIRECT INFORMATION GATHERING

When you have an opportunity to operate in the cultural environment or to interact with members of the cultural environment, you have an opportunity to directly gather information through active listening, observation, and inquiry. An active listener will ask open-ended questions in order to gain as much information as possible ("What do you think of X? How would you provide negative feedback in your environment?") and summary questions that will help to clarify what has been said or agreed to ("Now let me see if I understand you correctly. . . . You're saying that . . ."). Also, empathetic statements are a good way to elicit information, particularly when the issue seems personal or controversial ("It must be very difficult to work in these conditions!" or "This seems to be a big change for you!"). As you observe the responses and your environment, it is critical that you seek out patterns and understand their variation. The following list gives further tips on listening and observation skills:

- Concentrate and avoid distractions.
- Listen for central ideas and themes.
- Ask follow-up and probing questions.
- Check yourself and your assumptions.
- Try to interpret what you hear from the other's cultural perspective. Uncover the rationale.
- Restate and paraphrase to confirm and clarify.
- Listen to both content and delivery.
- Look for displays of emotions.
- Respect silences. Don't rush to fill in the gaps.
- Postpone evaluations; instead, seek verification and clarification of what you have observed.

Information generated in this way should help you to formulate hypotheses about the cultural configuration that characterizes colleagues, counterparts, partners, and clients. It is critical to keep in mind that these hypotheses will need to be tested, verified, and refined through subsequent interactions. The language of the Cultural Orientations Model can help you to organize, summarize, and refer to your findings.

Based on these hypotheses, you can identify potential cultural gaps and identify ways in which these culture gaps (1) may manifest themselves in behavior and (2) can be addressed in order to achieve a desired outcome.

Style Switching

Style switching is the ability to use a broad and flexible behavioral repertoire of cross-cultural skills that are appropriate to the given situation. It may be the result of cultural due diligence. Here is an example:

Jack Hanstead was appointed the head of a cross-functional global team in charge of preparing guidelines for packaging copy for the global organization. He was responsible for getting information from each of the regions and countries on their legal guidelines and requirements for copy.

His first action was to send two brief emails to his points of contact in each region, stating the information he needed from them. Of the four regions he was responsible for, only two contacts responded, and their emails provided none of what he had requested; rather, they provided information about themselves. After a few more days without any more information from his region contacts, Jack decided to write again to those people who had sent him empty emails, giving them a little background information about himself: his job role and title, why he was appointed to this team, and what previous experience he had. The day after he sent this email, both people wrote him back. Not only were their emails quite friendly, but they both said that they were excited to be working with him and that they hoped to arrange a phone conference to speak in more detail about the information he was requesting.

Astounded by these responses, Jack decided to send a third email to the other region contacts. In this email, he included information about himself (his role, his enthusiasm about working with these people, and his appreciation for their help) and provided a systemic explanation of the purpose of the request and how their input would be useful.

Not only did they immediately write him back, but they followed up with a phone call. Within the following week, all of the region contacts had provided him with the information he needed or were in the process of compiling that information.

Jack's ability to style-switch, to change from the short, impersonal, and functional email to a detailed, enthusiastic, and personal email, resulted in his receiving all the information he needed and creating a network of people that he could count on for future needs. In addition, he established trust, credibility, and rapport at an email level that could be enhanced with follow-up telephone calls and face-to-face meetings.

This example demonstrates that certain behaviors are easier to change than others. Although Jack was frustrated by his counterparts' initial lack of response, he was able to style-switch with relative ease in order to obtain the information he needed.

Style switching can become very difficult if you need to adopt a very different behavior that you feel may compromise your sense of identity and feeling of authenticity. It may help if you categorize your cultural preferences into nonnegotiable or core identifying features and negotiable identifying features.

The core cultural orientations are preferences and behaviors that are intricately tied to your sense of self. They are essentially nonnegotiable. You can become aware of the potential negative and positive aspects of these preferences and behaviors, but you will not feel comfortable altering them significantly. The negotiable cultural orientations consist of those preferences and behaviors in which you allow a range of flexibility and situational variability. This range of flexibility does not threaten your sense of self. The greater the number of behaviors that you include in the negotiable realm, the greater your ability to engage in style switching.

It is important to recognize that the core and negotiable realms manifest themselves behaviorally and that they are therefore different from values. Because each cultural environment associates different behaviors with a similar value, building an extensive and flexible behavioral repertoire allows you to extend the very essence of your self. In fact, the negotiable realm is the buffer through which your intentions, needs, requests, and decisions can be adequately translated—or, better, localized—across cultures.

Following are two examples of people we have encountered in our work who were confronted with a situation in which either their core or their negotiable cultural orientations were involved.

EXAMPLE 1

Martin Schutten, a native of Denmark, had worked at his company's home office in Denmark for two years when he was promoted to product manager. With this promotion, he was sent to Venezuela to work at the Latin American branch. His role would be to oversee a team of engineers.

Since he was unfamiliar with this plant and new to Venezuela, Martin hoped that the team he was overseeing would provide him with a little guidance concerning such things as regulations and procedures. While he was very familiar with the product and expected that things would be carried out in a certain fashion, he also liked giving his employees the freedom to make certain decisions on their own, without always coming to him. This had worked quite nicely for him in his home office.

His new team of engineers, however, was not what he expected. They were always asking him questions that he felt they could answer without him. They made no decisions on their own. When Martin asked them about ways to change certain things, they did not provide suggestions. He was astounded that this team of educated workers could not give him any ideas or feedback.

His team members, on the other hand, were disconcerted by the lack of guidance from their new manager. They couldn't believe that their boss was asking for their opinion or that he let them make certain decisions themselves. They felt that he was lacking in direction and confidence, and they believed that they could not function well without the guidance of a strong boss.

After a few weeks of ongoing confusion and frustration on both parts, Martin decided to seek the counsel of someone else. He contacted a colleague in Denmark who had lived and worked in Venezuela for six months but who was not affiliated with this present team of engineers. His colleague was eager to share information, as he had also had great difficulty integrating into his Venezuelan team. He told Martin that he had found that Venezuelans greatly valued a hierarchical orientation. They did what was asked of them without asking questions, never skipped hierarchical levels, did not enjoy and were uncomfortable with brainstorming, and expected their team leader to have all of the answers. Martin's colleague had also had a difficult time with these behaviors. But as time went by and he learned to style-switch, his rapport with his team was greatly improved and productivity increased.

Martin also enlisted the help of an informant within the organization who understood the organization and its culture. He asked his informant to provide tips and insights into directive behaviors that would make him more credible and successful with his team. In addition, Martin talked with other expatriates in the organization to get feedback and suggestions. After processing all this information, Martin realized why his team didn't brainstorm or make their own decisions and why they looked to him for so much guidance. The behaviors he was suggesting were not behaviors that their culture expected, reinforced, or valued. The engineers were used to being told what to do and were not used to contradicting or offering suggestions to a superior.

While he couldn't imagine having to give orders to his team and to answer all questions without being questioned in return, he desperately wanted to find a solution. Every day, he observed his team, and slowly he became a strong presence in their work area. He reinforced guidelines on a regular basis. He even practiced style switching at home. He gave more direction to his cleaning people, and he asked his cooking staff to prepare something specific rather than letting them make their own cuisine decisions. In addition, through verbal and nonverbal communication, he let his domestic help know that he was the only one to make final decisions.

While Martin identified with the equality orientation to power and had grown up in a milieu where this was always emphasized and reinforced, he felt that his success as a team leader in Venezuela depended on his ability to style-switch. Although it was very difficult, he was committed to making this change. His determination to learn about Venezuelan culture and to find ways to style-switch contributed to the success he had with his team. A short while after Martin started style switching, he gained the trust of his team and was able to establish credibility and rapport with the team members.

EXAMPLE 2

For six years, Diana Cruz had worked for the same company. One of her main reasons for choosing this company was its particularistic orientation. She could determine her work schedule, set up meetings when she thought it necessary, wear casual clothing, and decide, on an individual basis, the specific needs of her clients.

Shortly after she had received a promotion, her company was acquired by another company and most of her colleagues were laid off. She, however, had been greatly valued within the original company and was not laid off.

Soon after the acquisition, she started having difficulties with the new management and with company regulations. The acquiring company was very universalistic and had rigid policies and procedures. Diana had always valued having a flexible work schedule and being able to work odd hours to accommodate her busy personal life. With the new company, she had to comply with a set schedule. She felt that this was upsetting not only her outside needs but also her creativity within the company.

In addition, before the acquisition, when Diana wanted to schedule a meeting, she would individually contact each person who would be attending via an informal phone call, in person, or through email. If she wanted to schedule a meeting at the acquiring company, she needed to send a formal email to all the attendees at least one week prior to the meeting and provide the meeting agenda.

While Diana enjoyed her work, she had also enjoyed the freedom, flexibility, and consideration of her personal needs that her previous company had provided. She realized that if she was to continue with this company, she would need to comply with a long list of rules, regulations, and policies.

Shortly after the acquisition, she came to the decision that her particularistic orientation was a core orientation, and thus she was not willing to style-switch. She felt that style switching would compromise her identity. To the disappointment of her colleagues and superiors, Diana chose to take a new job that allowed her to maintain the integrity of this core value.

We have found that managers who are effective at style switching tend to have a strong and realistic sense of their identities and boundaries. When you think about yourself and your performance challenges and environment:

1. What are your core orientations, i.e., the ones that are intricately tied to your sense of identity and authenticity? How much would you be willing to switch your style, i.e., your behavior? Can you think of instances where your sense of self has been compromised by behavioral requirements?
2. What are your negotiable orientations, i.e., the ones that are least tied to your sense of identity? How far would you be willing to switch your style, i.e., your behavior, in these areas?

Cultural Dialogue

Cultural dialogue is the ability to illuminate the cultural underpinnings of behavior and performance, close cultural gaps, and create cultural synergy through conversation. According to Harris and Moran, cultural synergy "builds upon similarities and fuses differences resulting in more effective human activities and systems. The very diversity of people can be utilized to enhance problem solving by combined action."[11] This involves more than observation and active listening skills; it requires a better conversation along the principles outlined by William Isaacs in his important book *Dialogue and the Art of Thinking Together*. Isaacs sees dialogue as a powerful means

> to reach new understanding and, in doing so, to form a totally new basis from which to think and act. In dialogue, one not only solves problems, one dissolves them. We do not merely try to reach agreement, we try to create a new context from which many agreements may come. And we seek to uncover a base of shared meaning that can greatly help coordinate and align our actions with value.[12]

The ability to engage in cultural dialogue is a leadership skill that turns culture-based differences into a force field that creates both synergy and cohesion. Participation, empathy, inclusion, and joint exploration of deeply held beliefs and assumptions can foster shared insights, transforming the basic relationship and perspective of each individual involved. This is an increasingly critical tool for transcending social and cultural boundaries.

SUMMARY INSIGHTS

A byproduct of new technologies is their ability to profoundly change not just our concept of the world but also the very meaning of the words with which we refer to them. Almost irreverently they take language and alter it forever. Few words have been as affected by the Internet revolution as the words *connect* and *connectivity*. The shrill sounds of modems, telephone and cable connections, and IT infrastructure increasingly dominate our associations with these terms.

When the noted anthropologist Clifford Geertz described the globalizing world as one in which we are "tumbled" into a world of "endless connection" in which "it is increasingly difficult to get out of each other's way," he did not have IT in mind.[13] IT has given us the means to transcend boundaries of time and space at increasing speed and capacity, but our ability to truly *connect* rests on our interpersonal qualities and remains tenuous at best. The skills of style switching and the practices of cultural due diligence and cultural dialogue are key to our ability to truly connect and establish the interpersonal understanding and synergies that are the foundation and purpose for communication and interaction.

In this chapter we have explored the complex effect that culture has on communication and interaction. We have introduced a tool, a process, and the key elements of a cultural skill set. Throughout this discussion, we have applied the language of the Cultural Orientations Model consistently for building cultural competence. Having explored cultural variation on a macro, societal level in Chap. 4 and at the micro level of communication and interaction in this chapter, we can now turn to the specific management, leadership, and organizational challenges within which the macro and micro levels need to be reconciled.

6

CULTURAL COMPETENCE IN MARKETING AND SALES

"What managers do is the same around the world.
How they do it is determined by tradition and culture"

PETER DRUCKER

Now that we have explored the macro- and micro-level workings of cul-ture and the elements of cultural competence, we can turn our atten-tion to key applications of this information in the pursuit of a global vision. In this chapter, we focus on external applications, using marketing and sales, the business functions that directly connect the business to its cus-tomers, to illustrate how cultural competence needs to be integrated into the pursuit of key business functions. In Chap. 7, we focus on internal applications, discussing the salient applications of cultural competence to teamwork and collaboration, the critical link between an organization's global vision and individual performance.

An organization's access and connection to its customers is deeply rooted in culture, as culture is a fundamental determinant of a person's wants and needs, on the one hand, and the key to effectively positioning and selling goods or services, on the other. Values, perceptions, preferences, and behaviors are passed down through an individual's family and the surrounding culture and subcultures. A marketer's effectiveness is directly influenced by whether the choices it makes in communicating something about a good or service fit in with the local culture. If a chosen set of characteristics of descriptors is not aligned with the surrounding culture, then the success of a promotional campaign using that set of characteristics is in jeopardy.

The case of Wal-Mart , a U.S. general merchandise company, illustrates the ways in which cultural factors affect successful market segmentation and strategy formulation and the importance of culture for market penetration and adaptation of services. The company did not factor in either German pricing regulations or culture-based attitudes toward friendliness and possessions. What is considered service-oriented friendliness in the U.S. marketplace is seen by many Germans as hypocritical phoniness, unwanted intrusiveness, and lack of authenticity. Wal-Mart's chief executive officer, John B. Menzer, is quoted as having said, "We have screwed up in Germany. Our biggest mistake was putting our name up before we had the service and low prices."[1] In other words, Wal-Mart did not invest in cultural due diligence and was not prepared to adapt its approach to the customer and the marketplace. It did not build its strategy on the basis of cultural competence.

There are two schools of thought in the business community on how to deal with cultural diversity. One perspective is that a *global standardization* strategy is best in designing the marketing mix for a global marketplace, as has been demonstrated by the success of companies like Coca-Cola, McDonald's, and Sony. The argument here is that this approach will save on costs, promote one central brand or corporate image worldwide, and cause more goods to be sold to price-conscious consumers.

In some cases, global standardization has proved advantageous, but cultural differences are still far from disappearing. A global standardization approach assumes that the similarities among consumers across different countries outweigh any differences that may exist. Although companies may realize cost savings, they need to remember that competitors, both local and foreign, are seeking to offer more of what the customer in a particular country wants. Theodore Levitt, who promotes globalization through standardization, argues:

> The world is becoming a common marketplace in which people—no matter where they live—desire the same products and lifestyles. Global

companies must forget the idiosyncratic differences between countries and cultures and instead concentrate on satisfying universal drives.[2]

Supporters of standardization focus on the general convergence of consumption patterns and styles across countries. The demographic trends of aging populations, a fall in birth rates, and increased female employment seem to increase the similarities among major markets and cultures. Also, the benefits of product standardization across countries are many. Standardization simplifies decision making, reduces costs through economies of scale, results in exceptional operational efficiency because of the transferability of experience from one country to another, and gives a company a uniform, consistent worldwide image.

The contrary view argues that companies must focus on the specific geopolitical and cultural factors that characterize the consumers in particular countries and *tailor* or *individualize* their goods and services for those countries. The local approach contends that victory will go to the competitor who best adapts its offerings to the local market. Many companies find that a regional approach allows for uniformity of goods or services and a recognizable image without the constraints of standardization.

Devising separate policies and procedures in each country has been compared to an organ transplant: The critical question centers on acceptance or rejection. A host of adaptive measures such as product features, brand name, labeling, packaging, colors, materials, prices, sales promotion, advertising themes, media chosen, and execution can be used to address market conditions for a good or service at the country level. Many companies that believe in global standardization have learned that some degree of adaptation to local culture is required for success. Coca-Cola is less sweet or less carbonated in certain countries; McDonald's uses chili sauce instead of ketchup on its hamburgers in Latin America and uses lamb instead of beef in India. The risk is that a local approach will result in an excessive—that is, very costly—amount of adaptation.

In the end, circumstances may dictate which approach works best: global standardization or local responsiveness. However, when a company is seeking to successfully connect to customers in different markets and cultures, assuming until proven otherwise that cultural due diligence is worthwhile and that adaptation is required may simply be the safer assumption. Had Monsanto or Wal-Mart approached the European marketplace from this perspective, it might have realized its vision.

Ultimately, the focus of the global manager is to ensure that rejection is not a result of the organization's cultural myopia or even blindness. Demonstrated success in marketing and sales must be predicated upon the most basic of business principles: Know your competitor, know your audience, and know your customer—all of which are imbued with significant cultural overtones.

THE MARKETING-SALES CONTINUUM

Let's look more closely at the marketing and sales roles within organizations in order to comprehend the challenges faced by individuals as they try to incorporate their understanding of these cultural overtones into the process of delivering goods and services on an international basis. Marketing and sales are viewed as part of a single, integrated approach to the customer, a continuum in which sales are linked more and more to marketing as a partner, interacting in a most complex manner. However, although they are linked, marketing and sales are not interchangeable: Marketing describes the process that evokes interest within a potential customer before a sale, and sales represents the marketing effort required to realize a successful transaction. As a follow-up to sales, organizations must provide service and maintenance of goods or services with the object of promoting more sales.

Certain key attributes of each of these roles are essential to success in the global marketplace and are highly sensitive to cultural factors. The traditional marketing-sales plan is a detailed scheme indicating the ways in which a company intends to access, sell to, and service a specific consumer/buyer group. Product, price, promotion, and distribution are key elements of the planning process, as are service and support following implementation. This mix is successful when there is an in-depth understanding of customer-related data. The speed with which marketplace data change is a central challenge to the global marketing-sales team. Market potential can vary greatly and is affected by conditions and factors both within and outside the marketer's control. In addition, although markets move through a progression of stages to reach maturity, there is no set length of time over which this process occurs. It is simply a matter of timing and of consumer/buyer behavior or demand.

As a marketing-sales initiative moves beyond a domestic, single-country focus, additional factors become crucial—regulations, licensing, distribution, financing, exchange risk, and legal status, to name just a few. Every marketing effort must pass through a series of stages in order to reach the final consumer transaction. The potential customer's relationship with a good or service follows these stages: awareness of, affinity for, preference for, confidence in, and ultimately purchase of the good or service. Customers are the main concerns of marketers and salespeople. The product being offered can be any form of commodity or service without significantly changing the governing rule of the relationship. The rule is quite simple: The cost to the customer must reflect the customer's perception of the product's value. The marketer's job is to understand the relationship of cost to value when approaching customers. Despite the importance of this rule, many commercial failures occur as a result of factors such as poor interpersonal relationships, price blindness, quality defects, cultural myopia, bad packaging, and poor timing. Attention to all these factors is critical.

A key consideration in determining the usefulness of a particular marketing-sales process is the fluidity of markets in today's global environment. The marketplace is highly dynamic. Conditions change frequently and are difficult to predict: Interest rates and prices are in constant flux, new products and new competitors appear all the time, new wealth classes appear overnight, and new technology changes the nature of success constantly.

Dealing with customers who are at a distance from headquarters imposes added pressure on effective communication, logistics, and quality control. And although a car, a radio, or a soft drink may be universal, local cultures and style require that the specifics of the product vary constantly. Market penetration in the global marketplace is far more complex than dealing with expansion within the confines of a domestic market. Successful entry is easy to talk about and plan, but carrying it out requires a high level of skill and ability. When working globally, the marketer must keep in perspective the historical forces that have shaped the existing markets as well as anticipate future changes and forces that will create new prospects within the marketplace.[3]

CULTURAL COMPETENCE AND THE MARKETING-SALES CONTINUUM

Applying cultural competence to the marketing and sales functions involves two foci: the business professional and the consumer. The savvy business professional needs to understand key culture-dependent variables through which to relate to the customer base: language, aesthetics, values and norms, and social organization. These variables build upon and complement the ten basic dimensions of the Cultural Orientations Model. They permeate the way of life of any people.

Language

Language is the most important medium of communication and is often used to distinguish one culture from another. Although in many firms and industries English has become the default language of global business, businesspeople who speak the local language with a certain degree of proficiency are often able to gain valuable insights into the target market, its social organization, its values, and its ways of thinking. Knowing a local language allows individuals to recognize the great variety of nuances in the social fabric—a fact that is particularly significant for marketing and sales.

A complicating factor related to language is that few countries are mono-lingual and, conversely, the same language may be spoken across several cultures. For example, Switzerland has three major languages, French, German, and Italian, and in India there are as many as 17 national languages, including English, and hundreds of dialects.

Certain subtle aspects of language, such as intonation or volume of voice, can also convey mood and meaning. In Europe and in the United States, for example, a loud voice may indicate disagreement, whereas in Arab cultures, a loud voice may be used simply to get attention. In Korea, the concept of *kibun* is quite important to interpersonal communication, but this concept is unknown in the West. *Kibun* means "feeling" or "mood." Koreans know that in order to build a relationship effectively or enhance it over time, they must interact in a manner that will connect with the *kibun* of their colleagues.

Other factors related to the use of language are inherent in the communication dimension of the Cultural Orientations Model, specifically the *direct* or *indirect*, the *expressive* or *instrumental*, and the *high-context* or *low-context* uses of the language. Nonverbal behavior, such as hand gestures or eye contact, also plays a role in effective communication.

Aesthetics

Cultures also define themselves through aesthetic factors, such as the use of colors, forms, shapes, and sounds, and these factors can have an impact on critical dimensions of the marketing-sales continuum, such as negotiations, sales presentations, advertising and promotion, and closing. Color, for example, is a powerful and common tool available to marketers to create brand identification. It increases reinforcement and differentiation. However, colors also have strong symbolic value—in the United States and Europe, for example, black connotes mourning, but in many Far Eastern cultures white connotes mourning and black connotes bad luck or bad fortune. When John Player, the English cigarette manufacturer, attempted to launch its brand in Hong Kong with black and gold packaging at the beginning of the Chinese New Year, the launch, needless to say, was a disaster.

Values and Norms

Local values influence a customer's perceptions. They define the standards and models of behavior that influence the buying decision process. An international marketer needs to know the dominant values of the company's potential customers in all the country markets the company is targeting. Customer behavior is influenced by the value placed on such things as work, achievement, wealth, openness to risk, and material consumption, factors that are all given expression by a country or region's cultural orientations. In addition, specific information about such norms as holidays, vacation periods, work schedules, decision-making processes, demographics, age, and gender roles, among others, must be taken into consideration in product design, product development, and sales.

Levels of education also play a role in determining how products should be promoted. In cultures with a high level of illiteracy, for example, promotional materials using images may be more effective than materials that rely heavily on text. Other educational factors may also have a bearing on marketing and sales decisions. Some of these include the particular national focus of education and the role that elite schools play in society.

Social Organization

The family unit is the fundamental "building block" of a society. Some societies are organized around the immediate family, whereas other societies are organized around intact, extended family units. Ultimately, familial relations and familial structure influence who makes purchasing decisions and how these decisions are made.

With the exception of the decisions concerning daily foodstuffs, men make most purchasing decisions in patriarchal societies. In matriarchal societies like those of sub-Saharan Africa, women control the majority of consumer-based decisions, although decisions concerning major purchases, such as the purchase of cars or appliances, are made by men. In many Asian cultures, men occupy a dominant position in public. They constitute the majority of the workforce and earn the majority of the income. In private, however, the situation is reversed: At home, women make all decisions regarding purchases and investments.[4]

Table 6.1 identifies the critical areas in which cultural competence needs to be manifested in marketing and sales. The critical variables of culture are matrixed against the elements of the marketing-sales plan described earlier.

APPLYING THE CULTURAL ORIENTATIONS MODEL

In addition to enabling us to understand the variables to which cultural competence applies, as identified in Table 6.1, the Cultural Orientations Model enables us to develop a heightened acuity in approaching, communicating with, and appealing to the customer. The following is a brief summary of key considerations that a marketer or salesperson should be sensitive to in his or her pursuit of customer insight.

TABLE 6.1 Cultural Competence in Marketing and Sales

			Attributes		
Variables	**Price**	**Distribution**	**Sales**	**Advertising/promotion**	
Language: verbal and nonverbal	Style: bargaining vs. selling	Communicating for interpersonal impact	Selling style	Multiple languages and dialects	
Aesthetics: colors, forms/shapes, sounds	Packaging size given buying habits	Brand identification	Symbolic value of colors	Significant impact on choice of colors, shapes, and sounds Symbols and taboos	
Values and norms: perceptions, demographics, education	Attitudes toward bargaining/sales Educational and income level: lower prices to penetrate mass markets	Attitudes toward change Specialized outlets for various subcultures, including the rural-urban mix	Diverse cultural/terrain barriers that require broad sales force Varying attitudes toward work, time, achievement Motivation and control of the sales force	Language/words with different connotations Low literacy: simple instructions with graphics Euphemisms Translation	
Social organization: family, structures, buying process	Determination of buying influence: gender, family, hierarchy	Buyers accustomed to bargaining	Attitudes toward consumption, time-saving products	Selection of advertising/promotional vehicles	

254

Environment

In a *control* environment, clients will want to know if the good or service being offered will help them get more control of their life and the environment. Those clients who exhibit a *harmony* orientation will ask if the product is acceptable to others in the surrounding environment or whether, instead, it will give offense and alienate the client from others. If the clients or customers view the environment from a *constraint* perspective, they could be skeptical about the claims for the product. A constraint-oriented individual believes that a good or service can provide little control over the environment.

Time

Those individuals who demonstrate a *single-focus* orientation to time will respond to a marketer or salesperson with undivided attention. Single-focus individuals will be receptive to linear, point-by-point marketing or sales presentations or promotions. In contrast, a person with a *multifocus* orientation to time will be comfortable handling a variety of tasks at once, leaving the marketer or salesperson open to experiencing numerous interruptions in the interaction.

The fixed/fluid continuum is an important factor in effective marketing and sales. The individual with a *fixed* time orientation will want to begin and finish the sales presentation on time, as his or her schedule is tight and is organized into rational blocks or themes. The marketer or salesperson facing a customer with such an orientation should try to demonstrate flexibility in dealing with set slots of time so as not to pressure the potential customer into buying. A client with a *fluid* orientation to time will be less concerned with being precisely on time; rather, such a client will be inclined to take the amount of time required to accomplish what needs to be done, even if other appointments have to wait. In this instance, adhering to a formal set schedule of activities for its own sake is not appropriate.

Another continuum that affects marketing and sales is the past/present/future time continuum. An emphasis on the historical perspective, experience, and reputation of a company or consultant is most important from a *past*-oriented perspective. The key question might be, "How does this good or service fit in with what the company has provided before?"

For those with a *present* time orientation, it is important to know whether the good or service will satisfy some immediate need. This requires an effective management reply that demonstrates responsiveness and attention to the immediate needs of the client. Customers with a *future* view of time will wish to build a business relationship over the long term, both on a corporate level and on a personal level as well. They will also consider a product primarily from the perspective of its durability and its ability to continue meeting future needs.

Action

The being/doing continuum addresses highly personal considerations from the point of view of the marketer or salesperson. For those who demonstrate a *being* orientation, the main consideration is whether the good or service will improve their quality of life and personal relationships. Therefore, a "softer," more personal approach to selling is appreciated. If the customer has more of a *doing* orientation, an efficient, business-focused approach is more appropriate. For such an individual, the primary concern is whether the good or service being sold will help him or her become more productive and whether it will ensure that personal goals and objectives are met.

Communication

Communication is the dimension that most directly affects how effectively people work together. This is the reason that the communication dimension has more continua than any other cultural dimension in the Cultural Orientations Model.

The first continuum is the high-context–low-context continuum. For the client who demonstrates a *high-context* orientation, the most important need that effective communication with the marketer or salesperson fulfills is the building of a relationship of trust. The centrality of this need means that the closing of a sale will not be quick. Once trust is established, however, the chance of obtaining a sale is enhanced. In fact, if the trust relationship is properly built and maintained, the potential for obtaining repeat or referral business is high. The salesperson should provide contextual information leading up to an inevitable conclusion.

For the *low-context* person, facts and figures along with forthright conversation that leads the discussion to the exact point of the meeting are key. The marketer or salesperson may want to start with the conclusion and then provide the necessary contextual information as requested by the customer. The marketer or salesperson can expect to reach his or her objectives or close the sale expeditiously.

The second continuum of communication comprises the direct and indirect orientations. The client who is *direct* in her communication will not hesitate to be confrontational and will express objections to the topics being discussed in an open, direct manner. She is likely to ask the marketer or sales-person many questions, such as "How? What? When?" A marketer or sales-person with a direct orientation may be viewed as aggressive in indirect cultures and as forthright and refreshing in cultures with a more direct orien-tation. In those cultures where causing offense or losing face is an issue, an indirect style is more appropriate. A direct salesperson may be confused and frustrated by the seeming vagueness of an *indirect* person's interaction and responses. To address these circumstances, a direct salesperson may need to use examples and analogies to lead the indirect person to understanding, acceptance, and closure on a particular subject or decision. This will require additional time and effort on the part of direct communicators.

A marketer or salesperson can come into contact with two very different styles along the expressive-instrumental continuum of communication. The *expressive* individual speaks openly and displays his emotions, both positive and negative, during an interaction. As a result, the possibilities for embar-rassment and conflict are higher. On the other hand, the marketer or salesper-son will find it easier to know where she stands, as the client's opinions are clearly stated. The *instrumental* client will keep his emotions concealed or hidden. Such a person is difficult to "read," and the salesperson may not know his feelings about or position on a good or service until a sales closing is attempted. The instrumental client will also focus primarily on factual infor-mation concerning the good or service being offered.

Knowledge of the national or host culture is especially important in deal-ing with the formal-informal continuum. A thorough knowledge of the spe-cific customs of the prospect's culture that pertain to sales (e.g., status of buyer and seller, greetings, conversational topics, do's and taboos, etc.) is essential in a situation where the client exhibits a *formal* communication ori-entation. It is especially important for the marketer or salesperson to show respect by observing and demonstrating all the appropriate behaviors and cus-toms of the country. When operating in a business culture with an *informal* orientation, a lower level of protocol and a less stringent observation of cus-toms is called for, although respect should be communicated at all times.

Space

The matter of perceiving and dealing with one's physical surroundings is cap-tured by the private-public continuum. When a person has a *private* orienta-tion, meetings are likely to take place in quiet, secluded locations where privacy can be maintained. Such individuals will most likely maintain an impersonal social, physical distance with limited proximity to other people.

On the other hand, a *public*-oriented individual will prefer a crowded, noisy environment with little privacy. Such a client would be more comfortable with a closer physical distance.

Power

An understanding of the hierarchy-equality continuum is essential for successful marketing and sales. In cultures where *hierarchy* has a strong impact, individuals are concerned with proper deference to position and status, both within the workplace and at home. Under such circumstances, the marketer or salesperson may or may not be meeting with the decision maker. The chain of authority is pronounced, and the salesperson needs to gain respect before he or she can obtain access to higher officials in the hierarchy. Negotiations should be formal and dealings respectful. Within a culture with an *equality* orientation, the salesperson and the customer are regarded as being on relative equal terms. In this case, titles, status, and formal position are far less important in the marketing-sales interaction.

Individualism

The individualistic-collectivistic continuum plays a particularly important role in the decision-making phase of the marketing-sales process. When dealing with an *individualistic* person, the marketer or salesperson can expect a decision about a product or project to be made immediately. In this instance, it is advisable to sell the individual on the personal benefits presented by the product and to emphasize how the product will efficiently meet the client's personal needs and goals. In the *collectivistic* mode, decisions require a broader consultative approach; therefore, the client will need to refer to colleagues and others in order to reach a consensus decision. The collectivistic person operates and manages by maintaining ties to various central cliques and wants to know how the product or project can assist the group to be more effective. Since the group dynamic is central to making decisions, it is critical that the marketer or salesperson does not cause the client to lose face in front of others.

The second continuum within individualism is the universalistic-particularistic one. A client who has a *universalistic* orientation wants to be assured that he is being treated just like everyone else and that, therefore, the good or service he is being offered is identical in price, quality, etc., to the goods or services offered to all other customers under all circumstances. A *particularistic* customer, however, views herself and her needs as the exception to the rule. She views any formal agreement she may make as merely a guideline for conducting the purchase. The emphasis here is on personal relationships that enable particular agreements to be reached. It is tacitly understood that prices or quality may vary depending on how good the relations between the salesperson and the customer are.

Competitiveness

The competitive-cooperative continuum has a distinct impact on the relationship between the marketer or salesperson and the client across cultures. A *competitive* customer may be highly aggressive in pursuing the "best deal" or trying to outsmart the salesperson with a calculated approach. A *cooperative* customer will emphasize the quality of life and the interpersonal relationship(s) between the client and the salesperson. He values consensus over winning.

Structure

The manner in which an individual can be expected to process marketing and sales information and make decisions is reflected in the order-flexibility continuum. An *order* orientation is demonstrated by a client who needs a great deal of information and comprehensive documentation regarding the goods or services being discussed. Given this propensity, the client will take few risks until she is certain that she has received the details she needs in order to proceed with making a decision. By contrast, the *flexibility*-oriented client will make a decision with relatively little information or formal documentation. This client will be more willing to take risks or consider alternatives to proposals.

Thinking

The process of reflecting on information in order to reach a conclusion is the focus of the deductive-inductive continuum. The individual who thinks *deductively* will be satisfied with a limited amount of statistical data, preferring instead to engage in a conceptual-theoretical debate about the ideas behind the goods and services. The customer who demonstrates an *inductive* thinking process will insist on seeing the factual data relating to a good or service and to hear about other people's experiences with the product before drawing a conclusion. In this case, the marketer or salesperson will need to prepare all product data and narratives of customer experiences to which she can refer the customer to assist him in reaching a decision.

The linear-systemic continuum influences the speed with which the customer will reach a final decision. A *linear* person will want to hear a well-laid-out, logical argument telling him why he should purchase the product. Each element in the argument should be well defined and should support the previous point in a precise manner. In the context of interpersonal relations, this kind of thinking can appear to be impersonal and cold. When a client has a *systemic* orientation, the selling process is less direct and will probably involve circling around the issues and carefully considering the wider implications of the buying decision.[5]

THE GLOBAL, MULTICULTURAL MARKETING-SALES MODEL

From the previous discussion, a model emerges for global, multicultural marketing and sales that is composed of three principal phases: (1) global marketing environment, (2) global marketing strategy, and (3) global implementation. As summarized in the following list, each phase is made up of a series of essential action steps that—when executed properly and with full awareness of cultural variables—constitute a highly efficient and successful marketing and sales process.

Phase 1: Global Marketing Environment

- Understanding the global marketing environment
- Analyzing marketing opportunities in the global marketplace

Phase 2: Global Marketing Strategy

- Market segmentation
- Demographics
- Developing marketing strategies and partnerships
- Product decisions: global standards versus customization
- Pricing strategies for marketing
- Distribution channels for marketing
- Marketing communication: global advertising and promotion

Phase 3: Global Implementation

- The sales process: management
    Design
    Management
    Improvement

- The sales process: selling

    Identifying needs and prospecting

    Approaching the customer and building relationships

    Making the sales presentation and relating benefits

    Managing resistance, handling objections, and providing feedback

    Using influence and negotiation style(s)

    Understanding the techniques and methods that gain commitment (closing the sale)

    Maintaining the positive relationship established with the customer during the sale

A cross-cultural analysis of these phases pinpoints the significance of cultural dimensions in the marketing and sales process and enables marketers or salespeople to determine which elements of a marketing program can be standardized across multiple nations and which need to be adjusted to local customs. When successfully applied, knowledge and understanding of cultural dimensions enable marketers and salespeople to successfully penetrate targeted foreign markets and to enhance their organizational positioning within the global marketplace.[6] The phases are briefly described in the following sections.

Phase 1: Global Marketing Environment

UNDERSTANDING THE GLOBAL MARKETING ENVIRONMENT AND
ANALYZING OPPORTUNITIES
A fundamental characteristic of the global marketing and sales world is the broad diversity of the market environments in which organizations operate. Economic conditions within markets are key gauges of market potential and opportunity. Income is the single most critical marketing factor within a national or regional economic environment, whether it be discretionary per capita income or the gross domestic product of a developing country.

For example, in Japan, where environmental harmony and a collectivist orientation to individualism are prevalent cultural values, the changes required in order to move toward a postindustrial society are easier to handle because of the impact of Japanese cultural values on interpersonal and intragroup dynamics. Cultural characteristics and trends shape the view people have of themselves, of others, of nature, and of the marketplace. Generally speaking, cultural values persist (i.e., core beliefs and values persist over time), although secondary cultural attributes, such as attitudes toward marriage, do change over time. Furthermore, each culture contains subcultures (i.e., groups with specific shared values based on special experiences or circumstances). Overall, the marketer or salesperson must have a critical appreciation of the necessity of observing and understanding cultural values and shifts that might affect market opportunities. As mentioned, a range of demographic, economic, natural, technological, political, and cultural factors affects the market environments that companies encounter. In today's international environment, markets range from small open-air village exchanges to large regional trading blocs, such as ASEAN, NAFTA, MERCOSUR, EU, OPEC, GATT, CARICOM, and EFTA.

Economic variables as they relate to the various market characteristics of population, income, consumption patterns, infrastructure, geography, and attitudes toward foreign involvement in the economy are a starting point for the assessment of market potential by the international marketer. Economic data about these market characteristics provide a baseline for the collection of other, more market- or product-specific data.

Marketing is founded on the concept that all consumers have a variety of needs and that programs to address such needs must be tailored to each target consumer group. Since this applies within a country, it should apply even more consistently in foreign markets in which economic, political, and cultural conditions vary.[7]

Phase 2: Global Marketing Strategy

MARKET SEGMENTATION

The initial step taken by global marketers in preparation for a company's market expansion is a detailed analysis of the potential country or regional market. Despite the complexity of dealing with multiple national markets, organizations tend to approach countries and potential buyers by initially grouping them on the basis of their similarities and differences. The resulting market segmentation identifies groups of clients or customers that exhibit common buying behaviors at the regional, national, or transnational level.

The single most important task when evaluating data in this manner is to develop a strategy that can be used to reach a particular segment across multiple cultures without ignoring important cultural differences. In fact, results from various global marketing studies indicate that the closer you get to implementation, the more acute the need to pay particular attention to cultural differences becomes.

Once they have segment data, marketers target the countries or groups of people that are likely to be most responsive to marketing efforts and to buy the goods or services being offered. Once these groups are identified, the marketing and sales representatives must position their goods or services in the minds of their potential buyers. Cultural factors exert the broadest and deepest influence on consumer and business markets. Let us look at each of these processes to appreciate the impact of cultural dimensions on market decisions. Among the elements that need to be considered are three levels of evaluation: the culture itself, appropriate subculture(s), and social classes.

DEMOGRAPHICS

An important aspect of understanding culture as it pertains to market segmentation is to recognize that all cultures consist of smaller subcultures that offer their members more specific identification and socialization. Different immigrant nationalities, religions, racial groups, and geographical regions are subcultures. Many subcultures represent important market segments, and marketers often design products and marketing programs tailored to the needs of these segments. All societies exhibit social stratification, usually on the basis of income or ethnicity. Within these subcategories, additional culturally sensitive units may include people of a particular age, in a particular life-cycle stage, or with a particular occupation or lifestyle. The marketer's job is to understand the range of cultural differences represented by this social diversity so that he or she can properly position the product (good or service). Social customs, beliefs, values, and norms affect consumer choices, and a cultural understanding of different social groups in a market or region will help guide the design of goods or services at a global, regional, or country market level.

DEVELOPING MARKETING STRATEGIES AND PARTNERSHIPS

A critical element of global marketing strategy is determining how to link the company or organization to an increasingly competitive environment, i.e., selecting the markets to be entered or further penetrated. From a global marketing perspective, three factors may determine which countries to choose in this planning stage: (1) the individual appeal of a country market (e.g., India because of the size of its potential consumer market), (2) global strategic positioning (e.g., Israel because of its leading-edge high-technology design and development capability in the field of electronics), and (3) common dynamics in an economic zone (e.g., the NAFTA Southern Cone markets of Chile, Uruguay, Brazil, and Argentina). The key to developing a marketing and sales strategy is to conduct a detailed analysis of the industry and possible competitors within the market in order to establish a competitive advantage. This is an essential step in the planning process, in which key decisions are made about the extent of entry and which competitive strategy to adopt, the latter being determined by a choice among factors such as cost, differentiation, and focus. Furthermore, achieving a competitive advantage at the national level in a foreign country is dependent on the availability and condition of a number of resources: labor, natural resources, technical expertise, capital, and a working infrastructure. Each of these steps and the selection of resources have a distinct value within a given culture.

PRODUCT DECISIONS: GLOBAL STANDARDS VERSUS CUSTOMIZATION
The most important element of developing global marketing strategies is cross-cultural analysis, or the systematic comparison of similarities and differences in behavioral and physical aspects of different cultures. Cross-cultural analysis provides an approach to understanding market segments both across national boundaries and among groups within a society. The process of analyzing markets on a cross-cultural basis is helpful in deciding which elements of a marketing program can be standardized in multiple nations and which should be localized.

The most complicated problems in dealing with the cultural environment stem from the fact that one cannot learn culture, one has to live it.

PRICING STRATEGIES FOR MARKETING
The optimal price for a good or service is a balance between demand, as qualified by a client's willingness and ability to pay, and the need to cover costs and provide a margin of profit. Therefore, the global manager must develop pricing policies that address the specific environmental factors within each of the national or regional markets in which the company operates. Prices are constantly in flux and must be evaluated and adjusted regularly in light of product demand, competition, inflation/deflation, and local regulations.

In today's market, global organizations can pursue three alternative approaches to pricing. It is essential that the process recognize local income levels and competition. The three approaches reflect the environmental context of the market(s) and are described as follows:

1. *Ethnocentric*: A single price for a good or service is charged worldwide, with no adjustment for market-to-market conditions or potential profit.
2. *Polycentric*: The pricing approach is sensitive to local or regional market conditions.
3. *Geocentric:* This is a balanced approach that takes a midstream stance on pricing; global and local conditions over time drive the marketing and sales programs.[8]

DISTRIBUTION CHANNELS FOR MARKETING
Choosing a strategy for identifying and developing distribution channels is another key decision that global marketers are required to make. Distribution

channels are basically networks of individuals, service firms, or agencies that are highly diffuse points within national marketing systems. These points allow the flow of goods to and within markets and, when correctly structured, are a source of competitive advantage.

Establishing marketing distribution channels is one of the most challenging and difficult aspects of global marketing. Global marketing managers must understand that the formulation of distribution channel strategy is largely done by in-country management groups from within the company or through alliance partners. At the same time, the overall strategy must reflect the total marketing program as it relates to product design, price, and communications.

From a cross-cultural perspective, successful distribution channel strategy is influenced by several important factors:

- *Environment:* The strategy must respond to customers' need for a good or service that is conveniently available within, and appropriate to, the environment context.

- *Time:* The good or service must be available to customers at the times it is required or with less than the maximum tolerable delay.

- *Form:* The good or service must be prepared and packaged in a way that is acceptable to the customer (i.e., the size, color, shape, etc., must conform to cultural values within the market or region).

- *Relationships:* Making channel decisions involves a large number of interpersonal relationships that must be managed effectively. This includes spending the appropriate amount of time to reach, change, or terminate commitments and involves personal dedication to building relationships with distributors.

If properly managed at the country level with full attention to local customs, distribution channel agreements provide a valuable source of innovative new approaches that can enhance corporate strategy decisions.[9]

MARKETING COMMUNICATION: GLOBAL ADVERTISING AND PROMOTION

Effective global promotional programs involve an appropriate mix of elements, including indirect tools such as advertising, sales promotion, and publicity, that support the direct personal selling process. Of all the elements of the marketing mix, advertising decisions are the most critically affected by cultural differences in country markets. Customers respond in terms of their culture, style, feelings, value systems, attitudes, beliefs, and perceptions. The function of advertising is to interpret or translate the need/want-satisfying qualities of goods or services. Advertisements must therefore relate to cultural norms if they are to be effective. Among the diverse challenges and constraints of designing a global promotional campaign, for example, is the creation of a message that will appeal to the target culture—both customers/clients and the local personnel implementing the promotion. Reconciling the advertising and sales promotion effort with the cultural uniqueness of individual markets is one of the fundamental challenges facing the global marketer.

An effective promotional campaign involves a message directed at the target audience that leads that audience to understand the details of the good or service being offered and make the decision to buy or try the good or service. A key determinant in putting together the promotional message is the degree of standardization of the message or its customization for individual buying motives that needs to occur for the target country or region. This is one of the most widely debated areas in multinational or global marketing.

Standardization is supported by the contention that differences in the attitudes and needs of people across cultures are shrinking; therefore, individuals will respond to a single standardized campaign. In addition, marketers believe standardization provides cost advantages and allows a degree of control and leverage. This may occur across countries that share interests, similar levels of development, and/or a common language. Certain products, such as Coca-Cola, Mateus (wine), Levi-Strauss jeans, or Swatch watches, may have broad international brand recognition as the result of effective advertising and promotion and thus can be sold as a global brand throughout the world with a single message. Customization is more frequent in less-developed or developing countries, where a broad social range exists and local constraints fragment the markets. In such markets, the availability of various media to promote a product is limited, and the inherent costs of these media may be high. Examples of country-specific marketing programs are those of the Gillette Company, whose razors, blades, and toiletries have different names in different countries, such as Trac-II in the United States and G-II worldwide.

Crafting the promotional message involves understanding the linguistic nuances of the message as well as the general perceptual framework provided by the culture. Miscommunications and misunderstandings can occur as the result of a variety of factors, such as

- *Euphemisms in another language*: The Parker Pen Company promotional display for a brand of ink read in English " Avoid embarrassment; use Quink"; when translated into Spanish, it became "Evite embarazos; uso Quink," or "Avoid pregnancy; use Quink."
- *Incorrect translations of phrases*: Well-known examples of poor translations distorting the promotional message include the cases of Chevrolet and Ford in Latin American markets. The Chevrolet car name, Nova, and

the Ford car name, Fiera, mean "no go" and "ugly old woman," respectively, in Spanish. Coca-Cola's slogan "Coke adds life" became "Coke brings your ancestors back from the dead" when translated into Japanese.

- *Phonetic problems with brand names*: *Misair* sounds like the word for misery in French. *Bardok* sounds like the word for brothel in Russian.

- *Symbols:* An advertisement using an owl in India was ineffective because the owl is a symbol of bad luck in that country.

- *Unintended messages*: A detergent advertisement that showed soiled clothes on the left, a brand name soap in the middle, and clean clothes on the right worked in most countries—except in Arabic-language countries, where one reads from right to left. The resulting message thus read, "If you use our product on your clean clothes, they become dirty."

Other issues stem from the diversity of languages or dialects spoken in many countries, such as India and China. The large number of languages spoken in the world poses difficult questions for translators of promotional materials. Also, in areas where illiteracy is prevalent, marketers and salespeople need to rely much more heavily on effective images. Another matter to be aware of is the differences among subcultures, particularly linguistic or dialectic subcultures, that require tailoring the message to accommodate local needs and perceptions of good or services. The style of a written message in one language may be extremely difficult to translate into another language. Colors also have cultural overtones, and knowledge of local color symbolism is critical to success.[10]

Phase 3: Global Implementation

In the majority of companies, sales representatives have a critical role in determining the marketing mix. Salespeople are very effective in achieving a number of market objectives, especially those related to certain stages of the buying process, such as buyer education, negotiation, and sales closing. However, since a sales force is very costly, it is important that the company carefully consider when and how to use sales representatives to facilitate the marketing task.

The sales representative's mix of tasks varies with the state of the economy of the country in which he or she is working. Sales representatives perform one or more of the following tasks, each of which has a cultural dimension: prospecting, targeting, communicating, selling, servicing, information gathering, and allocating resources. In the new integrated view of marketing and sales, the salesperson decides on the types and mix of selling approaches that will define the market environment. In structuring these approaches, the sales representative needs to organize by territory, product, and market. The sales manager's responsibilities include adjusting pay scales, purchasing components, and training new salespeople and familiarizing them with the company, its history and products, the market(s) and competition, and the art of selling.

As the sales process is strongly dependent on personal selling (i.e., a direct market-customer focus), it is important that a company carefully consider when and how to use sales representatives to achieve its marketing objectives. The ultimate objectives of the sales force are customer satisfaction and company profit. The ultimate route to these objectives is the design and management of the sales force. All ten cultural dimensions are relevant to these objectives and affect the overall sales process.

THE SALES PROCESS

Today's customers range from individual consumers to large global and/or national organizations. In many country markets, each customer/client is treated as an individual market segment. Making contact on a direct personal level overseas requires the selection of specialized personnel. Ideally, they are directly recruited from the target country or market; this is frequently also mandated by law. Individuals from the target market have the critical language and cultural skills and understand the market's financial requirements. Furthermore, such individuals have full knowledge of the business protocol and negotiation techniques suitable to the company's image.

In today's diverse environment, it is important to view sales as encompassing a wide variety of styles and approaches. This diversity usually results from contrasting attitudes to personal relationship selling versus a transactional sales approach. A transactional sales approach emphasizes "making the sale" over spending time to cultivate the individual relationship as a means of achieving a sale. Personal relationship selling is grounded in the idea that customers and/or accounts require consistent, focused, and personal attention. Relationship selling requires a heavy investment in time and money, which may not be appropriate for all markets and companies.

Countries throughout Asia, for example, have a being orientation and stress the value of relationships in transacting business. This value affects business behavior and customs. The concepts of *quanxi* in China, *wa* in Japan, and *inhwa* in Korea speak directly to the relationship issue. Each of these concepts may be translated into English as "maintaining harmonious relations with the other." Their central place in business transactions indicates how important the concept of harmony is to the definition and maintenance of a business relationship in these countries.

- *Quanxi*: A dynamic element of Chinese culture, *quanxi* refers to a special relationship that two people have with each other, one in which they have agreed to exchange favors. An individual who refuses to return a favor loses face and is considered untrustworthy. Foreigners who wish to do business in China but have not established a *quanxi* relationship may very well have to deal with uninterested officials. To do business effectively in China, good personal connections must be established first. Decisions in China are made hierarchically, and superiors in each *quanxi* link must be in agreement.

- *Wa*: *Wa* is a Japanese concept that dictates that members of a group, be it a work team, a company, or a nation, cooperate with and trust one another. The Japanese prefer to do business with friends and do not like to deal with strangers. Before a business transaction can begin, the Japanese must situate the foreigner within a group context (a *wa* relationship must be established). The Japanese emphasize harmony and goodwill and prefer long-term relationships with business partners.

- *Inhwa*: A key factor influencing South Korean business behavior, *inhwa* stresses harmony by linking people of unequal rank, prestige, and power through a reciprocal and mutually beneficial system of loyalty. Subordinates defer to the judgments of their superiors, while superiors maintain a strong interest in the well-being of their subordinates. A corporation is viewed as a "family" or a "clan." As a consequence, Korean businesspeople prefer to establish personal ties with strangers before they transact business deals with them. As in China, a binding relationship in Korea is between individuals. *Inhwa* relationships are long-term, and cultivating them requires considerable time and much patience. Once these relationships are established, they must be continually maintained and strengthened.

A being orientation dominates in Latin American cultures as well. Therefore, interpersonal relationships between individuals are also critical to doing business in these cultures. The buyer-seller relationship is essential and is cultivated to build trust, confidence, and respect. The long-term nature of the relationship is very important. A mistaken emphasis on the transaction over interpersonal relations usually leads to a failed venture or contract.

A transactional sales approach, one in which relatively little or almost no time is spent on building personal relationships before moving to a sale, is appropriate in the United States, Canada, and many northern European countries. In many Western cultures (those of the United States and Europe), personal relationships play a diminished role in business interactions and are subservient to a focus on the product and production itself, including product characteristics, price, speed to market, and consummation of the sale. This approach is difficult for businesspeople from such places as Asia and Latin American to understand. The doing orientation that this approach represents may seem distant, impersonal, or too "businesslike" to those from being-oriented cultures, where the personal relationship is important.

Orientations to time are an equally important aspect of customer/client relationships. Multifocus salespeople will devote a lot of time to individuals as a means of developing a long-term relationship. Time spent learning about the other person is essential to enable the two parties to assess the viability of a long-term relationship, business venture, or exchange of goods or services. Such salespeople need the right amount of time and support for building a relationship. When delivering a sales pitch, the multifocus person may spend time developing an impressive presentation, but it will never replace rapport and a longer-term relationship. In multifocus cultures, therefore, a greater amount of time is spent in preparing and setting up sales calls and presentations. The past orientation to time also plays a large role in such cultures.

Single-focus individuals and their clients, in contrast, will favor elaborate sales presentations (overheads, multimedia) and will be prepared to move the discussion directly to concluding the sale of the product. These features substitute for much of the time devoted to building the relationship in multifocus cultures. For example, to a U.S. American or northern European, the presentation itself and the delivery of its key points are critical elements in the sales process. Therefore, a good presentation and strong group discussion/facilitation skills are critical to being effective.

DESIGNING AND MANAGING THE SALES FORCE
Objectives and Strategy

The high- and low-context cultural orientations to communication have an important impact on the strategic planning process. In low-context cultures, such as the United States, a written, specifically documented strategic sales plan is the absolute measure. For high-context cultures, however, the written plan is only the starting point in a long, evolving process in which participants form and manage networks of personal contacts and influence. In such cultures, plans are expected to change as individuals move into and out of the context in which the plan is evolving. As networks change, the plan moves forward, but with different support and input. Most Asian cultures are high-context. In these cultures, for example, details of strategic planning are not set until the roles, responsibilities, and hierarchical relationships of the individuals and groups involved have been determined. Another cultural dimension that affects the planning process is time. Different orientations to time can make the long-term strategic planning process full of challenges. In cultures in which there is a fluid orientation to time, schedules, deliverables, and flowcharts are seen as very flexible guidelines for completing a project. In contrast, in cultures with a fixed orientation to time, strategic planning is characterized by strict adherence to such things as precise objectives, plan milestones, and a tight schedule of deliverables. Goals or objectives are ulti-mately seen as much more critical, and the steps or events required to com-plete these goals are expected to evolve over time.

Structure and Size

The sales strategy will directly determine the organizational structure of the sales force, which may have one of four organizational formats: geographical or territorial, product, customer or market, and selling function. A single-prod-uct focus might benefit most from a territorial or function-based approach, whereas a multiproduct focus requires a product or market structure.

With a geographical or territorial organization, the salesperson will be required to put much time and effort into cultivating personal relationships and business ties. In other words, the salesperson needs to emphasize the being over the doing orientation on the action dimension. The emphasis here is on personal selling. The salesperson needs to understand how his or her per-sonal style fits into the local culture and how he or she can effectively bring about a sale. The design and shape of territories may be a function of natural barriers or of the particular ethnic groups present and their respective cultural influences, as well as being based on the workload or sales potential and travel times within a territory.

In the case of a product-based sales force, the organizational structure may arise because of the complex technical nature of the good or service or because of the sheer variety of the company's products. In either the territo-rial- or the product-structured approach, establishing personal relationships is central to success in the sales effort. The customer- or market-structured sales organization also requires the salesperson to establish close relationships (a being rather than a doing orientation) with different customer segments in order to attain a better and deeper understanding of unique customer needs.

The selling function sales structure is the most efficient for performing specialized selling activities (e.g., one sales force might specialize in

prospecting for and developing new accounts, while another sales force maintains and services existing customers). This structure is most prevalent in low-
context environments, where less emphasis is placed on the interpersonal side
of business relationships and greater emphasis is placed on concluding the
sale in a timely and efficient manner.[11]

Compensation

The management of sales force compensation is related to such issues as the
level and components of compensation and their relative importance in the
overall compensation plan. Compensation normally includes fixed (straight
salary) or variable (salary plus commissions, bonus, or profit sharing) salary,
expense allowances, and fringe benefits. In certain countries, mainly in Asia,
various cultural orientations combine to favor fixed over variable compensation. In Japan, for example, where the strong hierarchy orientation dictates
that family connections and seniority be rewarded, salary increases are based
on longevity within the company. Because the Japanese also have a collectivist orientation, commission systems are tied to the performance of the
entire sales force as a team. The economic aspirations of the individual are
deemphasized. Family background is most important in determining social
position. Since wealth therefore has only a very limited role in determining
status, straight salaries are considered more desirable and respectable.
However, in certain Western countries, especially the United States, where the
individualistic orientation holds sway, each salesperson strives to earn the
maximum amount of money possible. This results in a wide variety of sales
commission schemes, both fixed and variable.

Recruitment and Selection

The selection of effective and high-performing sales managers and representatives is at the very core of a successful sales organization. As market conditions
vary from country to country, adapting to changing cultural perspectives and
values is clearly one of the most challenging tasks facing the international salesperson. Companies seek to recruit and train only the top salespeople and to
avoid the risk of lower productivity as a result of hiring the wrong individuals.
Lack of understanding may hinder adaptation and adjustment to new situations,
leading to frustration and insecurity. The cost of making an inappropriate choice
is enormous, not just in lost sales but in the turnaround time and cost incurred
when one salesperson is replaced with another.

Once the appropriate market-driven and culturally driven selection criteria are determined, recruitment can begin. In some markets, such as those in

Asia and Latin America, the sales profession is lacking in prestige. Reasons for this lack of status include the view that sales is a job that requires deceit to bring success, is characterized by a high level of insecurity, and demands that individuals travel so much that they miss time with family and friends.

The diverse nature of markets in certain parts of the world, primarily in Asia, is also an important consideration when recruiting a sales force. Language and dialects alone make it difficult for an organization to field an adequate sales force. The multiplicity of languages can result in fragmented markets that are characterized by small, yet meaningful, sales segments. Centralized recruitment efforts may not be effective in addressing such a broad range of needs. The salesperson not only has to speak the particular language or dialect of the local market but must also have certain personality traits, including the ability to use personal connections to drive up sales.[12]

Managing and Improving Sales Training

The increasing level of sophistication among customers and clients demands that salespeople have an in-depth knowledge of the product, be highly efficient and reliable, and be able to provide additional product support or new ideas to the client. Time spent in training is time not out on the job selling; thus, while training is important, because of the investment required, both by the salesperson in the form of direct time and by the company in the form of materials, facilitators, etc., it must be managed in such a way that as much of it as possible occurs on the job. The staff's technical expertise is critical to maintaining an image of the company as competent, responsive to customers' needs, and having goods or services of the highest quality. Sales presentations and field procedures must all be geared toward displaying the capabilities of the company as well as its sales force.

In many cultures, local business practice may dictate the adoption of particular sales training techniques and methodology if training is to be effective in enhancing sales performance. The training process is successful only when the role of cultural orientations is taken into consideration. Individuals from different cultures learn differently. Adapting a training process to the host culture is the key to avoiding a culture clash resulting from an ethnocentric perspective. In collectivist cultures, for example, the group is the norm through which effective training and learning occurs. Everyone expects to learn in a team environment, and individual demonstrations of proficiency will occur only at or near the group norm. No one individual will distinguish him- or herself in the process. In countries with an individualistic orientation, such as the United States or most countries of Western Europe, an individual is expected to demonstrate individual initiative and to learn and excel on an individual basis. This creates a more competitive environment.

The direct, in-class approach to training may not always be appropriate. In Japan, training occurs on the job, with a mentor assigned to help the individual learn the products and sales techniques required to be successful. Individuals are rotated frequently (every year or two) throughout the organization. The assignment of a mentor to one individual is a very personalized approach. Performance appraisals, coaching, feedback, and critiques are all conducted in a formal, impersonal manner so that the individual does not lose face and remains focused on constructive criticism.[13]

Directing and Motivating the Sales Force

Supervision is an aspect of managing a sales force that addresses the interplay of individual and personal objectives and company objectives. Understanding the role of the sales force in an organization, what motivates people, and the types of stresses and concerns that the sales force has are critical to managing it successfully. Studies across various country markets with broadly diverse cultural environments show that the stress that sales force personnel experience in performing their job is highly similar. On the other hand, what motivates people tends to be considerably different across cultures.

The harmonization of individual and company objectives is a difficult task even in one's own market, let alone in a different country or region. From a U.S.-American perspective, company objectives take priority over personal preferences and social obligations, since the company is viewed as a social entity. People must feel a strong obligation to fulfill the requirements necessary for the company's success. The company takes precedence over family, friends, or other activities that might detract from what is best for the company. This view is not, however, universal across cultures. In many cultures, obligations to friends and family supersede obligations to one's company or profession.

Specific motivational incentives used in the United States, such as monetary and nonmonetary rewards (cash, honors, or identification with a larger group or organization) for outstanding performance, cannot be universally applied in other regions of the world. In northern Europe, for example, where personal income tax rates are quite high, noneconomic motivators work better. In high-context cultures, such as Latin America or Asia, economic rewards are less effective than social recognition. In Asia, for example, there is a strong belief that personal relationships are more important in daily life than the needs of the corporation. Paternalism, collectivism, the assurance of lifelong employment, and a hierarchical system based on seniority all serve to make the direct or open praise of good performance inappropriate. The norm in Japan is to blend with one's peers and associates, not to become the object of special public appreciation or consideration. Sales achievement awards are group-oriented and involve social acknowledgment rather than economic incentives. This is equally the case in Arab cultures, where a constraint orientation to the environment dictates that the individual is not responsible for personal achievements and should not expect to be rewarded for individual enterprise.

Evaluating the Sales Force

Performance reviews raise different issues for high- and low-context cultures. In low-context cultures, such as those of the United States and much of Western Europe, reviews are based on demonstrable and observable performance data, which are collected, analyzed, and shared directly with the salesperson in open discussions. In these cultures, the written word is treated quite formally and carries a large amount of weight and influence. In cultures where friendship or family ties may be more important than the organization, the criteria for selection, organization, and motivation are substantially different. In certain cultures, such as those of Latin America, organizations expand to accommodate the maximum number of friends and relatives. In high-context cultures, usually found in Asia, Latin America, and the Middle East, networks of interpersonal relations are still the primary channel for completing evaluations or assessments. Since personal ties and friendships are considered much more important than merit, the motivational levers are quite different.

The need to preserve face is the dominant motivator in high-context cultures. In many high-context countries, sharing objective performance data can be effective only if this is done in the context of a relationship or a personal communication. Such a communication may also be made nonverbally or indirectly, such as by assigning an individual to a lower-level assignment or by not including the individual in a meeting or team assignment.

The overall operations of the sales organization can be evaluated through a variety of quantitative measures (sales results, such as orders, sales volume, margins, or customer accounts; or sales efforts, such as sales calls, selling expenses, or customer service) and qualitative measures (territory management, marketing intelligence, follow-ups, and selling skills). These measures permit the assessment of performance in terms of effectiveness and efficiency. Evaluation of sales performance on the job requires a heightened sensitivity and a clear understanding of motivational factors on a country-by-country basis around the world. In high-context countries, the results of such an evaluation need to be expressed indirectly and with utmost discretion rather than directly and matter-of-factly as they often are in the United States and other low-context countries.

IMPROVING THE SALES MIX

The improvement of all components of the sales mix is an ongoing process that requires the international sales manager to constantly be in touch with the sales personnel. It also requires the international sales manager to remain aware of the cultural environments into which the sales force is being sent and/or in which and to which the sales force is making sales. Every member of a sales force must be committed to global learning to ensure his or her continued awareness of the culturally appropriate sales behaviors and strategies to produce successful sales.[14]

Of particular importance for improving one's sales strategies is monitoring one's relationships with the customer and improving one's negotiating abilities. The sales personnel and sales manager must inform themselves of the particular expectations a culture has for the long-term customer-salesperson relationship and seek to conform to these expectations. Negotiating tactics should also be reviewed regularly to ensure that they are in line with the current stage of the sales process and with cultural preferences.

Culture and the Sales Process

Selling is a multistep process, and none of these steps is culturally neutral. For our purposes, we have discerned seven discrete steps of selling. These steps are described below.

Step 1: Identifying Needs and Prospecting

The focus here is on strategizing, preparing for, and planning the sales call. In this step, cultural, financial, historical, economic, and political due diligence is used to determine an approach that will meet the needs of both the salesperson and the customer/client. Having a set of guidelines for analyzing the prospective market and identifying specific cross-cultural characteristics and values that would affect successful entry into that market is the key to success.

Step 2: Approaching the Customer and Building Relationships

The focus here is on identifying and communicating with an individual, a group, a network, or a company. This initial contact between parties can be straightforward, direct, and relatively brief and informal in low-context/doing cultures, such as the United States, or it may be formal and demanding of time, energy, and resources, as in Asian and Latin cultures. In low-context/doing cultures, the initial contact consists of a brief meeting in which the firm contacted reviews the proposal and data provided by another firm. Little time is spent building rapport. In high-context/being cultures, however, the successful salesperson will need to pay particular attention to developing a personal relationship first. This will give him or her organizational credibility and lead to effective sales.

Step 3: Making the Sales Presentation and Relating Benefits

The focus here is on gathering, assessing, and presenting information that is relevant to the customer/client's interests, issues, and needs. When personal relationships are built and the business network is penetrated, each side undergoes a period of orientation to the other's way of doing business, its organizational culture, the individuals involved, and the specific circumstances of the relationship. Each side and each person involved engages in a reassessment of the other. Each party seeks to understand its counterpart's goals, constraints, problem-solving approaches, and requirements. Based on this assessment, each side defines the business interests that will guide the future relationship. Then, based on this assessment and the resulting definition, all parties create an alignment. Depending on the cultural region, this phase requires varying degrees of attention, time, and resources.

Step 4: Managing Resistance, Handling Objections, and Providing Feedback

The focus here is on dealing with, handling, and responding to objections—one of the most difficult tasks in the selling process. During this phase, the salesperson also tries to obtain feedback to assist him or her in completing the sales call. The salesperson needs to respond with caution and attention, using active listening skills. She or he should not respond to an objection too quickly, especially in high-context cultures. In such cultures, taking time to pause and reflect is essential to making sure that the objection is clearly understood. Silence can be an effective tool in managing the exchange. Although more information may be appropriate when dealing with prospects from high-context cultures, providing too much information may emphasize the objections rather than the benefits of a good or service, as targeted information is the fundamental reason why an individual or organization makes a purchase. If the salesperson does not know the answer to an objection, he or she should defer to a higher authority and provide the additional information as soon as possible. To confirm the level of objection, it is best to use culturally appropriate questions. In direct cultures, closed-ended questions will usually yield the desired response. In indirect cultures, however, an open-ended question might prove more effective. In the indirect cultures of Asia, for example, the "yes" or "no" that results from a closed-ended question may have many shades of meaning. In such cultures, a buyer's "no" rarely means a complete turndown. A simple "yes" or "no" can mean "maybe" or even the opposite response. It is important for the salesperson to listen and remain attentive to sales clues. These might be the prospect's personality, facial expression, or word reactions. For example, in Japan a "yes" may mean "no, but " or "yes, maybe." Furthermore, in certain cultures, individuals do not respond unilaterally to questions, but instead defer to a broader group. Individuals from Arab cultures generally have a strong expressive orientation and thus frequently express themselves in very emotional terms, which might appear to be disapproving or negative. This, however, is not the way the response is meant.

Step 5: Using Influence and Negotiation Styles

The focus here is on bargaining with and persuading others through the use of logic/thinking styles, evidence, and influence strategies. This step depends on culture-based perspectives, values, and attitudes toward decision making as well as on the expectations of the customer/client, which have been defined in prior steps of the sales process. It is significant to note that bargaining between buyer and seller, with both striving to achieve an acceptable price, is quite common in many countries, especially in Asia or the Middle East. Since buyers in these regions expect to bargain, they often makes offers that are much lower than the asking price without realizing that such offers seems completely unreasonable to individuals from regions where bargaining is not practiced.

Step 6: Understanding the Techniques and Methods that Gain Commitment (Closing the Sale)

The focus here is on reaching and concluding a sales agreement. Review the use of concessions and compromises in reaching an agreement. The route to the conclusion of a sale may be long and circuitous in many parts of the world, especially since many foreign buyers view time quite differently from the way U.S. American or northern European buyers view it. For example, U.S. Americans are always in a hurry and are under great pressure to obtain results. Sometimes this leads them to back off from important objectives just to conclude a sale and move on to the next client.

The meaning and significance of an agreement differ across cultures as much as the ways in which the sales agreement is expressed. Cultural orientations have an impact on what is considered an agreement, how binding it is, how specific it is, and what its legal standing, ramifications, and duration are. In some cultures, a contract is the goal of a negotiation. In others, it is a platform from which business relationships are developed. The contract may also indicate an intention to continue the negotiation process when circumstances change. In such cases, a written agreement may simply mean the start of a long-term relationship, not the culmination of business talks. To the Chinese, for example, the conclusion of an agreement merely opens the prospect of a long term relationship. In fact, full closure of the deal is actually never realized; thus, it is important for both parties to be very specific about the content of the agreement and what actions will be taken as a result of it. A Chinese buyer will patiently continue to try to expand his expectations and objectives after a contract has been signed. Overall, it is important to be very patient when closing a deal in different cultures. If one moves too quickly to conclude a deal, one may be viewed with suspicion or distrust.

Step 7: Maintaining the Positive Relationship Established with the Customer during the Sale

The focus here is on following up on obligations and maintaining relationships after the conclusion of the business deal. The objective of any marketing and sales effort is to establish ongoing, repeat business. This ultimate phase in the sales process is perhaps the most critical for long-term and profitable relationships across cultural and national boundaries, yet it can be one of the most demanding. In high-context cultures, such as those of Asia or Latin America, maintaining client relationships is critical not only as a sine qua non to opening and closing an initial sale, but as an essential prelude to a much longer-term relationship. A Taiwanese or Brazilian client, for example, would expect an ongoing relationship with the salesperson to evolve, at both the personal and the professional level. Contracts or agreements are simply the beginning of a relationship in these cultures, with the legal stipulations given somewhat less emphasis than the personal contact. In low-context countries, quality after-sale service is inherent in the contract agreement itself and reflects the level of accountability each salesperson demonstrates in carrying out his or her job and ensuring timely sales for the company.[15]

SUMMARY INSIGHTS

This chapter has outlined applications of the Cultural Orientations Model to the customer-focused business functions of marketing and sales. As organizations pursue global business strategies, an understanding of the influence and impact of culture on management practice in general, and especially at a functional level, is a critical element in achieving competitive superiority.

Marketing and sales, in particular, require an acute sensitivity to local cultures in order to effectively position and sell the company's goods or services in a manner consonant with local market environments. Marketing and sales executives who spend their time and resources learning about the cultural differences and similarities among consumers and who use this knowledge to develop products, promotions, distributions, and sales strategies will ensure strategic competitive advantage for their companies and demonstrate leadership roles in their industry.

Our models of marketing and sales provide structured frameworks for mapping the specific applications of cultural competence to success in foreign markets. They can guide business professionals in conceptualizing, testing, and designing appropriate approaches and strategies for securing and improving their global market position.

7

TRANSLATING GLOBAL VISION INTO LOCAL ACTION: FOCUS ON MULTICULTURAL TEAMWORK AND COLLABORATION

Never doubt that a small group of thoughtful,
committed citizens can change the world,
indeed, it's the only thing that ever has.

MARGARET MEAD

Our exploration of the impact of culture has taken us from an investigation of the changes in organizational structure required in order to pursue global opportunities to a discussion of specific managerial skills, actions, and dilemmas. The realization of a global vision rests firmly on the ability to align and calibrate organizational structures and strategies with people—people who reflect and represent worldwide cultural diversity. This alignment and calibration are nothing more than building, nurturing, and cementing an organizational ethos (culture, climate, and identity) that is able to transcend differences and optimally integrate them for collective performance. That the reality is that global work is increasingly taking place in a virtual, technologically enabled environment only adds complexity to this already complex task.

In Chap. 1, we established that an organization needs a cadre of global managers and leaders who understand how to operate with a global mindset, a mindset of which cultural competence is a critical element. These are individuals who have internalized the idea that, in addition to their functional roles and expertise, they act as strategists, architects, coordinators, communicators, and facilitators. They have come to clearly understand that they are the agents of clarity and purpose in their sphere of influence, that their mandate is to counteract the proliferation of ambiguity and uncertainty and the blurring of just about everything that is inevitably unleashed by organizational globalization.

Consciously or unconsciously, these managers and leaders, when effective, operate with a high degree of cultural competence. They conduct cultural due diligence and apply style switching with the implicit awareness that there are multiple ways to attain a desired result—in fact, because of the multicultural scope of global projects, multiple ways to attain the targeted outcome are needed. They routinely engage in cultural due diligence and dialogue, as they are keenly aware that building the necessary foundation of trust, credibility, and rapport requires preparation and the acceptance of the idea that their own set of expectations and values cannot simply be projected onto others. They take their cultural mentoring seriously through active steps in their sphere of influence, assisting new employees or team members through the processes of cultural adjustment and adaptation; establishing common ground among diverse expectations, work practices, and approaches; enabling shared learning and development; and leading the culture of their organization. They actively establish the conditions of participation and representation that are necessary for global integration, alignment, and synergistic collaboration.

For many, the cultural orientations approach has become managerial shorthand for framing and steering the "soft side" of global performance. This concluding chapter is dedicated to discussing how the cultural orientations approach can assist the processes, mechanisms, and practices for translating a global vision into local actions.

FRAMING EFFECTIVE GLOBAL PERFORMANCE

It helps to take a look at what happens when a given initiative becomes global. The process starts with a desire to make a product, process, or service perform similarly or achieve similar results by preserving a maximum overall efficiency. Such a vision fuels both organizational structure and strategy. Once the conditions for maximum efficiency have been created and *hard* business parameters, such as sourcing, production, or manufacturing, have established the desired efficiency, organizations are shifting their attention to the complex, less quantifiable people processes. The litmus test of globalization lies specifically in the effectiveness with which a global vision has been translated into targeted and appropriate local actions. This process is essentially a megacommunication process, in which the mental picture of a typically small executive group is filtered and replicated to guide the actions of the organization's employee base.

This megacommunication process of filtering and replicating a vision involves three levels: the organizational, the individual, and the group or team. The last of these is the primary bridge between the organizational vision and individual action and deserves specific attention. Given the increased importance of effective communication, coordination, and management in dealing with global people processes, these processes have become a leadership imperative of the highest order. There are specific leadership levers at each level. The global performance development framework shown in Fig. 7.1 graphically displays these levels and the levers that are involved in the megacommunication and translation process. Figure 7.2 defines the various elements further.

As this process is essentially a communication process, it is subject to the cultural distortions discussed in Chap. 5. As its components define the global leadership domain of translating a global vision into local actions, reducing the distortions and creating a platform of shared understanding and integrated practices becomes an increased focus. This can be seen most clearly in the immediate performance environments of individuals, i.e., the teams and groups within which daily collaboration takes place. This level is the true frontier of operating globally, as it is the true locus of synergy and the place where integration is forged.

This frontier is defined by the requirement that groups of individuals transcend significant barriers of social, cultural, and geographic distance. In our work, we have come to call groups that effectively operate on this frontier

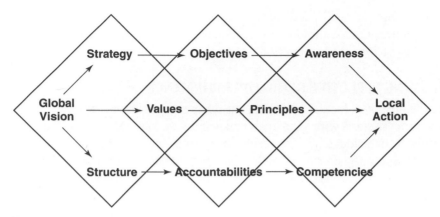

FIGURE 7.1   Global performance development framework.

Transcendent Teams.[1] In a globalizing organization, leadership needs to be directed toward enabling transcendent teamwork swiftly and through purposeful actions. The name captures the need for each individual to exercise and support such actions.

MEETING THE CHALLENGE OF TRANSCENDENCE

The key challenge for Transcendent Teams is to harness the power of true teamwork across distance. This amounts to a formidable challenge, since it is difficult enough to achieve the required synergy among people from similar backgrounds who share the same language and operate in the same location. If local culture is like gravity, as Trompenaars claims,[2] then Transcendent Teams are gravity-defying. The central question for both members and leaders of these teams is: *How can we create an identity and a process that will enable us to build cohesive teams that override, integrate, or coordinate the various modes of operation of each local environment, i.e., the gravity of each locale?*

In teams with geographically dispersed members, two realities coexist: the virtual or distant reality of the dynamics of the team across tangible and intangible distances and the actual or local reality of each team member's immediate environment, with its own norms and requirements. The conditions of the immediate environment, including time zone, language, socioeconomic reality, organizational structure, functional role, and cultural values, define a local reality that exerts a strong force on each individual team member. Transcendent teams will not be successful if team members remain so immersed in the local reality that they cannot properly enter the virtual or

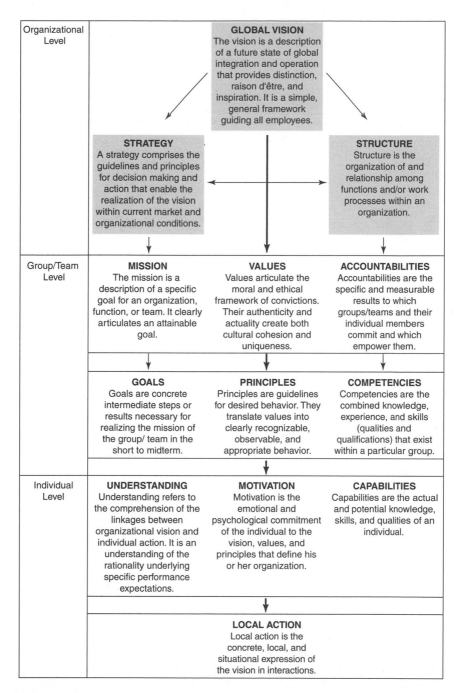

FIGURE 7.2

distant reality of the team. Scenario 7.1, "Battling Local Gravity," recounts the experiences of one team in dealing with local reality.

Scenario 7.1: Battling Local Gravity

A Spanish/U.S. research team at a U.S.-based technology company was having great difficulty building a cohesive identity. This was especially troublesome because the team was charged with a strategically important research and development project through which the company hoped to gain entry into a new market. The team was having significant difficulties because of the overriding power of local cultures, which reinforced negative stereotypes on both sides, and because of divergent operating models, processes, and practices. The dynamics of headquarters-subsidiary relations aggravated all these factors. The Spanish members felt that their U.S. colleagues did not solicit their opinions and perspectives and that decisions were made at headquarters without consideration or understanding of local realities. Consequently, they were not motivated to contribute fully to the team's work. They made sure that they met the minimum requirements, but beyond that they gave priority to other, local issues. Language difficulties and a lack of understanding of such U.S. business practices as brainstorming and frequent meetings (which they viewed as excessive) contributed to their sense of alienation. Their U.S. colleagues perceived them as being unreliable and uncommitted and viewed them as obstacles rather than assets. Both sides seemed to fortify their positions rather than create mutual trust and synergy. Because the project entailed technology developed in Spain, and because quick results were expected, the team leader was at a loss as to what to do about both the slow progress and the growing antipathy among the team members.

A successful Transcendent Team may start out as a group of separate individuals, each driven by and grounded in his or her local reality. However, this group develops into a team and learns to defy gravity; that is, it develops transcendence. Facilitating, and even accelerating, this transition is the key mission of the team leader, who needs to be equipped with the necessary awareness, knowledge, skills, and tools. This includes a thorough knowledge of both the team-development process and the phases of building cross-cultural effectiveness.

For a project team to achieve transcendence, all members of the team must be properly aligned with the team and the team culture. This means that they must overcome the forces of local gravity that make them resistant to becoming fully integrated into the team. Each petal in Fig. 7.3 represents a different person, and these people are pulled in different directions by local forces. These forces could derive from an individual's national or regional culture, from the culture of the individual's functional group (such as research and development, marketing and sales, or finance), or even from some other source, such as generational culture or family culture. Only when all team members are able to see their primary role on the team as being a member of that team (as opposed to being an expert in research and development, for example) will the team be able to properly achieve transcendence.

It is particularly important for leaders to focus on the process of building cross-cultural effectiveness or transcendence in the context of team development. Both team members and leaders need to pay close attention to the group processes required to maximize constructive and minimize destructive potential.

There are many models and frameworks that describe the various phases of team development. Among the most prominent are those developed by B. W. Tuckman,[3] Jon R. Katzenbach and Douglas K. Smith,[4] and Sylvia Odenwald.[5] All these models, with minor variations, describe a similar process of team development that seems to be captured most intuitively by Tuckman's stages of forming, storming, norming, and performing.

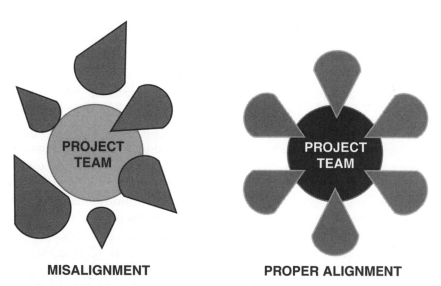

MISALIGNMENT   PROPER ALIGNMENT

FIGURE 7.3   Proper project team alignment.

What each model is missing, however, is a description of the process by which successful multicultural teams overcome cultural differences. This process, which is concurrent with other processes necessary to team formation, forms the core of the work of transcendence. The main aims of transcendence are to

1. Build cohesion through a strong team culture.
2. Overcome differences in cultural orientations among team members and leverage these differences for competitive advantage.
3. Transcend other sources of difference, such as time zones and locational and functional cultures.

Inspired by Milton Bennett's model for developing cross-cultural sensitivity[6] and our work with many different multicultural, global teams, we have developed a five-phase process for reaching transcendence.[7] These phases are as follows:

1. *Minimization*. In the minimization phase, barriers, differences, and key sources of social distance are recognized only on a superficial level. The most important of these sources are language and accent, location and time zones, functional culture, personal outlook, professional background, tenure, technology, organizational structure, and differing institutionalized systems and practices. The overall effect of these sources of social distance on productivity and collective performance in the consciousness of both the team leader and team members is minimized at best.

2. *Defense*. In the defense phase, as the awareness of the critical nature of the differences and sources of distance grows among team/group members, so do the defenses against change and adaptation. Differences and sources of distance are perceived as threats. Organizational, functional, and personal cultural differences can become amplified and in many situations serve as hiding places or even battlefields that significantly diminish productivity and collective performance.

3. *Acceptance*. Acceptance means that differences and sources of distance are taken seriously. They are recognized as critical obstacles to productivity and to collective performance, and team members exhibit an increased willingness to change and adapt. In this phase, cultural due diligence, style switching, dialogue, and mentoring are most effectively applied.

4. *Practice development*. Practice development means that the team consciously develops principles, guidelines, and practices to reduce social distance. Team/group members cultivate mindsets, competencies, and skills that measurably improve their effectiveness and collective performance. Communication and work protocols are established in order to

better facilitate cohesion. This requires each member to engage in conscious change, compromise, and style switching. The new practices and behaviors, such as new norms for the use of communication technology, emailing, or meeting management, may pull each group/team member out of his or her comfort zone and at times feel contrived or forced.

5. *Transcendence (or practice integration).* Transcendence means that the mindsets, principles, and practices that were consciously crafted and rehearsed in the previous phase become internalized and deeply engrained in the culture of the group/team. They become the source of cohesion upon which productivity and collective performance are based.

In the development of a Transcendent Team, these five phases are concurrent with the phases of regular team development, although the two processes occur at different paces. In our conceptualization, the five phases of regular team development are borrowed from Tuckman (forming, storming, norming, and performing), with a selection phase added.

For optimal Transcendent Team development, the phases of the two processes should be aligned as shown in Fig. 7.4. In order to form an effective and highly productive Transcendent Team, it is necessary that the team simultaneously pass through the five phases of transcendence and the five universal phases of team development. In Fig. 7.4, the universal phases are represented by the odometer's outer ring: selecting, forming, storming, norming, and performing. The five phases of transcendence are represented by the odometer's inner ring: minimization, defense, acceptance, practice development, and transcendence.

MANAGING TEAM DEVELOPMENT

In this section, we briefly examine the phases of team development, factoring in the challenge of overcoming critical barriers, many of which are either rooted in cultural differences or expressed through divergent cultural orientation patterns. We have organized our discussion around the five phases of regular team development. For each phase, we explore the role of culture and the steps necessary to achieve transcendence in a multicultural team.

Phase 1: Selecting

This phase consists of decisions concerning team membership. This is crucial for the ultimate success of the team insofar as the correct mix of talent, business units, and cultural backgrounds is key to achieving the team's goal. There are several things to consider when selecting people for a Transcendent Team.

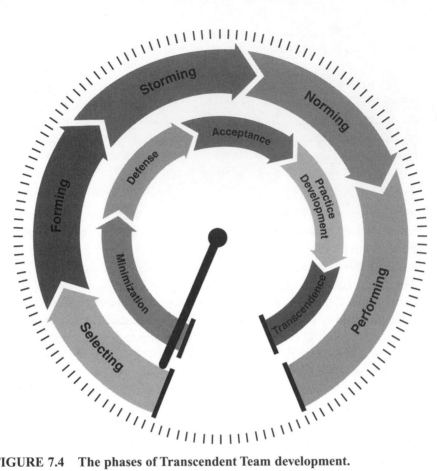

FIGURE 7.4   The phases of Transcendent Team development.

First, the composition of the team needs to be commensurate with the scope of the team's mission and objectives. For example, a global leadership team for a U.S. company with operations in more than 70 countries that is seeking to institute significant organizational changes will encounter great difficulty if it is composed only of representatives from the United States. It would be best if it had members representing several, or even many, of the more than 70 countries affected.

Second, the geographical location of team members is another key consideration. Members can relocate to a specific location, or they can remain at their local sites. The decision about location or relocation depends on a variety of factors:

- *The structure of the organization.* Global organizations may distinguish themselves by, for example, establishing centers of excellence or expertise; in most cases, this requires the co-location of team members.

- *Technology.* The technological infrastructure must enable members to communicate constantly and quickly and to access all relevant information as needed. Many organizations have been struggling with incompatible IT infrastructures, which cause frustration and underperformance (lack of productivity).

- *Assumptions and attitudes.* The general assumptions concerning and attitudes toward relocation, mobility, and expatriation on the part of (1) the organization and (2) the people involved are important. The latter are influenced by how acceptable and/or desirable mobility and expatriation are to the individuals in a given social environment. The former are governed by the level of institutional support for and understanding of the personal difficulties and challenges that cross-border and cross-cultural expatriation engenders. Lack of preparation and unresolved culture shock can significantly lower performance. Before deciding on the appropriate strategy for guiding expatriation, it is important to take the relevant organizational and social issues into consideration, assess the potential consequences for team performance, and ensure adequate support. For more information on the issue of international relocation, please consult any or all of the following books: *So You Are Going Overseas,*[8] *Survival Kit for Overseas Living,*[9] *Moving Your Family Overseas,*[10] and *In Another Dimension: A Guide for Women Who Live Overseas.*[11]

The following two scenarios illustrate how technology and assumptions can affect team development.

Scenario 7.2: Accessing the Intranet

At a team-building event for a global project team of a leading international provider of professional services, members discovered that the Latin American team members were not fully connected to the organization's intranet and that they did not have at their disposal the tools, databases, and information that they needed if they were to fully meet the expectations associated with their team roles. The lack of a global IT structure meant that the Latin American talent could not bring their full expertise and experience to bear on the project. This put them at a significant disadvantage for global as well as local projects.

Scenario 7.3: "They're No Longer Like Us"

A U.S.-based marketing organization relocated European managers to its Illinois headquarters to ensure that its European subsidiaries were represented at its center of decision making. Top management was surprised to find that most of the subsidiaries did not perceive this as a positive development and did not feel that they were well represented. Focus groups at the subsidiaries provided the insight that those who had been relocated were perceived as having become too "Americanized" to adequately represent the situation back home.

A third factor that should be borne in mind is that functional expertise alone is not a predictor of success on a Transcendent Team; in many cases, it is only a basic qualifying requirement for being selected. If it is not complemented by excellent interpersonal, communication, and leadership skills, upon which cross-cultural competency rests, functional expertise may not benefit the team.

Fourth, success at the local level may not translate into global success. An individual's success in a local environment does not guarantee his or her success in a global or multicultural environment. Cultural differences significantly affect success criteria. A global mindset and skill set are required to ensure effectiveness.

Finally, prior experience on a Transcendent Team does not guarantee success in future team collaborations. In the global business environment, Transcendent Teams are becoming increasingly common. However, there are many more teams in existence that are barely functioning than there are teams that are truly excelling. It is important that those team members with prior experience on Transcendent Teams have learned from their experience, particularly with respect to communication and cross-cultural sensitivity, and that they are willing to share and continue their learning. An individual's attitude toward continuous learning should be a major criterion for selection.

In summary, the key challenge is to ensure that the selection criteria are adequate and to check the underlying assumptions and beliefs that determine the selection process. As members are selected, it is essential that the team leader get a sense of the selected members' backgrounds, personality styles, and perspectives. These insights are critical to determining how the team members need to prepare for the forming stage of team development and to anticipating key issues for the team development process.

Phase 2: Forming

The formation phase is the initial phase of team development. It is during this phase that the groundwork is laid for all team processes and their ultimate success. The main tasks at this stage are becoming oriented, clarifying the mission and goals of the team and becoming committed to them, and generating a positive climate of enthusiasm and clarity of purpose and role.

On the interpersonal level, the main development task is to establish credibility, trust, and rapport among team members. On the group level, this translates into developing a collective sense of identity, cohesion, and purpose. The tasks of the team leader are to foster relationship building and team consciousness, provide direction, and ensure that the vision, mission, and goals of the team are understood and shared. To a great extent, it is the leader's responsibility to ensure that all these issues are adequately addressed. This requires a thorough understanding of how cultural orientations and other sources of distance might affect the team and its members.

As should already be clear from our earlier discussions, there is significant variation across cultures in the way in which credibility, trust, and rapport are established. When considering how a particular culture regards the establishment of trust and credibility, it is critical to consider the following:

- Is trust assumed and automatically extended, or is it earned and incrementally built? In highly industrialized countries, such as the United States, the Netherlands, and the United Kingdom, trust and open access are more readily extended up front, and are withdrawn only when experience shows that trust and access are not warranted. The reverse is true in cultures such as India and France, where trust is earned slowly, and skepticism and distrust are the initial conditions.

- Does credibility hinge on status, credentials, performance, or some combination of these three? In countries such as Japan, Mexico, Spain, France, and Germany, the hierarchy orientation of their cultures significantly affects the process of establishing credibility. Such markers of social status as age, position, and title help in building credibility in such cultures. On the contrary, in highly industrialized and advanced capitalist societies, such as the United States, Sweden, and the United Kingdom, the actual performance, actions, and activities of individuals at the time of the project are what establish credibility.

- Do "good" relationships rest on personal affinity and the development of closer ties or on maintaining distance? In cultures with a formal orientation, such as Germany and Japan, "good" collaborative relationships depend less on personal affinity and more on maintaining the appropriate level of formality and professional distance. In environments that value informality, such as the United States, affability is a key ingredient of a good relationship.

These issues play a large role in relationships among team members, but they also significantly affect the effectiveness of the team leader. For example, a team leader who is formal and instrumental in orientation, and who sees his or her credentials as the foundation for his or her credibility, may experience a significant "disconnect" with team members who are focused on achievement, affability, and the development of close bonds with fellow team members.

Such differences are not trivial. The critical development tasks of a Transcendent Team in the forming phase are to build relationships, set responsibilities, and establish a clear sense of purpose—and all these are intimately affected by cultural orientations. Team members need to devote time and energy to becoming acquainted and developing relationships of trust. Team leaders need to ensure that this time is available and is used optimally. In establishing appropriate ways to build relationships, it is important that the leader consider the specific cultural makeup of the team. Scenario 7.4, "The Functionality of Challenge," demonstrates how different the approach to disagreement and confrontation can be across cultures.

Scenario 7.4: The Functionality of Challenge

The U.S.-American leader of a U.S. team experienced significant problems in forming a multicultural team that included, among others, French and German employees. He found that the French and German team members often became embroiled in vociferous arguments over the processes and procedures to be followed. Whenever these arguments threatened to break out, the team leader tried to reduce the tension and smooth over the issue with general statements. After all, he felt, not only were these "debates" stalling the process, but they seemed inappropriately timed, destructive, and demoralizing. The team leader perceived the German and French members as hostile to each other and lacking in team spirit. Conversations with managers from both the German and French sides, however, revealed that the team members not only enjoyed their debates, but felt that their mutual criticism contributed significantly to the team's project by ensuring better quality. Each side welcomed the other side's criticism as a challenge and an opportunity to display their breadth of knowledge and professional competence. Conversely, both groups saw the team leader as weak and of questionable competence, as he seemed to back off from debate and gloss over important issues instead of clarifying them.

Critical impasses at the formation stage can be resolved through intensive face-to-face interaction and a balance of structured and unstructured occasions for team members to socialize and get to know one another. Geographically dispersed team members are at a disadvantage, since significant travel and expense are often necessary to enable such interactions.

CROSS-CULTURAL AWARENESS IN THIS PHASE

In the formation phase, cross-cultural awareness and skills are usually low and often coincide with the stages of minimization and defense—unless, of course, team members have had extensive prior experience on multicultural teams. Even team members with prior experience, however, may not fully realize all the implications of cultural diversity. They may find themselves working with individuals from backgrounds they have not previously encountered, they may feel overconfident about their understanding of cultural differences and thus be less receptive to new learning, or they may stereotype from their experiences with a few members of one culture, expecting others from that culture to conform.

In any case, cultural awareness will often be low and effective skills lacking. At the very least, skills will certainly not be the same among all members. It is important that cultural differences and the various ways in which these can affect a team be brought into the open at this stage. The goal is to heighten team members' awareness of cultural differences in order to make these differences a known focal point for the team, and to introduce a process and vocabulary that encourage an open dialogue about these differences. This is critical, since many cultural issues tend to be internalized by individuals, and so they are rarely acknowledged or discussed.

It is not essential, however, to address all layers of culture at this stage of team development. In fact, only those that are pertinent to developing a working relationship and to establishing mutual understanding and communication should be addressed. Among these issues are language, communication style and processes, and decision making.

Language.   Language is among the most fundamental and multifaceted issues for Transcendent Teams, yet it is rarely addressed honestly. It is often downplayed or overlooked altogether. Inevitably, team members will possess varying degrees of competency in and comfort levels with the language chosen for communication. This often leads to misunderstandings and embarrassment.

Although English is the lingua franca commonly used in cross-cultural business situations, the following issues are independent of the specific language used:

1. *Native versus second-language ability.* Native speakers of a language often underestimate the difficulty experienced by speakers who have acquired the language later in life. Native speakers often use idiomatic and/or colloquial expressions (including slang and local contractions— "gotcha" is an example) that leave many second-language speakers guessing. Embarrassed by their ignorance of these terms and expressions, they often dare not ask for clarification. The opposite may be true as well: Speakers for whom the language used is not native often superimpose the new vocabulary from this second language onto the grammatical structures of their native tongue. Their use of the second language often incorporates elements of their native language. Native speakers may therefore misunderstand or be puzzled by the expressions used, yet feel too embarrassed to ask.

   When native speakers are around people who seem to have an excellent command of the second language, they may be lured into a sense of comfort, with the result being an increase in the speed of their speech and a greater use of colloquial expressions and contractions. This is particularly the case with English speakers. Speakers of English as a second language (ESL) often have exceptionally well-developed business and professional language skills, but these individuals often are not used to an informal, social use of English. The problems that can arise from this discrepancy are often aggravated in the United States and Australia, where an informal use of language is part of business communication.

   Conversely, native speakers often lose sight of the fact that active language skills (speaking and writing) may not correlate with passive language skills (listening and reading). People who have obvious difficulties in speaking or writing may hear and read the language well.

2. *Accents.* Another language element that often creates difficulties in communication is accent. Second-language speakers often have an excellent command of the language, but speak the language in a way that is difficult for native speakers to understand. Native speakers, on the other hand, may have regional accents (for example, the southern Scottish, Indian, and U.S.-English accents) that are difficult for second-language speakers to comprehend. The difficulty in comprehending someone's accent can be

aggravated by the use of such technologies as the telephone and video-conferencing. While exposure to and interaction among team members will render these difficulties less significant over time, it is important that team members be aware that initially their accents can cause misunderstandings and that they be prepared to address the problem.

3. *Use of multiple languages.* When a Transcendent Team has several speakers of one or more languages that are not shared by other members of the team, standards for the use of these other languages must be established. If a team has two or more speakers that use the same language, should they use that language in team meetings? If they do, how will others who may not understand feel? It is not uncommon for team members to feel insecure, excluded, and alienated when colleagues use a language that they do not understand.

Communication style and process. Beyond language competency and usage, there are broader issues of communication style and process that need to be considered.

1. *Style.* Cultural orientations significantly affect the way we communicate. In particular, the formal-informal, direct-indirect, and expressive-instrumental continua of the COM need to be considered.

   - *The formal-informal continuum.* Different cultures and different generations within a culture exhibit different orientations toward formality and informality, particularly when initiating a relationship. In Germany, for example, where formality is traditionally a strong value, there is a marked generational difference that expresses itself in many ways, from forms of address to behavioral norms to acceptable clothing.

   - *The direct-indirect continuum.* The direct-indirect continuum of culture relates to the way in which team members make requests of one another, address problems, and resolve conflicts. Indirect communication is frequently found in environments that place a high emphasis on face saving, personal honor, and dignity. The communication styles commonly found in Latin America, East Asia, and the Middle East tend to emphasize indirectness. This means that subtle cues, including nonverbal ones, are frequently used to communicate disagreement. Direct refusals (as in the simple reply "no") are often considered impolite or even unacceptable. This can cause tension with individuals who have direct communication styles, such as those observed frequently in northern Europe, certain parts of the United

States, Canada, and Australia. These two styles of communication can clash in situations in which negative feedback is provided or when team members express disagreement. A direct communicator may be perceived as disrespectful, insensitive, and tactless. Indirect communicators, on the other hand, may be perceived as dishonest, evasive, weak, and fearful.

- *The expressive-instrumental continuum.* This continuum is of key importance, particularly with regard to evaluating a colleague, team member, or counterpart as professional and/or competent. People with an instrumental orientation tend to communicate in an objective and impersonal way. Often, this style is accompanied by frequent references to facts and external sources of data. For an instrumental communicator, emotions in work situations should be minimized. The opposite is true of expressive communicators. For them, emotions and emotive displays are key components of communication in the workplace. Passion is essential, and frequent references to personal experience are key to communicating effectively. From the perspective of an instrumental communicator, the expressive style seems unprofessional and incompetent.

2. *Communication processes.* Just as styles differ, so do expectations for communication processes. These include the use of communication technology and face-to-face meetings.

- *Communication technology.* In today's workplace, we are presented with a variety of choices of media and modes of communication. We may decide to walk over to someone's desk for an impromptu chat, use the intercom, leave a voice mail, send an email, schedule an appointment, send a fax, or conduct a videoconference. For the most part, we make these choices unconsciously, based on preferences that correlate with our patterns of cultural orientations. The efficacy of email and voice mail, for example, has been found to correlate significantly with the levels of rapport that have already been established in a relationship. Cultural context and cultural receptivity to these media also play an important role. Our choices of technology, however, are rarely based on a conscious consideration of these factors. More often, they are dictated by convenience and by hidden expectations concerning speed and responsiveness. The decision to send an email, for example, may be based on the hidden assumption that a speedy response will be received. When the speed of the response does not conform to our expectations, we may become impatient and accuse the recipient of lacking adequate communication skills. These experienced "delays" and frustrations may be the result of mismatched expectations.

As Table 7.1 illustrates, while they allow more instantaneous communication, the communication technologies at our disposal all have shortcomings. It is in person-to-person contact that the individual still has the greatest control over all aspects of communicating: words, format, voice tone, immediate feedback, nonverbal clues, environment, physical exchanges, and informal exchanges. Each communication technology is best suited for specific types of communication and requires different levels of context and rapport to be effective.

By developing general guidelines for communication during team formation, Transcendent Teams develop shared expectations for the use of technology and the structuring of messages.

- *Face-to-face meetings*. In order to build cohesion and energize its members, every team needs to emphasize face-to-face meetings among team members. Unstructured social time is a key element in building strong team relationships. Though this is necessary, it is often logistically difficult and expensive. Team members may have to travel great distances to come together, so that a considerable investment of time and money is required, as well as the sacrifice of personal time. To maintain and enhance the momentum of interpersonal relationships, teams need to meet frequently and consistently. An effort should be made to ensure that the burdens and sacrifices are evenly distributed. Local holidays also need to be taken into account when scheduling face-to-face meetings.

Decision making. The issue of decision making is a key consideration for every Transcendent Team. It lies at the heart of team culture, since decision-making processes reflect the team members' values and the degree of integration and trust among the team members. Individuals who are empowered to make certain decisions will feel trusted and valued. On the other hand, excluding individuals from the decision-making process can signal distrust and thus be highly demotivating.

In addition, individual team members may have very different expectations concerning decision-making processes. How much data, reflection, and analysis are necessary before a decision can, or should, be made? When are decisions necessary? These are issues that no team can solve easily. The

TABLE 7.1   The Efficacy of Communication Technology

	Email	Voice mail	Telephone conference	Video-conference	Face-to-face meetings
Words	√	√	√	√	√
Control over format		√	√	√	√
Voice tone		√	√	√	√
Immediate feedback			√	√	√
Nonverbal clues				√	√
Environment				√	√
Physical exchange					√
Informal exchange					√

Intrinsically Most Suited for

                Participative discussion and debate

                Reaching agreement and understanding

                Discussing sensitive issues

Factual information sharing

Exchange of data

Clarification or summarizing meeting results

Low Context		**High Context**
High Level of Rapport	←——————→	**Low Level of Rapport**

Source: This table has been adapted from *Globally Speaking: Skills and Strategies for Success with Asia*, Video Two, (San Francisco, Calif.: Meridian Resources Associates, Inc., 1997) and from Marian Stoltz-Loike, *Managing a Global Work Force: A Cross-Cultural Guide* (New York: Warren Gorham & Lamont, 1989).

potential solutions will reflect the personalities and cultural orientations of the individuals involved.

All the issues discussed here are essential to the formation stage. Addressing them at the beginning and demonstrating awareness of the various and differing needs concerning decision making are key to a team's success.

Phase 3: Storming

The storming phase is key to the formative development of a Transcendent Team. It entails a sense of conflict and crisis as team members become fully aware of the implications of culture and cultural differences for the management of work and problem-solving activities.

Up to this point, team members have generally been enthusiastic about their mission. The team has operated according to the foundation laid in the formation phase, and members have gathered experience with the different personalities, work styles, and cultural orientations of their fellow members. Guidelines for collaboration have slowly been taking hold. Up until now team members' experiences have been both positive and negative, but now hidden tensions between functional areas, cultural groups, and individual personalities begin to surface. Enthusiasm usually begins to decline. Team members become more conscious of the constraints, requirements, and conditions of meeting the team's objectives. Critical team development tasks tend to center around establishing clarity regarding roles, responsibilities, expectations, and work practices. Increasingly, task-related details and processes become an issue.

As tensions rise to the surface during the storming phase, it is imperative that the team sustain a positive climate, while at the same time resolving contentious issues and establishing clarity. As conflict and friction are experienced, a key leadership task becomes managing and facilitating conflict in a positive way and harnessing the opportunities contained in every crisis.

The cultural orientations of team members significantly affect the events and outcome of this stage. While the surface elements of culture tend to be the focal point of understanding cultural differences during the forming phase, deeper levels of culture affect the storming phase. This is due to the fact that default behaviors that reflect culture-based preferences tend to emerge most strongly in a conflict or crisis situation, and the ability of individuals to switch styles diminishes.

The most relevant cultural dimensions for this phase are structure, competitiveness, individualism, power, space, and environment. Table 7.2 outlines the importance of each of these dimensions.

CROSS-CULTURAL AWARENESS IN THIS PHASE

When the crisis inherent in this stage is positively managed and facilitated, it forces team members to examine and confront the deeper manifestations of culture. Team members will now realize that there are profound differences between themselves and others, beyond the levels of language and communication. The learning inherent in this stage should move a team out of a minimization mindset into one of acceptance.

TABLE 7.2   An Overview of the Central Cultural Dimensions in the Storming Phase of Transcendent Team Development

Cultural dimension	Role in storming phase
Structure	Order-oriented individuals have difficulties with ambiguity and uncertainty. They tend to be risk-averse and resistant to change. As leaders, they tend to map out precise guidelines, but they may not have provided for all contingencies. Anxiety and tension result as the order-oriented team members try to establish certainty and predictability in a situation that offers none.
Competitiveness	Latent conflict between functional groups and/or sites may create a sense of internal competition that ultimately is destructive to the cohesion of the team and therefore to the achievement of the team's transcendence goal. While external competition can add to the team's cohesion, internal competition is highly corrosive. It is critical that resource allocation, reward, recognition, and compensation systems be designed and aligned so as to minimize internal competition.
Individualism	Individualistic-oriented members may disassociate themselves from the team process and assert their uniqueness and individuality. They may also assert territorial claims to decision making and other aspects of the work that they regard as their domain. This can be highly damaging to team relations and to the development of team cohesion. This tendency can be especially pronounced in team members whose value to the organization lies in their unique skills and competency base, such as research scientists, consultants, or sales managers.
Power	Hierarchy-oriented individuals may expect the leader to provide the clarity that the team seems to lack at this point. When a leader does not fulfill this expectation, the leader's credibility and effectiveness tend to drop in the eyes of hierarchy-oriented members. Team members' motivation may suffer as well. Equality-oriented individuals, on the other hand, may expect to share in the clarification process. They will expect to be heard and to have their positions fully considered. They assume that any decisions clarifying issues and procedures will be made by the team as a whole. If these expectations are not met, the equality-oriented team members may feel demotivated.
Space	The psychological dimension of space is most significantly involved in this phase, particularly as it relates to territorial behavior. Particularly in cross-functional environments,

(continues)

Cultural dimension	Role in storming phase
	individuals with a private orientation to space may be more prone to apprehension about loss of authority and power as well as about sharing information.
Environment	As conflict occurs, orientations toward the environment may influence the resultant behavior and positions of team members. Control-oriented individuals will tend to take charge and actively engage in conflict. Harmony-oriented individuals will strive for a balance and offer a position that is already a compromise. Constraint-oriented individuals may expect explicit guidelines, general clarity, and conflict resolution mechanisms to be provided

This is not an automatic process, however; it needs to be carefully facilitated by the team leader. A skilled leader may even take steps to accelerate the crisis component of this phase, realizing that a team must face and resolve these crisis elements before it can perform effectively.

If the issues that arise in this phase are not resolved appropriately, the team may become stuck at a level of bare functionality or pure dysfunction. Unfortunately, cultural differences can play a significant role in whether conflicts are solved well. In fact, they can become a political battleground.

Some of the biggest conflicts faced by team members in globalizing organizations result from members' fears of losing control over their domains. The protective reactions that arise when others move into a member's "territory" are a consequence of feelings of invasion and encroachment. When team members feel threatened, they will engage in protective behavior designed to keep the "intruders" out. This leads to politicking and various tactical behaviors in which cultural differences often become amplified and suddenly emerge as insurmountable barriers.

Phase 4: Norming

During this stage, the team establishes norms and operating principles and practices to govern team processes, all the while taking into consideration the diverse perspectives, personalities, styles, weaknesses, and strengths of its members. This stage essentially consists of defining and creating the operational platform on which the team's performance culture will be built.

This is an important step for any team, but it is particularly crucial when local gravity must be overcome in order to develop team transcendence on a multicultural team. It requires each team member to make a commitment to the constant and continued pursuit of learning and to the conscious adaptation of behaviors.

Following are some of the key issues related to culture and distance that need to be considered, discussed, and put into action.

STANDARDS FOR MANAGING ACROSS TIME ZONES

In many organizations, global managers find themselves on the phone or in videoconferences with colleagues around the world at all hours of the day and night. This often entails a significant sacrifice of family life and leisure time. Needless to say, members of Transcendent Teams need to feel that the inconveniences and burdens of global teaming are shared equally. Expecting the same people to be available at the same odd hours every week, for example, can create resentment, particularly when such sacrifices are not openly acknowledged.

Travel and meeting locations also are an issue. A team should make sure that it is not always the same people who are required to travel every time a meeting or event takes place. In many organizations, employees at the subsidiaries travel more frequently than their counterparts at headquarters. The location of meetings should be chosen so that each site gets an opportunity to act as host (thereby increasing exposure to and mutual understanding of local realities), or in such a way as to minimize everyone's need for travel.

When scheduling conference calls, videoconferences, and the like, it is important to factor in the local social environment within which team members operate. In cooperative- and order-oriented cultural environments, individuals may be less inclined to make sacrifices that threaten their quality of life or that infringe upon prior social obligations. National and religious holidays also need to be taken into consideration.

These considerations are especially important for U.S. corporations, which provide relatively little vacation time and observe few national holidays. The U.S. corporate environment is one in which employees readily spend extra time at work. Individual, personal achievement and a pragmatic attitude that dictates that people do whatever it takes to get the job done are both highly valued. Managers in many U.S. organizations assume that their international counterparts (1) are motivated by the same values of achievement and pragmatism, and (2) are equally willing or able to sacrifice personal time. Scenario 7.5 "U.S./European Issues," illustrates how differently someone's work ethic may be perceived depending on whether the perceiver is from a doing- or a being-oriented culture.

Scenario 7.5: U.S./European Issues

Jason Brown, a U.S. manager in Sweden, had tremendous difficulty establishing a rapport and his credibility with his Swedish counterparts. He would frequently stay late in the office, and he was often the first one on the job in the morning. After only a few weeks, many of his Swedish colleagues started to suspect that something was wrong with Brown's family life. Since the balance of family and work life is prized in Sweden and since family obligations are taken as seriously as work obligations, they found it difficult to understand how their U.S. colleague could consistently assign work obligations a higher priority than spending time with his family.

Such differences in attitudes toward work and personal time often lead to difficulties and misunderstandings. Absences from work due to vacations and holidays can lead to interruptions in work flow and work processes if they are not adequately planned for. Information and expertise are temporarily inaccessible and therefore are unavailable to the team. Furthermore, team members who work in cultures where there are fewer holidays, less vacation time, and a higher level of competitiveness tend to assume that their colleagues with more vacation time, more holidays, and cooperative cultural patterns are less productive. This hidden assumption can have a significant impact on relations among team members. While many studies suggest that there is no direct correlation between hours at work and productivity, the subjective impression nevertheless exists. It is difficult to correct and can erode social relationships and trust among team members.

DEADLINES AND TIME LINES

The cultural dimension of time poses a significant challenge for Transcendent Teams, since team members can differ widely in their orientation along the fixed-fluid continuum. When deadlines, appointments, and time lines are set, team members may understand them very differently. There may be a variety of assumptions concerning (1) how binding they are and (2) what degree of variance or negotiability exists.

An individual with a fluid orientation may perceive a given deadline or time line as an expression of good faith and desire, but assume that unforeseen circumstances and interference will automatically change the deadline. Such a person expects an inherent flexibility in time lines and often perceives them as inherently negotiable.

Individuals with a fixed orientation, on the other hand, tend to view dead-lines and time lines as firm. They expect strict adherence to them and do not allow them to be negotiated. They may also expect employees to do whatever it takes to meet deadlines, measuring professional behavior, reliability, and trust on the basis of adherence to time lines.

INFORMATION SHARING AND EXCHANGE

One of the biggest complaints from teams is that information is not shared appropriately. The concept of local gravity discussed earlier has a tremendous effect on this process.

We are more likely to relate important facts and information about an issue to people who are physically close to us but uninvolved in the issue than to those who are physically distant. We may recount a meeting or presentation in great detail to a colleague whom we see regularly at the water cooler or cof-feemaker, but who has nothing to do with the project, while forgetting to inform colleagues abroad who may be part of the project. When we do tell these colleagues about the meeting, our accounts are often restricted to the facts. We often leave out our subjective evaluation and the personal qualities of our experience—information that is often crucial for proper interpretation and understanding.

Communicating through email can be equally problematic. Evidence sug-gests that people are more likely to send an email message to someone a few offices or cubicles away than to someone in another part of the world. For most people, email has become an additional way of sharing information and communicating that is integrated into a local repertoire of casual chatting, shared lunches, and informal meetings. These email messages may include or allude to contextual information that is not shared by distant colleagues or team members. Thus, what falls by the wayside is the subjective, emotional, contextual information that lends meaning to a message beyond the words seen on the screen.

The cultural dimension of space also has great impact on information-sharing behavior. In private-oriented environments and for people with this orientation, access to and the sharing of information are not key values. In fact, often the opposite is true; secrecy and information hoarding are not only expected but reinforced and rewarded. When information is used to mark ter-ritory and fend off unwanted "intruders," teams whose effectiveness rests on the swift access to and processing of information may experience severe dif-ficulties. In these situations, it is important to check for any of the following culturally related issues:

- Whether the individuals, organizations, or functions involved are threatened in any way or apprehensive about the changes that are inevitably required as a result of global operations
- Whether the cultural environment and social background of the individuals involved are ones in which information sharing is approached from a different perspective (often, a strong hierarchy and/or order orientation creates differing expectations)
- Whether the expectations for information-sharing behavior are clearly articulated, explained, and realistic

Processes, guidelines, tools, and rewards need to be established in order to facilitate the development of the process of the desired information-sharing behavior in a Transcendent Team. Rewards and recognition systems must reflect the high value placed on information-sharing behaviors. Some organizations that are team-based, yet maintain individualized reward, recognition, and compensation processes, are putting in place synergy measures: ways in which individuals document any input by and assistance from others.

COMMUNICATION STYLE AND PROCESSES REVISITED
Once actual communication among team members has taken place, it is time to revisit the ground rules that were established when the team was formed. The most important areas to be revisited in this phase are (1) problem solving, (2) conflict management, and (3) decision making. Ultimately, these are the three areas of greatest concern and with the greatest potential for friction. Any team, whether monocultural or multicultural, is likely to be very unclear about these processes; cultural differences can only add to the inherent sources of frustration.

CROSS-CULTURAL AWARENESS IN THIS STAGE
During this phase, the focus of cultural awareness has shifted from the differences that exist among team members to the commonality that can be established among them. This means that emphasis is placed on building and cementing the culture of the team itself. Operating agreements, guidelines, and principles are discussed and agreed upon. These will require each member to engage in adaptive behaviors to transcend her or his individual comfort zones and to adopt some new practices.

Phase 5: Performing

If the previous four phases have been managed successfully, the team will have created its own specific principles, guidelines, practices, and expectations—that is, it will have created its own culture. It is this culture that ultimately enables the team to transcend the various sources of social distance and to exert the gravity-defying power required. This strong team culture will enable all members to focus increasingly on task-related issues. Because this new team culture is highly vulnerable, it will have to be carefully monitored, maintained, and nurtured. Following are the key features of teams in this stage:

- The team should have moved from a low-context to a high-context communication style, enabled primarily by personal face-to-face experiences among its members. A solid, foundational level of trust should exist, and procedures for the team's pursuit of its objectives should be in place.

- The team should have established its basic organization and interaction processes. These includes the process through which work gets done and the ways in which team members communicate with and relate to one another. Establishing these processes entails maintaining a balance between the doing and being orientations to action.

- The team should have established its identity, a high degree of cohesion, and a sense of collectivism. This means that team members should trust one another, be committed to the team, and provide assistance to one another. The team should have developed its own unique, distinctive culture, with individuals feeling a sense of pride in their membership. A key element in this development is that the team celebrates its successes and develops unique features. Enabling identity, cohesion, and collectivism should be key goals of the team leadership.

- The team should be aware of its tendency to exclude, which is a function of cohesion and collectivism. Too much cohesion and collectivism can establish a sense of exclusivity or cliquishness that inhibits the absorption of new talent and resources. It may also inhibit the continued flexibility that allows the team to adapt when changes are necessary. Maintaining flexibility and openness is another key goal of team leadership.

CROSS-CULTURAL ISSUES: FROM PRACTICE TO TRANSCENDENCE
As a team moves through the various phases of development, particularly the crises of the storming phase, team members develop the relationship platform and interpersonal understanding required for their collective performance. Through continuous monitoring and guidance by a skilled team leader, the team culture comes to incrementally supersede the social distance that operates among team members. The commitment, motivation, collaborative mindsets, and interdependent partnering skills of team members allow for the

shared development and integration of conscious operational practices; that is, the team develops the culture of transcendence.

Key cultural orientation indicators of a Transcendent Team culture are

- A moderate to high level of context
- A balance between the being and doing orientations
- A high degree of collectivism
- A high degree of structural flexibility that allows the team to retain its dynamism and the capacity to change

Teams that exhibit these key team culture indicators will have established a sound collaborative platform on which collective performance can rest. The most significant implication of this is that three prerequisites are critical for enabling a Transcendent Team:

- The team leader must be skilled in developing, managing, and maintaining the team culture and establishing his or her own authority, credibility, trust, and rapport with team members. The team leader needs to ensure that performance expectations are high and that team culture development is included as a performance goal.
- Team leaders must invest time and energy in tracking and managing the development of their team's culture. Important categories and cultural dimensions need to be evaluated alongside specific team-development issues.
- Team members must be encouraged to develop a collaborative mindset. Since accelerating team development and expeditiously attaining a transcendent operating mode is a key imperative in many globalizing organizations, preparing employees with the requisite awareness, mindsets, and competencies is a necessary development objective. This objective entails not only individual development but also organizational development. It is of key strategic importance to aligning training and development efforts with organizational goals.

SUMMARY INSIGHTS

We have come full circle in our journey, which started with the phenomenon of globalization and the role of culture within it and moved on to the leadership focus and actions required for building cultural synergy and integration as the foundation on which the actualization of a global vision so critically relies. Our discussions have taken us through abstract and strategic macro issues as well as concrete and tactical micro issues. The complexities of doing business globally are characterized precisely by the inescapable realization that global work requires first and foremost being conscious of the interrelated nature of formerly separated management and organizational domains. Our work in this area has led us to some general recommendations for practice and development that are targeted at the organizational level, the team/group level, and the individual level. Since they are general in nature, each organization, team, and individual is challenged to establish specific practices conducive to establishing a "culture of multiculturalism" upon which global effectiveness so critically hinges.

Recommendations for Organizational Practices and Development

- Develop, communicate, and reinforce a global vision based on the requirements for global mindsets and cultural competence.
- Create an atmosphere in which cultural differences are openly recognized, discussed, and valued (use a consistent vocabulary to address cultural differences).
- Embed cultural and cross-cultural competence into all management and leadership development initiatives and tools.
- Develop and communicate operating approaches and principles (distinguish between core and negotiable principles).
- Foster learning through the creation of knowledge and information sharing (e.g., meeting practices, knowledge base).

Recommendations for Team/Group Practices and Development

- Include cultural self- and other-awareness measures in formal and informal team development processes.
- Develop team norms (i.e., a team culture) based on an understanding of the multiculturalism of the team's members, including norms and principles for using communication technologies.
- Develop and practice new member integration processes based on explicit cultural introductions.
- Foster continuous learning (e.g., global meeting locations with associated learning activities, cultural briefings).
- Incorporate the practice of cultural due diligence into the operating procedures of the team in order to manage the performance environment of the team.

Recommendations for Individual Leadership Practices and Development

- Actively continue building (1) cultural self- and other-awareness and (2) the skill of style switching.
- Pursue global learning through the use of knowledge and information resources (include Web-based resources, books, papers, etc.).
- Hone and apply listening, observation, and inquiry skills for building cultural knowledge.
- Differentiate between culture-based form and content for decision-making processes.
- Develop an awareness of how your culture-based preferences are amplified in your team and how they affect team performance (beware of your blind spots).
- Continuously develop and practice the art of style switching in order to direct, motivate, and align people successfully.
- Be alert to the danger that cultural differences become a scapegoat for other organizational performance issues.

Notes

Chapter 1

1 "Setting a Course for the New Global Landscape," *Financial Times* (London), January 30, 1998.

2 Michel Camdessus, "Making Globalization Work for Workers," Address to the 24th Congress of the World Confederation of Labor, Bangkok, Thailand, December 2, 1997.

3 Benjamin Barber, *Jihad vs. McWorld: How Globalism and Tribalism Are Reshaping the World* (New York: Ballantine Books, 1995).

4 Rosabeth Moss Kanter, *World Class: Thriving Locally in the Global Economy* (New York: Simon & Schuster, 1996).

5 Vijay Govindarajan and Anil K. Gupta, *The Quest for Global Dominance: Transforming Global Presence into Global Competitive Advantage* (San Francisco: Jossey-Bass, 2001), chaps. 1 and 2.

6 "Setting a Course for the New Global Landscape."

7 Colin Coulson-Thomas, *Creating the Global Company: Successful Internationalization* (New York: McGraw-Hill, 1992), pp. 12–13.

8 Michael J. Marquardt and Nancy O. Berger, *Global Leaders for the 21st Century* (Albany, N.Y.: State University of New York Press, 2000).

9 Jacques Delcourt and Philippe de Woot (eds.), *Les Defis de la globalization— Babel ou Pentecote?* (Louvain, Belgium: Presses universitaires de Lovain, 2000); Robert Gilpin and Jean M. Gilpin, *The Challenge of Global Capitalism* (Princeton, N.J.: Princeton University Press, 2000); John Micklethwait and Adrian Woodridge, *A Future Perfect: The Challenge and Hidden Promise of Globalization* (New York: Time Books, 2000).

10 Reginal Dale, "The Globalization Conundrum," *France*, Winter 2000–2001, pp. 31–34; Agence France Press, "France's Anti-Globalization Hero Gets Jail Terms for McDonald's Attack," September 13, 2000; Jean Marc Vittoli, "La Mondialisation prise en otage," *L'Expansion*, no. 657, November 22–December 5, 2001.

11 *Global Trends 2015: A Dialogue about the Future with Non Government Experts*, National Intelligence Council (National Foreign Intelligence Board), NIC 2000-02, December 2000, pp. 15–17.

12 "Annual Survey of World's Top 500 Industrial Corporations," *Financial Times*, August 2001.

13 *Global Trends 2015*, pp. 34–35.

14 Ibid., pp. 36–40.

15 Fred Harmon, *Business 2010: Five Forces that Will Reshape Business* (Washington, D.C.: Kiplinger Books, 2001).

16 Richard S. W. Judy and Carol D'Amico, *Workforce 2020, Work and Workers in the 21st Century* (Indianapolis, Ind: Hudson Institute, 1997).

17 William E. Halal, "The Top 10 Emerging Technologies," *Futurist*, July–August 2000; Marquardt and Berger, *Global Leaders*, pp. 5–16; H. Wayne Hodgins, *Into the Future: A Vision Paper*, National Governors' Association (NGA) and American Society for Training and Development (ASTD), 2000, pp. 5–7.

18 John L. Daniels and N. Caroline Daniels, *Global Vision: Building New Models for the Corporation of the Future* (New York: McGraw-Hill, 1993).

19 Govindarajan and Gupta, *Quest for Global Dominance,* pp. 223–245.

20 Hodgins, *Into the Future*, pp. 12–15.

21 Hodgins, *Into the Future*, pp. 39–43; *Global Trends 2015*, pp. 38–39; Judy and D'Amico, *Workforce 2020*, pp. 15–25.

22 "Globalization and the Knowledge Economy," Management Consultancies Association Report, August 1999.

23 Christopher A. Bartlett and Sumantra Ghoshal, *Managing Across Borders: The Transnational Solution* (Boston: Harvard Business School Publishing, 1998).

24 Loc. cit.

25 Jeffrey E. Garten, *The Mind of the CEO* (New York, Perseus Publishing, 2001).

26 Sarah Anderson and John Cavanagh, "Top 200—The Rise of Global Corporate Power," Institute for Policy Studies (IPS), 2001.

27 Rosabeth Moss Kanter, *Rosabeth Moss Kanter on The Frontiers of Management* (Boston: Harvard Business Publishing, 1997).

28 Samuel Huntington, *The Clash of Civilizations and the Remaking of World Order* (New York: Simon & Schuster, 1997).

29 Francis Fukuyama, *Trust: The Social Virtues and the Creation of Prosperity* (New York: The Free Press, 1995), pp. 5–6.

30 Alison Maitland, "Throw the Rule-Book Out of the Window," *Financial Times*, February 8, 2000.

31 World Economic Forum and Harvard University, *The Global Competitiveness Report* (Oxford University Press, 2000).

32 Edgar Schein, *Organizational Culture and Leadership* (San Francisco: Jossey-Bass, 1996).

33 Anne Fisher, *Fortune*, January 24, 1995.

34 Garten, *Mind of the CEO*, pp. 83–84.

35 Robert Heller, "Connect the Dots," *CIO Magazine*, March 1, 2001.

Chapter 2

1 Edward T. Hall, *The Silent Language* (New York: Doubleday Books, 1990), p. xv.

2 Alfred L. Kroeber and Clyde Kluckhohn, *Culture: Critical Review of Concepts and Definitions,* vol. 1, no. 1 (Cambridge, Mass.: Peabody Museum, 1952).

3 Ludwig Wittgenstein, *Culture and Value* (Chicago: University of Chicago Press, 1984).

4 Michael Carrithers, *Why Humans Have Cultures* (Oxford: Oxford University Press, 1992).

5 See Geert Hofstede, *Culture's Consequences* (Newbury Park, Calif.: Sage Publications, 1984) and Alfons Trompenaars, *Riding the Waves of Culture: Understanding Cultural Diversity in Business* (London: The Economist Books, 1993) as the most recognized examples.

6 Erich Wolf, *Europe and the People without History* (London: University of California Press, 1982).

7 José Ortega y Gasset, "Unity and Diversity," in *Europe in History as a System* (New York: W. W. Norton, 1962).

8 Benjamin Barber, *Jihad vs. McWorld: How Globalism and Tribalism Are Reshaping the World* (New York: Ballentine Books, 1996).

9 Hofstede, *Culture's Consequences.*

10 See, for example, a comprehensive treatment in Helen Spencer-Oatey, *Culturally Speaking: Managing Rapport in Talk Across Cultures* (New York: Continuum International Publishing Group, Inc., 2000).

11 Carl Coon, *Culture Wars and the Global Village: A Diplomat's Perspective* (Amherst, N.Y.: Prometheus Books, 2000).

12 See the works of sociologist William G. Sumner (1840–1910).

13 See Joerg Schmitz, *Cultural Orientations Guide* (Princeton, N.J.: Training Management Corporation, 2000), p. vii; also, Robert Rosen et al., *Global Literacies* (New York: Simon and Schuster, 2000), p. 34, identifies distinct *layers* of culture beyond the concept of national culture.

14 Ruth Benedict, *Patterns of Culture* (London: Routledge and Kegan Paul, 1935), p. 15.

15 Clyde Kluckhohn, "Universal Categories of Culture," in *Anthropology Today*, ed. S. Tax (Chicago: University of Chicago Press, 1962), pp. 317–318.

16 Talcott Parsons, "The Pattern Variables," in *On Institutions and Social Evolution: Selected Writings*, ed. Leon H. Mayhem (Chicago: University of Chicago Press, 1982), pp. 106–114.

17 Edward T. Hall, "The Silent Language in Overseas Business," *Harvard Business Review*, May–June 1960, p. 92.

18 Louis E. Boone, *Quotable Business* (New York: Random House, 1992), p. 186.

19 Charles Hampden-Turner and Alfons Trompenaars, *The Seven Cultures of Capitalism* (New York: Doubleday, 1993).

20 Ibid., p. 4.

21 Edward C. Stewart and Milton J. Bennett, *American Cultural Patterns: A Cross-Cultural Perspective*, rev. ed. (Yarmouth, Me: Intercultural Press, 1991), pp. 28–30.

22 Stephen H. Rhinesmith, *A Manager's Guide to Globalization: Six Keys to Success in a Changing World* (Homewood, Ill.: Business One–Irwin, 1993), pp. 77–79.

23 Hampden-Turner and Trompenaars, *Seven Cultures of Capitalism*, p. 34.

24 Lawrence E. Harrison, *Who Prospers?* (New York: Basic Books, 1992).

25 Joel Kotkin, *Tribes: How Race, Religion, and Identity Determine Success in the New Global Economy* (New York: Random House, 1993).

26 Francis Fukuyama, *Trust: The Social Virtues and the Creation of Prosperity* (New York: Free Press, 1995).

27 See, for example, Stephan Dahl, *Intercultural Skills for Business* (London: ECE, 2000).

28 Arthur R. Radcliff-Brown, *Structure and Function in Primitive Society* (London: Cohen and West, 1952). See also Seymour Martin Lipset, "Values and Democracy," in *Culture and Society: Contemporary Debates,* eds. J. Alexander and S. Seidman (New York: Press Syndicate of the University of Cambridge, 1990).

29 Erving Goffman, *The Presentation of Self in Everyday Life* (New York: Doubleday, 1959).

Chapter 3

1 Edward Hall has called *situation* the building block of culture and devoted an entire chapter to its importance. See Edward T. Hall, *Beyond Culture* (New York: Doubleday, 1990), chap. 9.

2 Derald Wing Sue and David Sue, *Counseling the Culturally Different: Theory and Practice,* 2d ed. (New York: John Wiley & Sons, 1990), pp. 140–143.

3 Hall, *Beyond Culture*, p. 2.

4 Ibid., p. 6.

5 Nancy Adler, *International Dimensions of Organizational Behavior*, 2d ed. (Boston: PWS-Kent, 1991), p. 31.

6 Kluckhohn and Strodtbeck, *Variation in Value Orientations* (Evanston, Ill.: Row, Peterson, 1961), p. 340.

7 Edward C. Stewart and Milton J. Bennett, *American Cultural Patterns: A Cross-Cultural Perspective,* rev. ed. (Yarmouth, Me.: Intercultural Press, 1991), pp. 28–30.

8 Richard Mead, *Cross-Cultural Management Communication* (New York: John Wiley, 1990), pp. 134-135.

9 Lisa Adent Hoecklin, *Managing Cultural Differences for Competitive Advantage,* Special Report No. P656 (London: The Economist Intelligence Unit, 1993), p. 22.

10 Hall, *The Silent Language,* p. 176.

11 Bob Hagerty, "Trainers Help Expatriate Employees Build Bridges to Different Cultures," *The Wall Street Journal,* June 14, 1993.

12 Charles Hampden-Turner and Alfons Trompenaars, *The Seven Cultures of Capitalism* (New York: Doubleday, 1993), p. 22.

13 Stephen Rhinesmith, *Cultural Organizational Analysis: The Interrelationship of Value Orientations and Managerial Behavior,* Publication Series No. 5 (Cambridge, MA: McBer and Company, 1971), p. 35.

14 Peter Senge, *The Fifth Discipline: The Art and Practice of the Learning Organization* (New York: Doubleday, 1990), p. 3.

15 Stewart and Bennet, *American Cultural Patterns,* p. 41.

16 Hoecklin, *Managing Cultural Differences,* p. 49.

17 This message was forwarded to us in preparation for a consulting assignment. It has been modified slightly to remove all references that could identify any of the parties involved.

Chapter 4

1 Margaret Nydell, *Understanding Arabs* (Yarmouth, Me.: Intercultural Press, 1996), p. 68.

2 Ellen Feghali, "Arab Cultural Communication Patterns," *International Journal of Intercultural Relations,* vol. 21, 1997, p. 358.

3 Mark Cohen, *Under Crescent and Cross* (Princeton, N.J.: Princeton University Press, 1995), p. 59.

4 Nydell, *Understanding Arabs,* p. 119.

5 Ibid., p. 44.

6 Ibid., p. 29.

7 Ibid., p. 82.

8 Loc. cit.

9 Alfons Trompenaars, *Riding the Waves of Culture: Understanding Diversity in Global Business* (London: The Economist Books, 1993), p. 161.

10 Feghali, "Arab Cultural Communication Patterns," p. 352.

11 Trompenaars, *Riding the Waves of Culture*, p. 40.

12 Loc. cit.

13 Halim Barakat, *The Arab World: Society, Culture, and the State* (Los Angeles: University of California Press, 1999), p. 63.

14 Lee Kuan Yew, as cited in Training Management Corporation, *Doing Business in Asia* (Princeton, N.J.: Princeton Training Press, 2000), p. 14.

15 Loc. cit.

16 David Rearwin, *The Asia Business Book* (Yarmouth, Me.: Intercultural Press, 1991), p. 76.

17 Rearwin, *The Asia Business Book*, p. 27.

18 Rearwin, *The Asia Business Book*, p. 31.

19 Engholm, *When Business East Meets Business West*, p. 107.

20 Trompenaars, *Riding the Waves of Culture*, p. 158.

21 Elisabeth Marx, *Breaking Through Culture Shock: What You Need to Succeed in International Business* (San Rafael, Calif.: World Trade Press, 1989), p. 63.

22 Polly Platt, *French or Foe? Getting the Most out of Visiting, Living, and Working in France* (Skokie, Ill.: Cultural Crossings, 1996), p. 32.

23 Ibid., p. 37.

24 Ibid., p. 206.

25 Richard Hill, *We Europeans* (Brussels: Europublications, 1995), p. 85.

26 Trompenaars, *Riding the Waves of Culture*, p. 59.

27 Hill, *We Europeans*, p. 84.

28 Ibid., p. 41.

29 Timothy Garton Ash, "The Puzzle of Central Europe," *The New York Review of Books*, 18 March 1999, p. 2.

30 Hill, *We Europeans*, p. 210.

31 Yale Richmond, *From Nyet to Da: Understanding the Russians* (Yarmouth, Me.: Intercultural Press, 1995), p. 41.

32 Ibid., p. 40.

33 Dimiter Kriazov, Sherry E. Sullivan, and Howard S. Tu, "Business Success in Eastern Europe: Understanding and Customizing HRM." *Business Horizon*, vol. 43, no. 1, 2000, p. 14.

34 Vladimir Kvint, "Don't Give Up on Russia," *Harvard Business Review*, May–June 1993, p. 72.

35 Christopher Earley and Miriam Erez, *The Transplanted Executive: Why You Need to Understand How Workers in Other Countries See the World Differently* (New York: Oxford University Press, 1997), p. 63.

36 Kvint, "Don't Give Up on Russia," pp. 71–72.

37 Marshall Goldman et al., "The Russian Investment Dilemma," *Harvard Business Review*, May–June 1994, p. 41.

38 Richmond, *From Nyet to Da*, p. 38.

39 Training Management Corporation, *Doing Business in North America* (Princeton, N.J.: Princeton Training Press, 2000), p. 20.

40 Ibid., p. 56.

41 Pang Guek Chen, and Robert Barlas, *Culture Shock! Canada* (Portland, Oreg: Graphic Arts Center, 1992), p. 64.

42 Richard Mead, *Cross-Cultural Management Communication* (London: John Wiley and Sons, 1990), p. 116.

43 Eva S. Kras, *Management in Two Cultures: Bridging the Gap between U.S. and Mexican Managers* (Yarmouth, Me.: Intercultural Press, 1995), p. 46.

44 Ibid., pp. 26–27.

45 Mary Murray Bosrock, *Put Your Best Foot Forward: South America* (Franklin, Mo.: Conquest Corporation, 1997), p. 111.

46 Rosa Daskal Albert, "A Framework and Model for Understanding Latin American and Latino/Hispanic Cultural Patterns" in *Handbook of Intercultural Training*, 2d ed. (Thousand Oaks, Calif.: Sage, 1996), p. 335.

47 Geert Hofstede, *Culture's Consequences* (Newbury Park, Calif.: Sage Publications, 1984).

48 William Hutchinson, Cynthia Poznanski, and Laura Todt-Stockman, *Living in Colombia: A Guide for Foreigners* (Yarmouth, Me.: Intercultural Press, 1987), p. 88.

49 Trompenaars, *Riding the Waves of Culture,* p. 34.

50 Training Management Corporation, *Doing Business in Latin America* (Princeton, N.J.: Princeton Training Press, 2000), p. 26.

51 Ibid., p. 28.

Chapter 5

1 Derald Wing Sue and David Sue, *Counseling the Culturally Different: Theory and Practice*, 2d ed. (New York: John Wiley & Sons, 1990).

2 Alfons Trompenaars, *Riding the Waves of Culture: Understanding Diversity in Global Business* (New York: Irwin Professional Publishing, 1994), p. 6.

3 Nancy Adler, *International Dimensions of Organizational Behavior* (Boston: PWS-Kent, 1991), p. 83.

4 Edward T. Hall and Mildred Reed Hall, *Understanding Cultural Differences* (Yarmouth, Me.: Intercultural Press, 1989). In *The Silent Language*, Hall devotes an entire chapter to the view of culture as communication (chap. 5, "Culture Is Communication").

5 Herbert Kohl, *From Archetype to Zeitgeist: Powerful Ideas for Powerful Thinking* (Boston: Little, Brown, 1992), p. 203. *Synergy* comes from the Greek *synergos*, which means "working together," and it describes those benefits that can materialize from collaboration.

6 Mildred Sikkema and Agnes Niyekawa, *Design for Cross-Cultural Learning* (Yarmouth, Me.: Intercultural Press, 1987), p. 32.

7 See, for example, *Doing Business Internationally: The Resource for Business and Social Etiquette*, 5th ed. (Princeton, N.J.: Princeton Training Press, 1999); Terri Morrison, Wayne Conaway, and George Borden, *Kiss, Bow or Shake Hands* (Holbrook, Mass.: Adams Media Corporation, 1994); Norine Dresser, *Multicultural Manners* (New York: John Wiley & Sons, 1996); or Roger Axtell, *Gestures: The Do's and Taboos of Body Language Around the World* (New York: John Wiley & Sons, 1991).

8 According to Joerg Schmitz/Training Management Corporation, *Cultural Orientations Guide: Building Cross-Cultural Effectiveness* (Princeton, N.J.: Princeton Training Press, 2000), a *culture gap* is defined as "the difference in cultural orientations between individuals or between an individual and a social context."

9 According to Schmitz/Training Management Corporation, *Cultural Orientations Guide, social distance* is defined as "the level of comfort or discomfort that operates between individuals or groups as a result of differences in cultural orientations."

10 The Cultural Orientations Model, COM, Cultural Orientations Indicator, and COI are all trademarks of Training Management Corporation; Registration 75-652669, 75-652654, and 75-652670.

11 P. R. Harris and R. T. Moran, *Managing Cultural Differences* (Houston: Gulf Publishing, 1991), p. 155.

12 William Isaacs, *Dialogue and the Art of Thinking Together* (New York: Doubleday, 1999).

13 Clifford Geertz, *Works and Lives: The Anthropologist as Author* (Stanford, Calif.: Stanford University Press, 1992), p. 147.

Chapter 6

1 Daniel Rubin, "Culture Clash Confounds Wal-Mart in Germany," *The Philadelphia Inquirer,* December 29, 2001.

2 Theodore Levitt, "The Globalization of Markets," *Harvard Business Review*, May–June 1983, pp. 99–102.

3 Erin Keown and Kirsten Jensen, "Multi-Cultural Marketing" (Seattle, Wash.: The Chamber of Small Business Action Council, November 30, 2000).

4 Hans Mühlbacher, Lee Dahringer, and Helmuth Leihs, *International Marketing: A Global Perspective* (London: International Thomas Business Press, 1999), pp. 169–211; Michael R. Czinkota and Ilkka A. Ronkainen, *International Marketing*, 9th ed. (New York: Dryden Press, 1996), pp. 36–53.

5 James R. Walton, *Commitment and Trust in Cross-Cultural Marketing Relationships: The Effect of Cultural Adaptation* (Lubbock, Tex.: Texas Tech University, November 30, 2000).

6 Czinkota and Ronkainen, *International Marketing*, pp. 242–263.

7 Kamran Kashani, *Managing Global Marketing: Cases and Text* (Boston, Mass.: PWS Kent Publishing Company, 1992), pp. 83–99.

8 Michael R. Czinkota, Ilkka A. Ronkainen, and John J. Tarrant, *The Global Marketing Imperative* (Lincolnwood, Ill.: NTC Business Books, 1995), pp. 133–146.

9 Czinkota and Ronkainen, *International Marketing*, pp. 442–471.

10 Simon Anholt, *Another One Bites the Grass: Making Sense of International Advertising* (New York: John Wiley & Sons, 2000), pp. 18–130; Marieke de Mooij, *Global Marketing and Advertising: Understanding Cultural Paradoxes* (London: SAGE Publications, 1998), pp.15–38.

11 Charles M. Futrell, *Sales Management: Teamwork, Leadership, and Technology* (New York: Dryden Press, 1998), pp. 267–297.

12 Philip R. Cateora, *International Marketing* (Chicago: Irwin, 1996), pp. 526–535.

13 Futrell, *Sales Management*, pp. 377–411.

14 Jeffrey Edmund Curry, *International Marketing: Approaching and Penetrating the Global Marketplace* (San Rafael, Calif.: World Trade Press, 1999), pp. 158–163.

15 Robert D. Hisrich and Ralph W. Jackson, *Selling and Sales Management* (Hauppauge, N.Y.: Barron's Educational Series, 1993).

Chapter 7

1 Joerg Schmitz, *Transcendent Teams* (Princeton N.J.: Princeton Training Press, 2000).

2 Alfons Trompenaars, *Riding the Waves of Culture: Understanding Diversity in Global Business* (New York: Irwin Professional Publishing, 1994), p. 6.

3 B. W. Tuckman, "Developmental Sequence in Small Groups," *Psychological Bulletin*, vol. 63, 1965, pp. 384–399.

4 Jon R. Katzenbach and Douglas K. Smith, *The Wisdom of Teams: Creating the High Performance Organization* (Boston, Mass.: Harvard Business School Press, 1993).

5 Sylvia Odenwald, *Global Solutions: Moving from Collision to Collaboration* (New York: Irwin Professional Publishing, 1996).

6 Milton J. Bennett, "Towards a Development Model of Intercultural Sensitivity," in *Education for Intercultural Experience*, ed. Michael Paige (Yarmouth, Me.: Intercultural Press, 1993).

7 Our work with numerous global, multicultural teams at the following organizations has helped us develop and frame the Transcendent Team concept and approach: American Express, Air Products and Chemicals, AT&T, Berlex, Citigroup, Corning, Ernst & Young, IBM, Lucent Technologies, Merck, National Semiconductors, PPG, Schering AG, and Wunderman.

8 Stewart J. Black and Hal B. Gregersen, *So You Are Going Overseas: Employer Workbook* (San Diego, Calif.: Global Business Publishers, 1998).

9 Robert L. Kohls, *Survival Kit for Overseas Living: For Americans Planning to Live and Work Abroad* (Yarmouth, Me.: Intercultural Press, 1984).

10 Rosalind Kalb and Penelope Welch, *Moving Your Family Overseas* (Yarmouth, Me.: Intercultural Press, 1992).

11 Nancy Piet-Pelon and Barbara Hornby, *In Another Dimension: A Guide for Women Who Live Overseas* (Yarmouth, Me.: Intercultural Press, 1985).

Index

About the Authors

Danielle Medina Walker is founder and president of Training Management Corporation. Fluent in four languages, Ms. Walker has worked and consulted extensively with major companies in North America, Asia, Europe, and the Middle East, and is coauthor of several books on achieving global professional success. She can be reached at dwalker@tmcorp.com.

Thomas Walker is chief operating officer of Training Management Corporation (TMC), a recognized leader in the field of global management and cross-cultural consulting and training. A veteran of over two decades in international human resources development, Walker spent a number of years both living and working overseas. He can be reached at twalker@tmcorp.com.

Joerg Schmitz is senior director of Training Management Corporation. A cultural anthropologist by training, Schmitz specializes in consulting on strategic global learning initiatives and delivering management training to global companies and organizations both in the United States and overseas. He can be reached at jschmitz@tmcorp.com.

SIGN UP FOR YOUR CULTURAL PROFILE ASSESSMENT USING THE CULTURAL ORIENTATIONS INDICATOR (COI)®

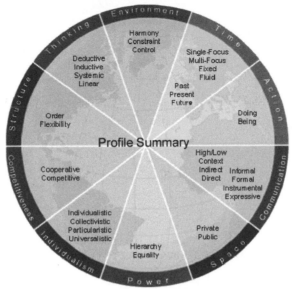

Cultural Orientations Model™ Framework

Today, understanding and identifying cultural differences is an essential skill for global managers and leaders. Developing cultural self-awareness and effective behavioral strategies to minimize the cultural gaps that occur when contrasting value orientations of different social groups arise is key to working in today's diverse, multicultural business environment.

The Cultural Orientations Model (COM)™, designed by Training Management Corporation, has been used by thousands of employees of Fortune 1000 companies worldwide to enhance one's cross-cultural skills and abilities to…

• Understand the importance and complexity of culture in business
• Develop a more comprehensive grasp of individual and organizational behaviors
• Improve communication processes and structures
• Adapt management practices to local demands
• Appreciate difference in behavior from a cultural perspective
• Prepare for difficult business challenges
• Improve multicultural and global teamwork

To obtain your own COI® profile, please contact us at: info@tmcorp.com

For a demo, visit our website at:
http://www.tmcorp.com

Training Management Corporation
600 Alexander Road _ Princeton _ NJ 08540
Tel: 609-951-0525 _ Fax: 609-951-0395

Web: http://www.tmcorp.com _ E-mail: info@tmcorp.com